Shojo Beat

ORESAMA TEACHER

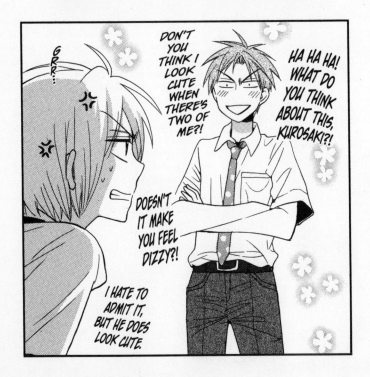

HA HA HA! WHAT DO YOU THINK ABOUT THIS, KUROSAKI?!
DON'T YOU THINK I LOOK CUTE WHEN THERE'S TWO OF ME?!
DOESN'T IT MAKE YOU FEEL DIZZY?!
GRR...
I HATE TO ADMIT IT, BUT HE DOES LOOK CUTE.

Vol. 7

Story & Art by

Izumi Tsubaki

ORESAMA TEACHER

Story & Characters

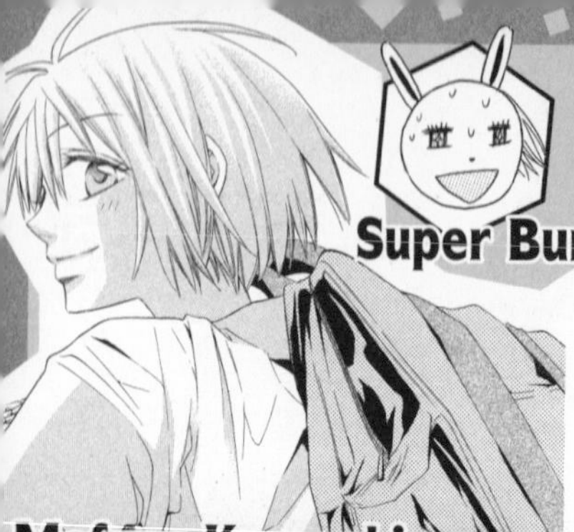
Super Bun!

Mafuyu Kurosaki

Former leader of a high school gang. Currently enjoying living alone. She plans on having an ordinary, modern high school life at Midorigaoka Academy…

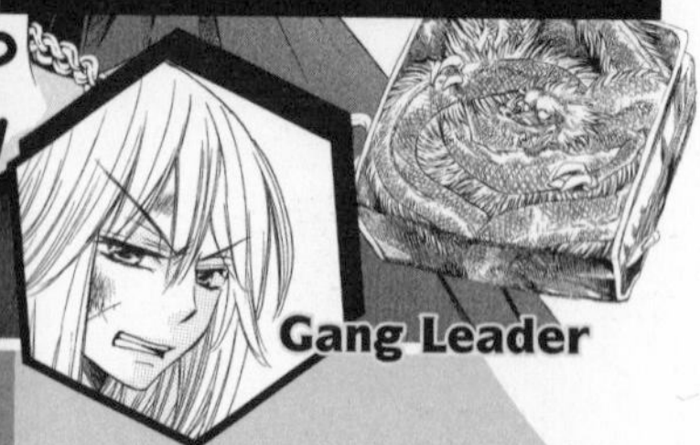
Gang Leader

Mafuyu Kurosaki was the successful leader of a high school gang who united Saitama Prefecture under her flag. But she got too active in her role and was caught by the police. When her angry mother "suggested" she transfer to the remote Midorigaoka Academy, Mafuyu saw it as her chance to start over as a sparkling coed.

Unfortunately, her childhood friend Takaomi Saeki is her new homeroom teacher—the very person who set her on the path to delinquency! With Takaomi around, Mafuyu's high school life once again starts to stray from the straight and narrow.

★Mafuyu fights to save her first new friend, Hayasaka, from his troubles. But in order to hide her identity, she wears a rabbit mask and becomes Super Bun… Other times she disguises herself as a boy named Natsuo. The Public Morals Club is busy every day!

Midorigaoka Academy's Public Morals Club

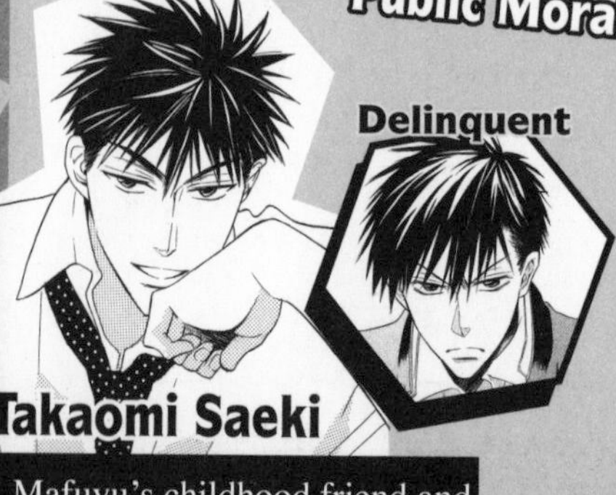
Delinquent

Takaomi Saeki

Mafuyu's childhood friend and new homeroom teacher. He is also a former delinquent. He became a teacher for a reason, but what was it?!

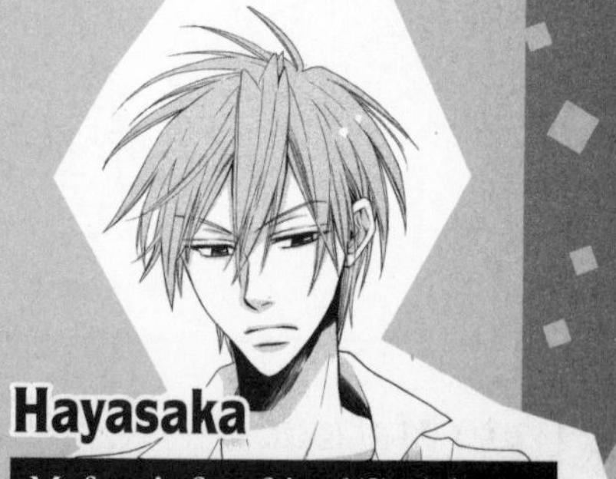

Hayasaka

Mafuyu's first friend(?). A lone-wolf delinquent. He'll take on anyone who wants to fight him! Admires Super Bun.

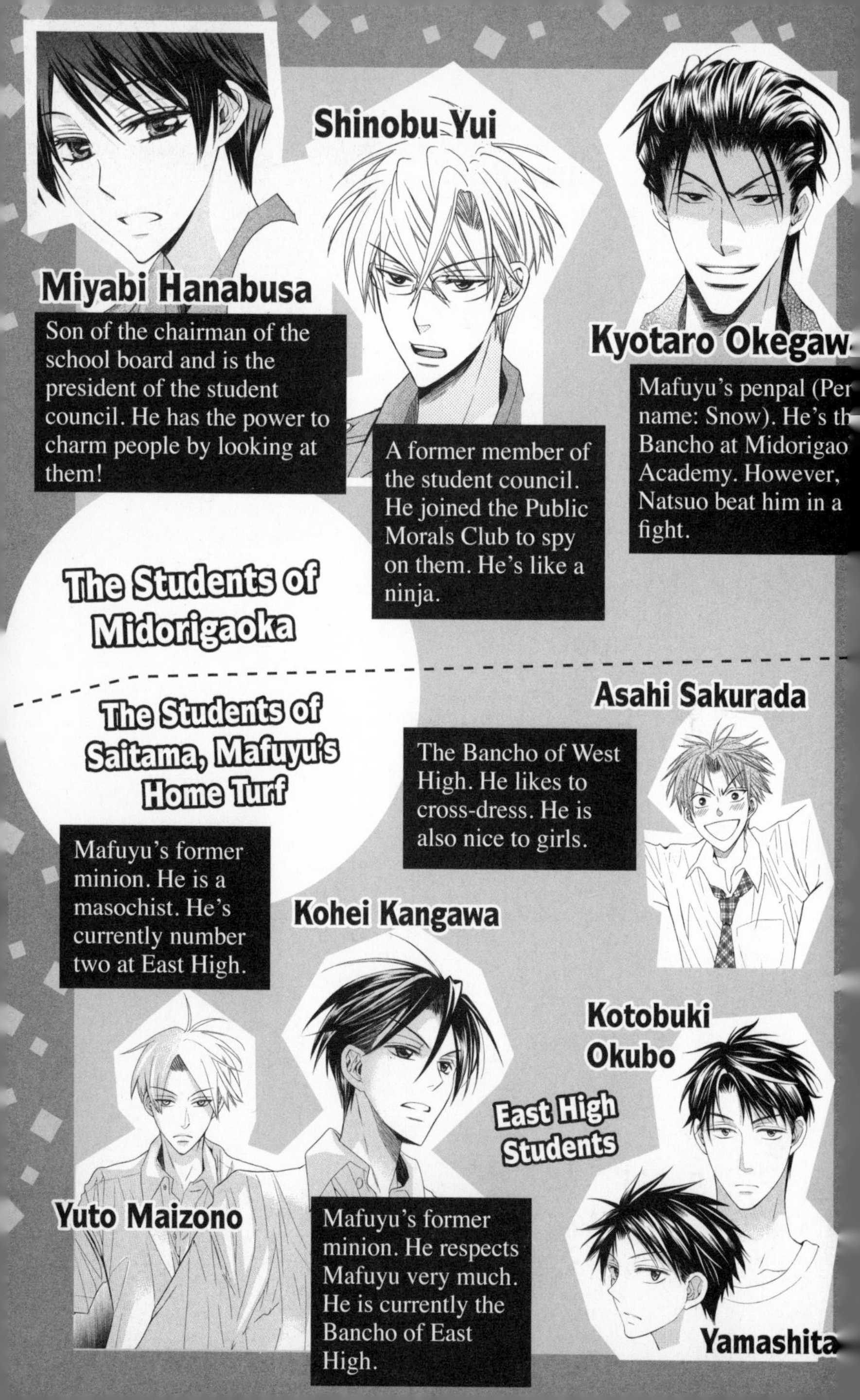
Miyabi Hanabusa
Son of the chairman of the school board and is the president of the student council. He has the power to charm people by looking at them!
Shinobu Yui
A former member of the student council. He joined the Public Morals Club to spy on them. He's like a ninja.
Kyotaro Okegaw
Mafuyu's penpal (Per name: Snow). He's th Bancho at Midorigao Academy. However, Natsuo beat him in a fight.
The Students of Midorigaoka
The Students of Saitama, Mafuyu's Home Turf
Asahi Sakurada
The Bancho of West High. He likes to cross-dress. He is also nice to girls.
Mafuyu's former minion. He is a masochist. He's currently number two at East High.
Kohei Kangawa
Kotobuki Okubo
East High Students
Yuto Maizono
Mafuyu's former minion. He respects Mafuyu very much. He is currently the Bancho of East High.
Yamashita

ORESAMA TEACHER

Volume 7
CONTENTS

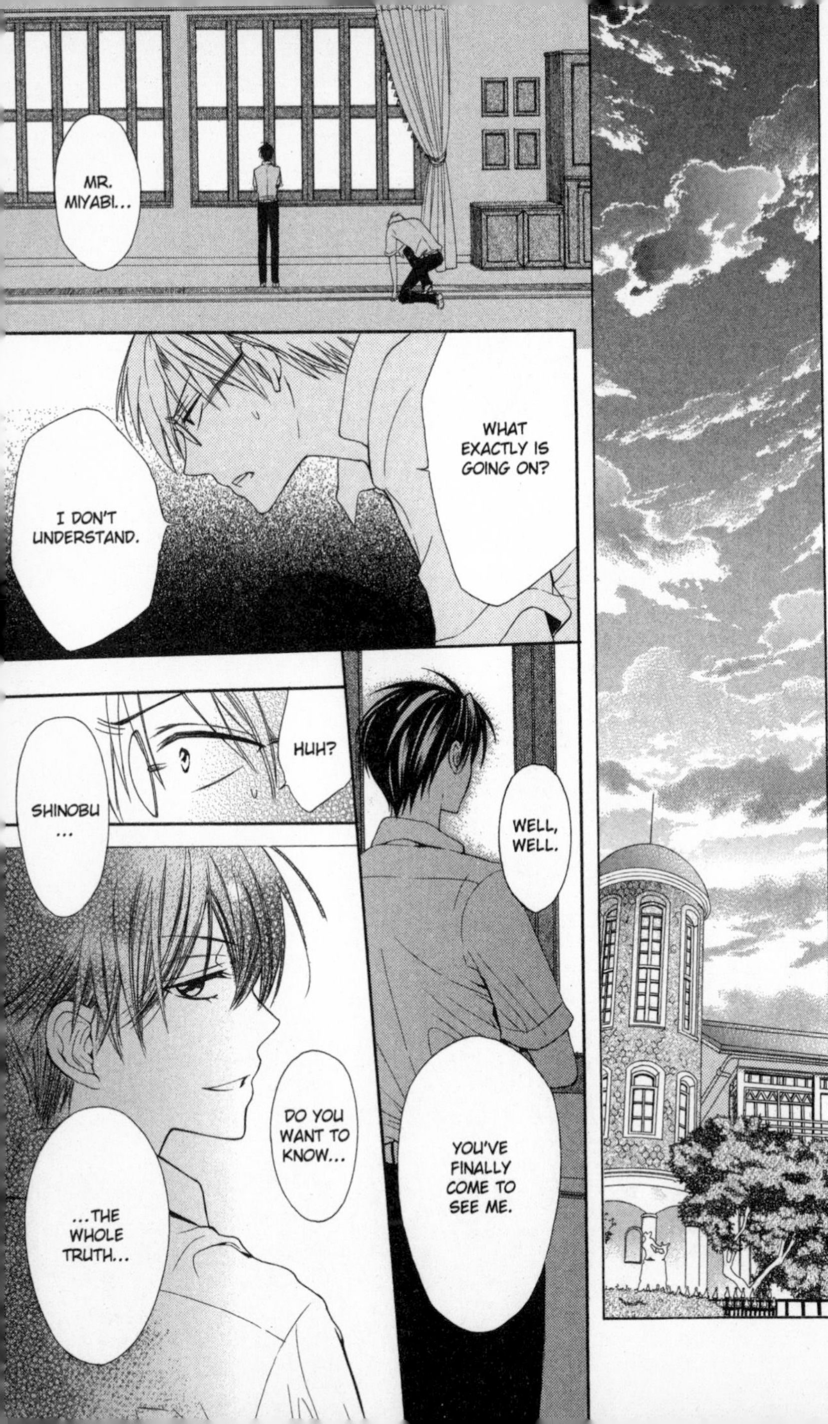
MR. MIYABI...
WHAT EXACTLY IS GOING ON?
I DON'T UNDERSTAND.
WELL, WELL.
YOU'VE FINALLY COME TO SEE ME.
HUH?
SHINOBU...
DO YOU WANT TO KNOW...
...THE WHOLE TRUTH...

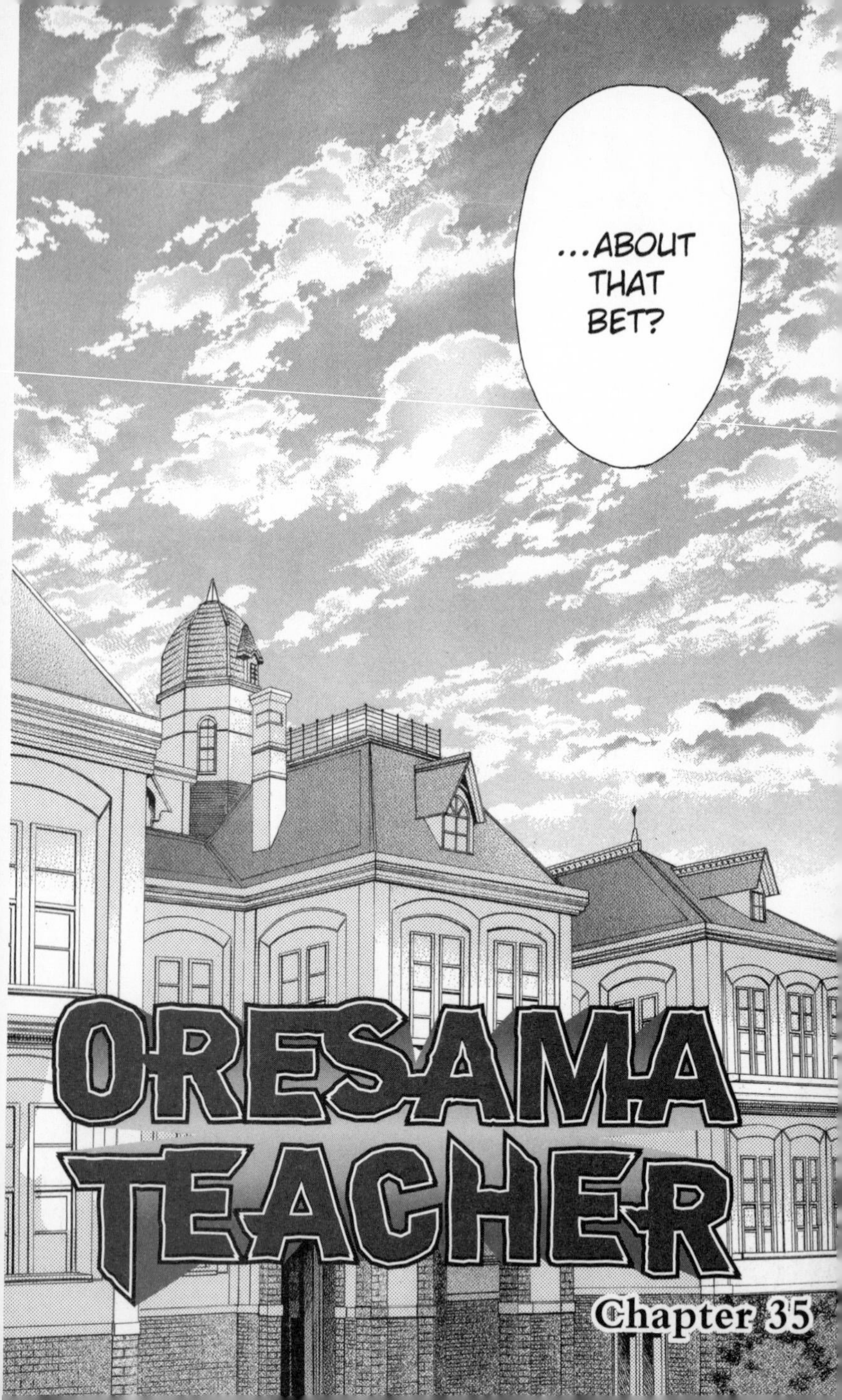
...ABOUT THAT BET?
ORESAMA TEACHER
Chapter 35

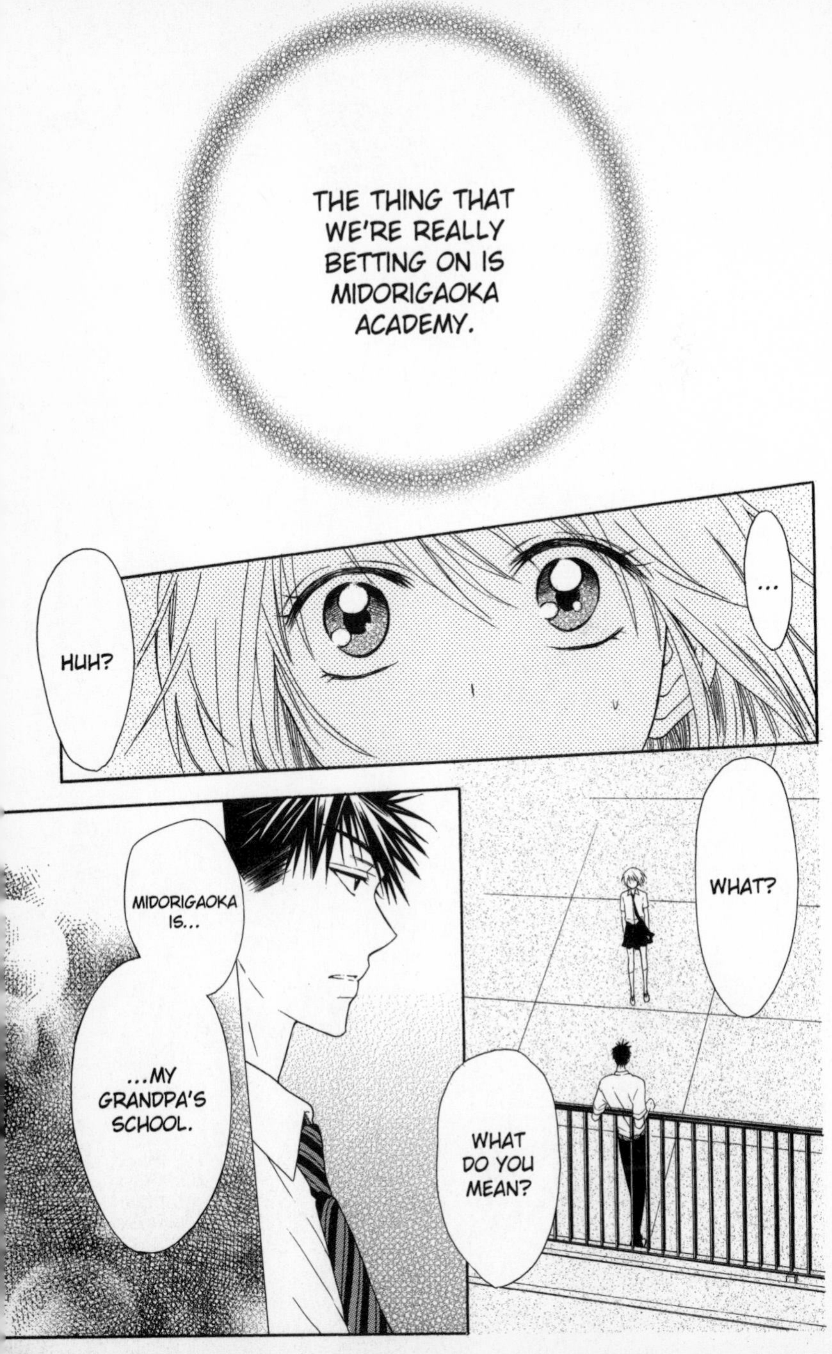
THE THING THAT WE'RE REALLY BETTING ON IS MIDORIGAOKA ACADEMY.
...
HUH?
WHAT?
WHAT DO YOU MEAN?
MIDORIGAOKA IS...
...MY GRANDPA'S SCHOOL.

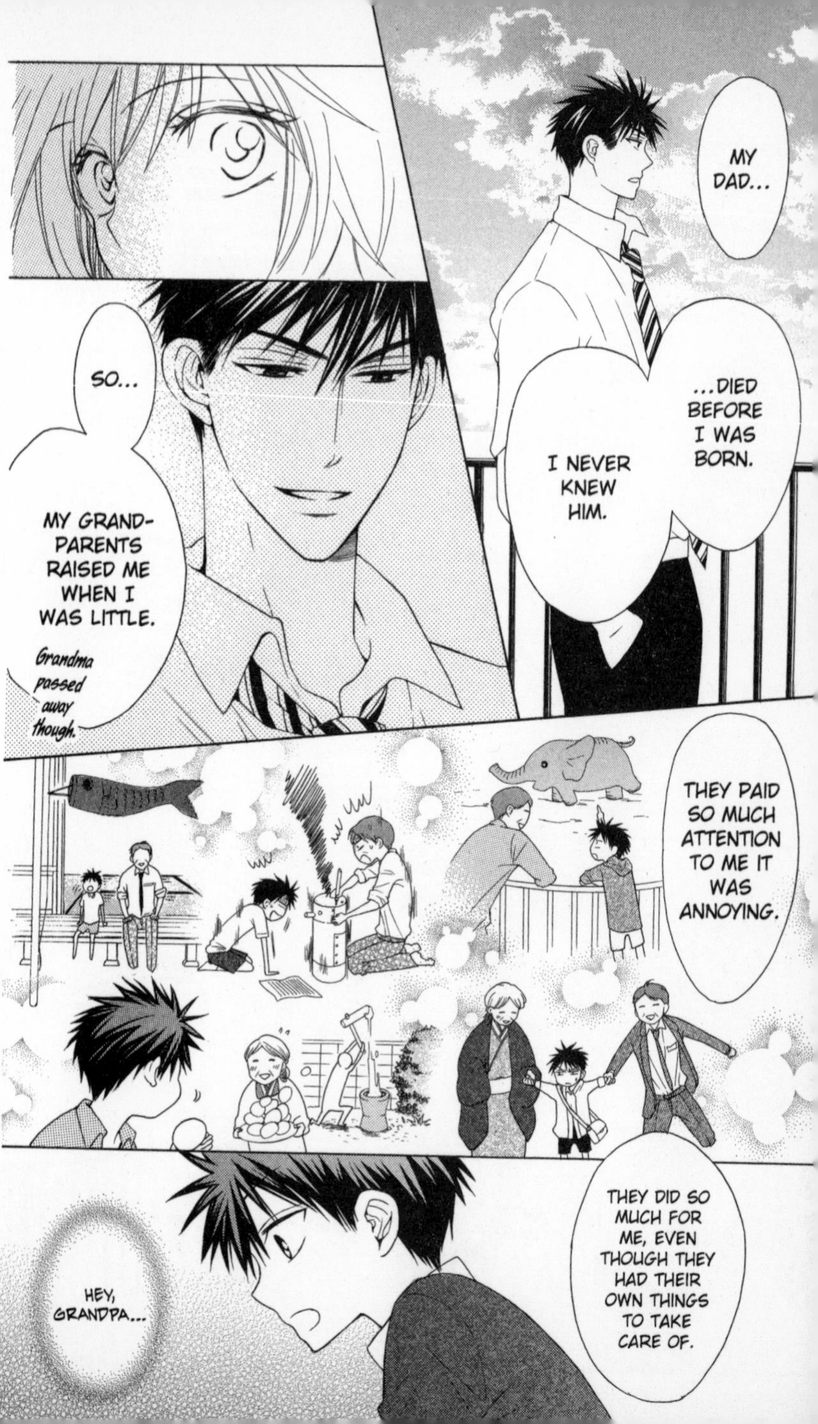
MY DAD...
...DIED BEFORE I WAS BORN.
I NEVER KNEW HIM.
SO...
MY GRAND-PARENTS RAISED ME WHEN I WAS LITTLE.
Grandma passed away though.
THEY PAID SO MUCH ATTENTION TO ME IT WAS ANNOYING.
THEY DID SO MUCH FOR ME, EVEN THOUGH THEY HAD THEIR OWN THINGS TO TAKE CARE OF.
HEY, GRANDPA...

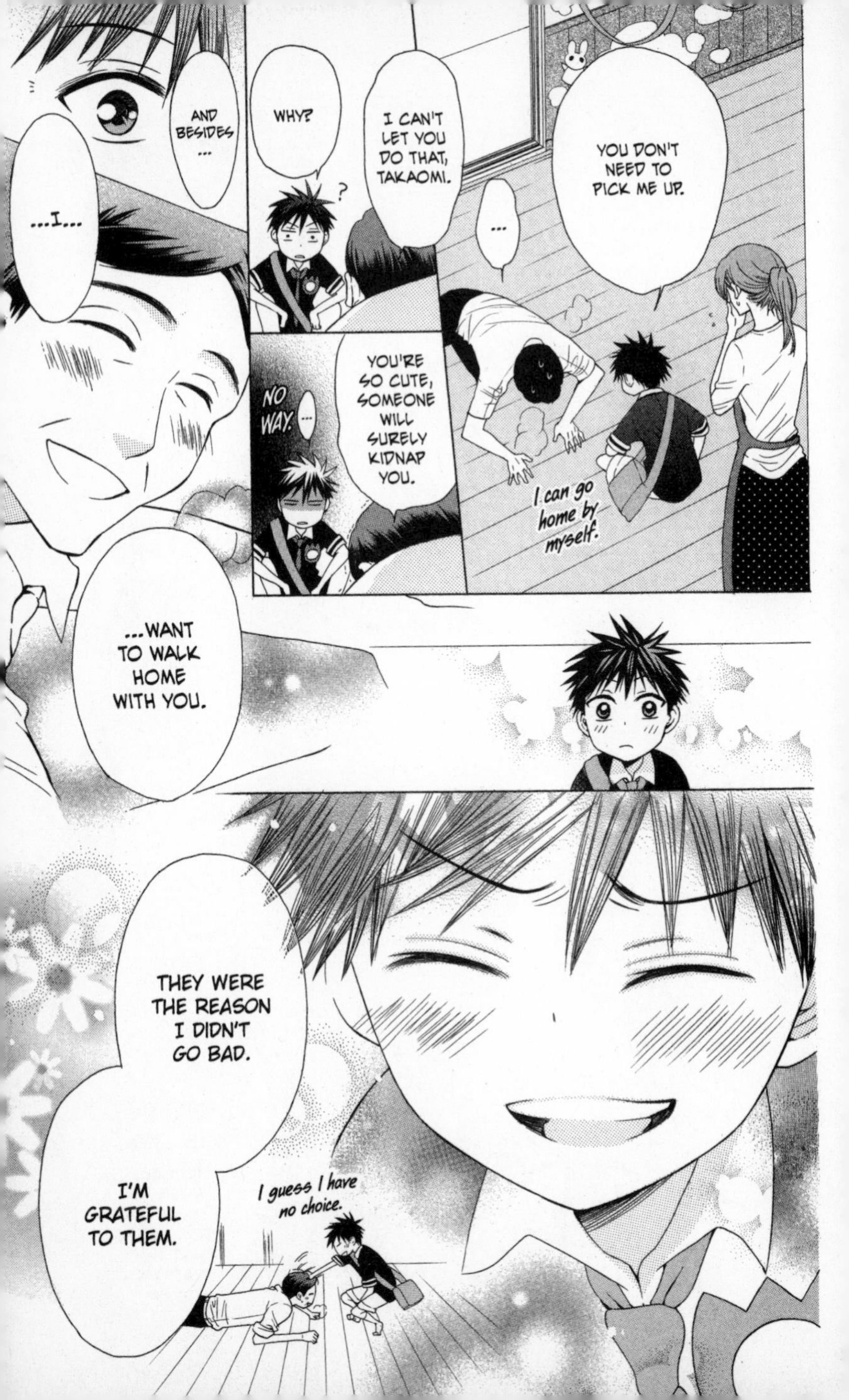

YOU DON'T NEED TO PICK ME UP.
...
I can go home by myself.
I CAN'T LET YOU DO THAT, TAKAOMI.
WHY?
?
YOU'RE SO CUTE, SOMEONE WILL SURELY KIDNAP YOU.
NO WAY.
...
AND BESIDES...
...I...
...WANT TO WALK HOME WITH YOU.
THEY WERE THE REASON I DIDN'T GO BAD.
I'M GRATEFUL TO THEM.
I guess I have no choice.

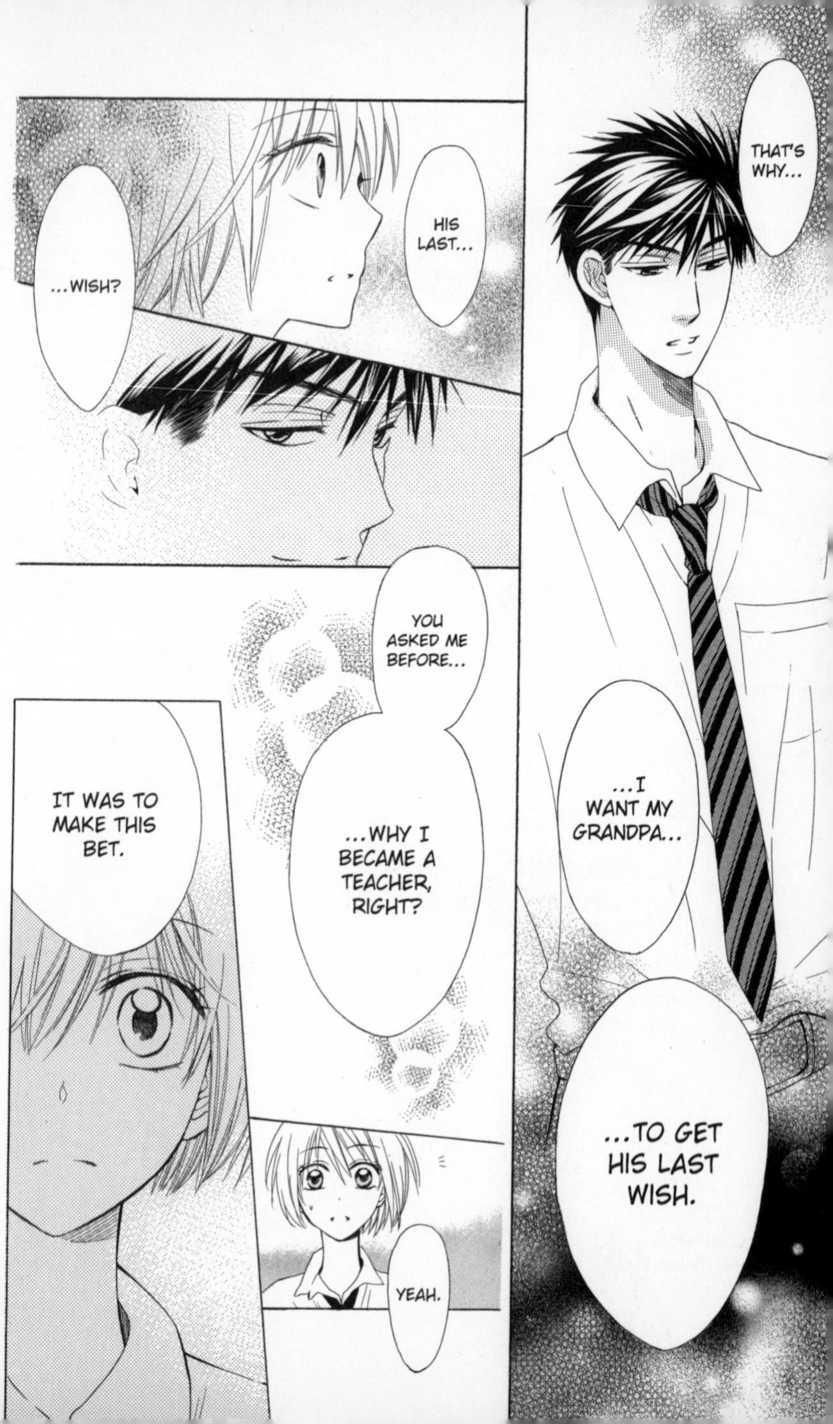
THAT'S WHY...
...I WANT MY GRANDPA...
...TO GET HIS LAST WISH.
HIS LAST...
...WISH?
YOU ASKED ME BEFORE...
...WHY I BECAME A TEACHER, RIGHT?
YEAH.
IT WAS TO MAKE THIS BET.

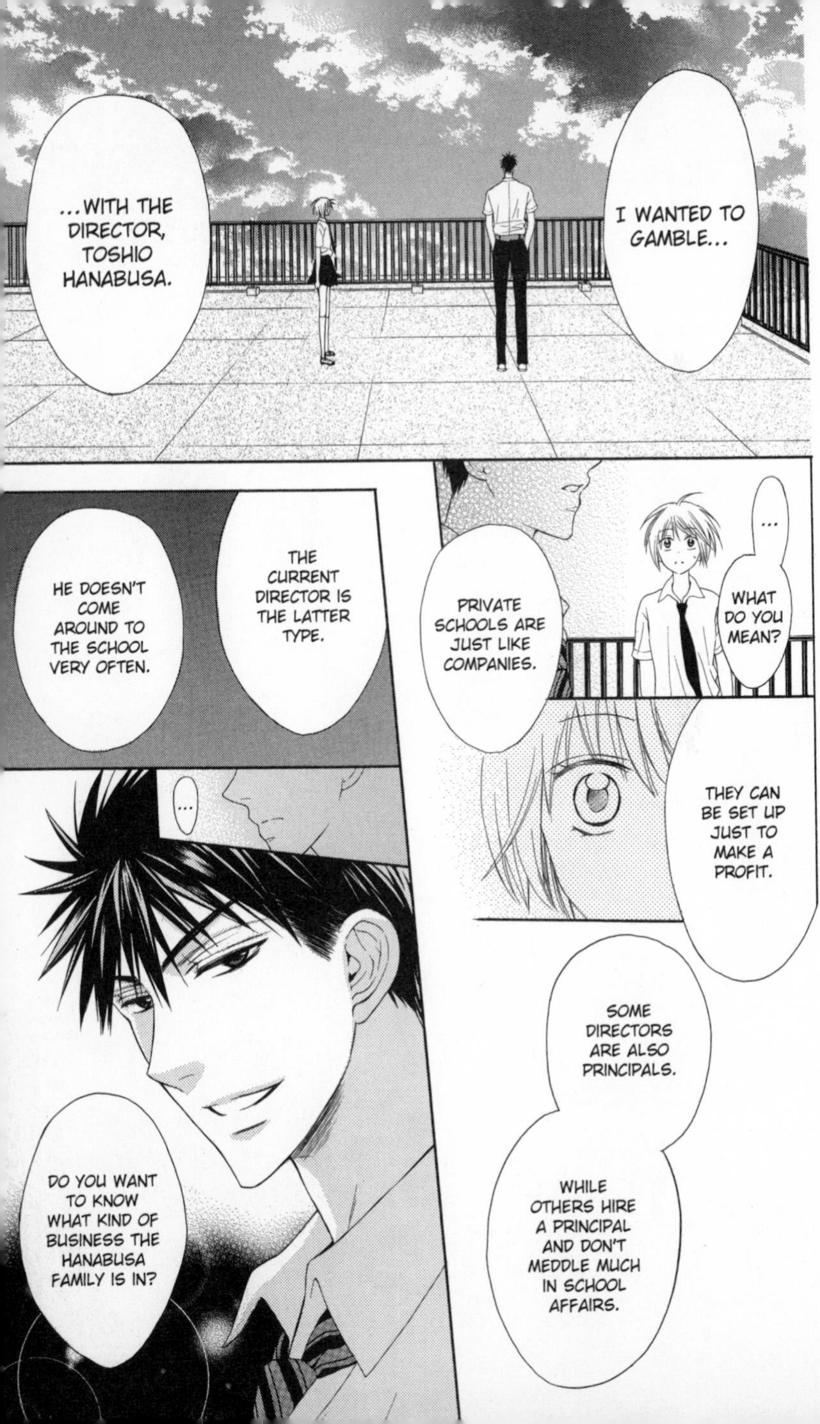

I WANTED TO GAMBLE...
...WITH THE DIRECTOR, TOSHIO HANABUSA.
...
WHAT DO YOU MEAN?
PRIVATE SCHOOLS ARE JUST LIKE COMPANIES.
THEY CAN BE SET UP JUST TO MAKE A PROFIT.
SOME DIRECTORS ARE ALSO PRINCIPALS.
WHILE OTHERS HIRE A PRINCIPAL AND DON'T MEDDLE MUCH IN SCHOOL AFFAIRS.
THE CURRENT DIRECTOR IS THE LATTER TYPE.
HE DOESN'T COME AROUND TO THE SCHOOL VERY OFTEN.
...
DO YOU WANT TO KNOW WHAT KIND OF BUSINESS THE HANABUSA FAMILY IS IN?

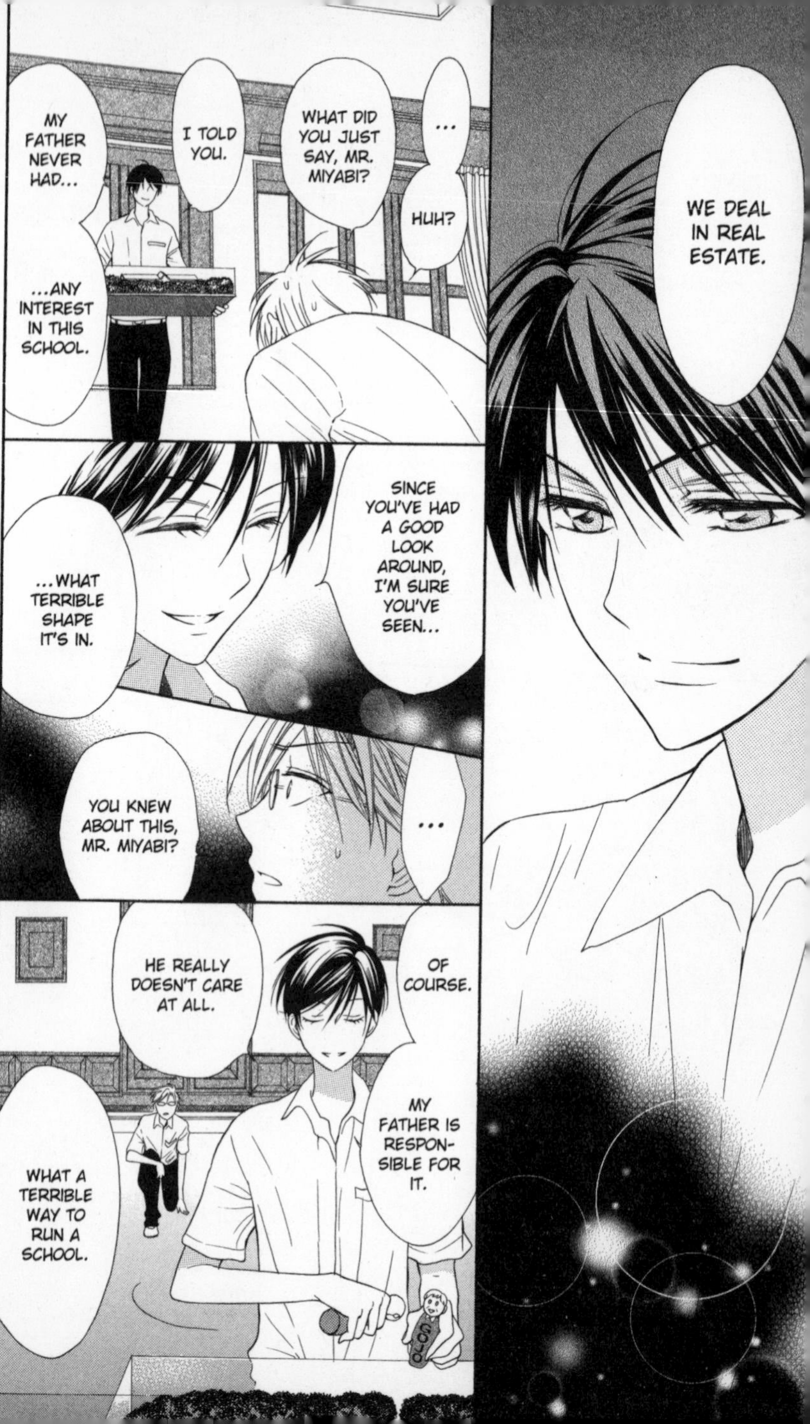
WE DEAL IN REAL ESTATE.
...
WHAT DID YOU JUST SAY, MR. MIYABI?
HUH?
I TOLD YOU.
MY FATHER NEVER HAD...
...ANY INTEREST IN THIS SCHOOL.
SINCE YOU'VE HAD A GOOD LOOK AROUND, I'M SURE YOU'VE SEEN...
...WHAT TERRIBLE SHAPE IT'S IN.
...
YOU KNEW ABOUT THIS, MR. MIYABI?
OF COURSE.
HE REALLY DOESN'T CARE AT ALL.
MY FATHER IS RESPON-SIBLE FOR IT.
WHAT A TERRIBLE WAY TO RUN A SCHOOL.

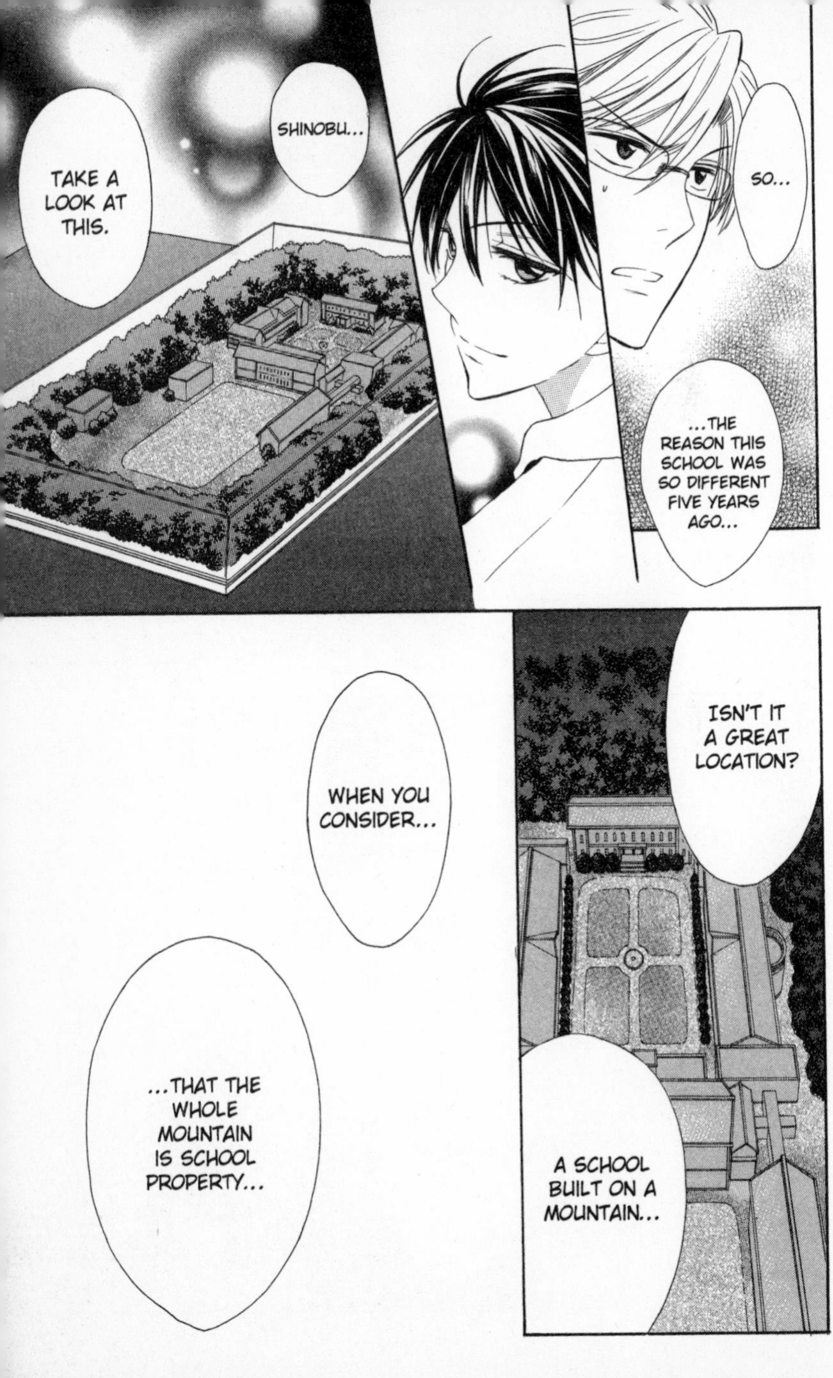
SO...
...THE REASON THIS SCHOOL WAS SO DIFFERENT FIVE YEARS AGO...
SHINOBU...
TAKE A LOOK AT THIS.
ISN'T IT A GREAT LOCATION?
A SCHOOL BUILT ON A MOUNTAIN...
WHEN YOU CONSIDER...
...THAT THE WHOLE MOUNTAIN IS SCHOOL PROPERTY...

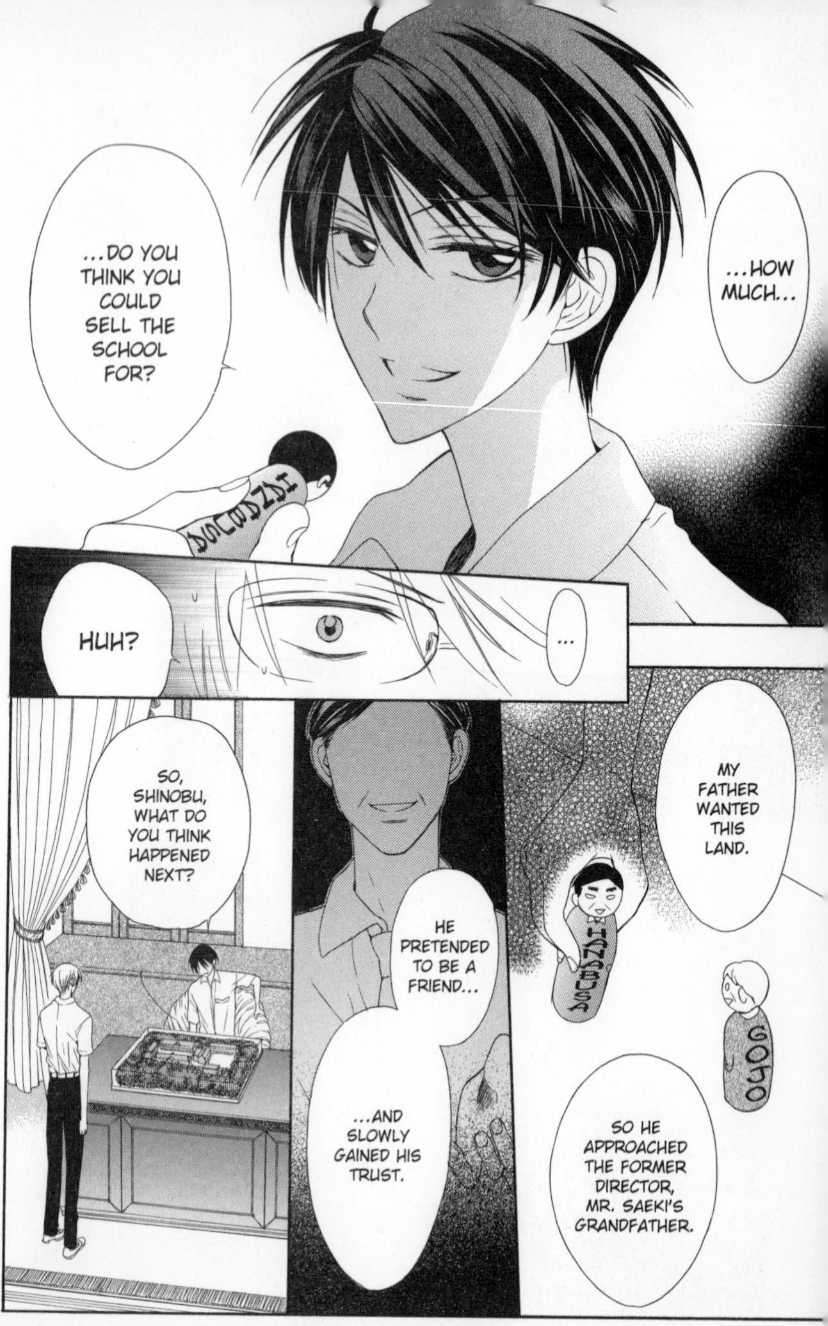

...HOW MUCH...
...DO YOU THINK YOU COULD SELL THE SCHOOL FOR?
...
HUH?
MY FATHER WANTED THIS LAND.
HANABUSA
GOJO
SO HE APPROACHED THE FORMER DIRECTOR, MR. SAEKI'S GRANDFATHER.
HE PRETENDED TO BE A FRIEND...
...AND SLOWLY GAINED HIS TRUST.
SO, SHINOBU, WHAT DO YOU THINK HAPPENED NEXT?

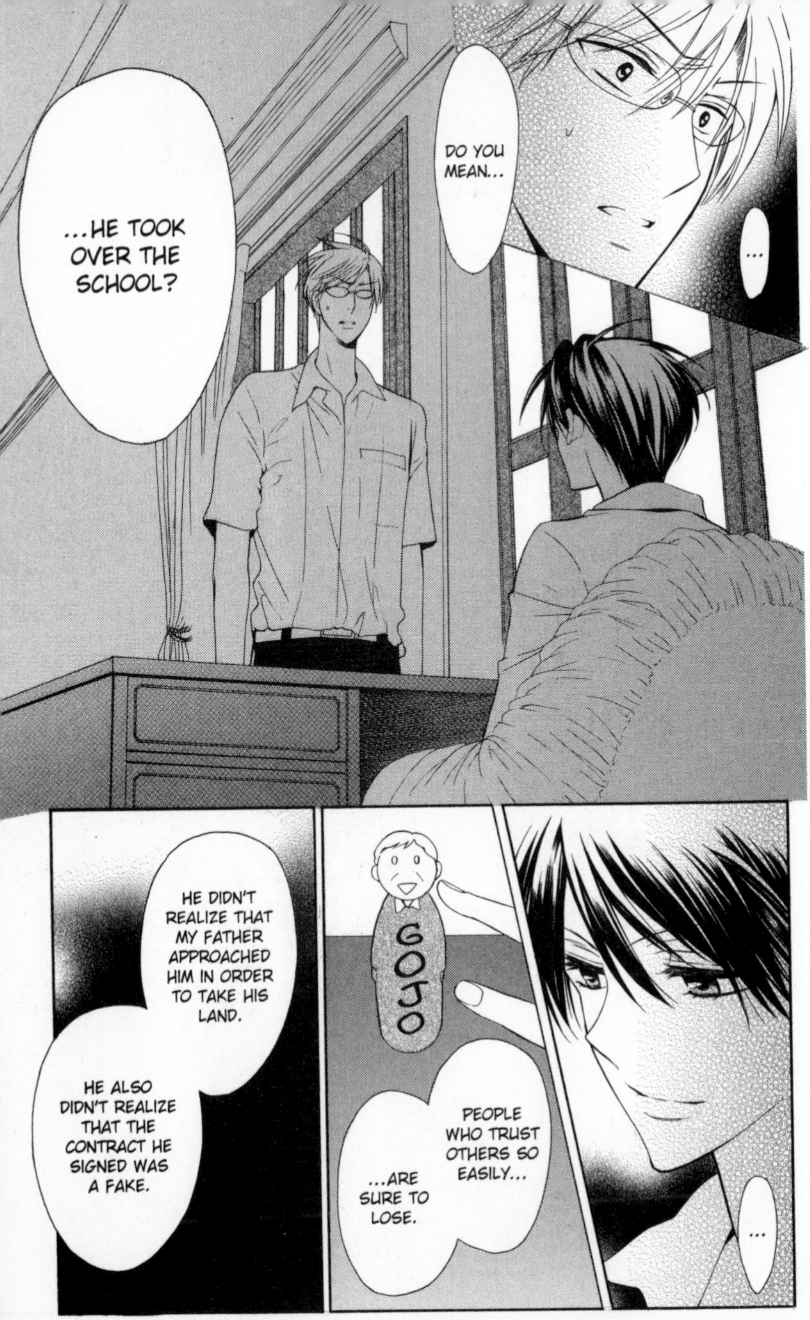

DO YOU MEAN...
...HE TOOK OVER THE SCHOOL?
...
GOJO
PEOPLE WHO TRUST OTHERS SO EASILY...
...ARE SURE TO LOSE.
...
HE DIDN'T REALIZE THAT MY FATHER APPROACHED HIM IN ORDER TO TAKE HIS LAND.
HE ALSO DIDN'T REALIZE THAT THE CONTRACT HE SIGNED WAS A FAKE.

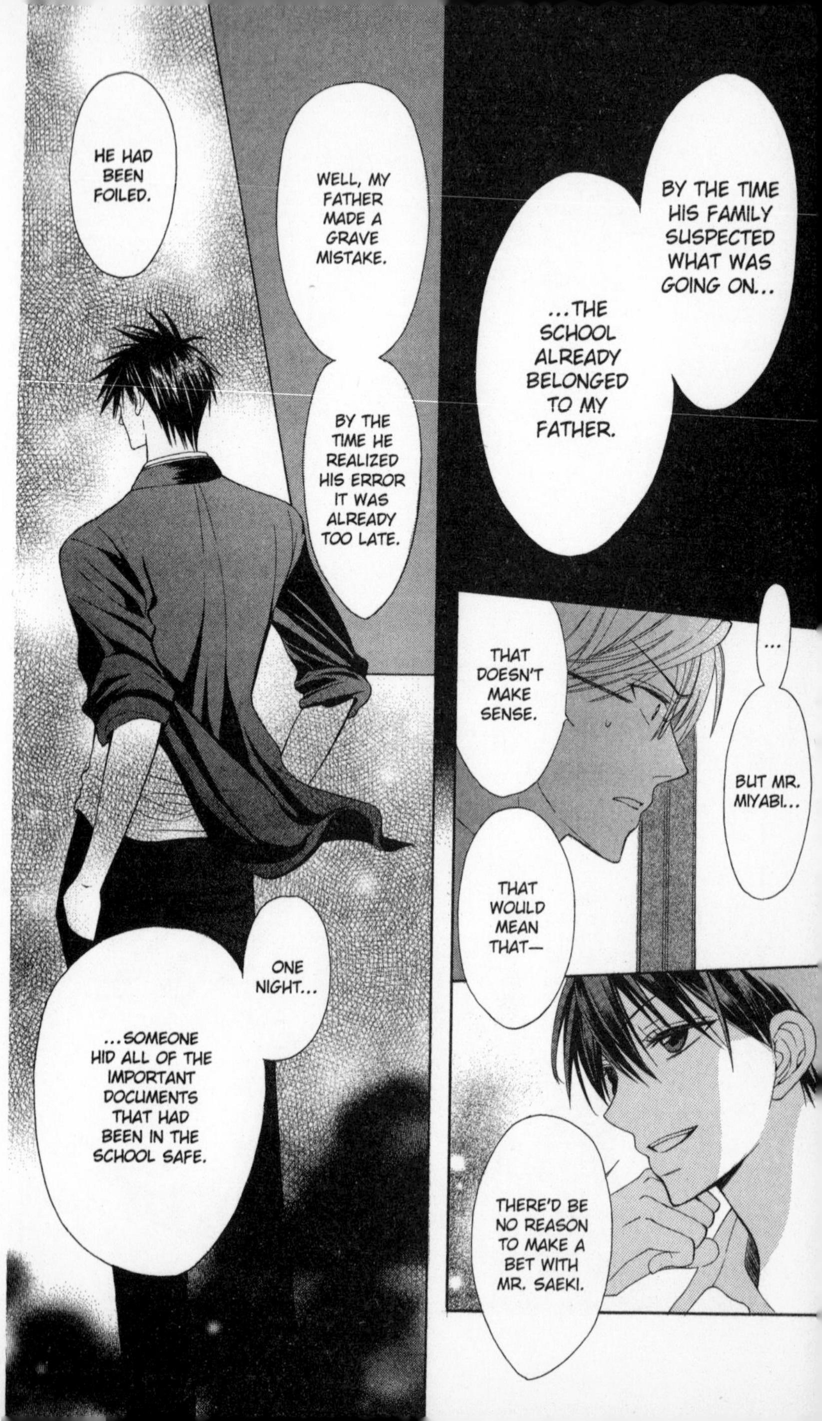
BY THE TIME HIS FAMILY SUSPECTED WHAT WAS GOING ON...
...THE SCHOOL ALREADY BELONGED TO MY FATHER.
...
BUT MR. MIYABI...
THAT DOESN'T MAKE SENSE.
THAT WOULD MEAN THAT—
THERE'D BE NO REASON TO MAKE A BET WITH MR. SAEKI.
WELL, MY FATHER MADE A GRAVE MISTAKE.
BY THE TIME HE REALIZED HIS ERROR IT WAS ALREADY TOO LATE.
HE HAD BEEN FOILED.
ONE NIGHT...
...SOMEONE HID ALL OF THE IMPORTANT DOCUMENTS THAT HAD BEEN IN THE SCHOOL SAFE.

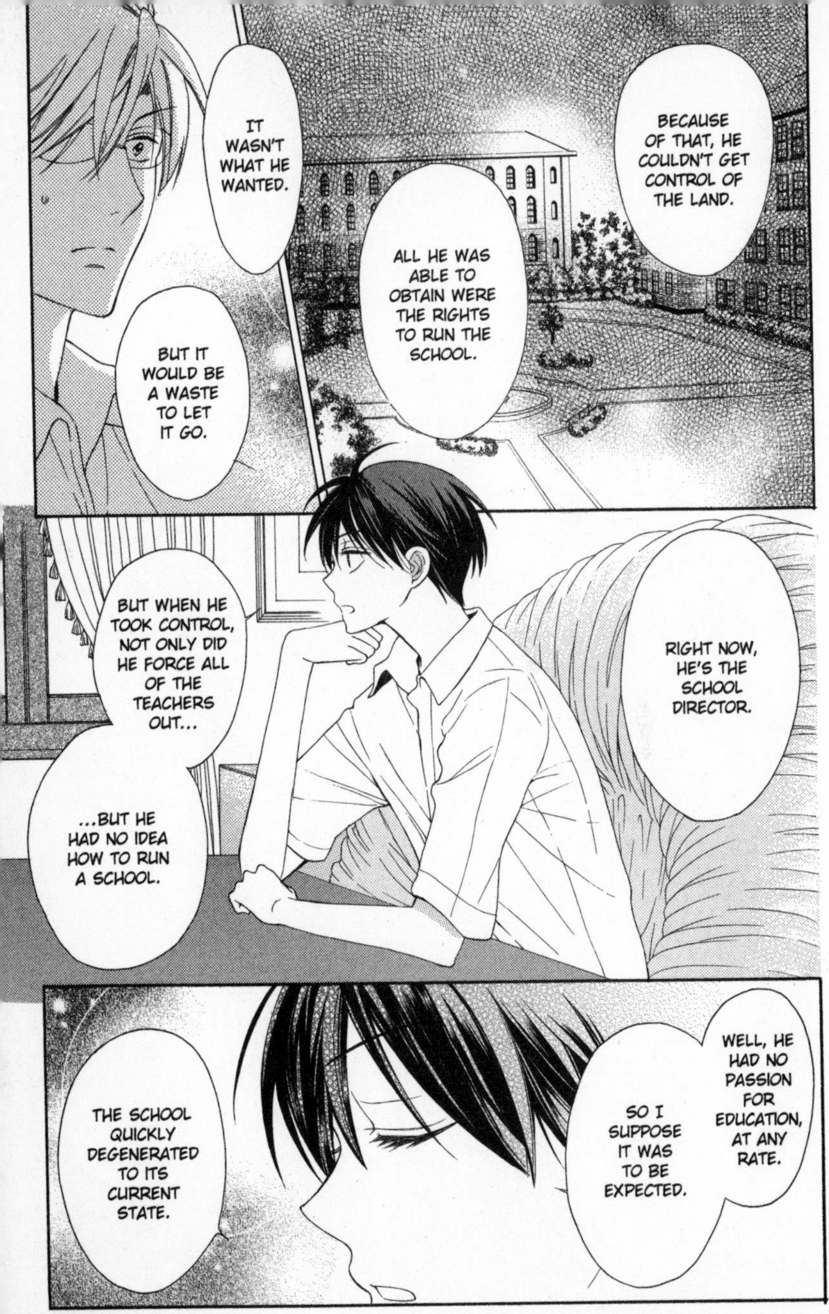
BECAUSE OF THAT, HE COULDN'T GET CONTROL OF THE LAND.
ALL HE WAS ABLE TO OBTAIN WERE THE RIGHTS TO RUN THE SCHOOL.
IT WASN'T WHAT HE WANTED.
BUT IT WOULD BE A WASTE TO LET IT GO.
RIGHT NOW, HE'S THE SCHOOL DIRECTOR.
BUT WHEN HE TOOK CONTROL, NOT ONLY DID HE FORCE ALL OF THE TEACHERS OUT...
...BUT HE HAD NO IDEA HOW TO RUN A SCHOOL.
WELL, HE HAD NO PASSION FOR EDUCATION, AT ANY RATE.
SO I SUPPOSE IT WAS TO BE EXPECTED.
THE SCHOOL QUICKLY DEGENERATED TO ITS CURRENT STATE.

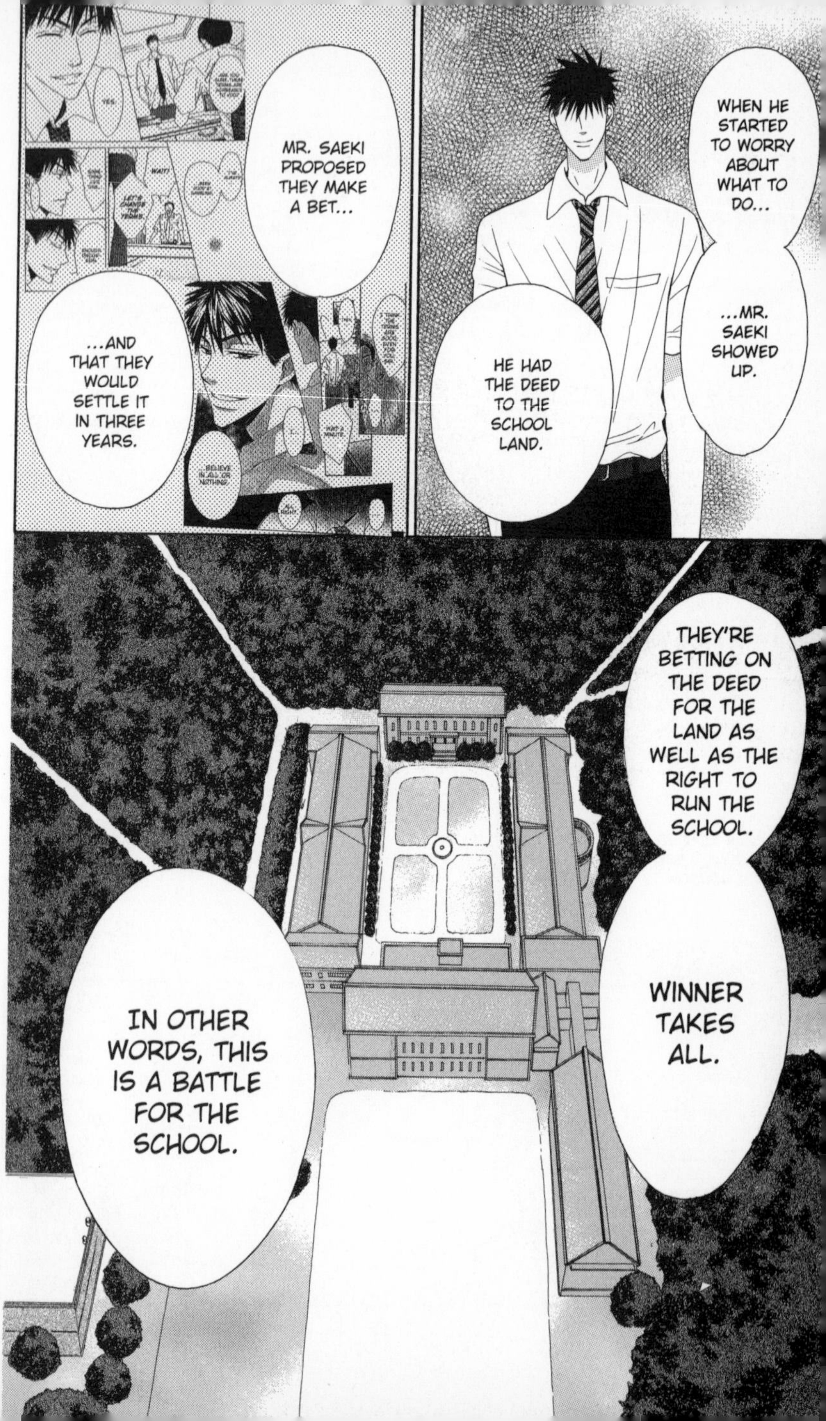
WHEN HE STARTED TO WORRY ABOUT WHAT TO DO...
...MR. SAEKI SHOWED UP.
HE HAD THE DEED TO THE SCHOOL LAND.
MR. SAEKI PROPOSED THEY MAKE A BET...
YES.
WAIT!
LET'S CHANGE THE TERMS.
...AND THAT THEY WOULD SETTLE IT IN THREE YEARS.
...BELIEVE IN ALL OR NOTHING.
ALL RIGHT.
THEY'RE BETTING ON THE DEED FOR THE LAND AS WELL AS THE RIGHT TO RUN THE SCHOOL.
WINNER TAKES ALL.
IN OTHER WORDS, THIS IS A BATTLE FOR THE SCHOOL.

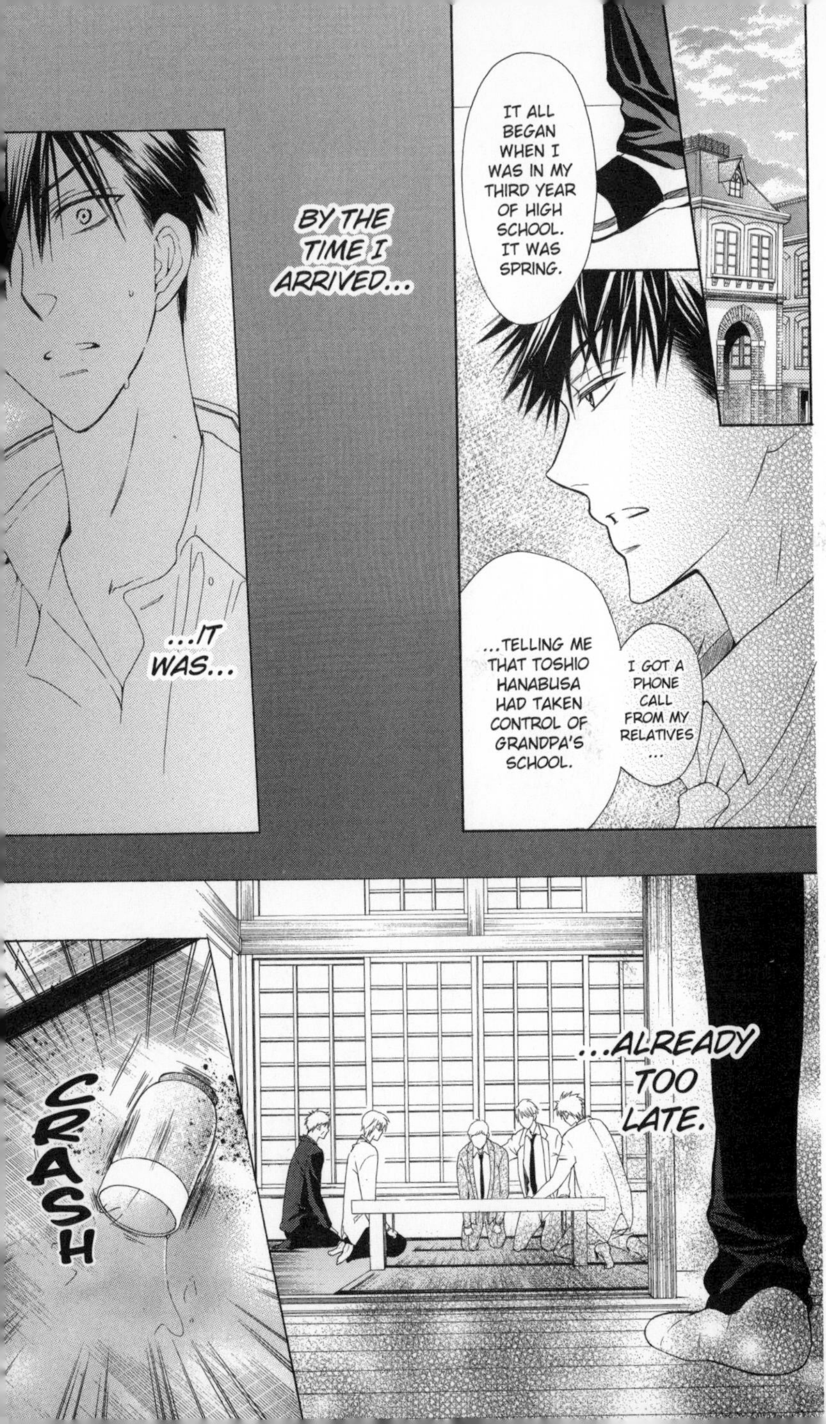
IT ALL BEGAN WHEN I WAS IN MY THIRD YEAR OF HIGH SCHOOL. IT WAS SPRING.
I GOT A PHONE CALL FROM MY RELATIVES ...
...TELLING ME THAT TOSHIO HANABUSA HAD TAKEN CONTROL OF GRANDPA'S SCHOOL.
BY THE TIME I ARRIVED...
...IT WAS...
...ALREADY TOO LATE.
CRASH

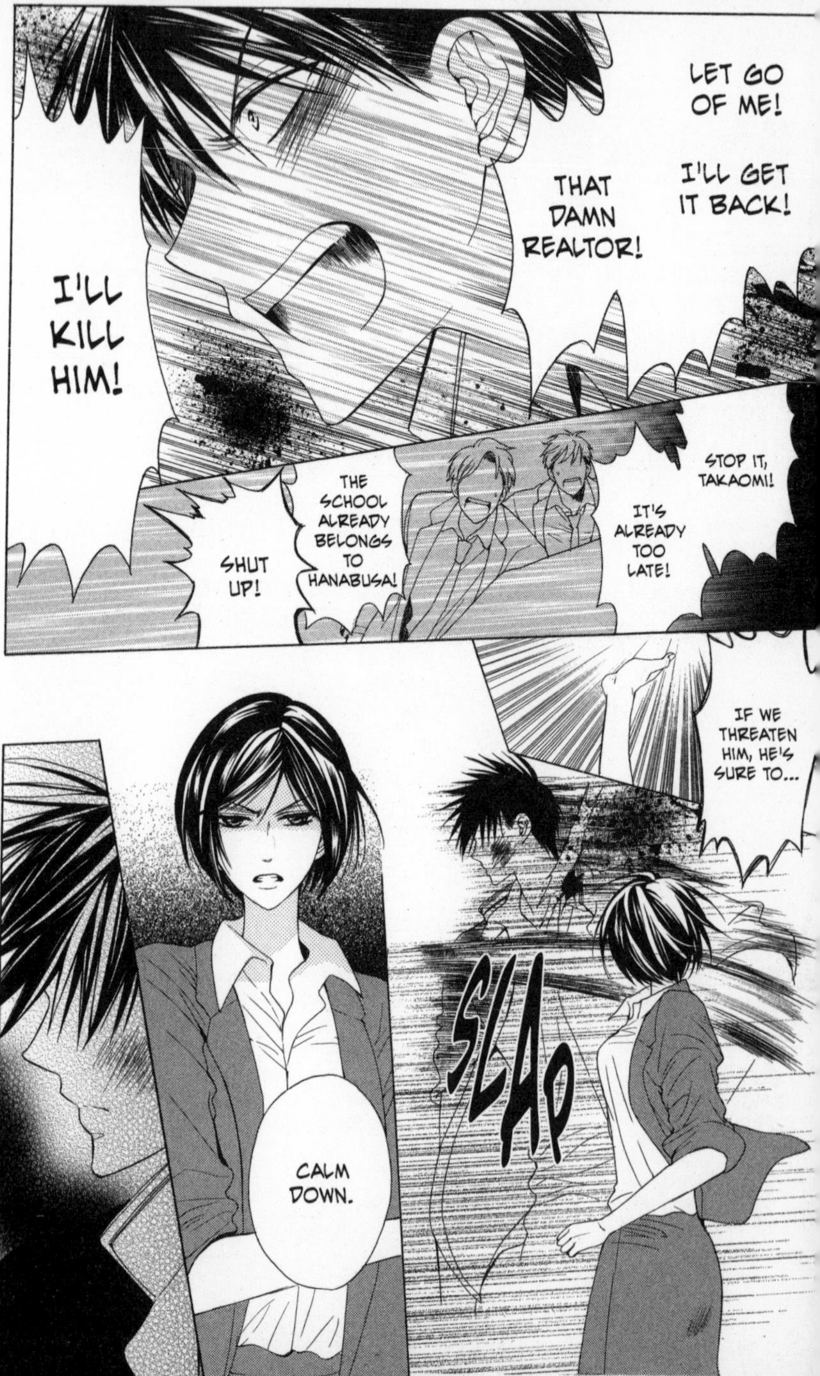
LET GO OF ME!
I'LL GET IT BACK!
THAT DAMN REALTOR!
I'LL KILL HIM!
STOP IT, TAKAOMI!
IT'S ALREADY TOO LATE!
THE SCHOOL ALREADY BELONGS TO HANABUSA!
SHUT UP!
IF WE THREATEN HIM, HE'S SURE TO...
SLAP
CALM DOWN.

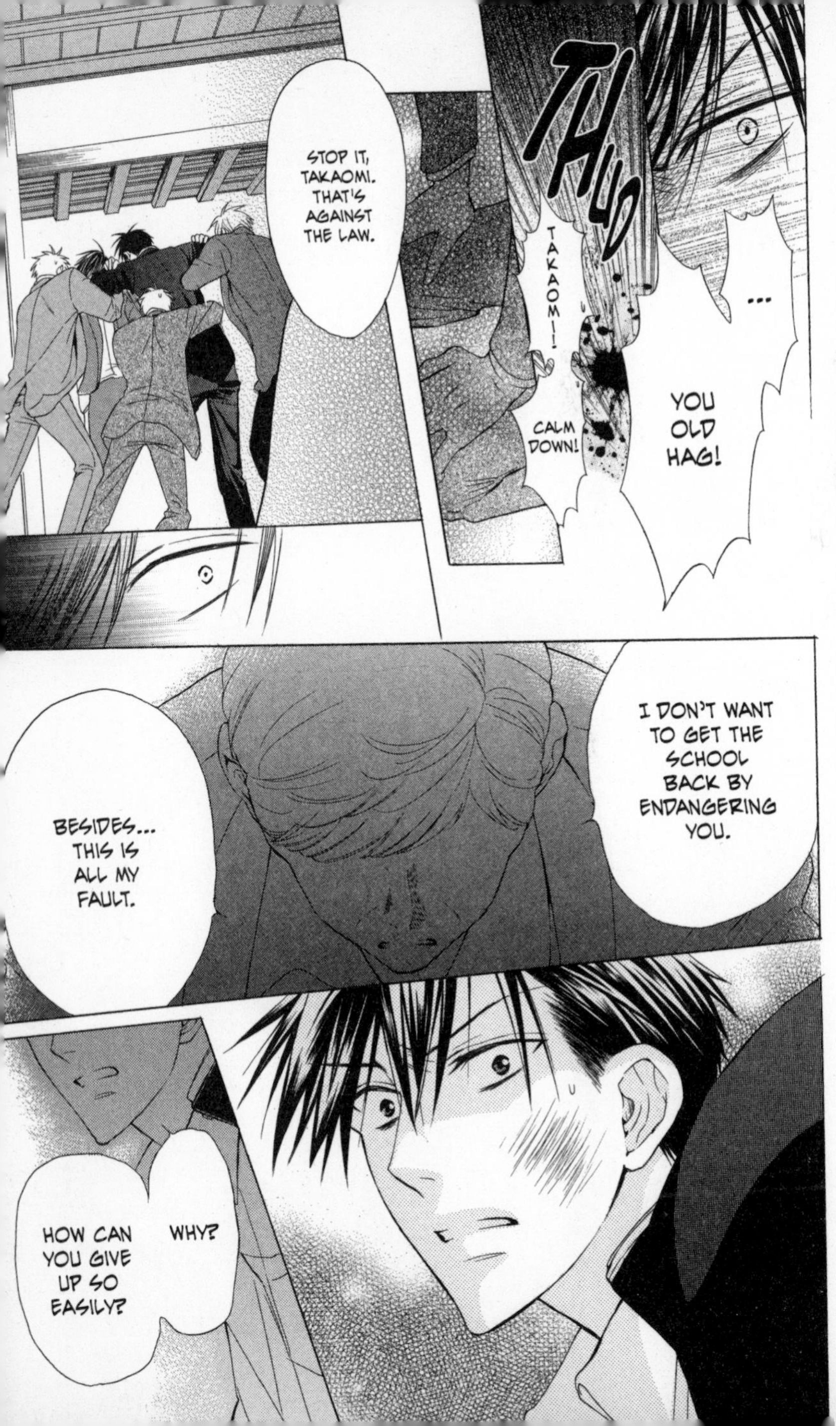
THUD
...
YOU OLD HAG!
TAKAOMI!!
CALM DOWN!
STOP IT, TAKAOMI. THAT'S AGAINST THE LAW.
I DON'T WANT TO GET THE SCHOOL BACK BY ENDANGERING YOU.
BESIDES... THIS IS ALL MY FAULT.
WHY?
HOW CAN YOU GIVE UP SO EASILY?

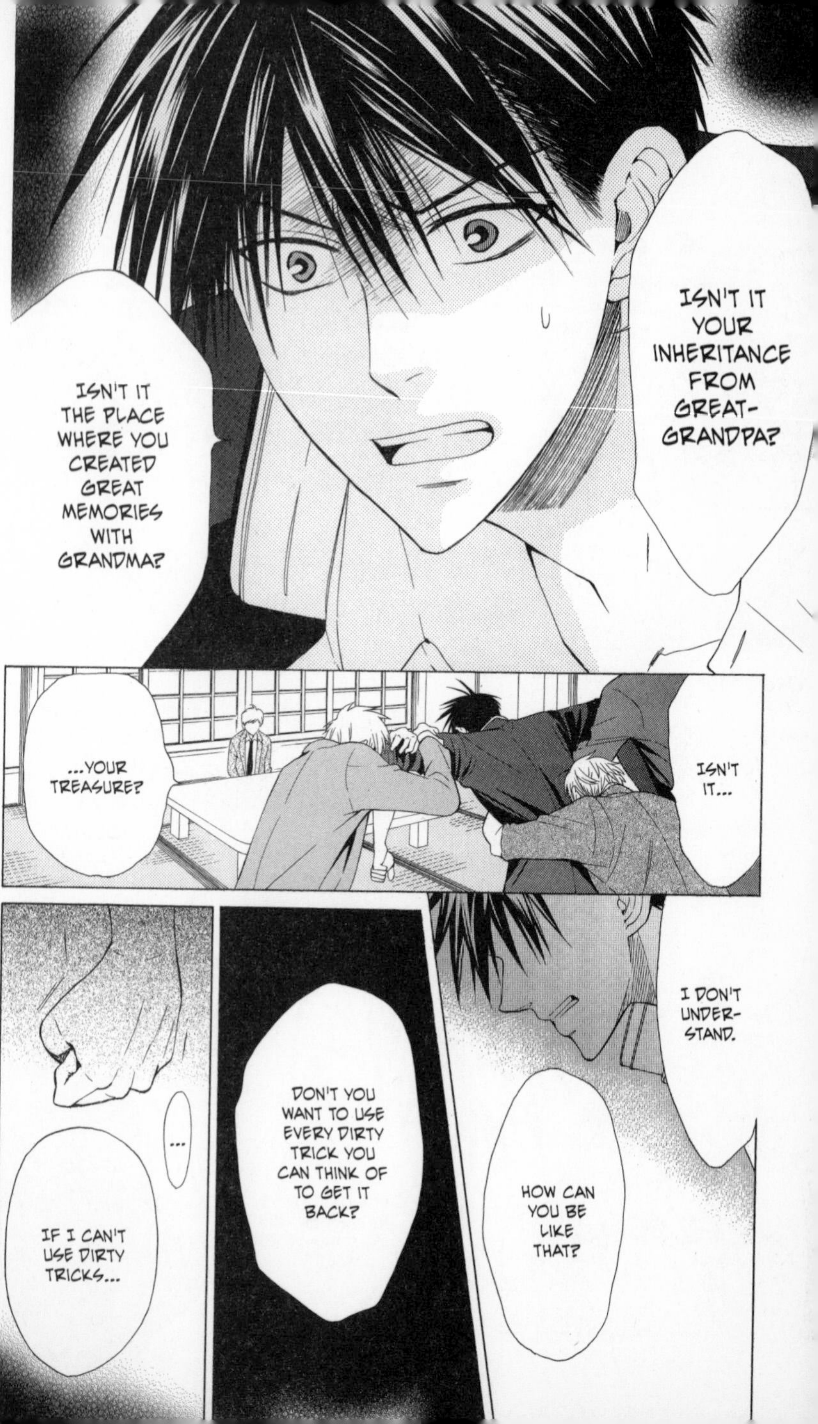
ISN'T IT YOUR INHERITANCE FROM GREAT-GRANDPA?
ISN'T IT THE PLACE WHERE YOU CREATED GREAT MEMORIES WITH GRANDMA?
ISN'T IT...
...YOUR TREASURE?
I DON'T UNDER-STAND.
HOW CAN YOU BE LIKE THAT?
DON'T YOU WANT TO USE EVERY DIRTY TRICK YOU CAN THINK OF TO GET IT BACK?
...
IF I CAN'T USE DIRTY TRICKS...

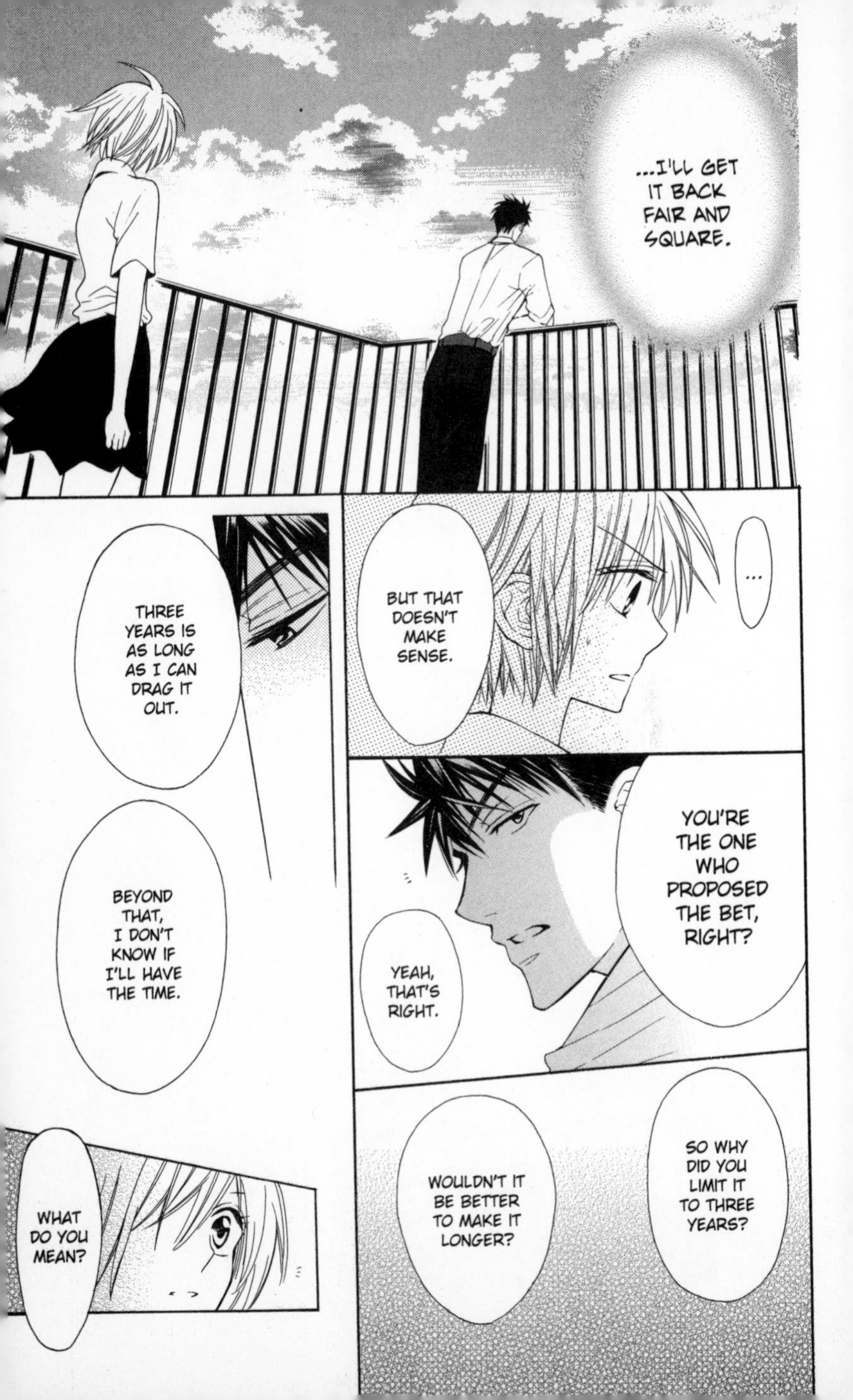
...I'LL GET IT BACK FAIR AND SQUARE.
...
BUT THAT DOESN'T MAKE SENSE.
YOU'RE THE ONE WHO PROPOSED THE BET, RIGHT?
YEAH, THAT'S RIGHT.
SO WHY DID YOU LIMIT IT TO THREE YEARS?
WOULDN'T IT BE BETTER TO MAKE IT LONGER?
THREE YEARS IS AS LONG AS I CAN DRAG IT OUT.
BEYOND THAT, I DON'T KNOW IF I'LL HAVE THE TIME.
WHAT DO YOU MEAN?

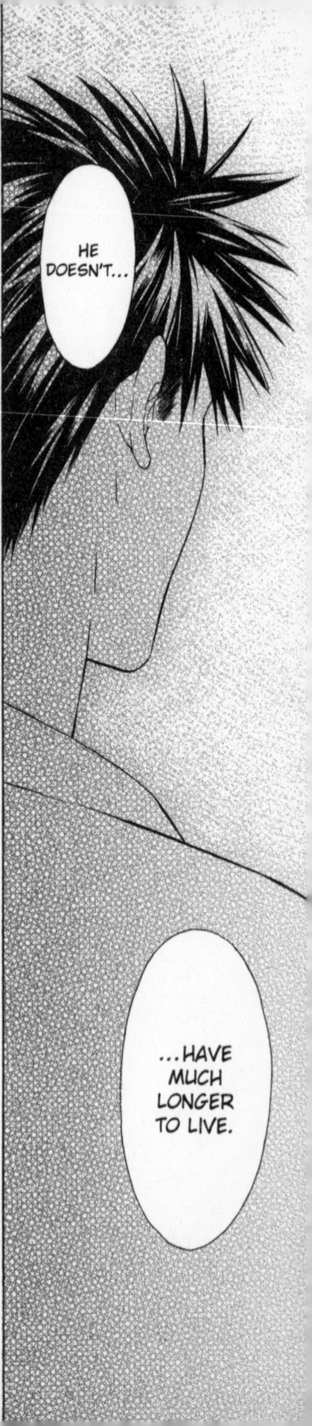
HE DOESN'T...
...HAVE MUCH LONGER TO LIVE.

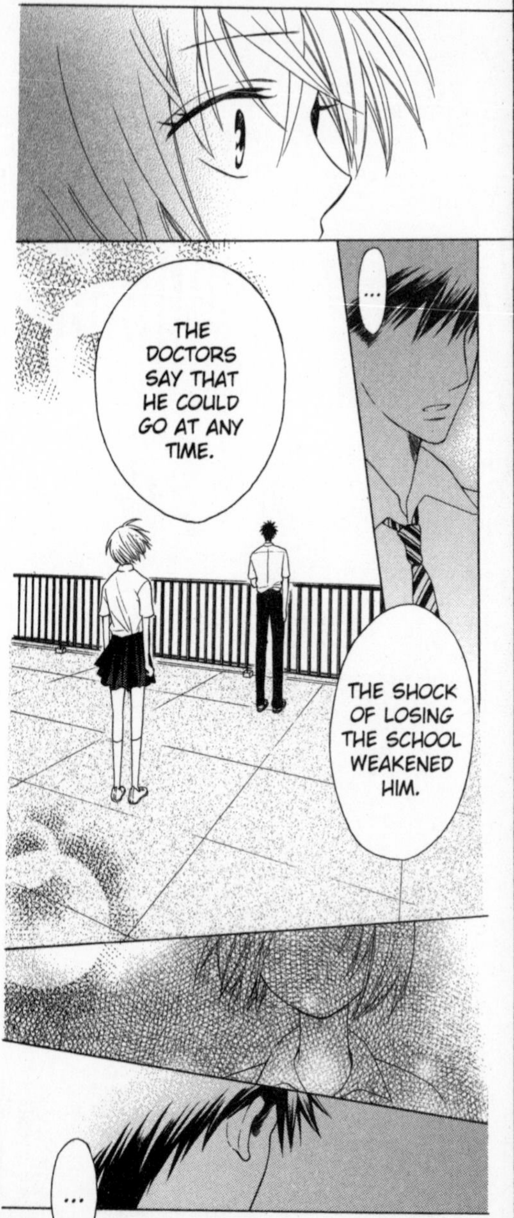
...
THE DOCTORS SAY THAT HE COULD GO AT ANY TIME.
THE SHOCK OF LOSING THE SCHOOL WEAKENED HIM.
...

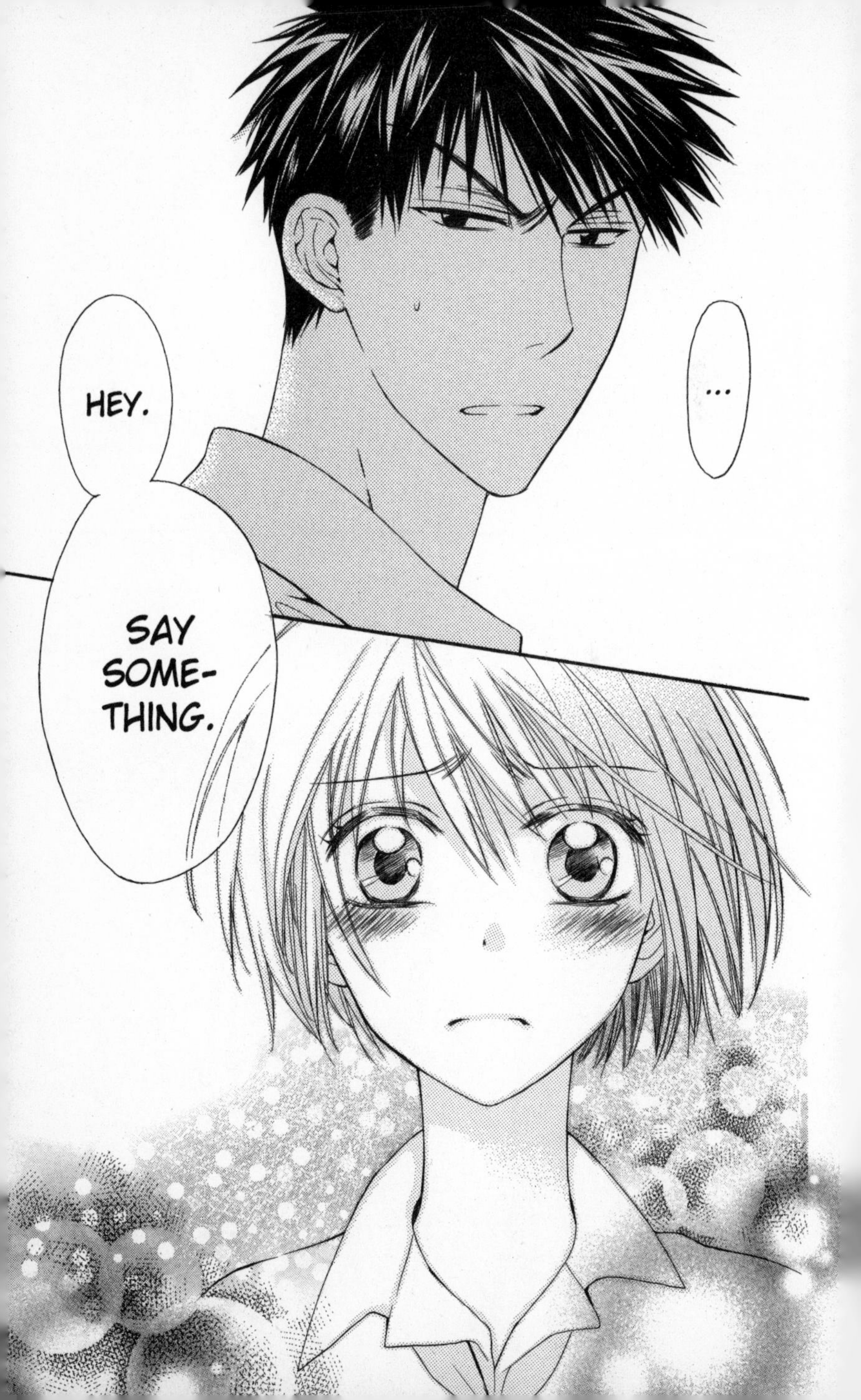
...
HEY.
SAY SOME-THING.

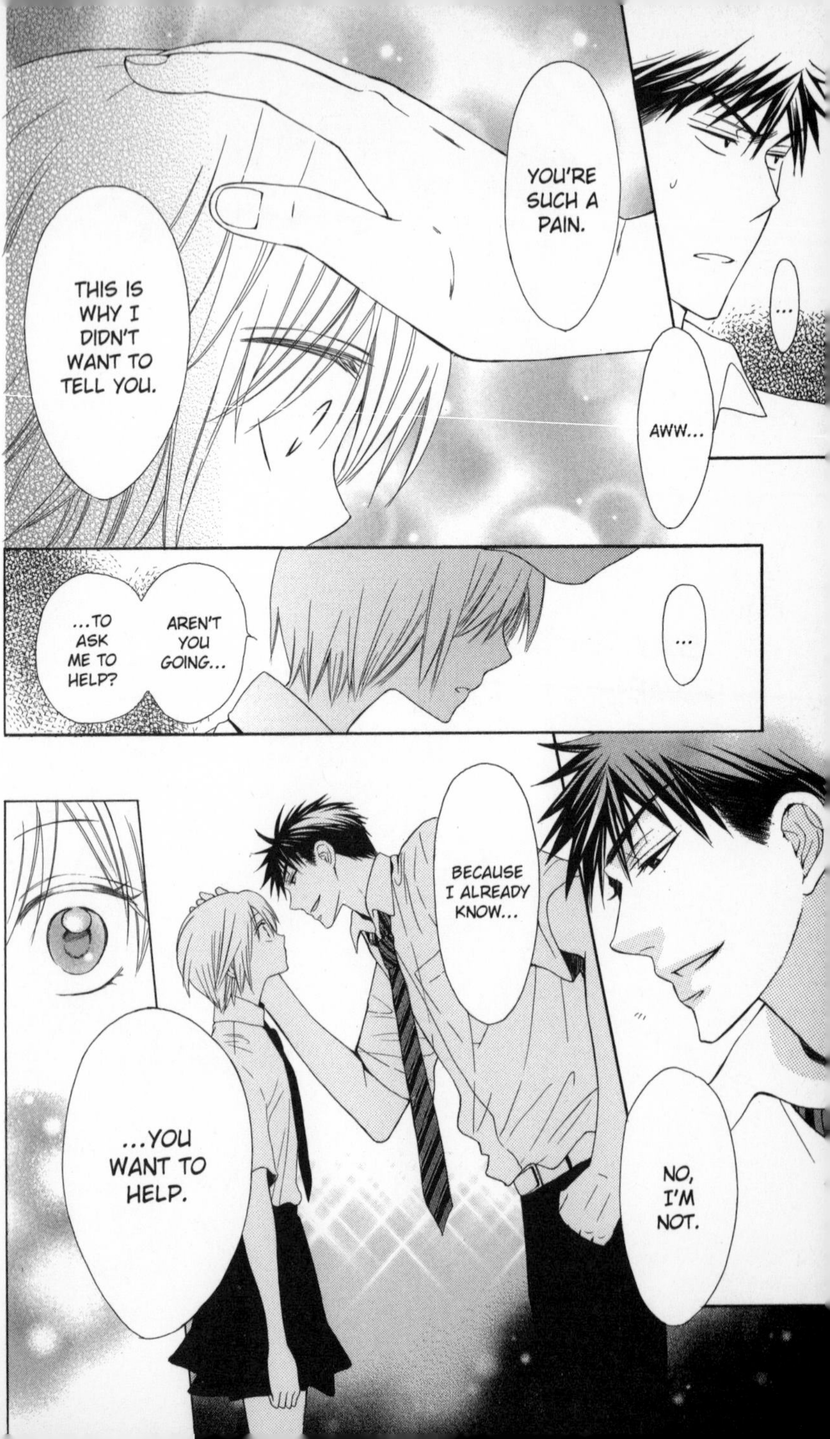
YOU'RE SUCH A PAIN.
...
AWW...
THIS IS WHY I DIDN'T WANT TO TELL YOU.
...
AREN'T YOU GOING...
...TO ASK ME TO HELP?
BECAUSE I ALREADY KNOW...
NO, I'M NOT.
...YOU WANT TO HELP.

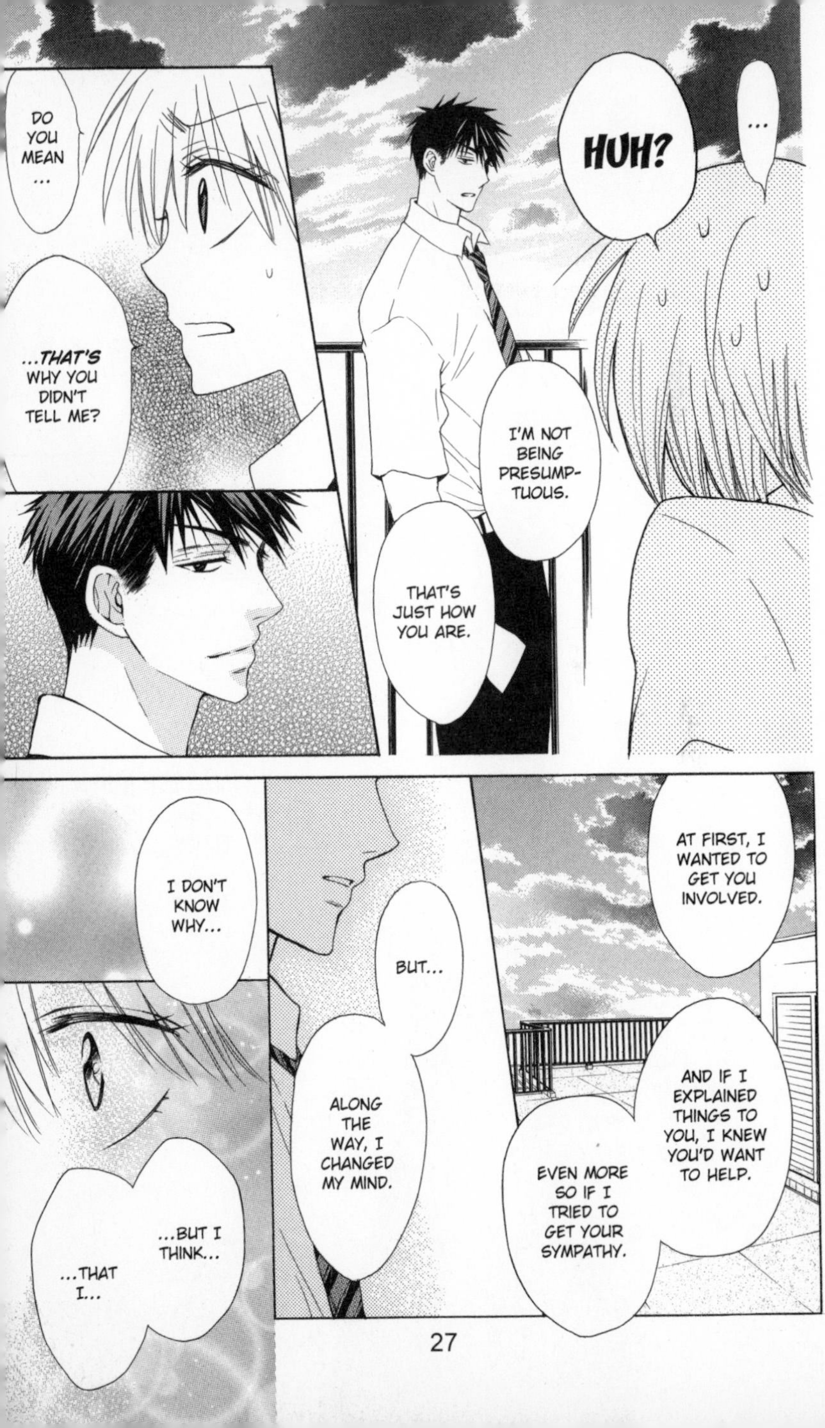
...
HUH?
I'M NOT BEING PRESUMPTUOUS.
THAT'S JUST HOW YOU ARE.
DO YOU MEAN ...
...*THAT'S* WHY YOU DIDN'T TELL ME?
AT FIRST, I WANTED TO GET YOU INVOLVED.
AND IF I EXPLAINED THINGS TO YOU, I KNEW YOU'D WANT TO HELP.
EVEN MORE SO IF I TRIED TO GET YOUR SYMPATHY.
BUT...
ALONG THE WAY, I CHANGED MY MIND.
I DON'T KNOW WHY...
...BUT I THINK...
...THAT I...

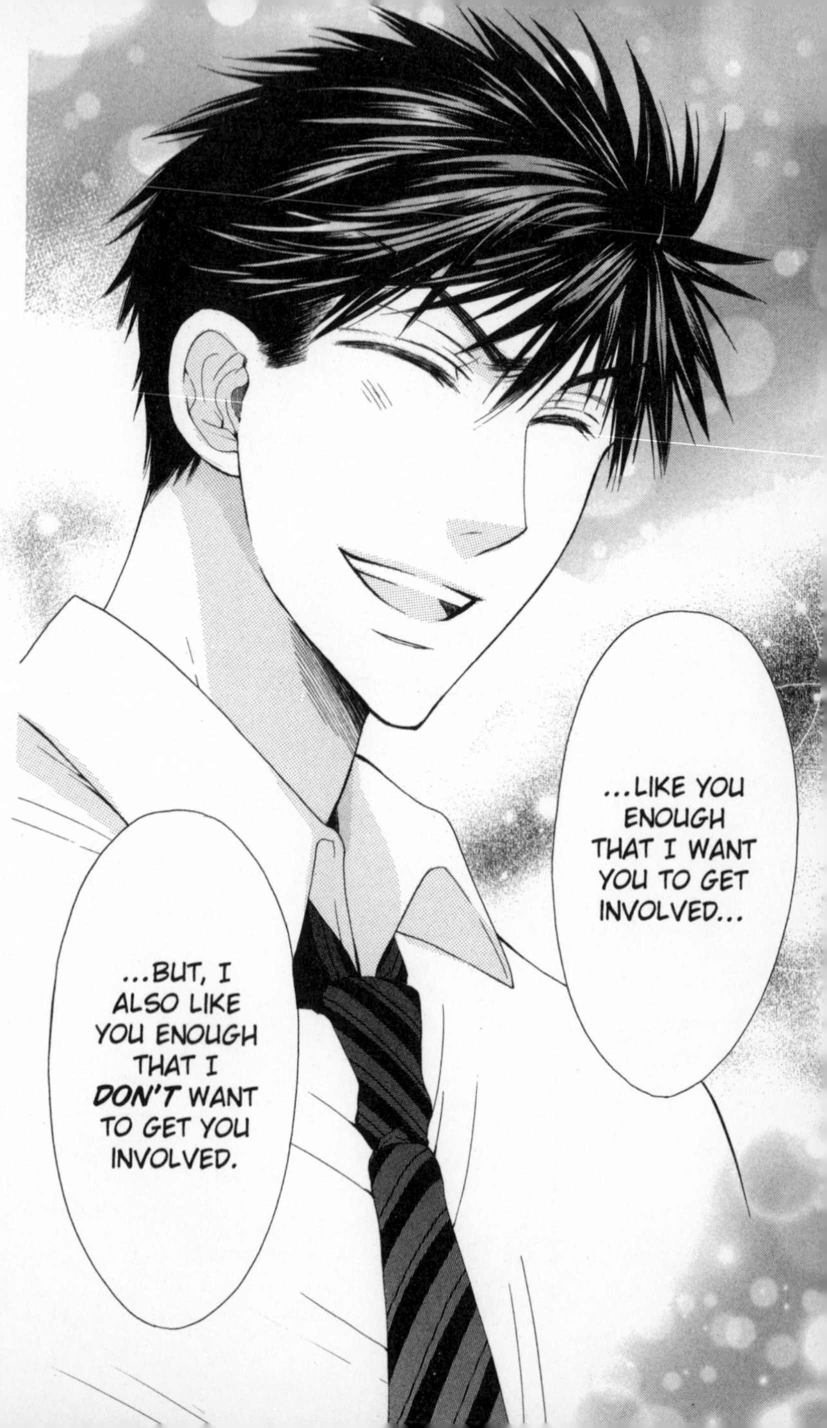
...LIKE YOU ENOUGH THAT I WANT YOU TO GET INVOLVED...
...BUT, I ALSO LIKE YOU ENOUGH THAT I *DON'T* WANT TO GET YOU INVOLVED.

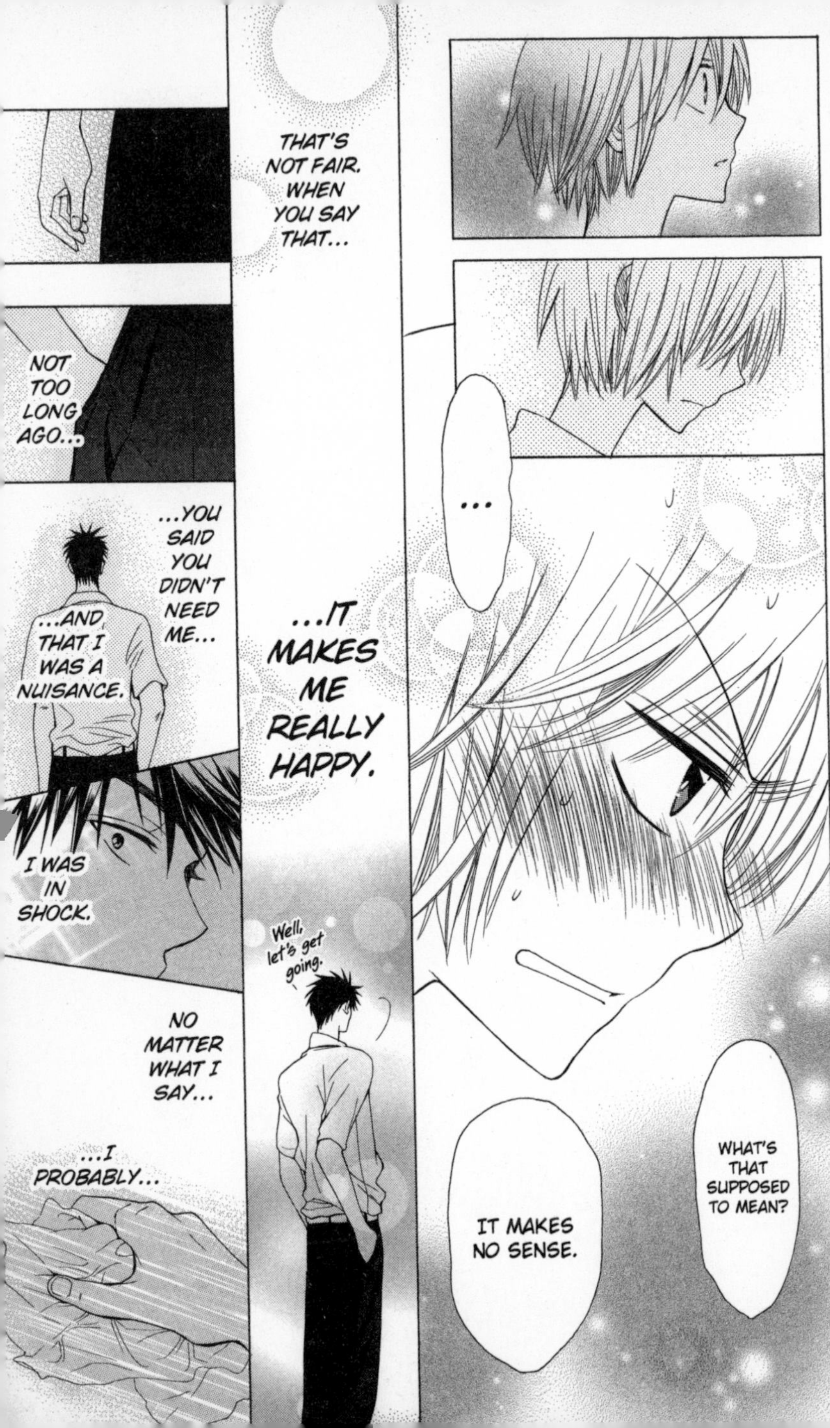
...
WHAT'S THAT SUPPOSED TO MEAN?
IT MAKES NO SENSE.
THAT'S NOT FAIR. WHEN YOU SAY THAT...
...IT MAKES ME REALLY HAPPY.
Well, let's get going.
NOT TOO LONG AGO...
...YOU SAID YOU DIDN'T NEED ME...
...AND THAT I WAS A NUISANCE.
I WAS IN SHOCK.
NO MATTER WHAT I SAY...
...I PROBABLY...

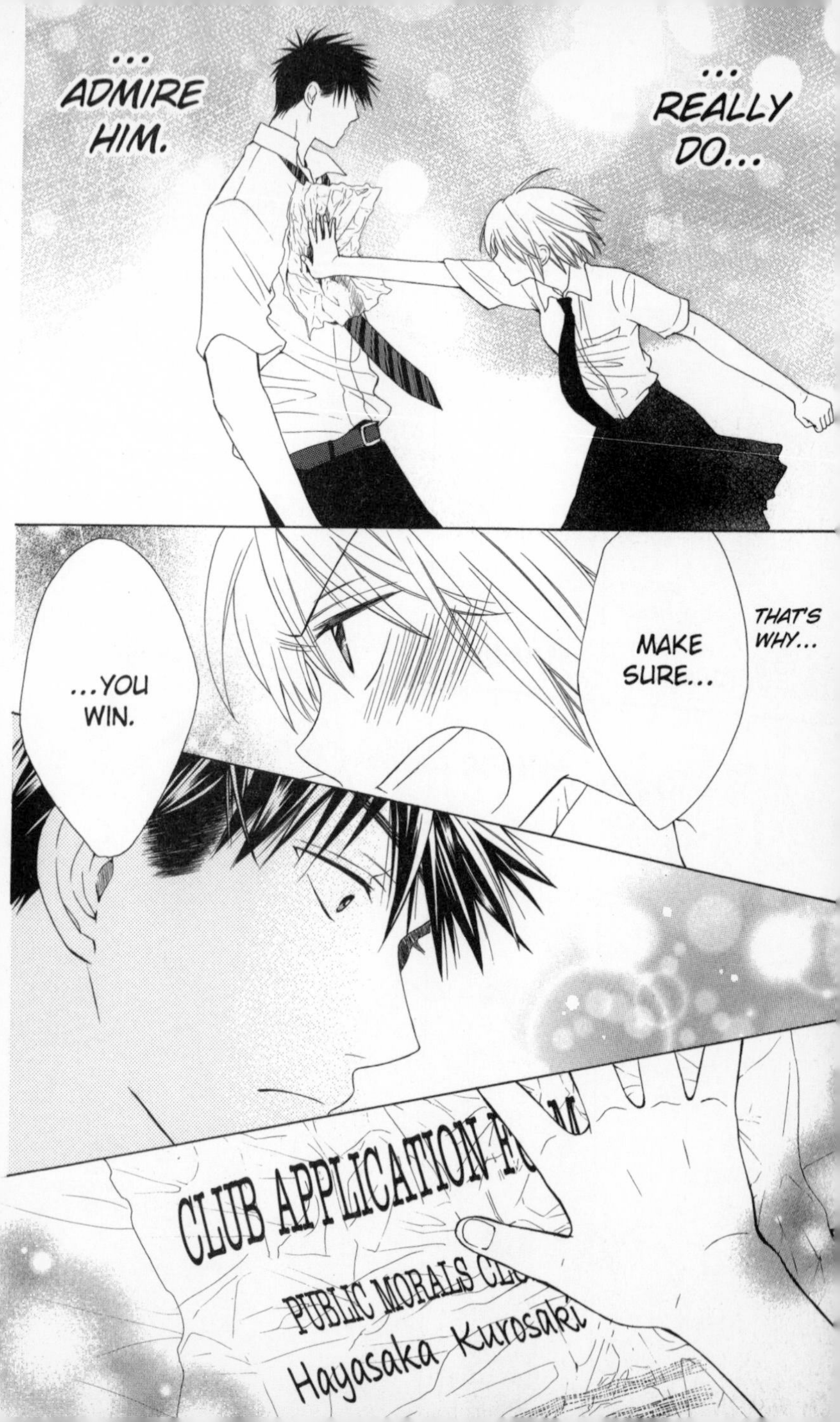
...
REALLY
DO...
...
ADMIRE
HIM.
THAT'S WHY...
MAKE SURE...
...YOU WIN.
CLUB APPLICATION
PUBLIC MORALS
Hayasaka Kurosaki

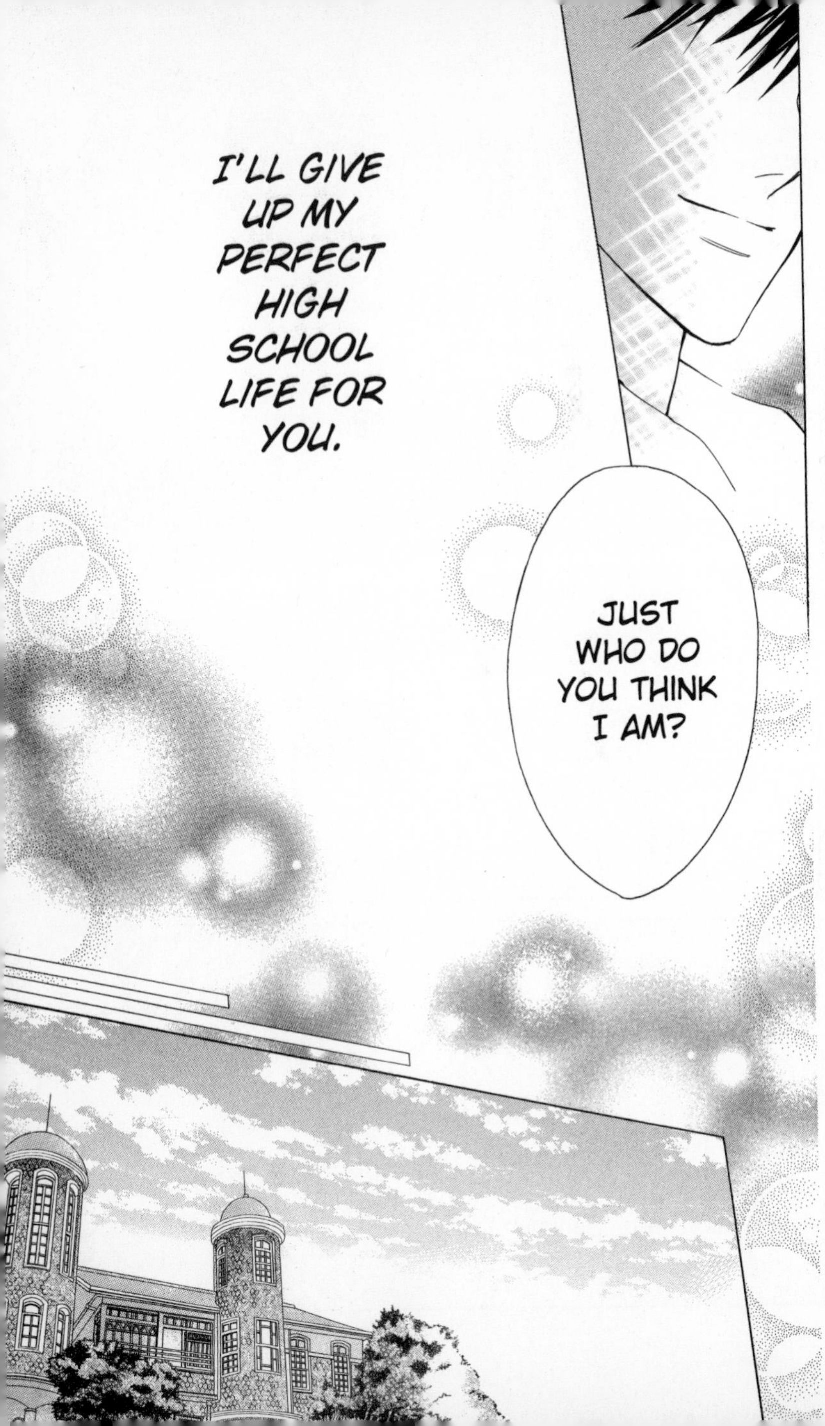
JUST WHO DO YOU THINK I AM?
I'LL GIVE UP MY PERFECT HIGH SCHOOL LIFE FOR YOU.

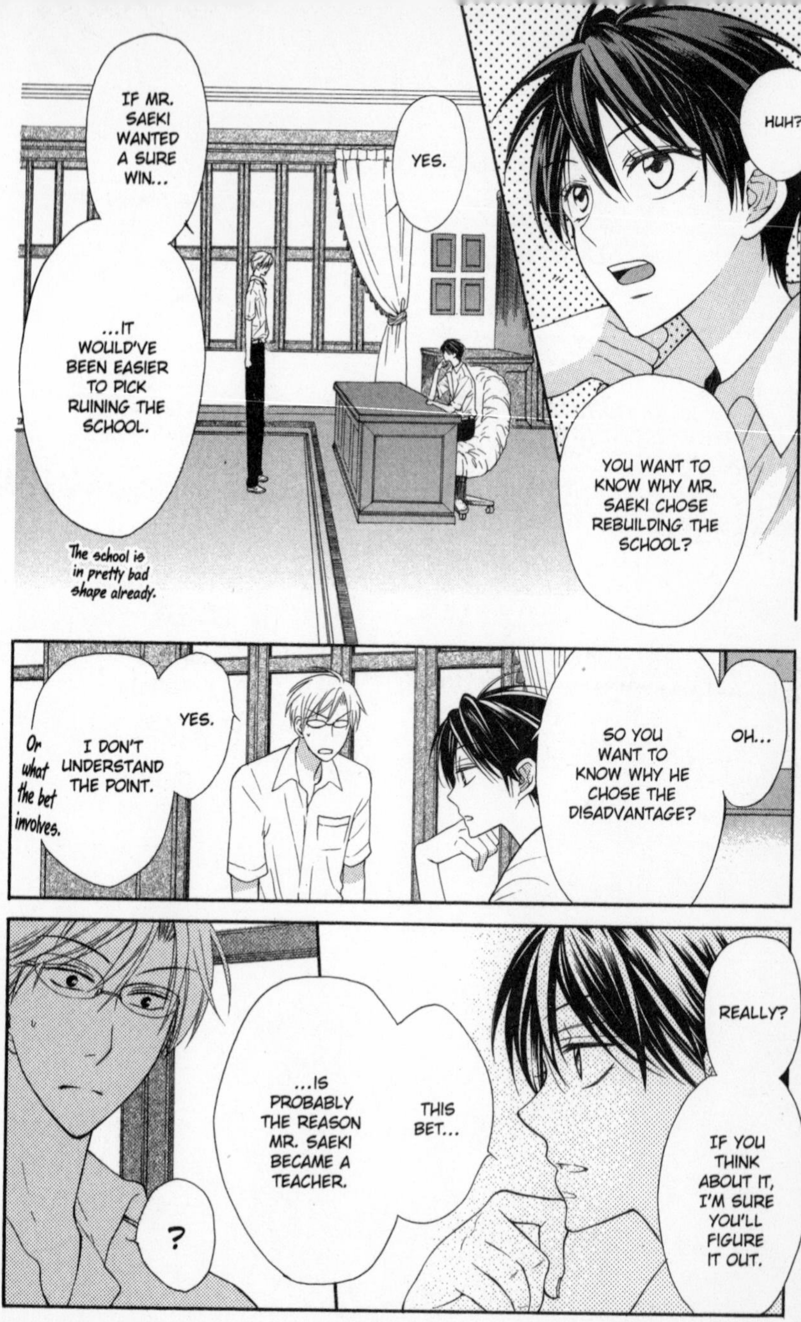
HUH?
YOU WANT TO KNOW WHY MR. SAEKI CHOSE REBUILDING THE SCHOOL?
YES.
IF MR. SAEKI WANTED A SURE WIN...
...IT WOULD'VE BEEN EASIER TO PICK RUINING THE SCHOOL.
The school is in pretty bad shape already.
OH...
SO YOU WANT TO KNOW WHY HE CHOSE THE DISADVANTAGE?
YES.
I DON'T UNDERSTAND THE POINT.
Or what the bet involves.
REALLY?
IF YOU THINK ABOUT IT, I'M SURE YOU'LL FIGURE IT OUT.
THIS BET...
...IS PROBABLY THE REASON MR. SAEKI BECAME A TEACHER.
?

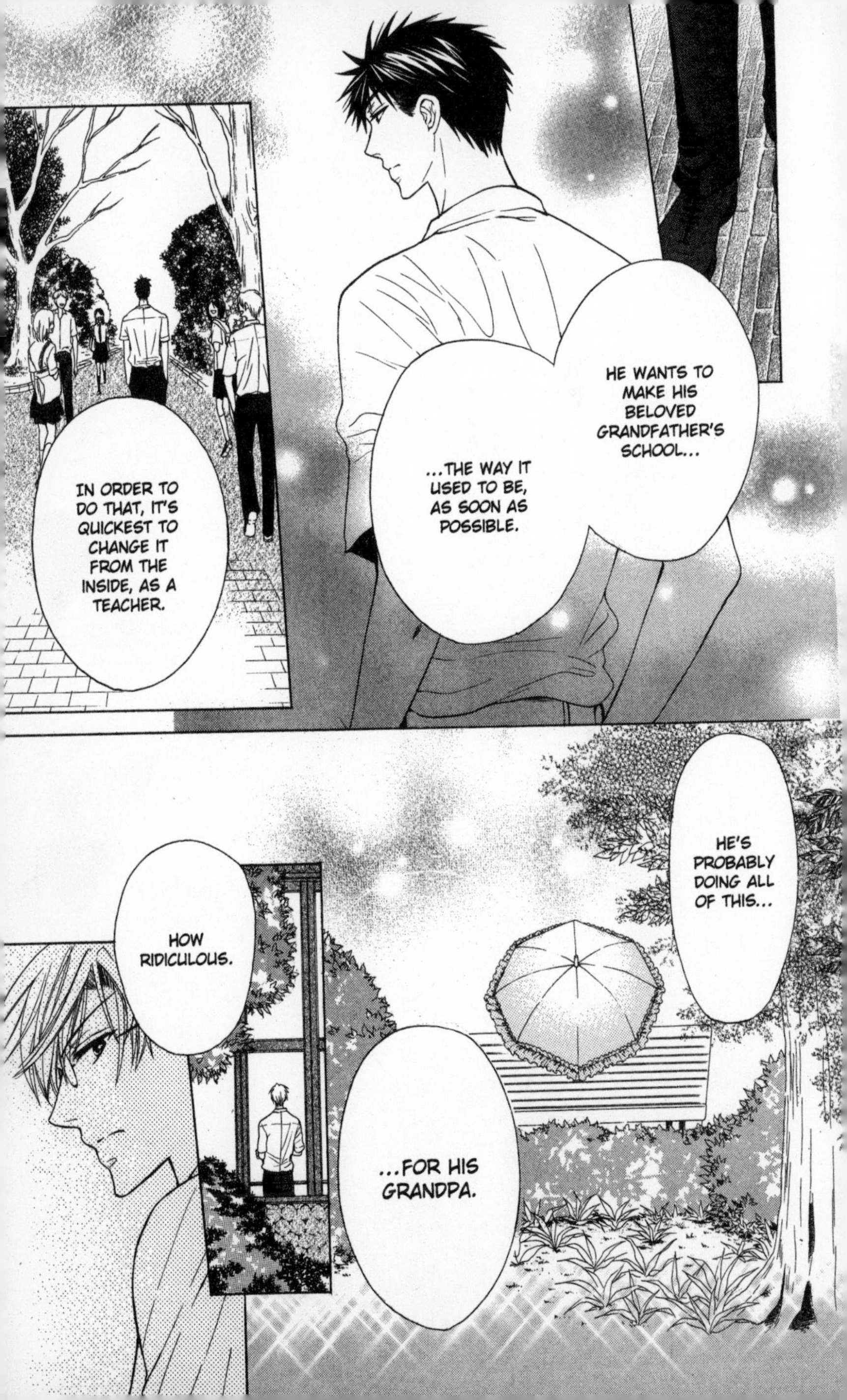
HE WANTS TO MAKE HIS BELOVED GRANDFATHER'S SCHOOL...
...THE WAY IT USED TO BE, AS SOON AS POSSIBLE.
IN ORDER TO DO THAT, IT'S QUICKEST TO CHANGE IT FROM THE INSIDE, AS A TEACHER.
HE'S PROBABLY DOING ALL OF THIS...
...FOR HIS GRANDPA.
HOW RIDICULOUS.

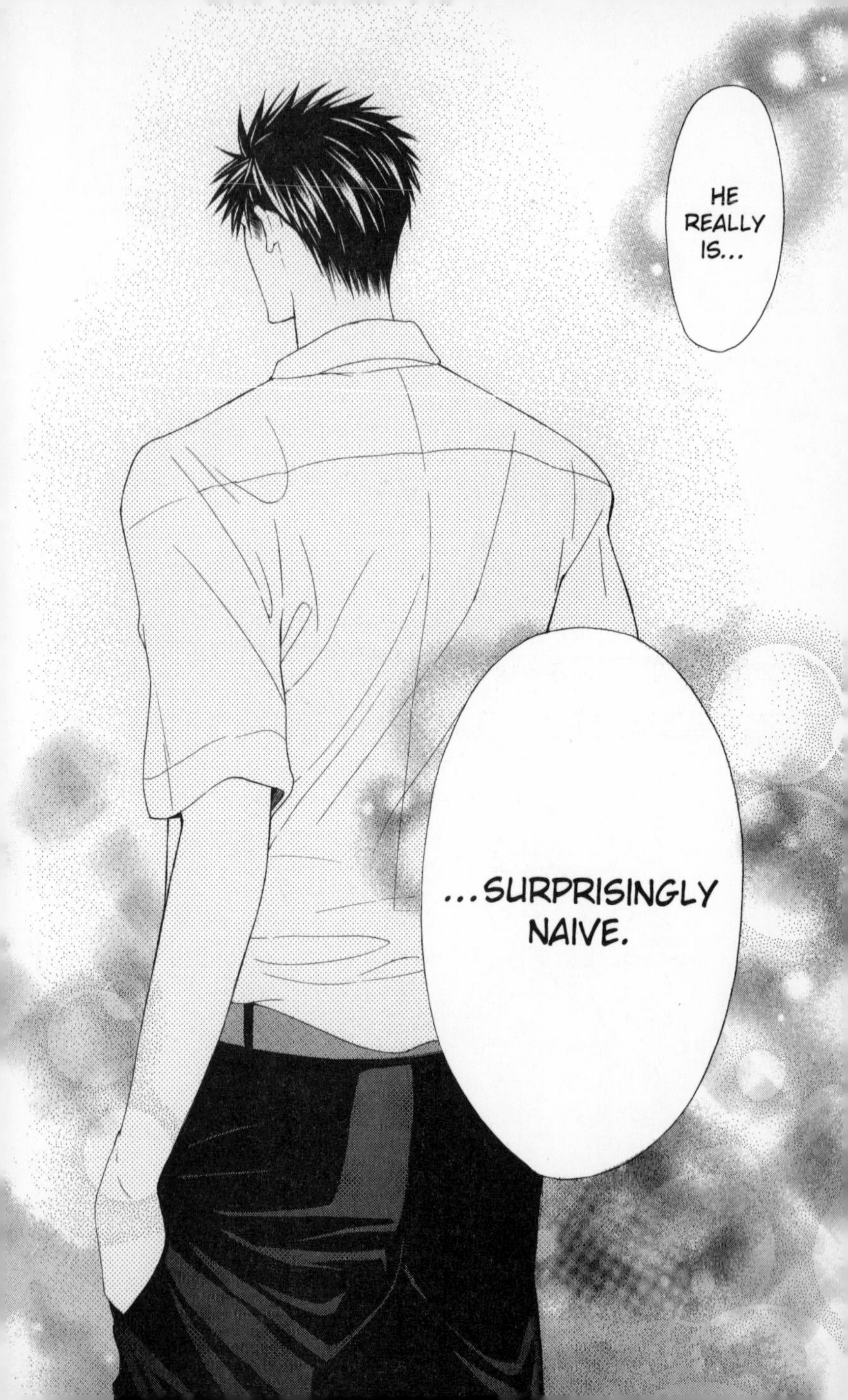
HE REALLY IS...
...SURPRISINGLY NAIVE.

Chapter 36

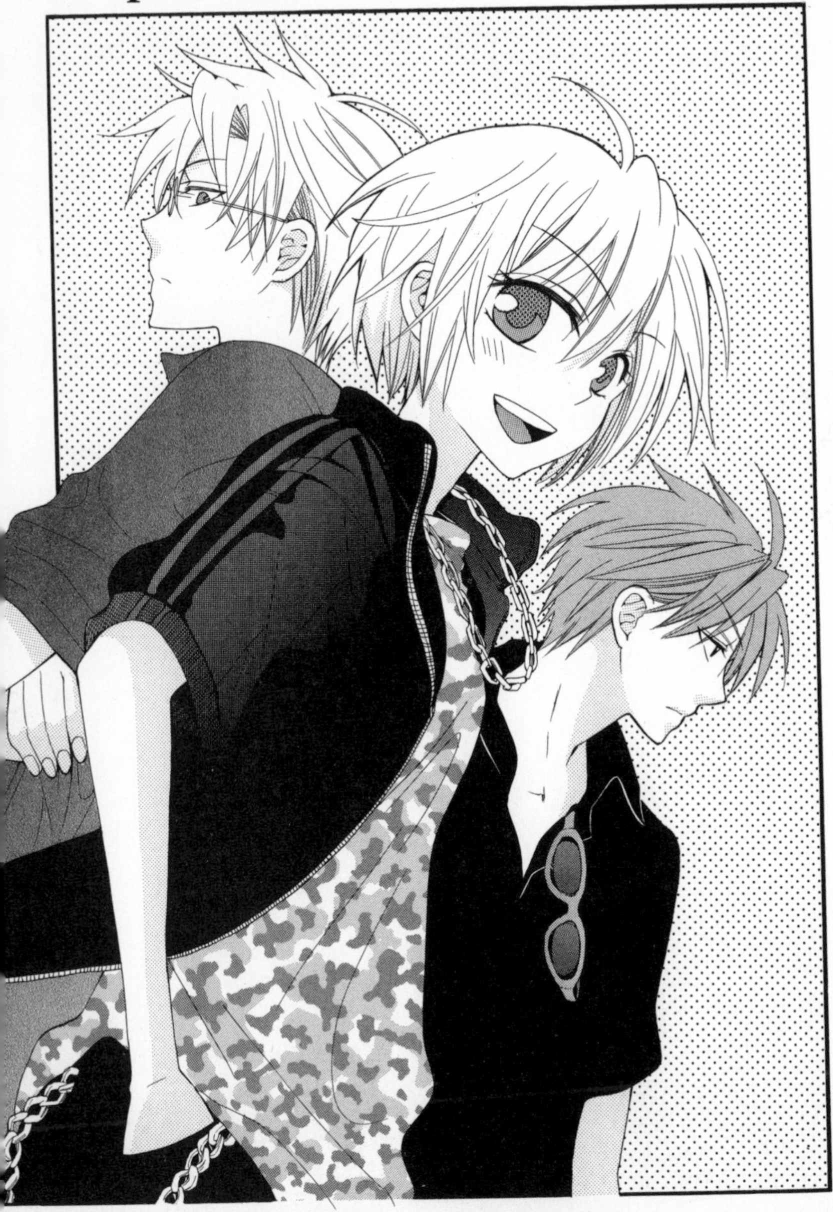

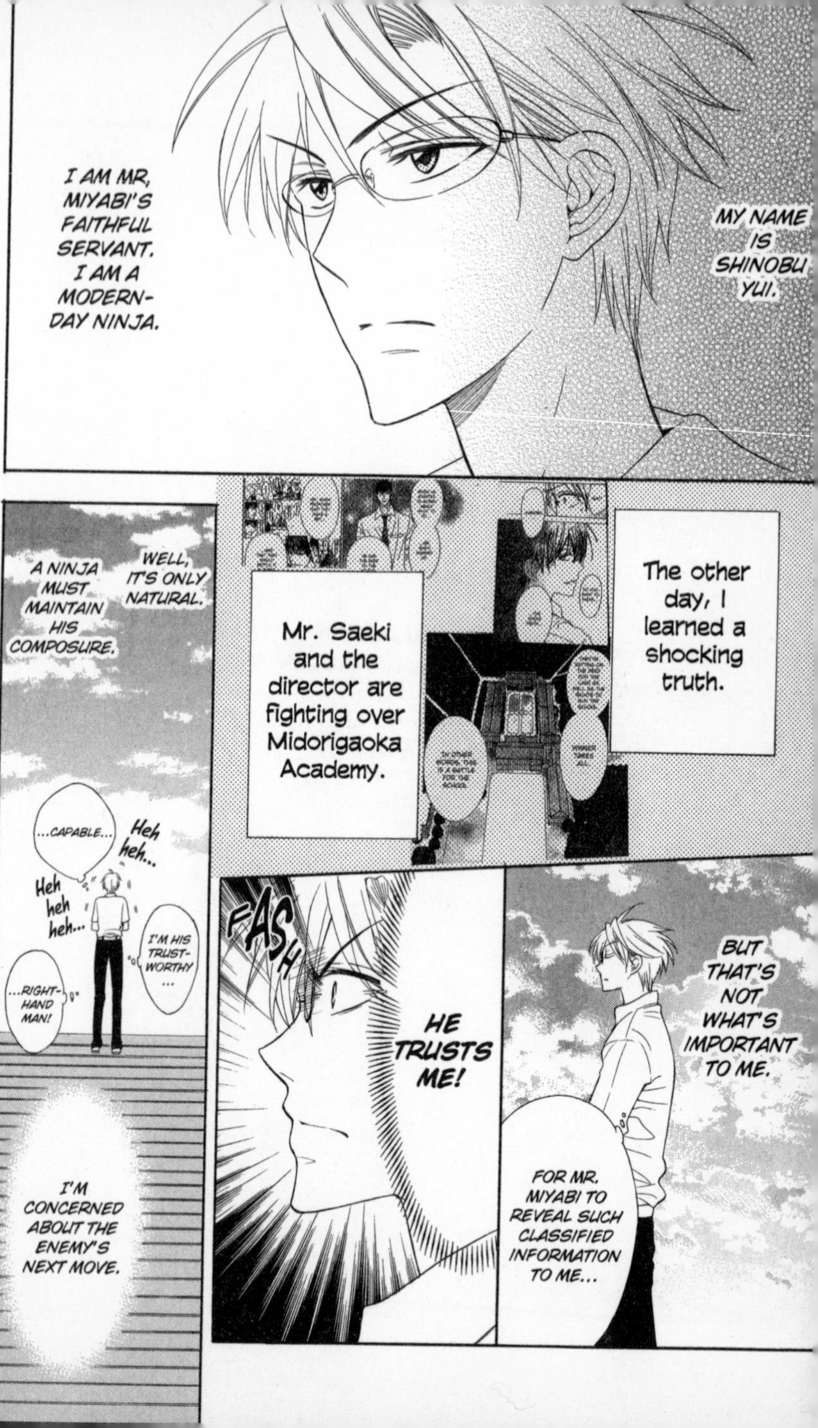

MY NAME IS SHINOBU YUI.
I AM MR. MIYABI'S FAITHFUL SERVANT. I AM A MODERN-DAY NINJA.
The other day, I learned a shocking truth.
Mr. Saeki and the director are fighting over Midorigaoka Academy.
BUT THAT'S NOT WHAT'S IMPORTANT TO ME.
FOR MR. MIYABI TO REVEAL SUCH CLASSIFIED INFORMATION TO ME...
FASH
HE TRUSTS ME!
WELL, IT'S ONLY NATURAL.
A NINJA MUST MAINTAIN HIS COMPOSURE.
Heh heh...
...CAPABLE...
Heh heh heh...
I'M HIS TRUST-WORTHY...
...RIGHT-HAND MAN!
I'M CONCERNED ABOUT THE ENEMY'S NEXT MOVE.

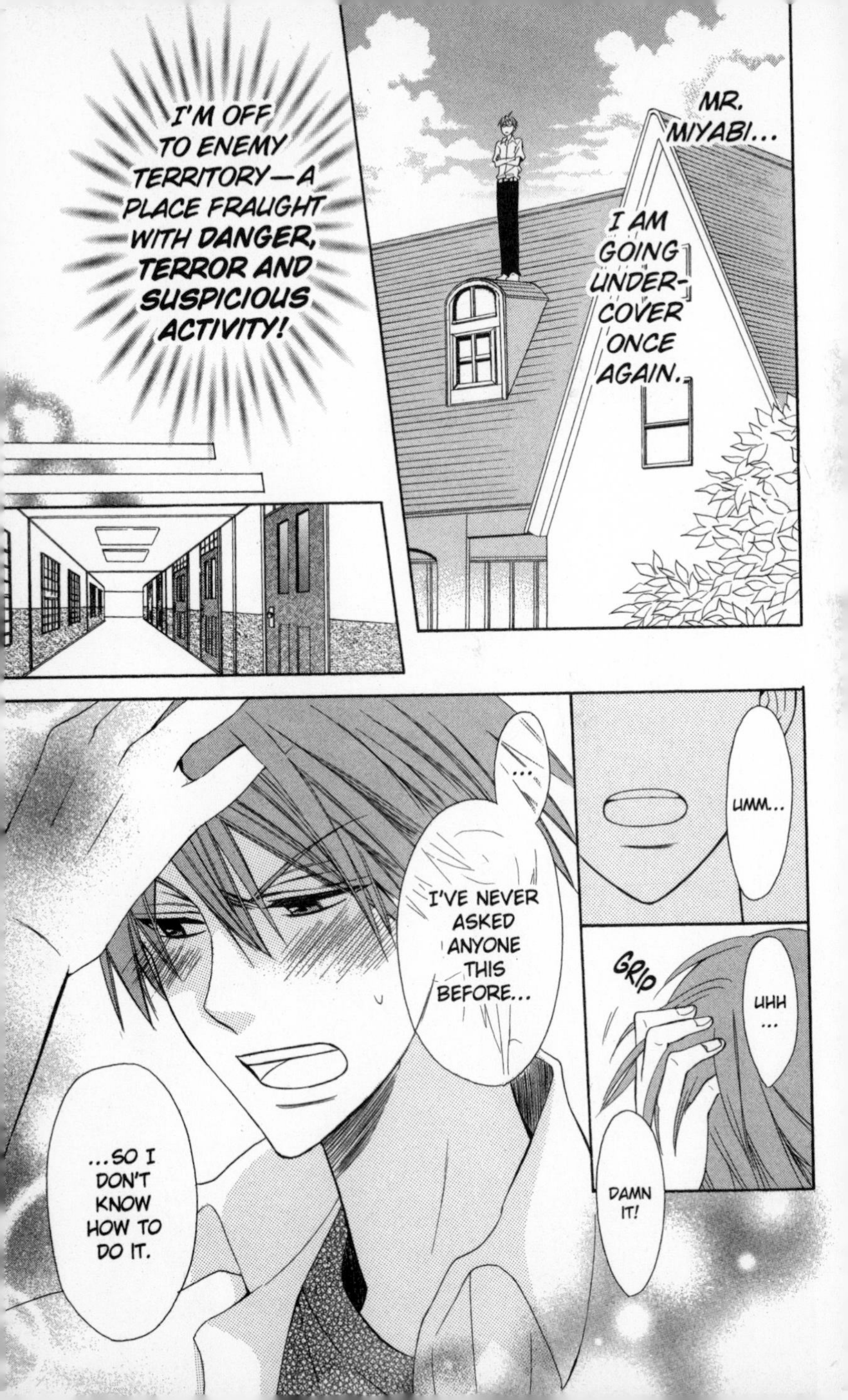
MR. MIYABI...
I AM GOING UNDER-COVER ONCE AGAIN.
I'M OFF TO ENEMY TERRITORY—A PLACE FRAUGHT WITH DANGER, TERROR AND SUSPICIOUS ACTIVITY!
UMM...
GRIP
UHH...
DAMN IT!
...
I'VE NEVER ASKED ANYONE THIS BEFORE...
...SO I DON'T KNOW HOW TO DO IT.

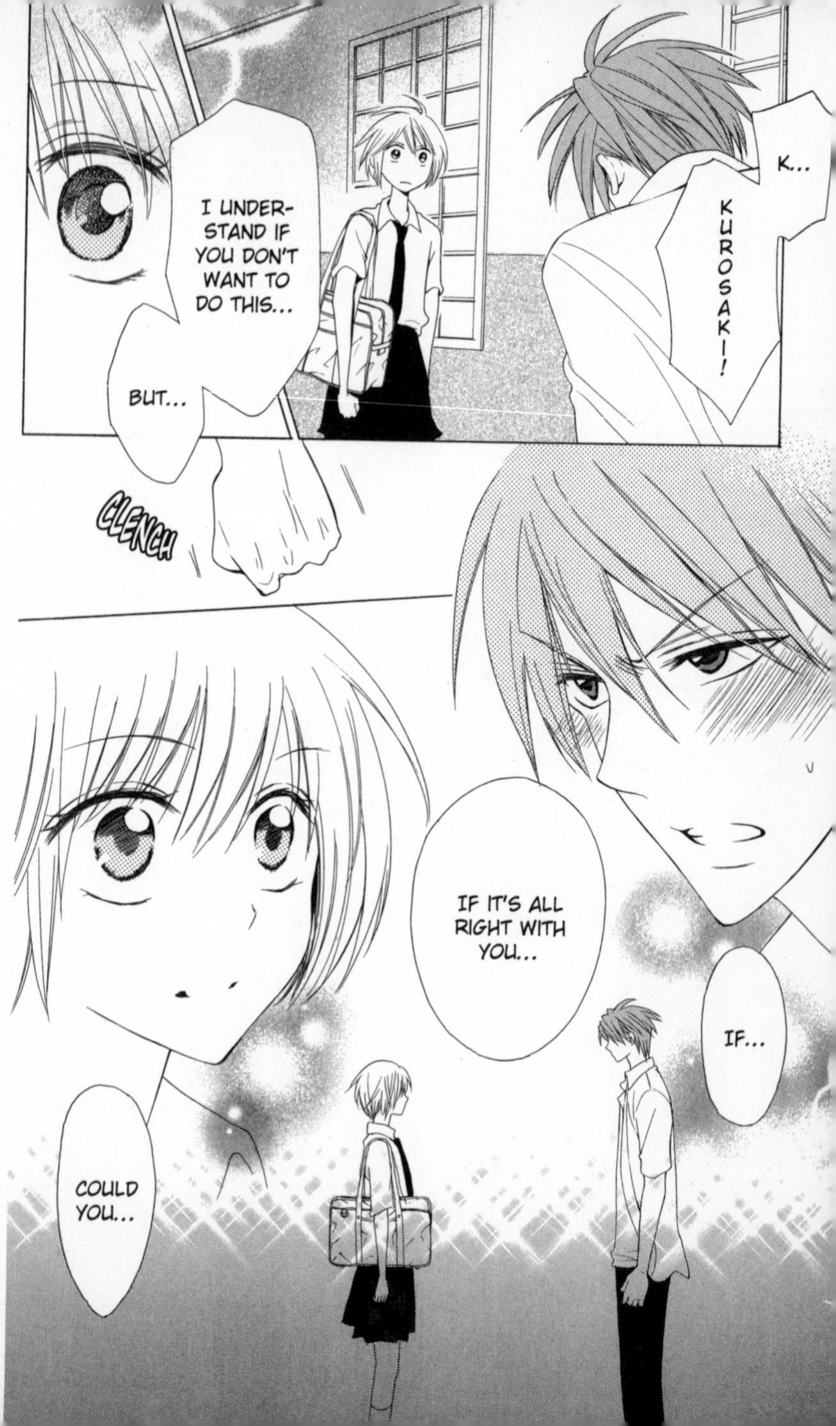
K...
KUROSAKI!
I UNDERSTAND IF YOU DON'T WANT TO DO THIS...
BUT...
CLENCH
IF...
IF IT'S ALL RIGHT WITH YOU...
COULD YOU...

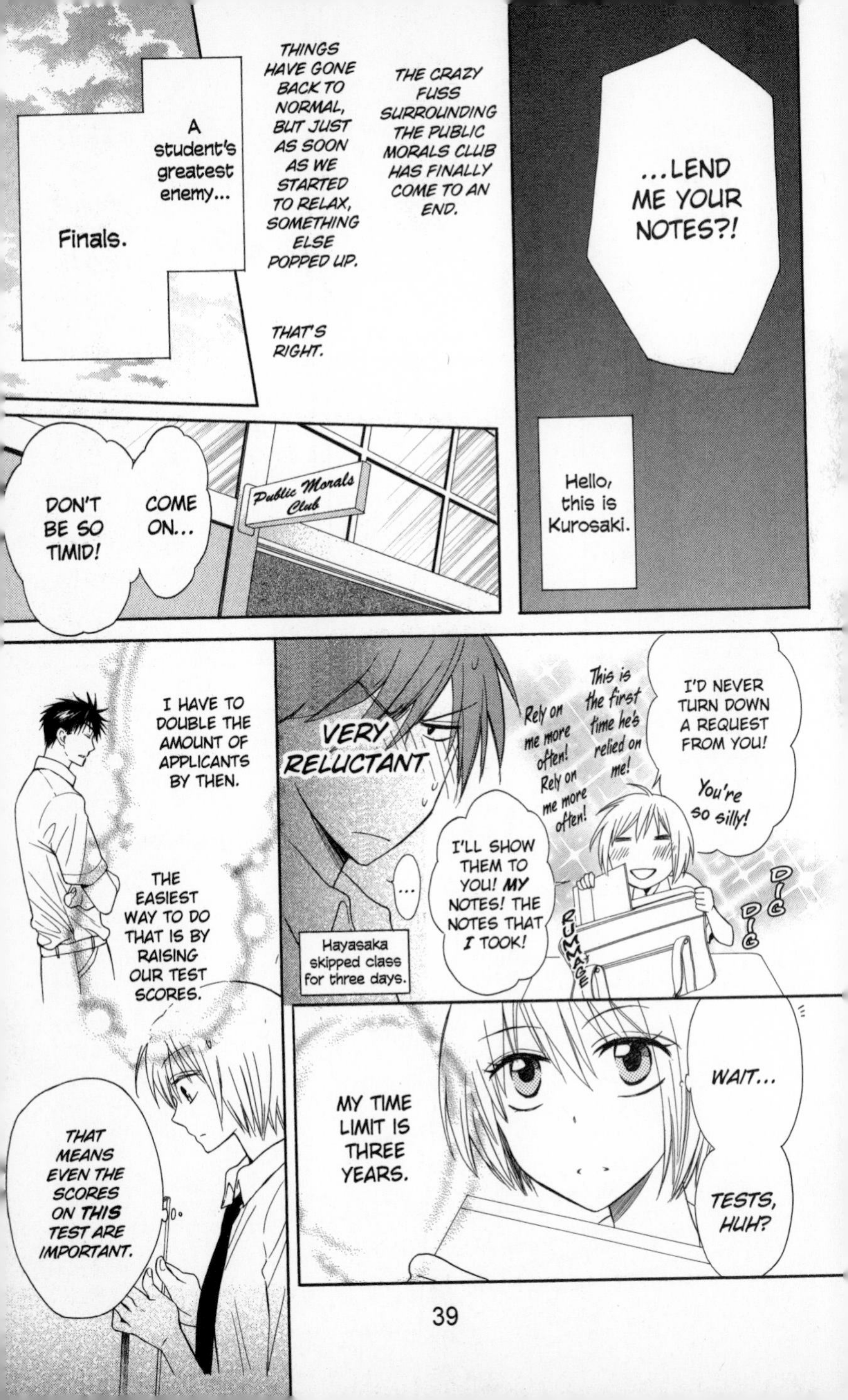
...LEND ME YOUR NOTES?!
Hello, this is Kurosaki.
THE CRAZY FUSS SURROUNDING THE PUBLIC MORALS CLUB HAS FINALLY COME TO AN END.
THINGS HAVE GONE BACK TO NORMAL, BUT JUST AS SOON AS WE STARTED TO RELAX, SOMETHING ELSE POPPED UP.
THAT'S RIGHT.
A student's greatest enemy...
Finals.
Public Morals Club
COME ON...
DON'T BE SO TIMID!
I'D NEVER TURN DOWN A REQUEST FROM YOU!
You're so silly!
This is the first time he's relied on me!
Rely on me more often! Rely on me more often!
VERY RELUCTANT
I'LL SHOW THEM TO YOU! MY NOTES! THE NOTES THAT I TOOK!
...
DIG DIG
RUMMAGE
Hayasaka skipped class for three days.
WAIT...
TESTS, HUH?
MY TIME LIMIT IS THREE YEARS.
I HAVE TO DOUBLE THE AMOUNT OF APPLICANTS BY THEN.
THE EASIEST WAY TO DO THAT IS BY RAISING OUR TEST SCORES.
THAT MEANS EVEN THE SCORES ON THIS TEST ARE IMPORTANT.

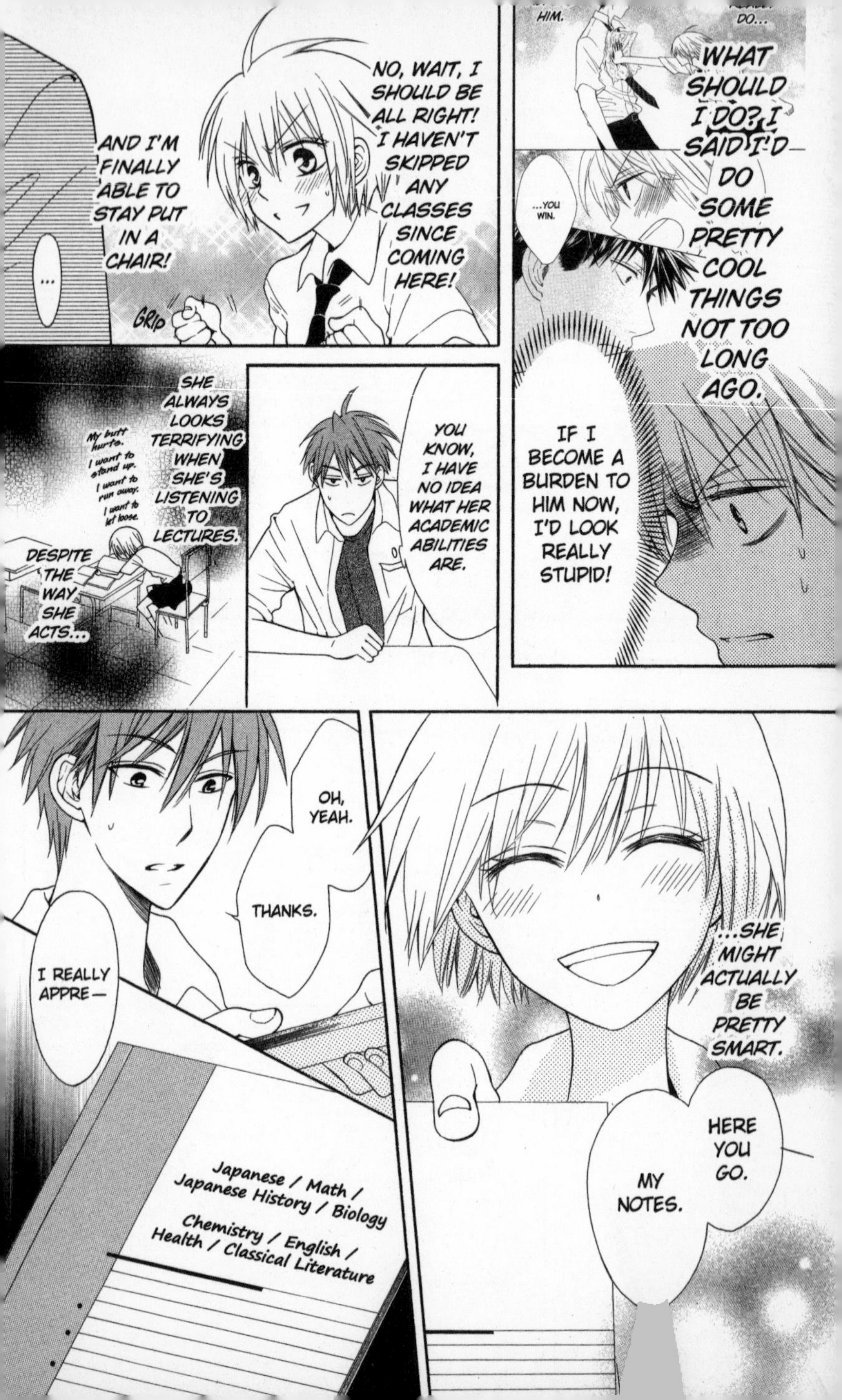
HIM.
DO...
WHAT SHOULD I DO? I SAID I'D DO SOME PRETTY COOL THINGS NOT TOO LONG AGO.
...YOU WIN.
IF I BECOME A BURDEN TO HIM NOW, I'D LOOK REALLY STUPID!
NO, WAIT, I SHOULD BE ALL RIGHT! I HAVEN'T SKIPPED ANY CLASSES SINCE COMING HERE!
AND I'M FINALLY ABLE TO STAY PUT IN A CHAIR!
GRIP
...
YOU KNOW, I HAVE NO IDEA WHAT HER ACADEMIC ABILITIES ARE.
SHE ALWAYS LOOKS TERRIFYING WHEN SHE'S LISTENING TO LECTURES.
My butt hurts. I want to stand up. I want to run away. I want to let loose.
DESPITE THE WAY SHE ACTS...
...SHE MIGHT ACTUALLY BE PRETTY SMART.
HERE YOU GO.
MY NOTES.
OH, YEAH.
THANKS.
I REALLY APPRE—
Japanese / Math / Japanese History / Biology
Chemistry / English / Health / Classical Literature

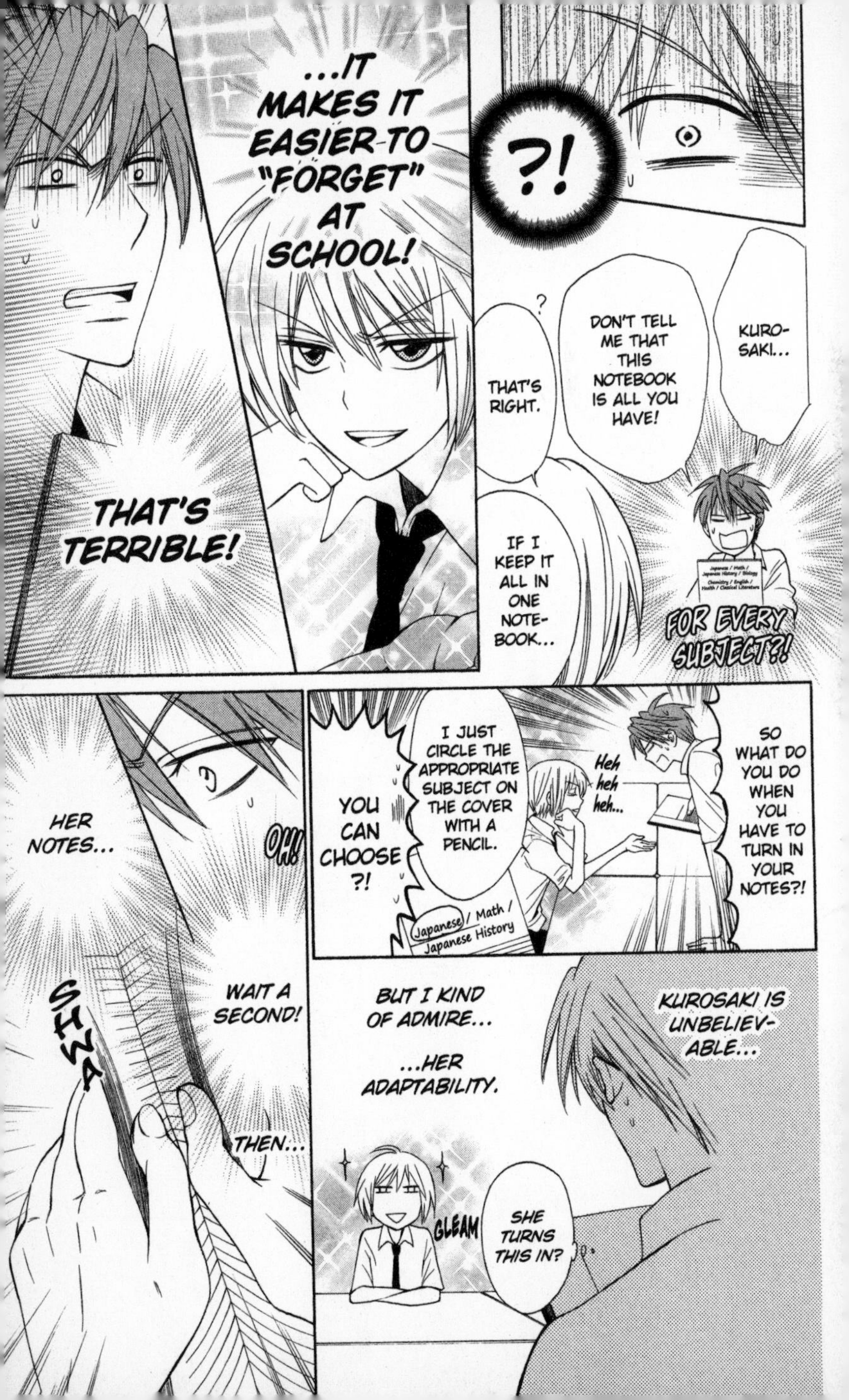
?!
KURO-SAKI...
DON'T TELL ME THAT THIS NOTEBOOK IS ALL YOU HAVE!
FOR EVERY SUBJECT?!
THAT'S RIGHT.
IF I KEEP IT ALL IN ONE NOTE-BOOK...
...IT MAKES IT EASIER TO "FORGET" AT SCHOOL!
THAT'S TERRIBLE!
SO WHAT DO YOU DO WHEN YOU HAVE TO TURN IN YOUR NOTES?!
Heh heh heh...
I JUST CIRCLE THE APPROPRIATE SUBJECT ON THE COVER WITH A PENCIL.
YOU CAN CHOOSE ?!
Japanese / Math / Japanese History
KUROSAKI IS UNBELIEV-ABLE...
SHE TURNS THIS IN?
GLEAM
BUT I KIND OF ADMIRE...
...HER ADAPTABILITY.
OH!
HER NOTES...
WAIT A SECOND!
THEN...
SHWA

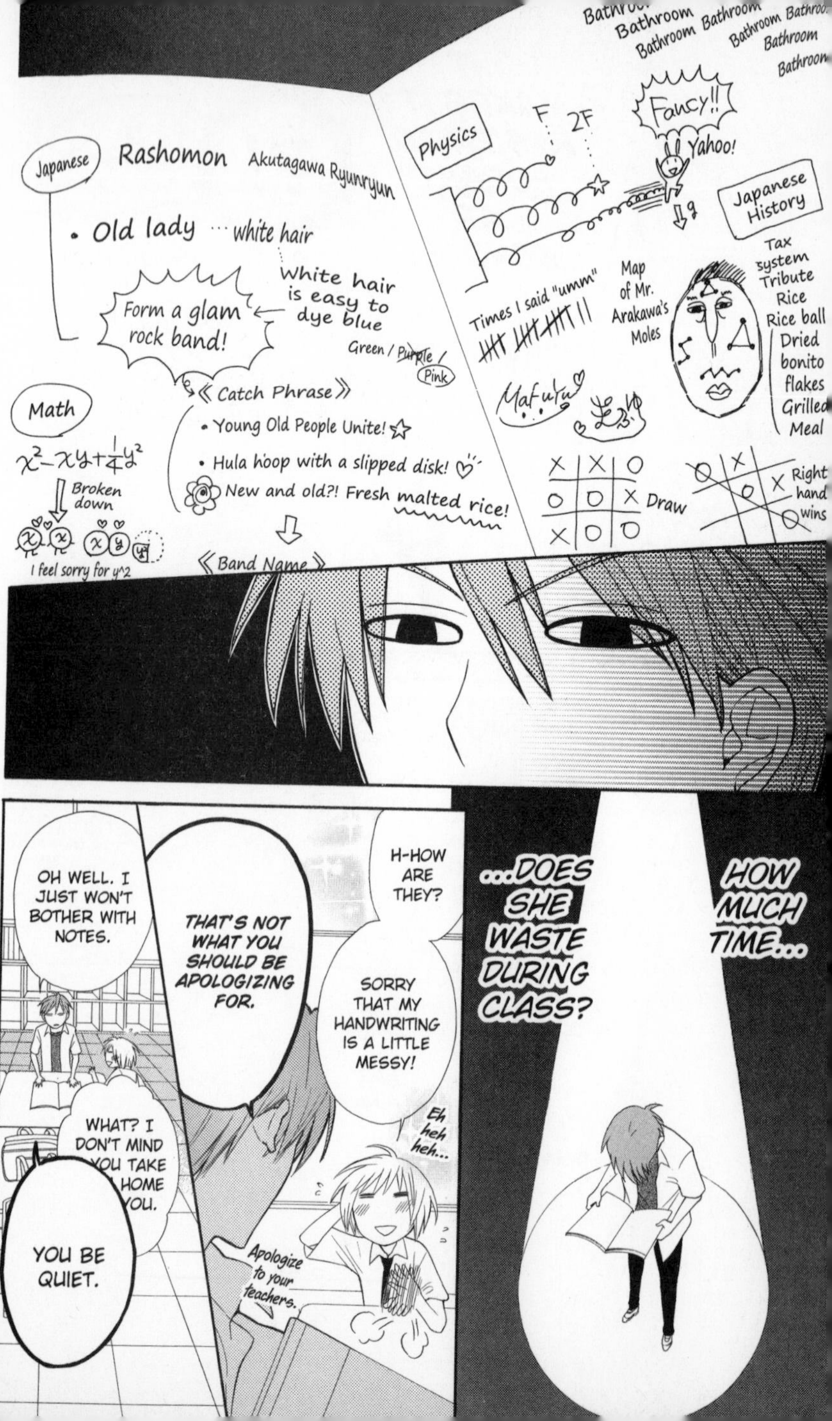

Bathroom Bathroom Bathroom Bathroom Bathroom Bathroom Bathroom
Physics
F
2F
Fancy!!
Yahoo!
g
Japanese History
Tax system
Tribute
Rice
Rice ball
Dried bonito flakes
Grilled Meal
Times I said "umm"
Map of Mr. Arakawa's Moles
Mafuyu
Draw
Right hand wins
Japanese
Rashomon
Akutagawa Ryunryun
• Old lady ... white hair
White hair is easy to dye blue
Green / Purple / Pink
Form a glam rock band!
《Catch Phrase》
• Young Old People Unite!
• Hula hoop with a slipped disk!
New and old?! Fresh malted rice!
《Band Name》
Math
$x^2-xy+\frac{1}{4}y^2$
Broken down
I feel sorry for y^2
HOW MUCH TIME...
...DOES SHE WASTE DURING CLASS?
H-HOW ARE THEY?
SORRY THAT MY HANDWRITING IS A LITTLE MESSY!
Eh heh heh...
THAT'S NOT WHAT YOU SHOULD BE APOLOGIZING FOR.
Apologize to your teachers.
OH WELL. I JUST WON'T BOTHER WITH NOTES.
WHAT? I DON'T MIND
YOU BE QUIET.

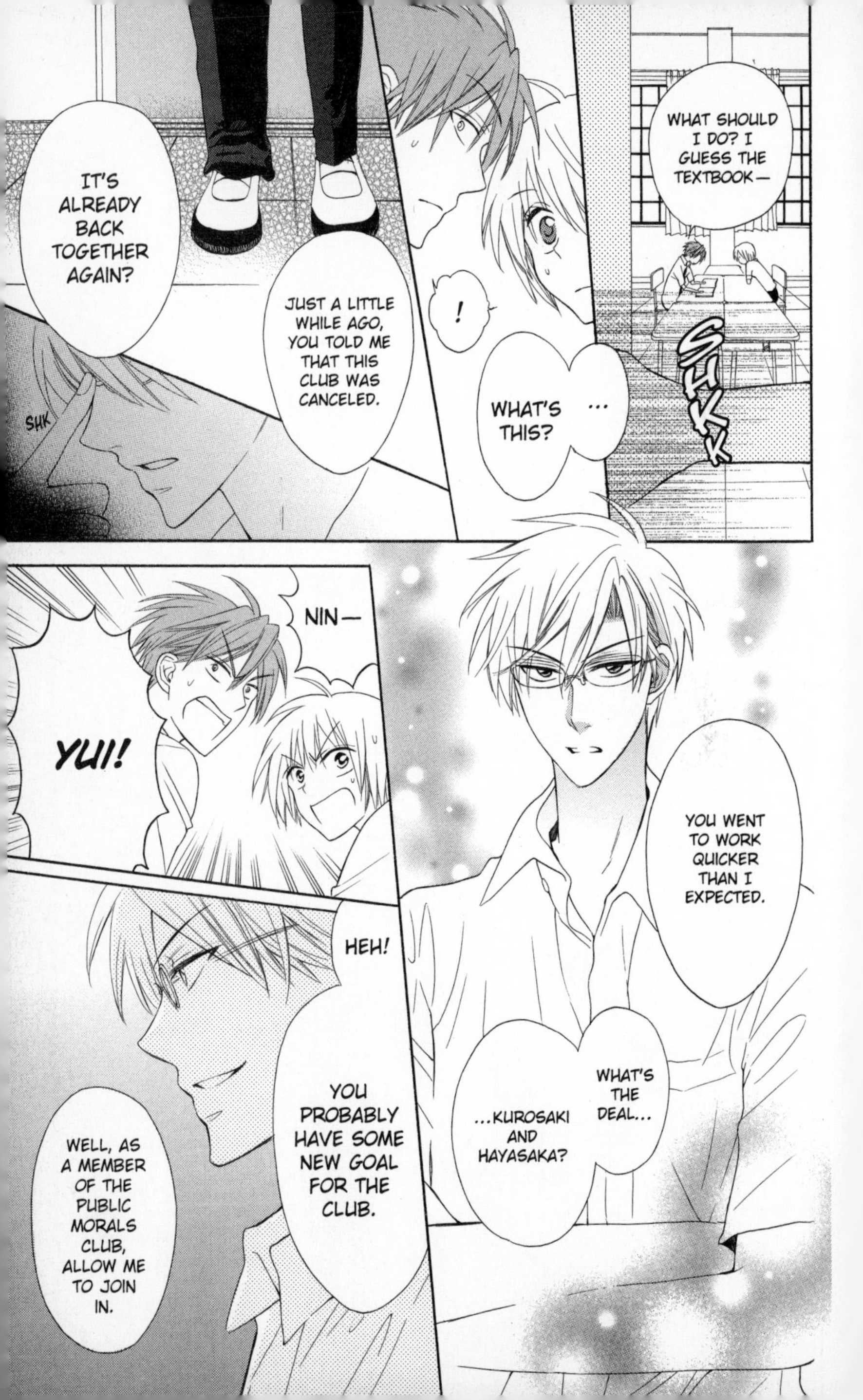
WHAT SHOULD I DO? I GUESS THE TEXTBOOK—
SHKK
!
WHAT'S THIS? ...
IT'S ALREADY BACK TOGETHER AGAIN?
JUST A LITTLE WHILE AGO, YOU TOLD ME THAT THIS CLUB WAS CANCELED.
SHK
YOU WENT TO WORK QUICKER THAN I EXPECTED.
WHAT'S THE DEAL... ...KUROSAKI AND HAYASAKA?
NIN—
YUI!
HEH!
YOU PROBABLY HAVE SOME NEW GOAL FOR THE CLUB.
WELL, AS A MEMBER OF THE PUBLIC MORALS CLUB, ALLOW ME TO JOIN IN.

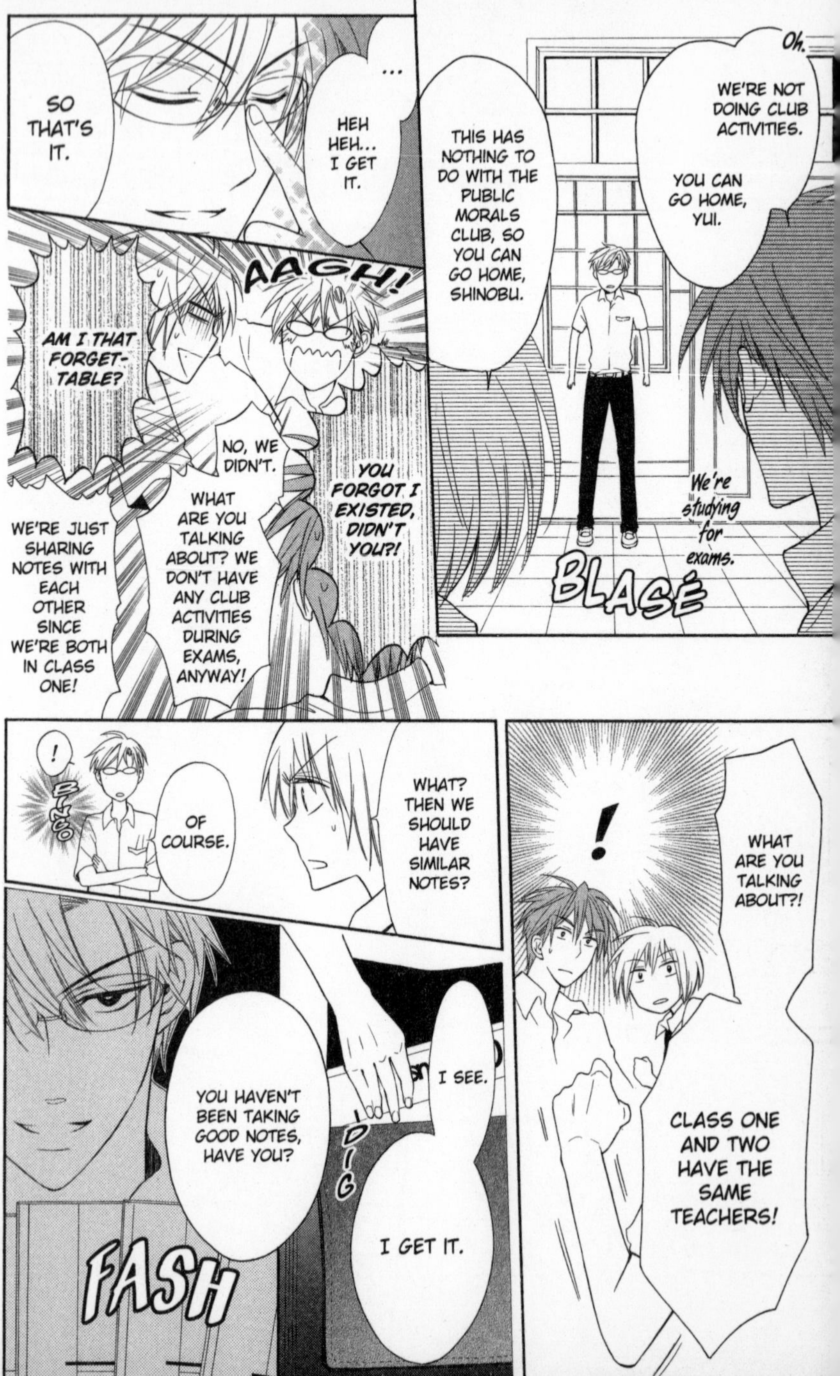
Oh.
WE'RE NOT DOING CLUB ACTIVITIES.
YOU CAN GO HOME, YUI.
THIS HAS NOTHING TO DO WITH THE PUBLIC MORALS CLUB, SO YOU CAN GO HOME, SHINOBU.
We're studying for exams.
BLASÉ
...
HEH HEH... I GET IT.
SO THAT'S IT.
AAGH!
YOU FORGOT I EXISTED, DIDN'T YOU?!
AM I THAT FORGET-TABLE?
NO, WE DIDN'T.
WHAT ARE YOU TALKING ABOUT? WE DON'T HAVE ANY CLUB ACTIVITIES DURING EXAMS, ANYWAY!
WE'RE JUST SHARING NOTES WITH EACH OTHER SINCE WE'RE BOTH IN CLASS ONE!
!
WHAT ARE YOU TALKING ABOUT?!
CLASS ONE AND TWO HAVE THE SAME TEACHERS!
WHAT? THEN WE SHOULD HAVE SIMILAR NOTES?
OF COURSE.
!
BINGO
I SEE.
I GET IT.
DIG
YOU HAVEN'T BEEN TAKING GOOD NOTES, HAVE YOU?
FASH

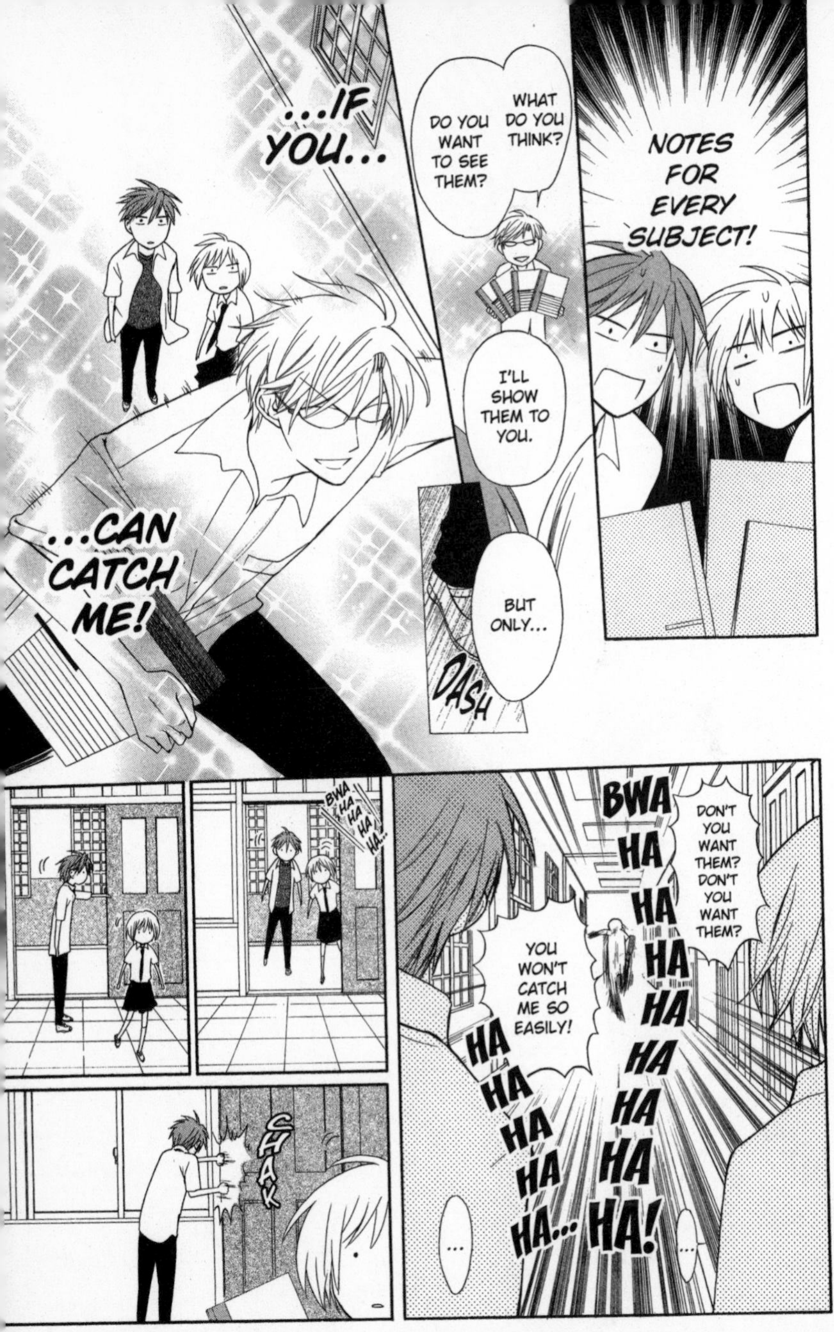
NOTES FOR EVERY SUBJECT!
WHAT DO YOU THINK?
DO YOU WANT TO SEE THEM?
I'LL SHOW THEM TO YOU.
BUT ONLY...
DASH
...IF YOU...
...CAN CATCH ME!
BWA HA HA HA HA HA HA HA HA HA HA HA!
DON'T YOU WANT THEM? DON'T YOU WANT THEM?
YOU WON'T CATCH ME SO EASILY!
HA HA HA HA HA HA...
...
...
BWA HA HA HA HA...
CHAK

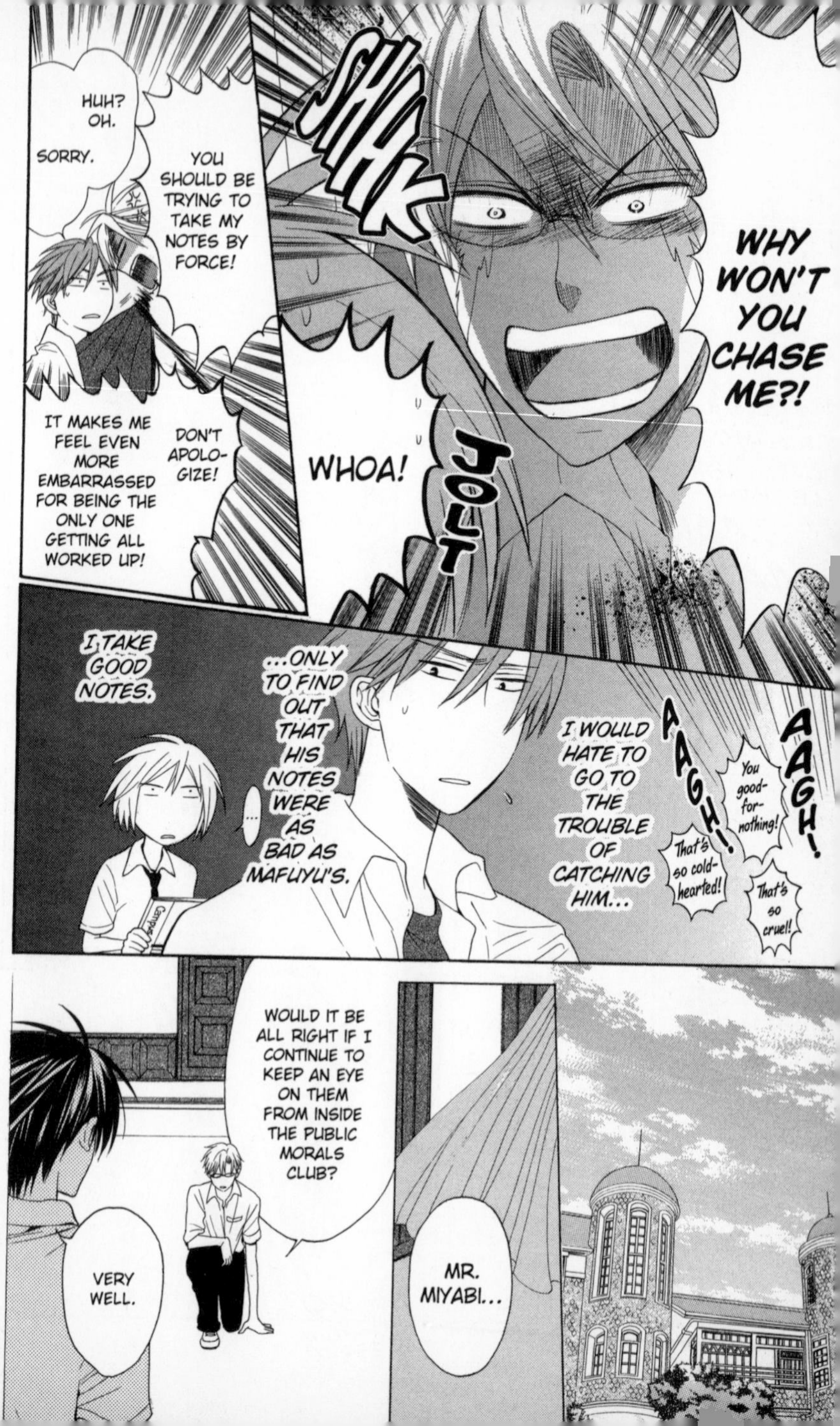
SHAK
WHY WON'T YOU CHASE ME?!
JOLT
WHOA!
HUH? OH.
SORRY.
YOU SHOULD BE TRYING TO TAKE MY NOTES BY FORCE!
DON'T APOLOGIZE!
IT MAKES ME FEEL EVEN MORE EMBARRASSED FOR BEING THE ONLY ONE GETTING ALL WORKED UP!
AAGH!
You good-for-nothing!
That's so cruel!
AAGH!
That's so cold-hearted!
I WOULD HATE TO GO TO THE TROUBLE OF CATCHING HIM...
...ONLY TO FIND OUT THAT HIS NOTES WERE AS BAD AS MAFUYU'S.
...
I TAKE GOOD NOTES.
MR. MIYABI...
WOULD IT BE ALL RIGHT IF I CONTINUE TO KEEP AN EYE ON THEM FROM INSIDE THE PUBLIC MORALS CLUB?
VERY WELL.

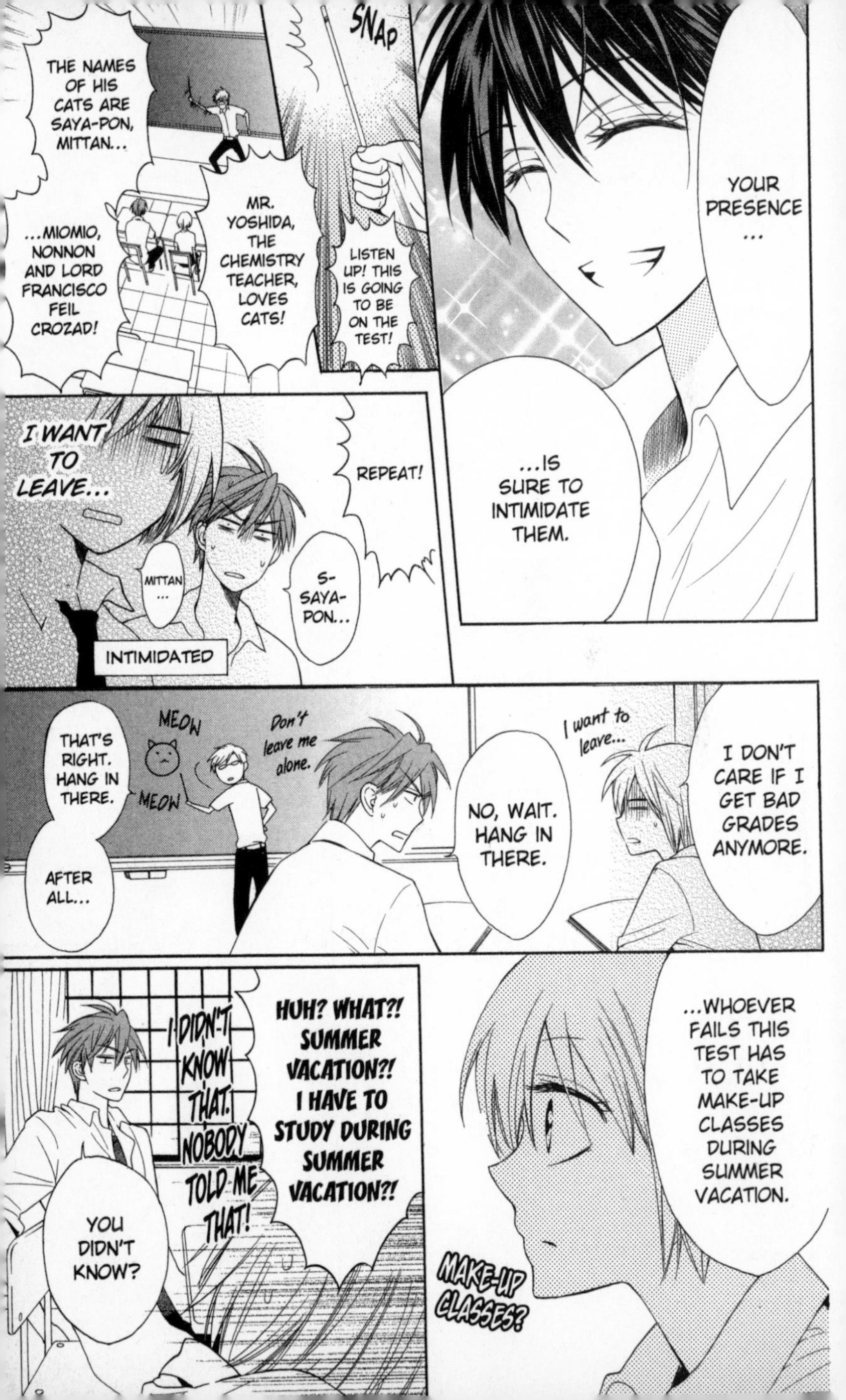

YOUR PRESENCE…
…IS SURE TO INTIMIDATE THEM.
SNAP
LISTEN UP! THIS IS GOING TO BE ON THE TEST!
MR. YOSHIDA, THE CHEMISTRY TEACHER, LOVES CATS!
THE NAMES OF HIS CATS ARE SAYA-PON, MITTAN…
…MIOMIO, NONNON AND LORD FRANCISCO FEIL CROZAD!
REPEAT!
S-SAYA-PON…
MITTAN…
I WANT TO LEAVE…
INTIMIDATED
I DON'T CARE IF I GET BAD GRADES ANYMORE.
I want to leave…
NO, WAIT. HANG IN THERE.
Don't leave me alone.
MEOW
MEOW
THAT'S RIGHT. HANG IN THERE.
AFTER ALL…
…WHOEVER FAILS THIS TEST HAS TO TAKE MAKE-UP CLASSES DURING SUMMER VACATION.
MAKE-UP CLASSES?
HUH? WHAT?! SUMMER VACATION?! I HAVE TO STUDY DURING SUMMER VACATION?!
I DIDN'T KNOW THAT. NOBODY TOLD ME THAT!
YOU DIDN'T KNOW?

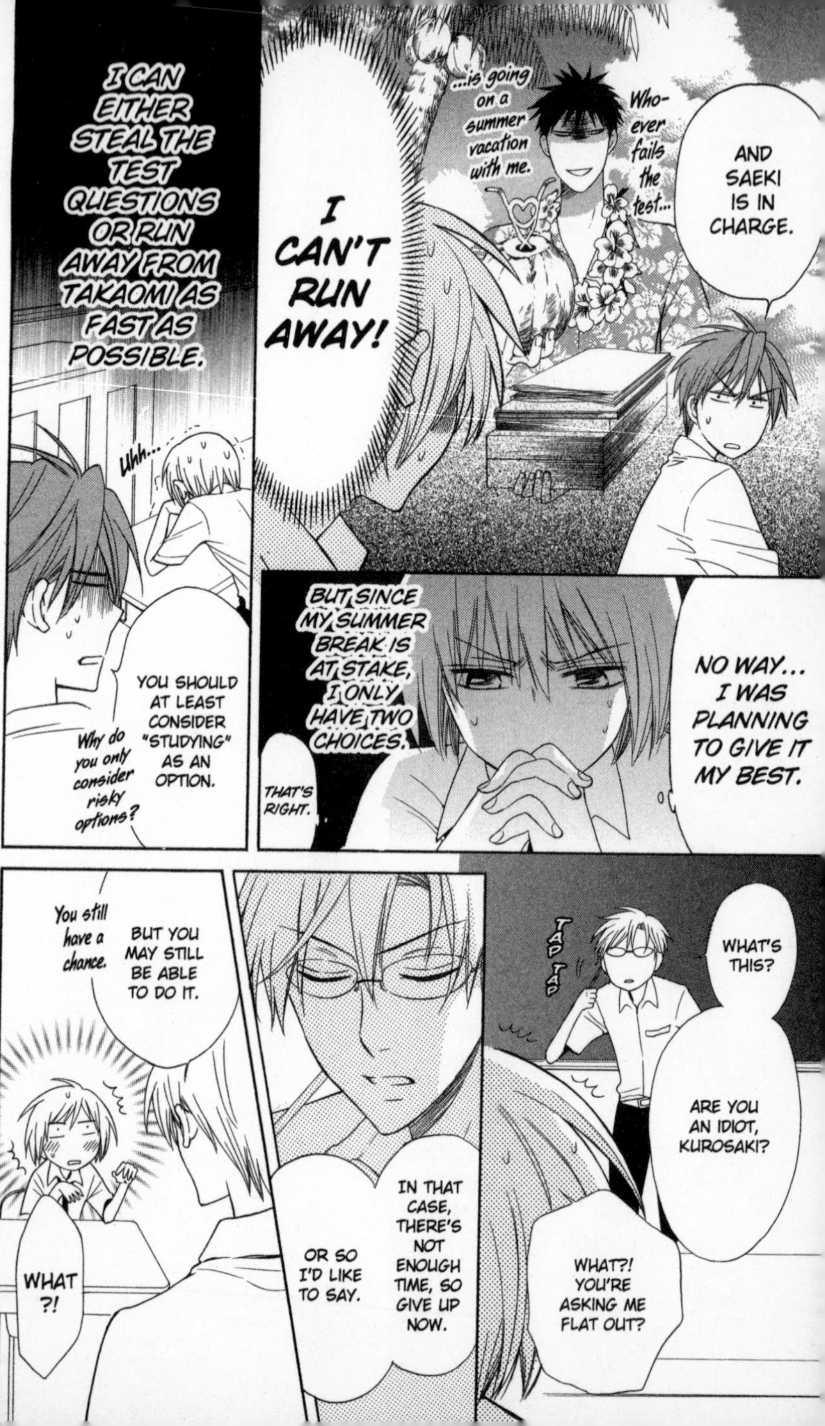
AND SAEKI IS IN CHARGE.
Whoever fails the test...
...is going on a summer vacation with me.
I CAN'T RUN AWAY!
NO WAY... I WAS PLANNING TO GIVE IT MY BEST.
BUT SINCE MY SUMMER BREAK IS AT STAKE, I ONLY HAVE TWO CHOICES.
THAT'S RIGHT.
I CAN EITHER STEAL THE TEST QUESTIONS OR RUN AWAY FROM TAKAOMI AS FAST AS POSSIBLE.
Uhh...
YOU SHOULD AT LEAST CONSIDER "STUDYING" AS AN OPTION.
Why do you only consider risky options?
TAP TAP
WHAT'S THIS?
ARE YOU AN IDIOT, KUROSAKI?
WHAT?! YOU'RE ASKING ME FLAT OUT?
IN THAT CASE, THERE'S NOT ENOUGH TIME, SO GIVE UP NOW.
OR SO I'D LIKE TO SAY.
BUT YOU MAY STILL BE ABLE TO DO IT.
You still have a chance.
WHAT?!

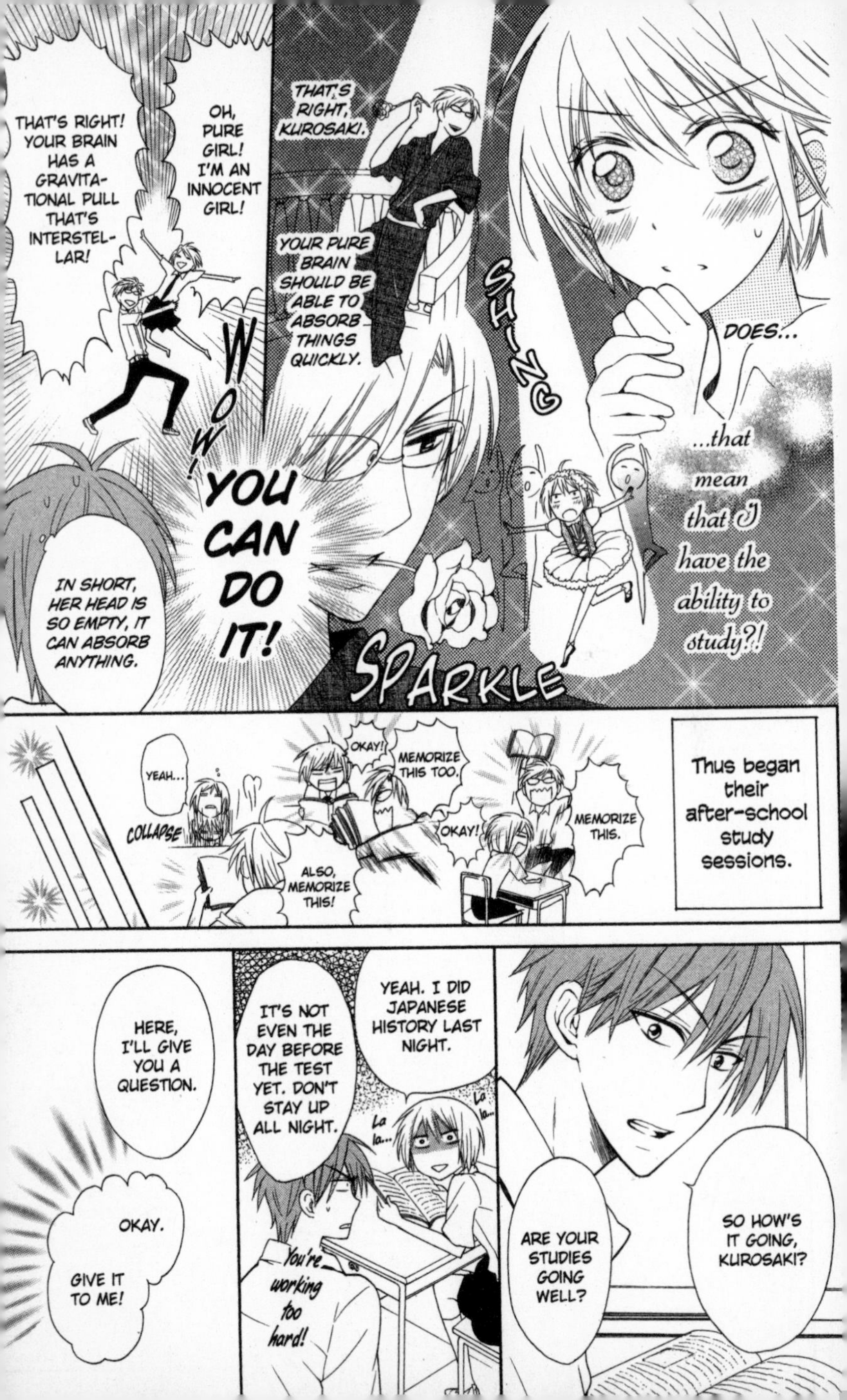

DOES...
...that mean that I have the ability to study?!
SHING
SPARKLE
THAT'S RIGHT, KUROSAKI.
YOUR PURE BRAIN SHOULD BE ABLE TO ABSORB THINGS QUICKLY.
WOW!
YOU CAN DO IT!
OH, PURE GIRL! I'M AN INNOCENT GIRL!
THAT'S RIGHT! YOUR BRAIN HAS A GRAVITATIONAL PULL THAT'S INTERSTELLAR!
IN SHORT, HER HEAD IS SO EMPTY, IT CAN ABSORB ANYTHING.
Thus began their after-school study sessions.
MEMORIZE THIS.
OKAY!
MEMORIZE THIS TOO.
OKAY!
ALSO, MEMORIZE THIS!
YEAH...
COLLAPSE
SO HOW'S IT GOING, KUROSAKI?
ARE YOUR STUDIES GOING WELL?
YEAH. I DID JAPANESE HISTORY LAST NIGHT.
IT'S NOT EVEN THE DAY BEFORE THE TEST YET. DON'T STAY UP ALL NIGHT.
La la...
La la...
You're working too hard!
HERE, I'LL GIVE YOU A QUESTION.
OKAY.
GIVE IT TO ME!

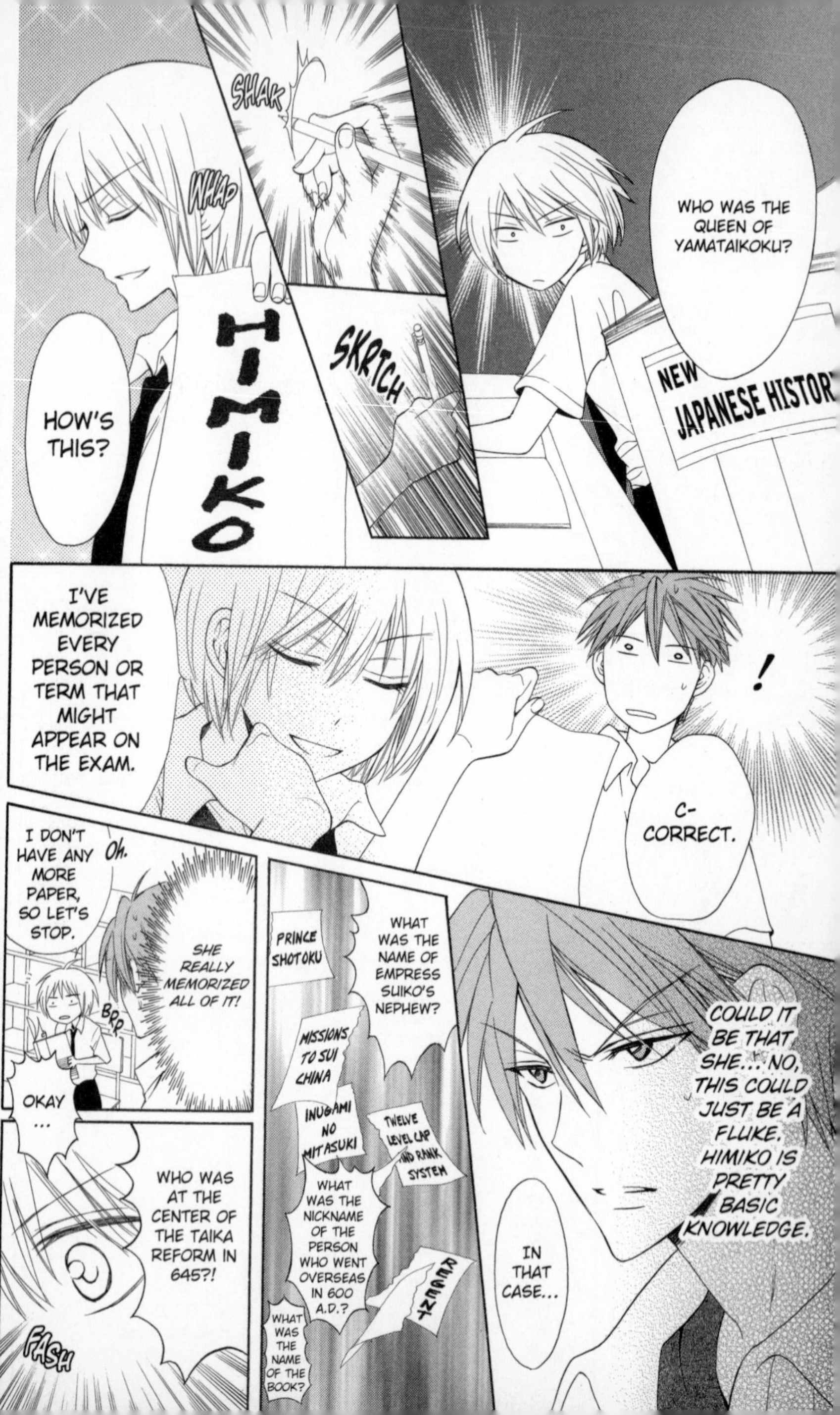
WHO WAS THE QUEEN OF YAMATAIKOKU?
NEW JAPANESE HISTORY
SKRTCH
SHAK
WHAP
HIMIKO
HOW'S THIS?
!
C-CORRECT.
I'VE MEMORIZED EVERY PERSON OR TERM THAT MIGHT APPEAR ON THE EXAM.
COULD IT BE THAT SHE... NO, THIS COULD JUST BE A FLUKE. HIMIKO IS PRETTY BASIC KNOWLEDGE.
IN THAT CASE...
WHAT WAS THE NAME OF EMPRESS SUIKO'S NEPHEW?
PRINCE SHOTOKU
MISSIONS TO SUI CHINA
INUGAMI NO MITASUKI
TWELVE LEVEL CAP AND RANK SYSTEM
WHAT WAS THE NICKNAME OF THE PERSON WHO WENT OVERSEAS IN 600 A.D.?
REGENT
WHAT WAS THE NAME OF THE BOOK?
I DON'T HAVE ANY MORE PAPER, SO LET'S STOP.
Oh.
SHE REALLY MEMORIZED ALL OF IT!
BRP
OKAY...
WHO WAS AT THE CENTER OF THE TAIKA REFORM IN 645?!
FASH

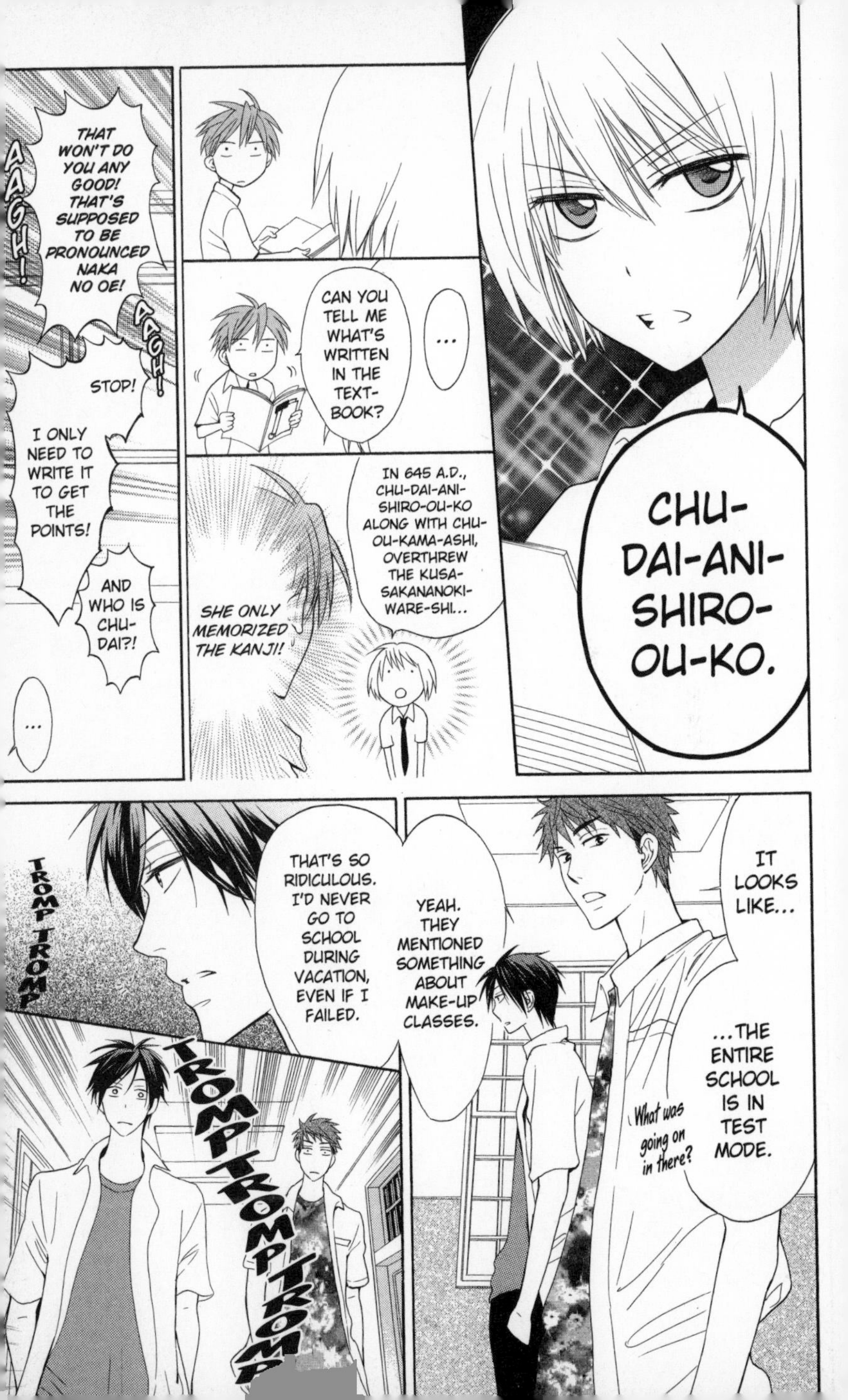
CHU-DAI-ANI-SHIRO-OU-KO.
...
CAN YOU TELL ME WHAT'S WRITTEN IN THE TEXT-BOOK?
IN 645 A.D., CHU-DAI-ANI-SHIRO-OU-KO ALONG WITH CHU-OU-KAMA-ASHI, OVERTHREW THE KUSA-SAKANANOKI-WARE-SHI...
SHE ONLY MEMORIZED THE KANJI!
THAT WON'T DO YOU ANY GOOD! THAT'S SUPPOSED TO BE PRONOUNCED NAKA NO OE!
AAGH!
AAGH!
STOP!
I ONLY NEED TO WRITE IT TO GET THE POINTS!
AND WHO IS CHU-DAI?!
...
IT LOOKS LIKE...
...THE ENTIRE SCHOOL IS IN TEST MODE.
What was going on in there?
YEAH. THEY MENTIONED SOMETHING ABOUT MAKE-UP CLASSES.
THAT'S SO RIDICULOUS. I'D NEVER GO TO SCHOOL DURING VACATION, EVEN IF I FAILED.
TROMP TROMP
TROMP TROMP TROMP TROMP

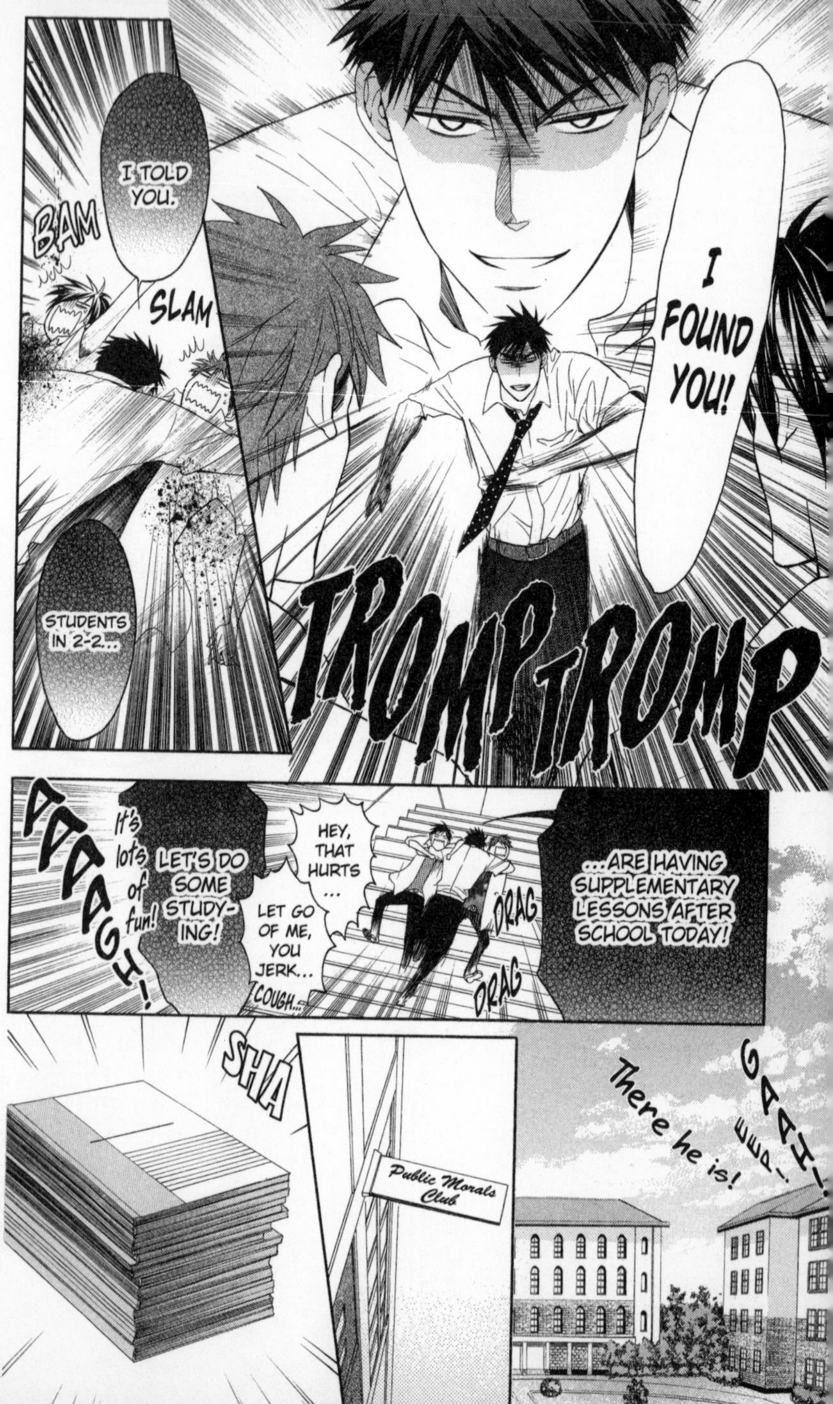

I FOUND YOU!
TROMP TROMP
I TOLD YOU.
BAM
SLAM
STUDENTS IN 2-2...
...ARE HAVING SUPPLEMENTARY LESSONS AFTER SCHOOL TODAY!
DRAG
DRAG
HEY, THAT HURTS...
LET GO OF ME, YOU JERK... COUGH...
LET'S DO SOME STUDY-ING!
It's lots of fun!
AAAAGH!
GAAAH-!
There he is!
Public Morals Club
SHA

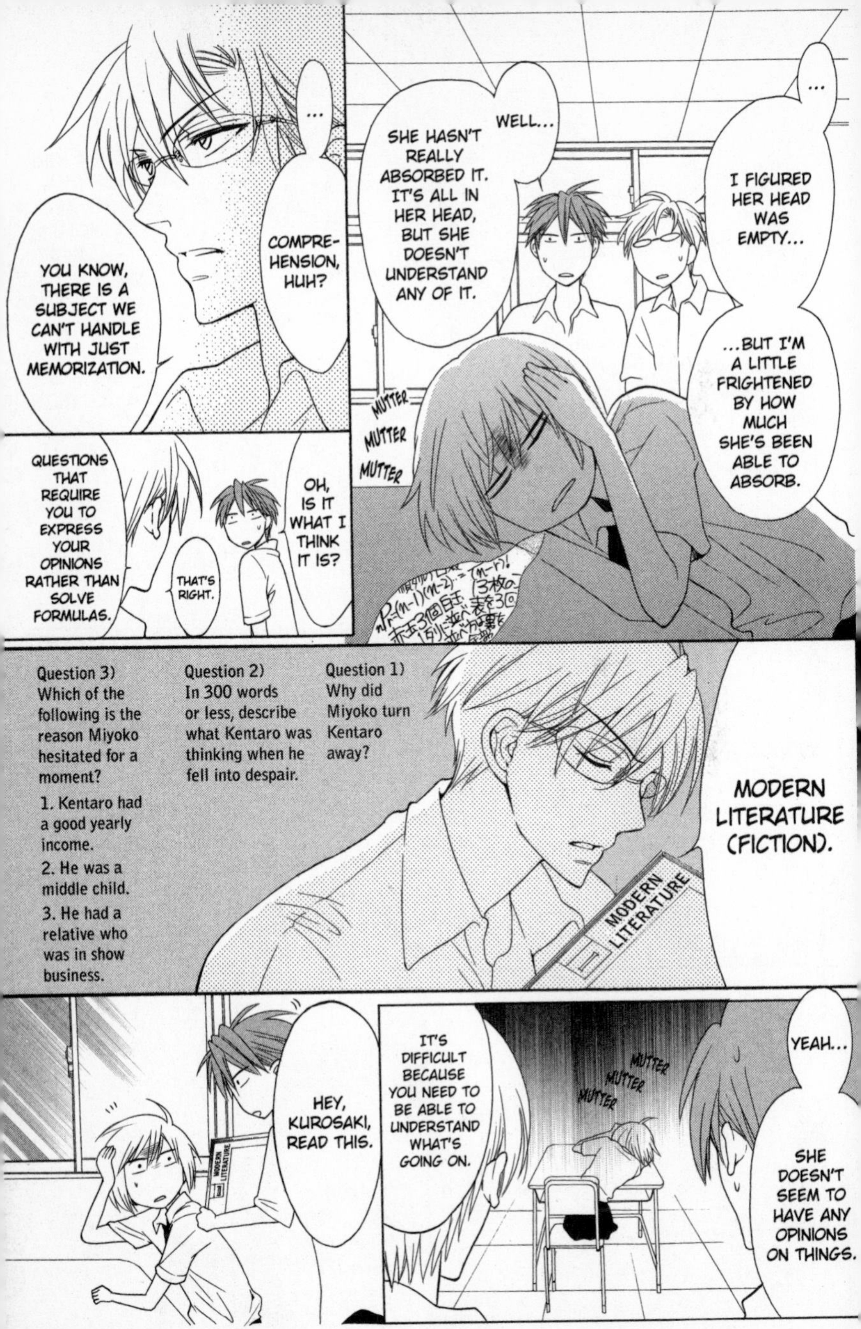
...
I FIGURED HER HEAD WAS EMPTY...
...BUT I'M A LITTLE FRIGHTENED BY HOW MUCH SHE'S BEEN ABLE TO ABSORB.
WELL...
SHE HASN'T REALLY ABSORBED IT. IT'S ALL IN HER HEAD, BUT SHE DOESN'T UNDERSTAND ANY OF IT.
MUTTER
MUTTER
MUTTER
...
COMPREHENSION, HUH?
YOU KNOW, THERE IS A SUBJECT WE CAN'T HANDLE WITH JUST MEMORIZATION.
OH, IS IT WHAT I THINK IT IS?
THAT'S RIGHT.
QUESTIONS THAT REQUIRE YOU TO EXPRESS YOUR OPINIONS RATHER THAN SOLVE FORMULAS.
MODERN LITERATURE (FICTION).
MODERN LITERATURE
Question 1) Why did Miyoko turn Kentaro away?
Question 2) In 300 words or less, describe what Kentaro was thinking when he fell into despair.
Question 3) Which of the following is the reason Miyoko hesitated for a moment?
1. Kentaro had a good yearly income.
2. He was a middle child.
3. He had a relative who was in show business.
YEAH...
SHE DOESN'T SEEM TO HAVE ANY OPINIONS ON THINGS.
MUTTER
MUTTER
MUTTER
IT'S DIFFICULT BECAUSE YOU NEED TO BE ABLE TO UNDERSTAND WHAT'S GOING ON.
HEY, KUROSAKI, READ THIS.
MODERN LITERATURE

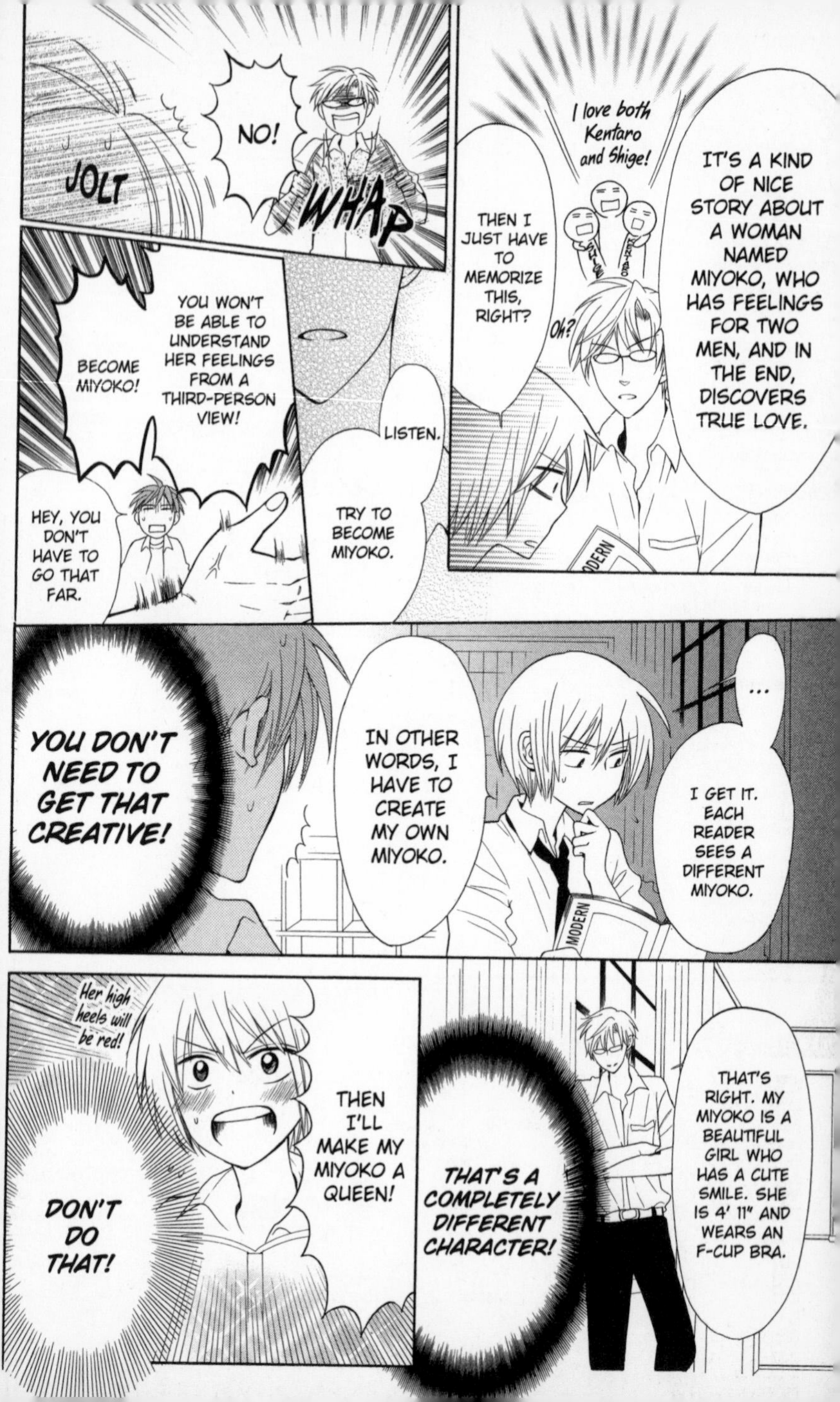
IT'S A KIND OF NICE STORY ABOUT A WOMAN NAMED MIYOKO, WHO HAS FEELINGS FOR TWO MEN, AND IN THE END, DISCOVERS TRUE LOVE.
I love both Kentaro and Shige!
THEN I JUST HAVE TO MEMORIZE THIS, RIGHT?
Oh?
WHAP
NO!
JOLT
LISTEN.
TRY TO BECOME MIYOKO.
YOU WON'T BE ABLE TO UNDERSTAND HER FEELINGS FROM A THIRD-PERSON VIEW!
BECOME MIYOKO!
HEY, YOU DON'T HAVE TO GO THAT FAR.
...
I GET IT. EACH READER SEES A DIFFERENT MIYOKO.
IN OTHER WORDS, I HAVE TO CREATE MY OWN MIYOKO.
YOU DON'T NEED TO GET THAT CREATIVE!
THAT'S RIGHT. MY MIYOKO IS A BEAUTIFUL GIRL WHO HAS A CUTE SMILE. SHE IS 4' 11" AND WEARS AN F-CUP BRA.
THAT'S A COMPLETELY DIFFERENT CHARACTER!
THEN I'LL MAKE MY MIYOKO A QUEEN!
Her high heels will be red!
DON'T DO THAT!

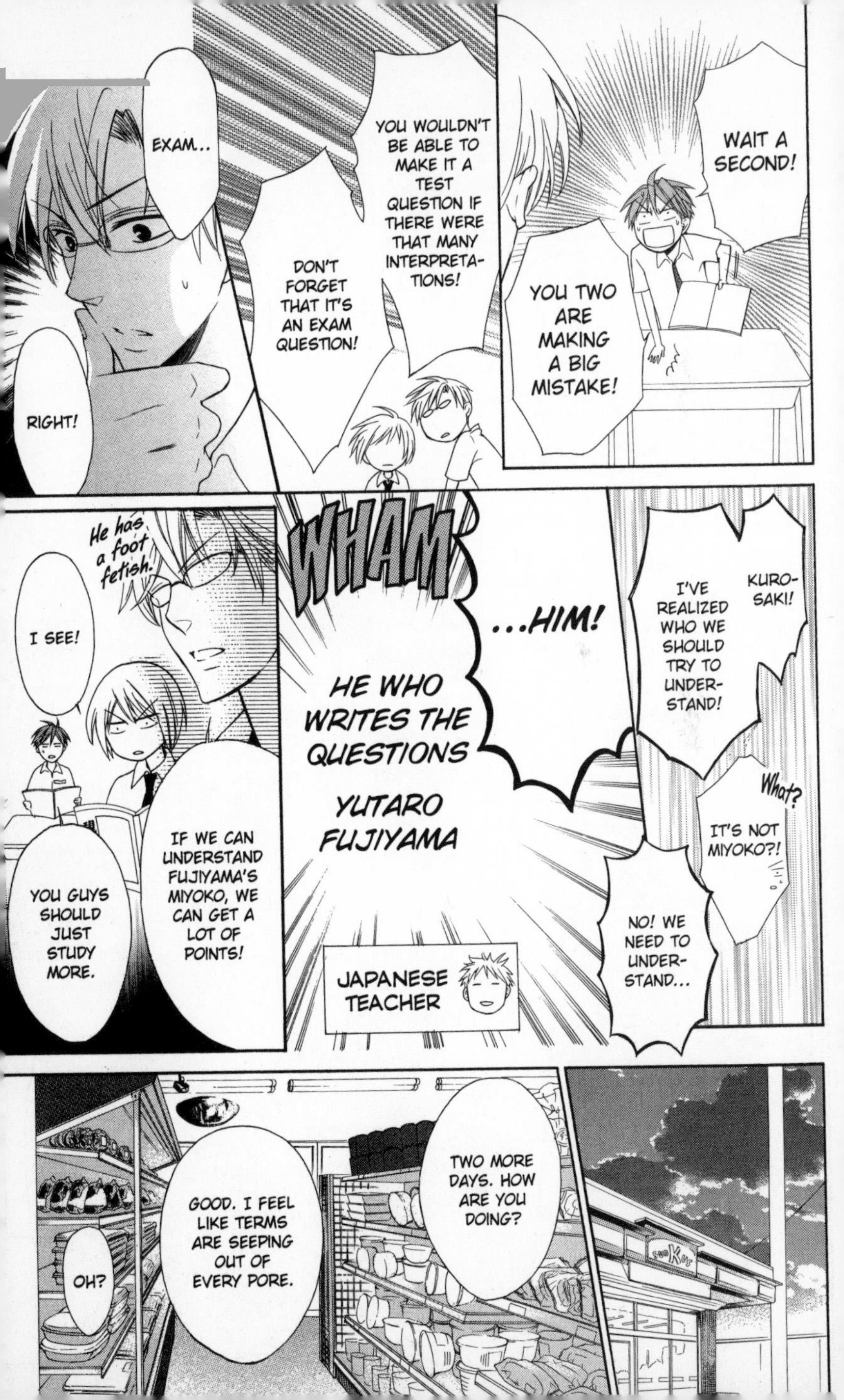
WAIT A SECOND!
YOU TWO ARE MAKING A BIG MISTAKE!
YOU WOULDN'T BE ABLE TO MAKE IT A TEST QUESTION IF THERE WERE THAT MANY INTERPRETA-TIONS!
DON'T FORGET THAT IT'S AN EXAM QUESTION!
EXAM...
RIGHT!
KURO-SAKI!
I'VE REALIZED WHO WE SHOULD TRY TO UNDER-STAND!
What?
IT'S NOT MIYOKO?!
NO! WE NEED TO UNDER-STAND...
...HIM!
WHAM
HE WHO WRITES THE QUESTIONS
YUTARO FUJIYAMA
JAPANESE TEACHER
IF WE CAN UNDERSTAND FUJIYAMA'S MIYOKO, WE CAN GET A LOT OF POINTS!
I SEE!
He has a foot fetish.
YOU GUYS SHOULD JUST STUDY MORE.
TWO MORE DAYS. HOW ARE YOU DOING?
GOOD. I FEEL LIKE TERMS ARE SEEPING OUT OF EVERY PORE.
OH?

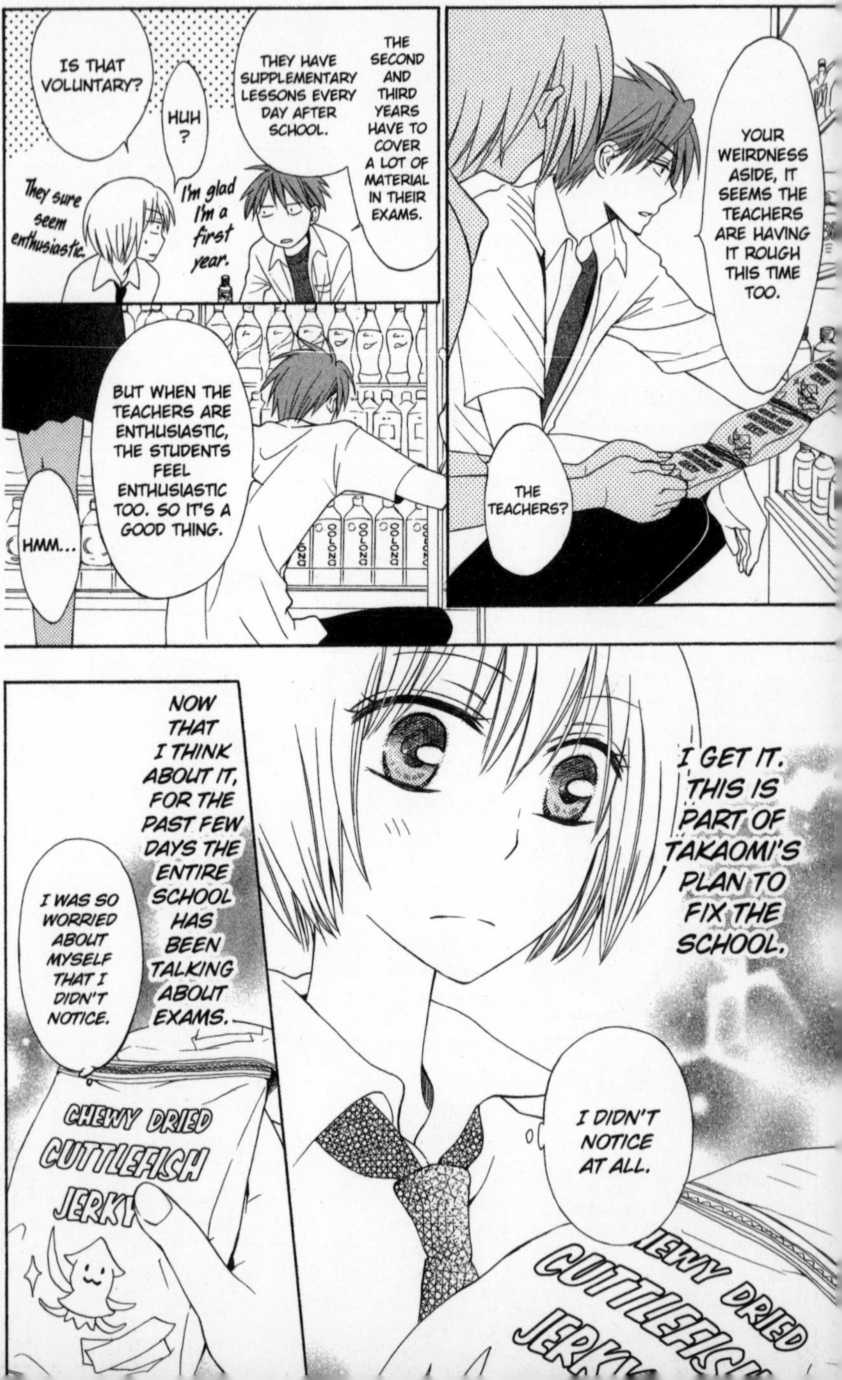
YOUR WEIRDNESS ASIDE, IT SEEMS THE TEACHERS ARE HAVING IT ROUGH THIS TIME TOO.
THE TEACHERS?
THE SECOND AND THIRD YEARS HAVE TO COVER A LOT OF MATERIAL IN THEIR EXAMS.
THEY HAVE SUPPLEMENTARY LESSONS EVERY DAY AFTER SCHOOL.
HUH?
IS THAT VOLUNTARY?
I'm glad I'm a first year.
They sure seem enthusiastic.
BUT WHEN THE TEACHERS ARE ENTHUSIASTIC, THE STUDENTS FEEL ENTHUSIASTIC TOO. SO IT'S A GOOD THING.
HMM...
I GET IT. THIS IS PART OF TAKAOMI'S PLAN TO FIX THE SCHOOL.
NOW THAT I THINK ABOUT IT, FOR THE PAST FEW DAYS THE ENTIRE SCHOOL HAS BEEN TALKING ABOUT EXAMS.
I WAS SO WORRIED ABOUT MYSELF THAT I DIDN'T NOTICE.
I DIDN'T NOTICE AT ALL.
CHEWY DRIED CUTTLEFISH JERKY

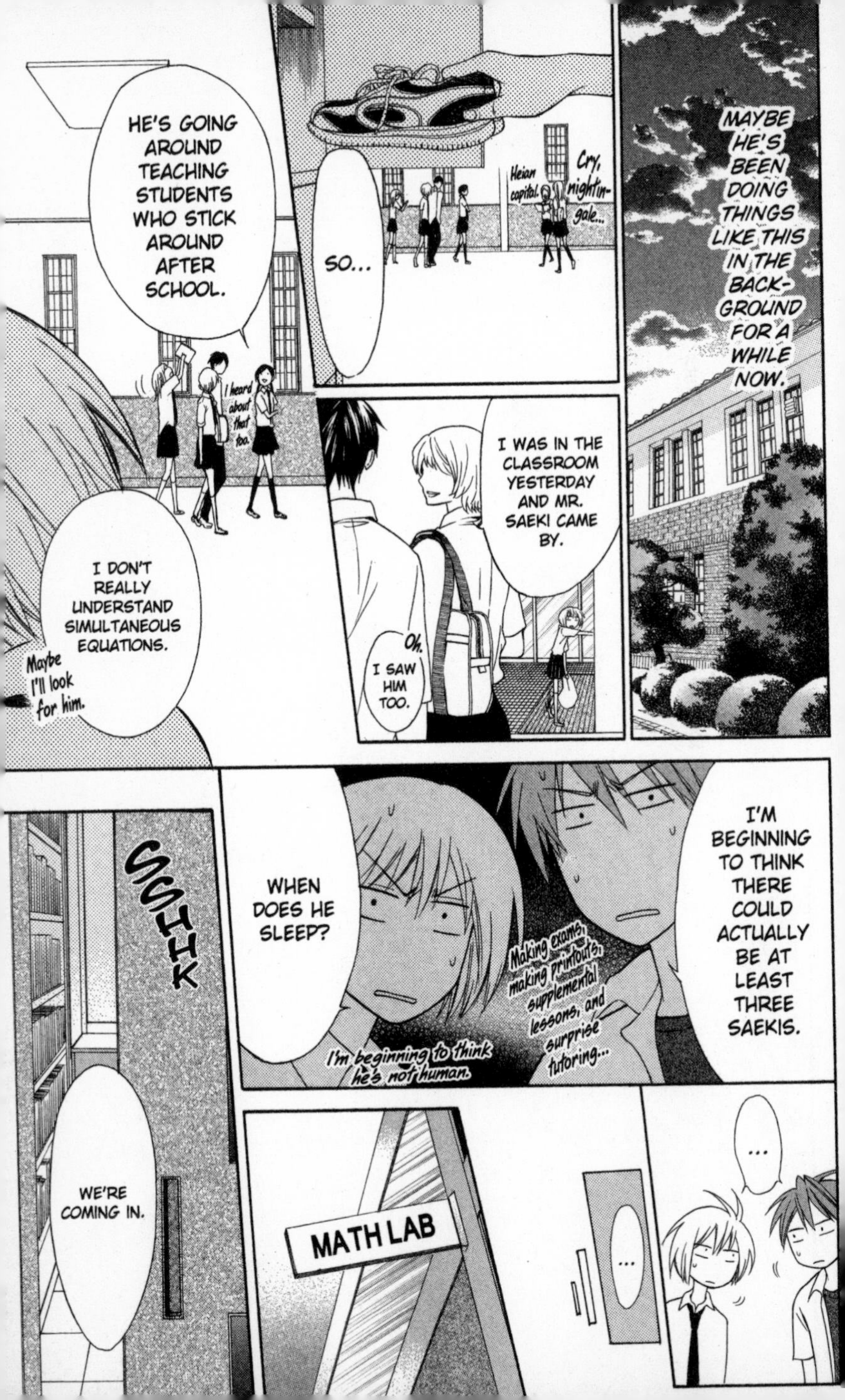
MAYBE HE'S BEEN DOING THINGS LIKE THIS IN THE BACKGROUND FOR A WHILE NOW.
SO...
Cry, nightingale...
Heian capital.
I WAS IN THE CLASSROOM YESTERDAY AND MR. SAEKI CAME BY.
Oh. I SAW HIM TOO.
HE'S GOING AROUND TEACHING STUDENTS WHO STICK AROUND AFTER SCHOOL.
I heard about that too.
I DON'T REALLY UNDERSTAND SIMULTANEOUS EQUATIONS.
Maybe I'll look for him.
I'M BEGINNING TO THINK THERE COULD ACTUALLY BE AT LEAST THREE SAEKIS.
WHEN DOES HE SLEEP?
Making exams, making printouts, supplemental lessons, and surprise tutoring...
I'm beginning to think he's not human.
...
...
MATH LAB
SSHHK
WE'RE COMING IN.

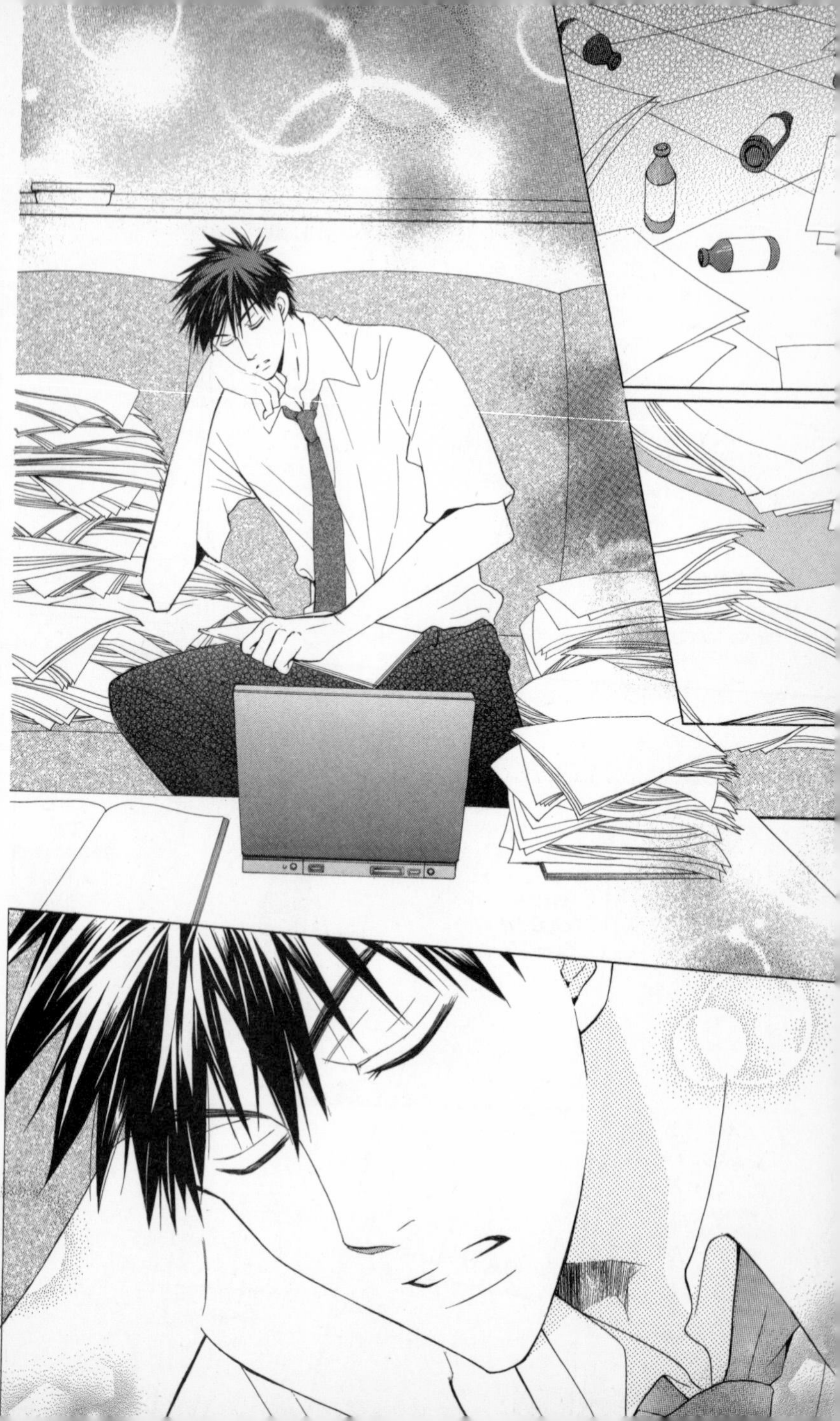

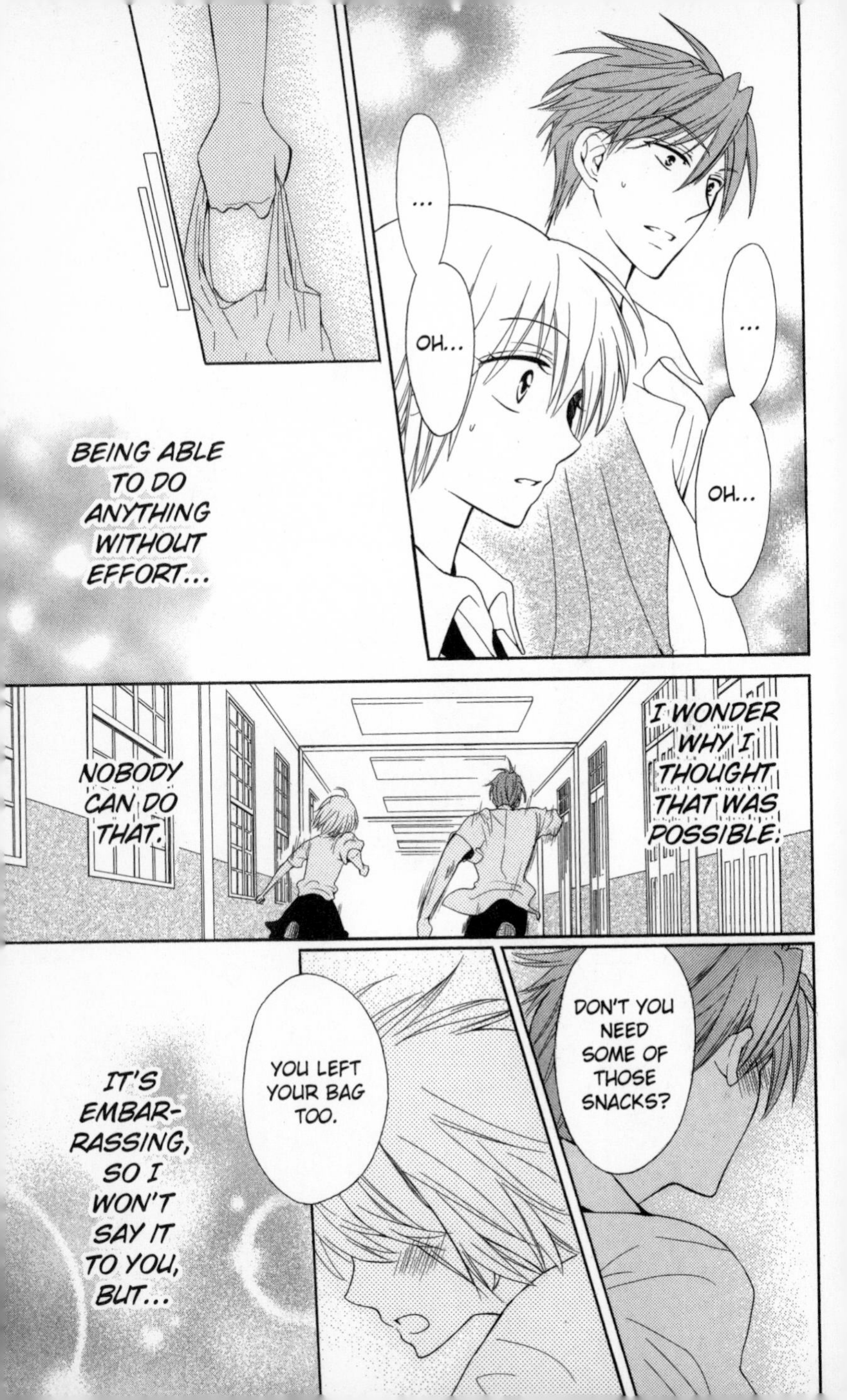
...
OH...
...
OH...
BEING ABLE TO DO ANYTHING WITHOUT EFFORT...
I WONDER WHY I THOUGHT THAT WAS POSSIBLE.
NOBODY CAN DO THAT.
DON'T YOU NEED SOME OF THOSE SNACKS?
YOU LEFT YOUR BAG TOO.
IT'S EMBARRASSING, SO I WON'T SAY IT TO YOU, BUT...

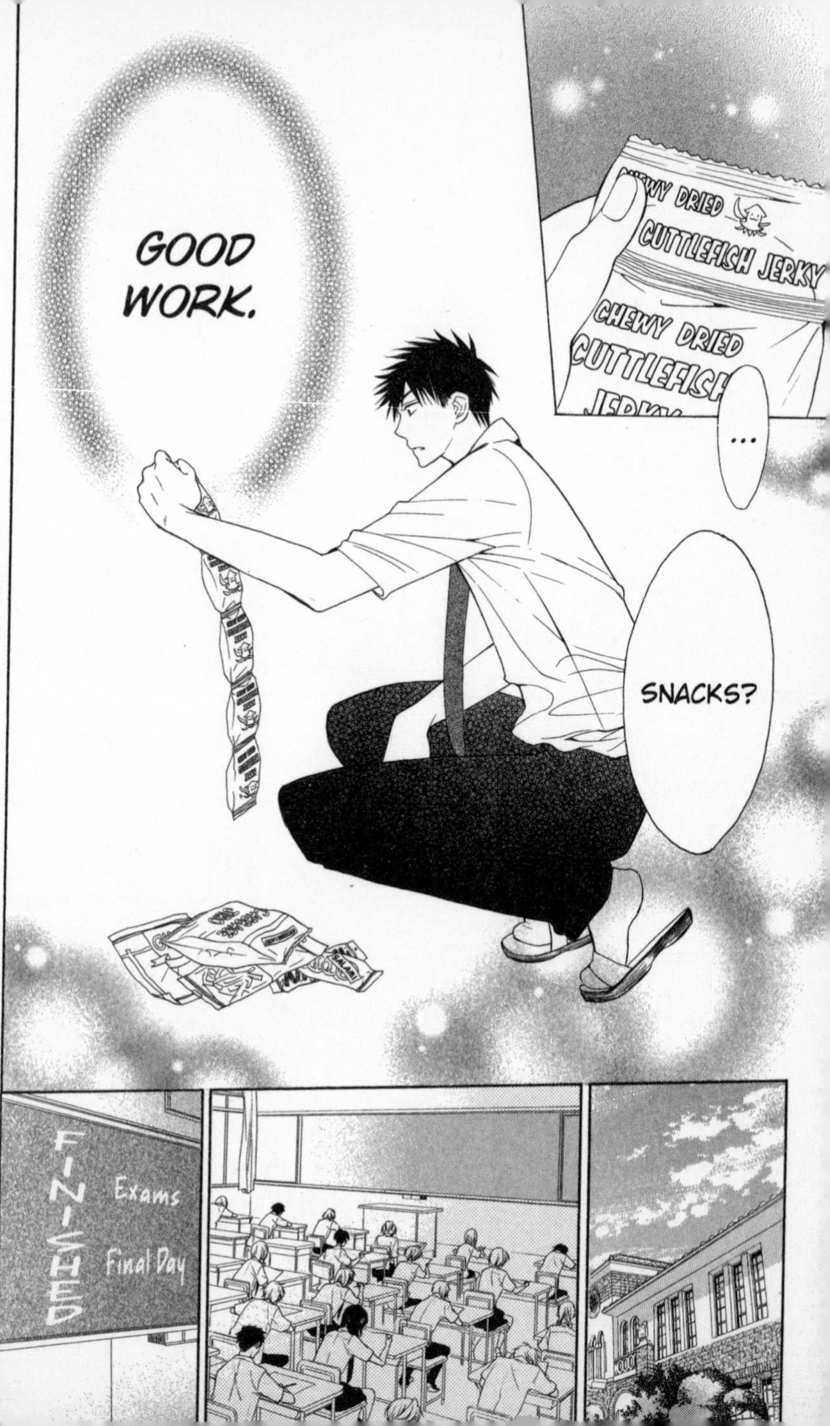
CHEWY DRIED CUTTLEFISH JERKY
CHEWY DRIED CUTTLEFISH
...
GOOD WORK.
SNACKS?
FINISHED
Exams Final Day

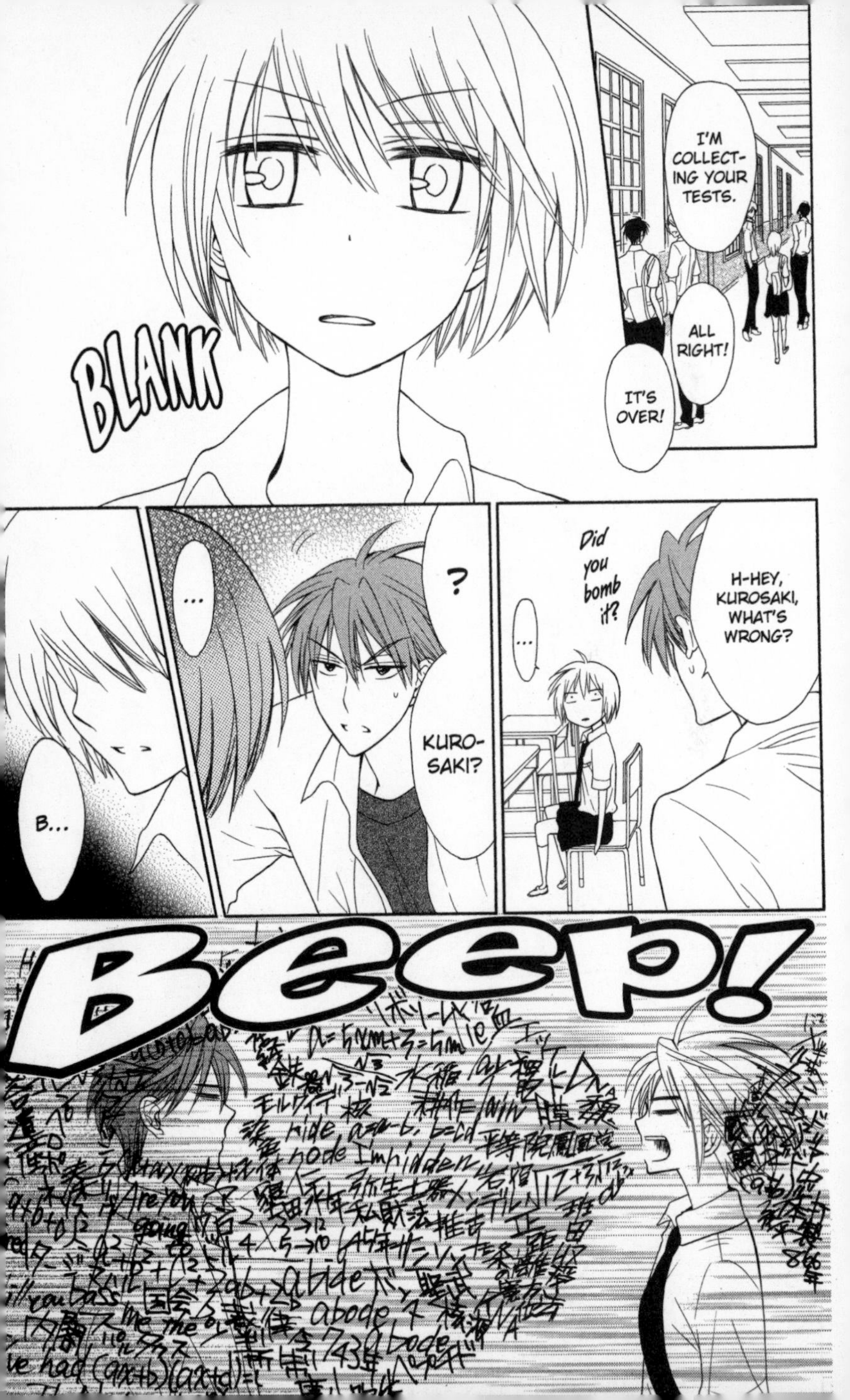
I'M COLLECTING YOUR TESTS.
ALL RIGHT!
IT'S OVER!
BLANK
H-HEY, KUROSAKI, WHAT'S WRONG?
Did you bomb it?
...
?
KURO-SAKI?
...
B...
Beep!

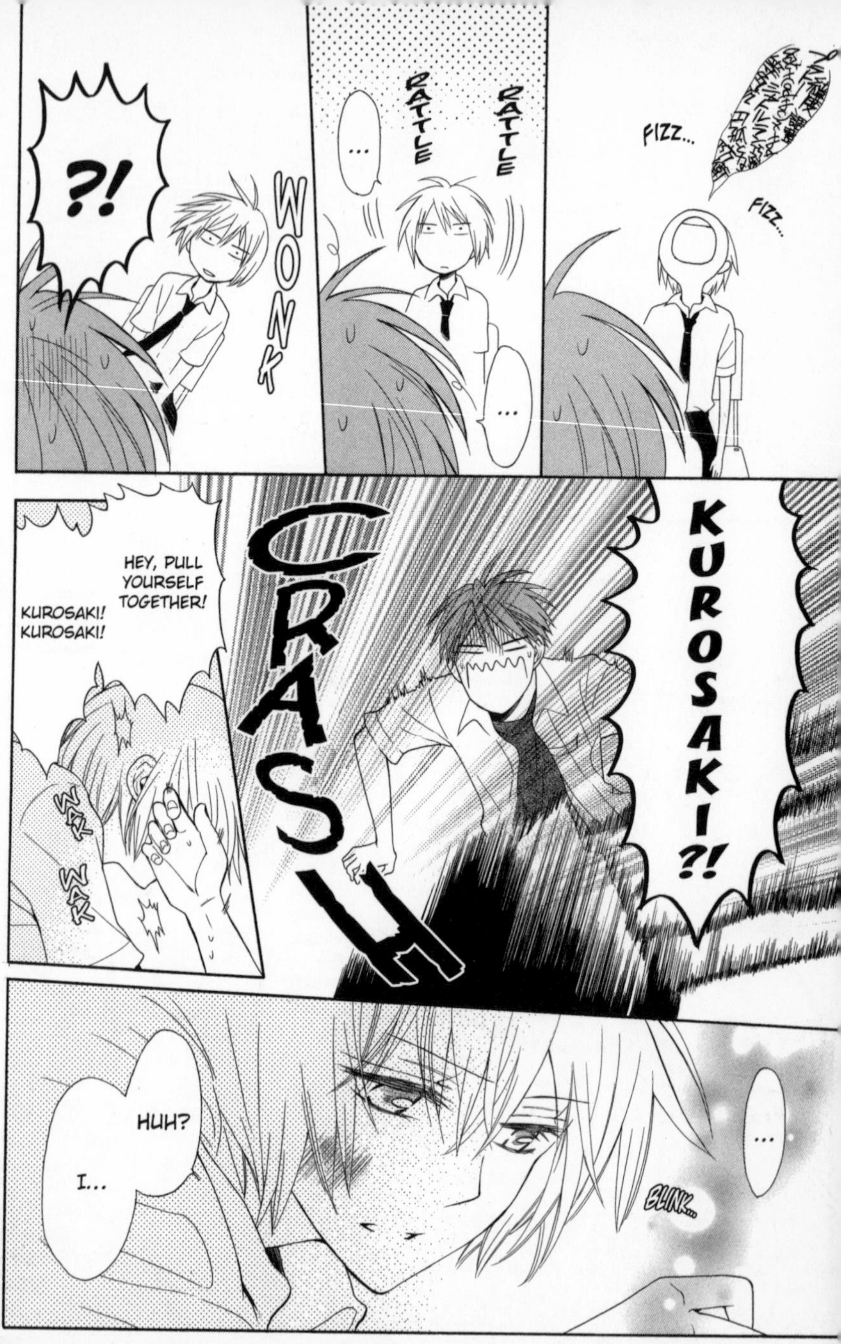
FIZZ...
FIZZ...
RATTLE
RATTLE
...
...
WONK
?!
KUROSAKI?!
CRASH
HEY, PULL YOURSELF TOGETHER!
KUROSAKI! KUROSAKI!
...
BLINK...
HUH?
I...

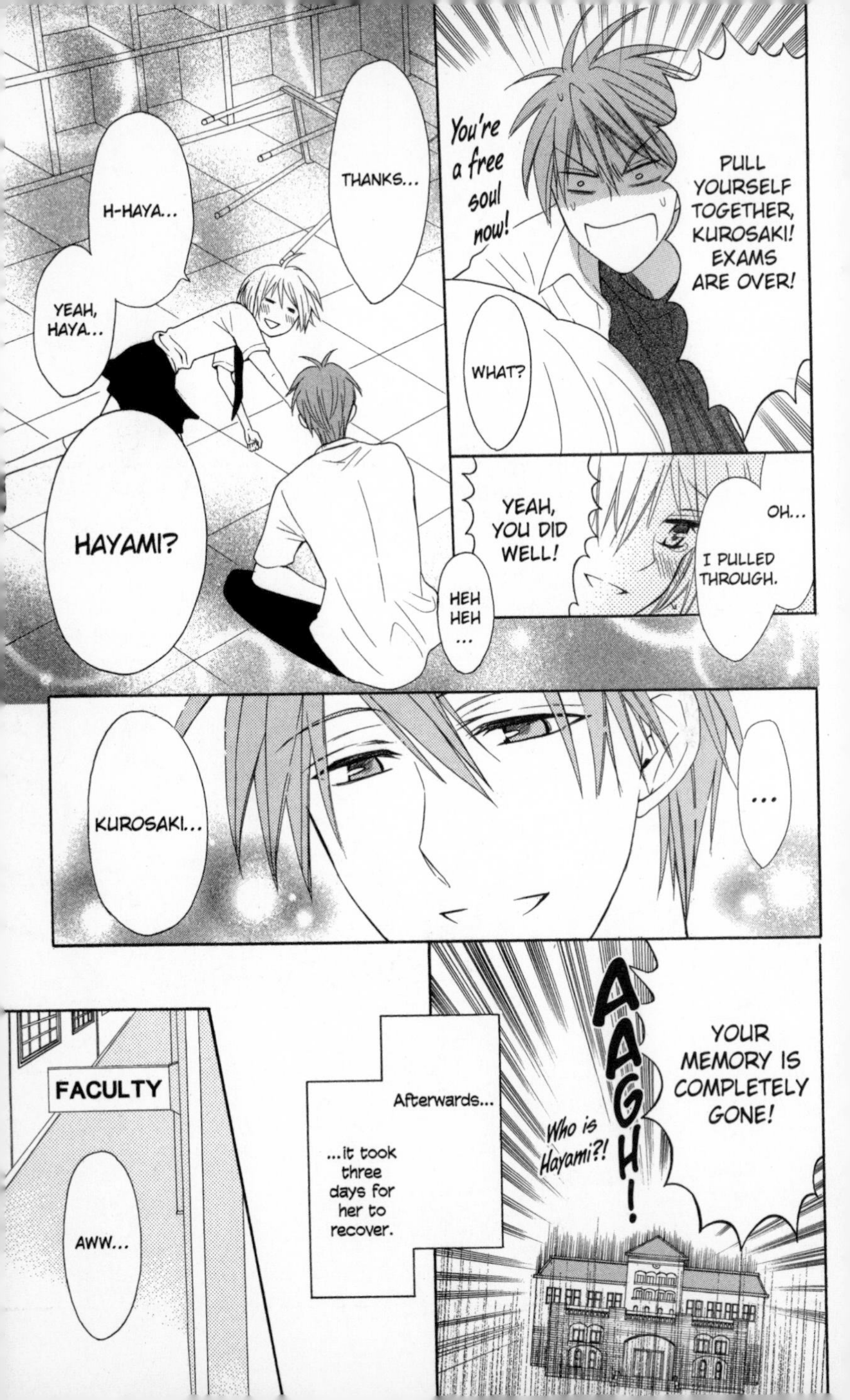

PULL YOURSELF TOGETHER, KUROSAKI! EXAMS ARE OVER!
You're a free soul now!
WHAT?
OH...
I PULLED THROUGH.
YEAH, YOU DID WELL!
HEH HEH ...
THANKS...
H-HAYA...
YEAH, HAYA...
HAYAMI?
...
KUROSAKI...
YOUR MEMORY IS COMPLETELY GONE!
AAGH!
Who is Hayami?!
Afterwards...
...it took three days for her to recover.
FACULTY
AWW...

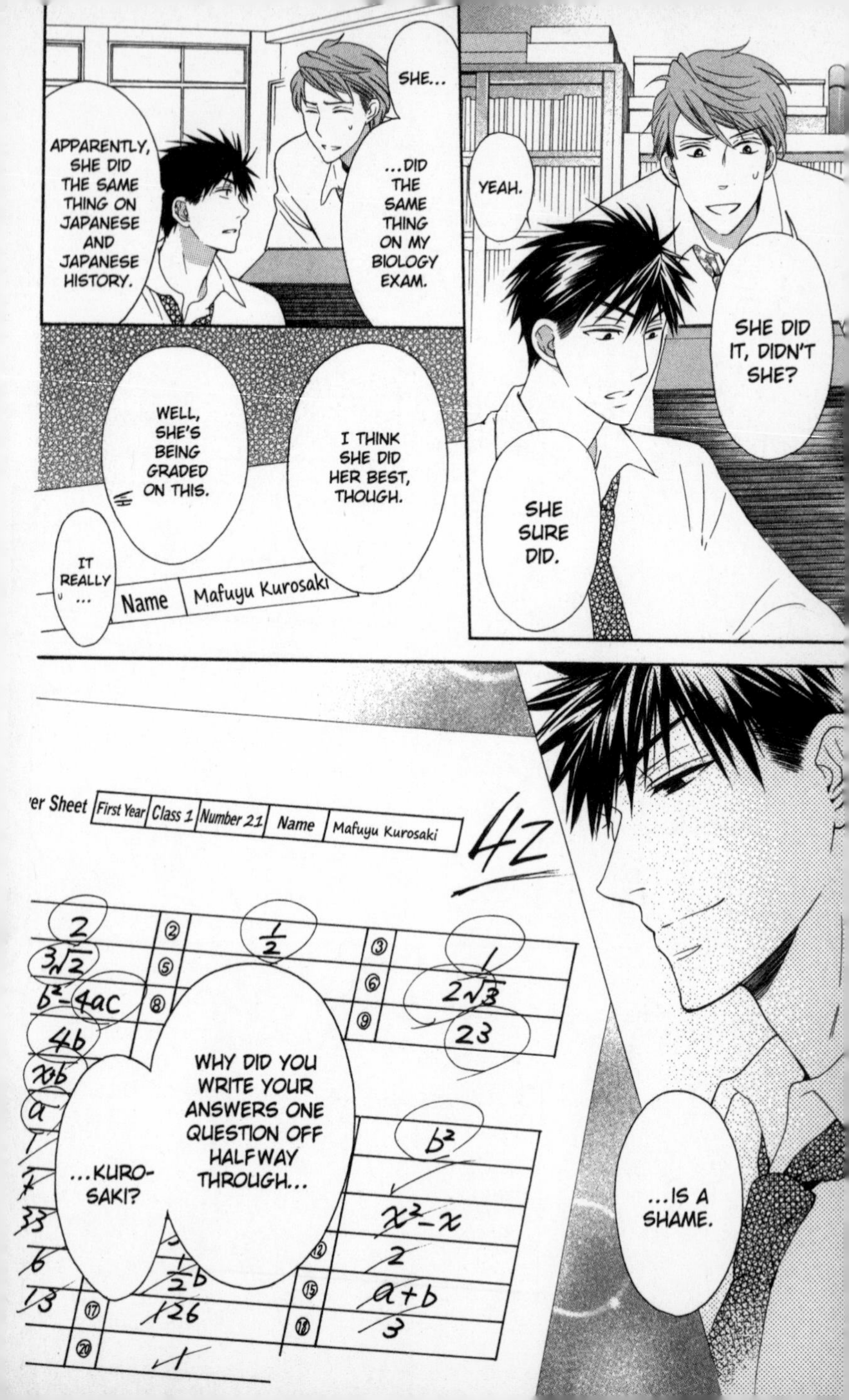
SHE DID IT, DIDN'T SHE?
YEAH.
SHE SURE DID.
SHE...
...DID THE SAME THING ON MY BIOLOGY EXAM.
APPARENTLY, SHE DID THE SAME THING ON JAPANESE AND JAPANESE HISTORY.
I THINK SHE DID HER BEST, THOUGH.
WELL, SHE'S BEING GRADED ON THIS.
IT REALLY...
Name Mafuyu Kurosaki
...IS A SHAME.
er Sheet First Year Class 1 Number 21 Name Mafuyu Kurosaki
42
WHY DID YOU WRITE YOUR ANSWERS ONE QUESTION OFF HALFWAY THROUGH...
...KURO-SAKI?

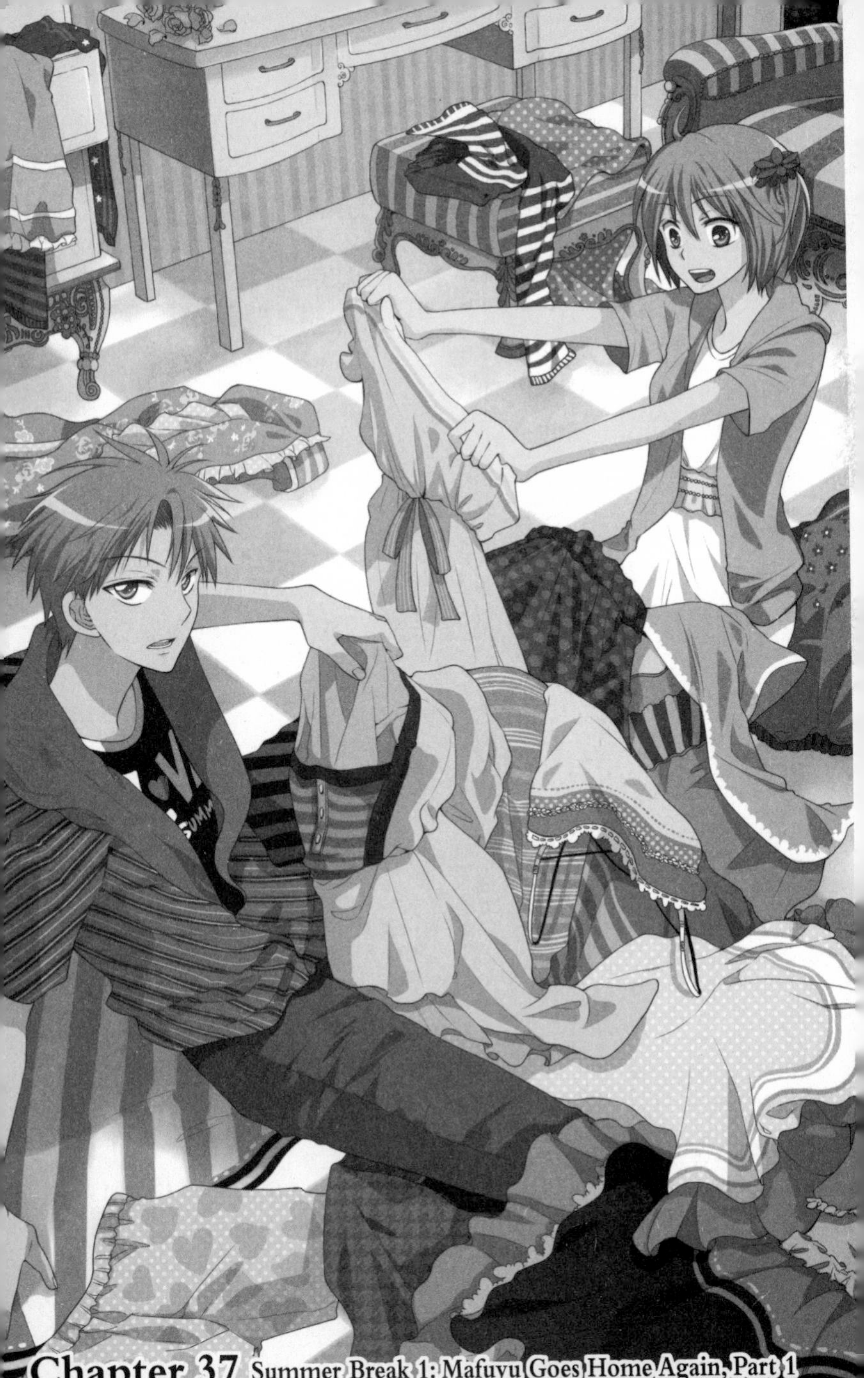

Chapter 37 Summer Break 1: Mafuyu Goes Home Again, Part 1

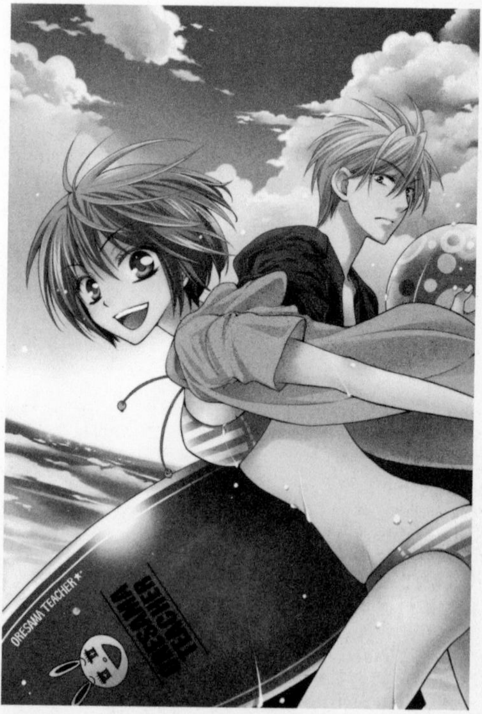
ORESAMA TEACHER★

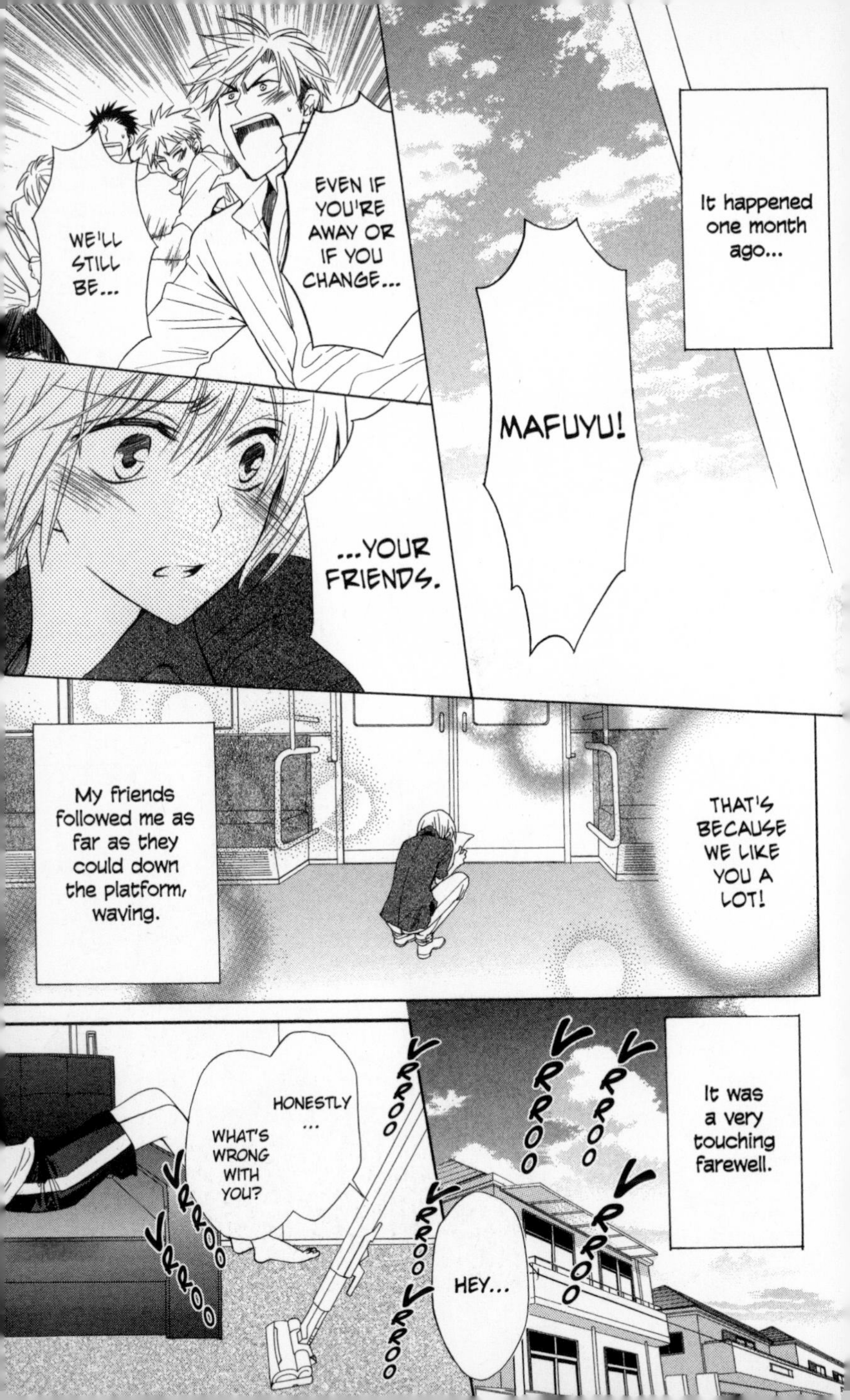
It happened one month ago...
MAFUYU!
EVEN IF YOU'RE AWAY OR IF YOU CHANGE...
WE'LL STILL BE...
...YOUR FRIENDS.
THAT'S BECAUSE WE LIKE YOU A LOT!
My friends followed me as far as they could down the platform, waving.
It was a very touching farewell.
VRROO VRROO VRROO VRROO VRROO VRROO
HEY...
HONESTLY ...
WHAT'S WRONG WITH YOU?
VRROO VRROO

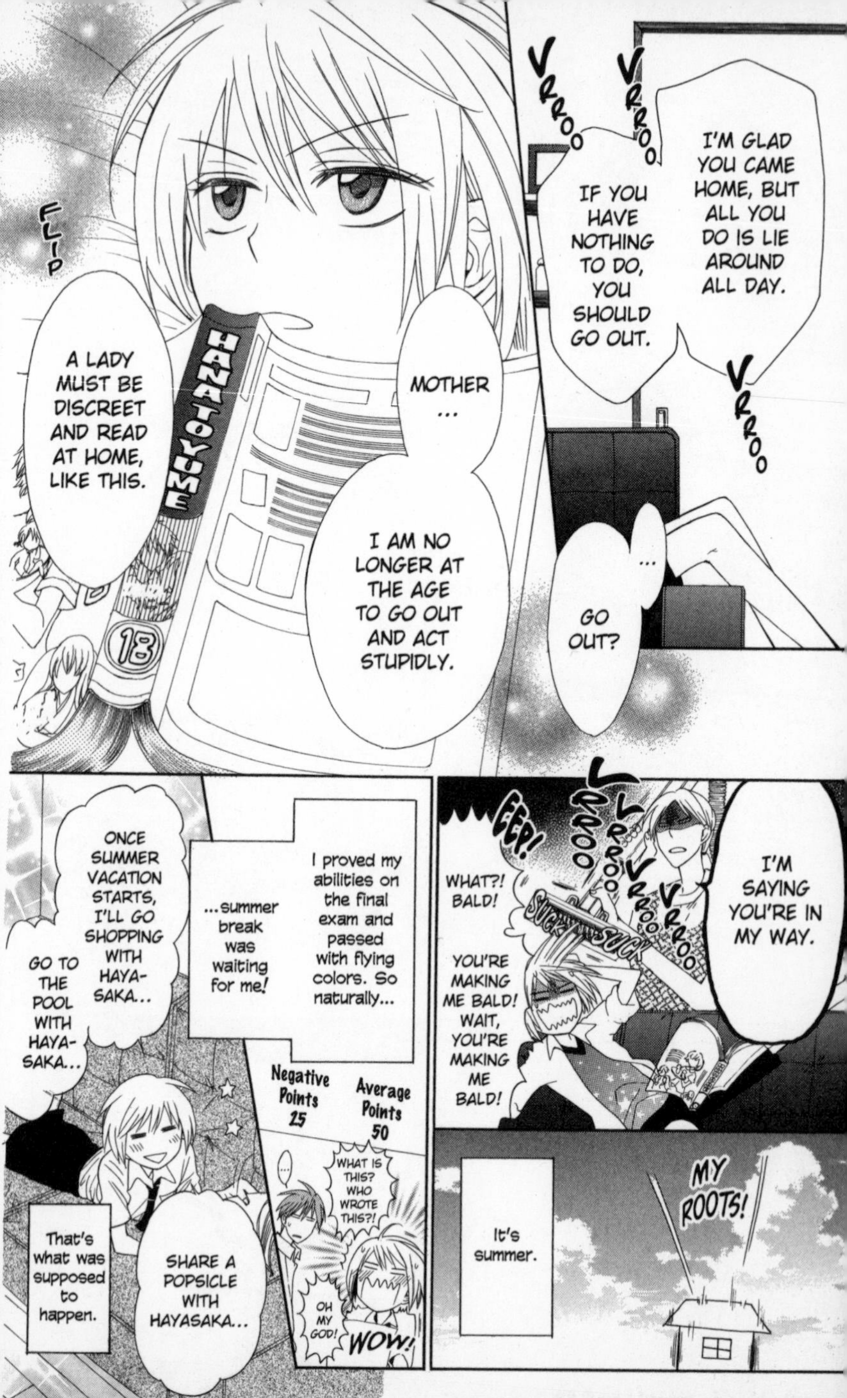
VRROO
VRROO
I'M GLAD YOU CAME HOME, BUT ALL YOU DO IS LIE AROUND ALL DAY.
IF YOU HAVE NOTHING TO DO, YOU SHOULD GO OUT.
VRROO
...
GO OUT?
MOTHER ...
I AM NO LONGER AT THE AGE TO GO OUT AND ACT STUPIDLY.
FLIP
HANATOYUME
18
A LADY MUST BE DISCREET AND READ AT HOME, LIKE THIS.
I'M SAYING YOU'RE IN MY WAY.
VRROO
VRROO
VRROO
VRROO
VRROO
EEP!
SUCK SUCK
WHAT?! BALD!
YOU'RE MAKING ME BALD! WAIT, YOU'RE MAKING ME BALD!
MY ROOTS!
It's summer.
I proved my abilities on the final exam and passed with flying colors. So naturally...
...summer break was waiting for me!
Negative Points 25
Average Points 50
WHAT IS THIS? WHO WROTE THIS?!
...
OH MY GOD!
WOW!
ONCE SUMMER VACATION STARTS, I'LL GO SHOPPING WITH HAYA-SAKA...
GO TO THE POOL WITH HAYA-SAKA...
SHARE A POPSICLE WITH HAYASAKA...
That's what was supposed to happen.

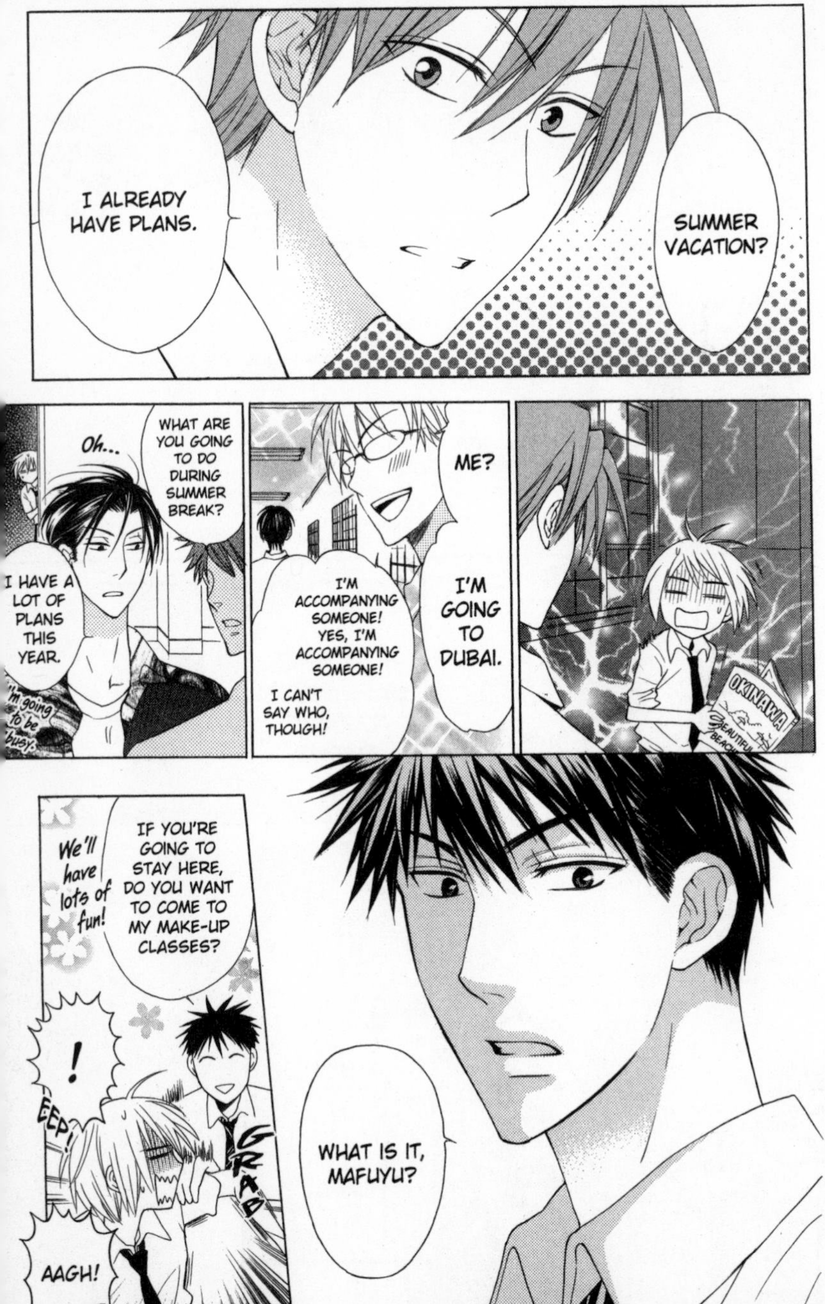
SUMMER VACATION?
I ALREADY HAVE PLANS.
OKINAWA
BEAUTIFUL
ME?
I'M GOING TO DUBAI.
I'M ACCOMPANYING SOMEONE! YES, I'M ACCOMPANYING SOMEONE!
I CAN'T SAY WHO, THOUGH!
WHAT ARE YOU GOING TO DO DURING SUMMER BREAK?
Oh...
I HAVE A LOT OF PLANS THIS YEAR.
I'm going to be busy.
WHAT IS IT, MAFUYU?
IF YOU'RE GOING TO STAY HERE, DO YOU WANT TO COME TO MY MAKE-UP CLASSES?
We'll have lots of fun!
!
EEP!
GRAB
AAGH!

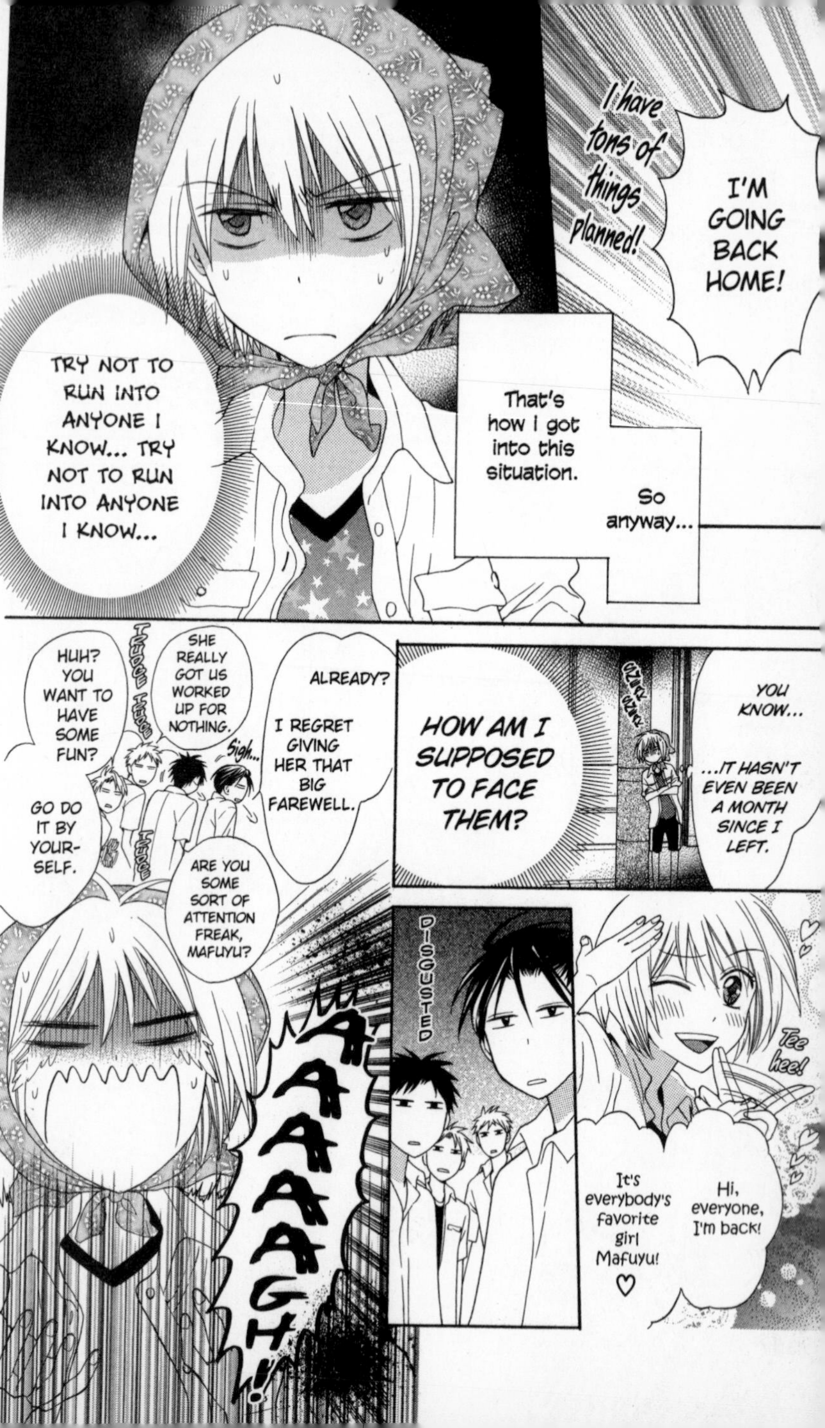
I'M GOING BACK HOME!
I have tons of things planned!
That's how I got into this situation.
So anyway...
TRY NOT TO RUN INTO ANYONE I KNOW... TRY NOT TO RUN INTO ANYONE I KNOW...
YOU KNOW...
...IT HASN'T EVEN BEEN A MONTH SINCE I LEFT.
HOW AM I SUPPOSED TO FACE THEM?
Hi, everyone, I'm back!
It's everybody's favorite girl Mafuyu! ♡
Tee hee!
DISGUSTED
ALREADY?
I REGRET GIVING HER THAT BIG FAREWELL.
SHE REALLY GOT US WORKED UP FOR NOTHING.
Sigh...
HUH? YOU WANT TO HAVE SOME FUN?
GO DO IT BY YOURSELF.
TRUDGE TRUDGE
TRUDGE
ARE YOU SOME SORT OF ATTENTION FREAK, MAFUYU?
AAAAAAGH!!

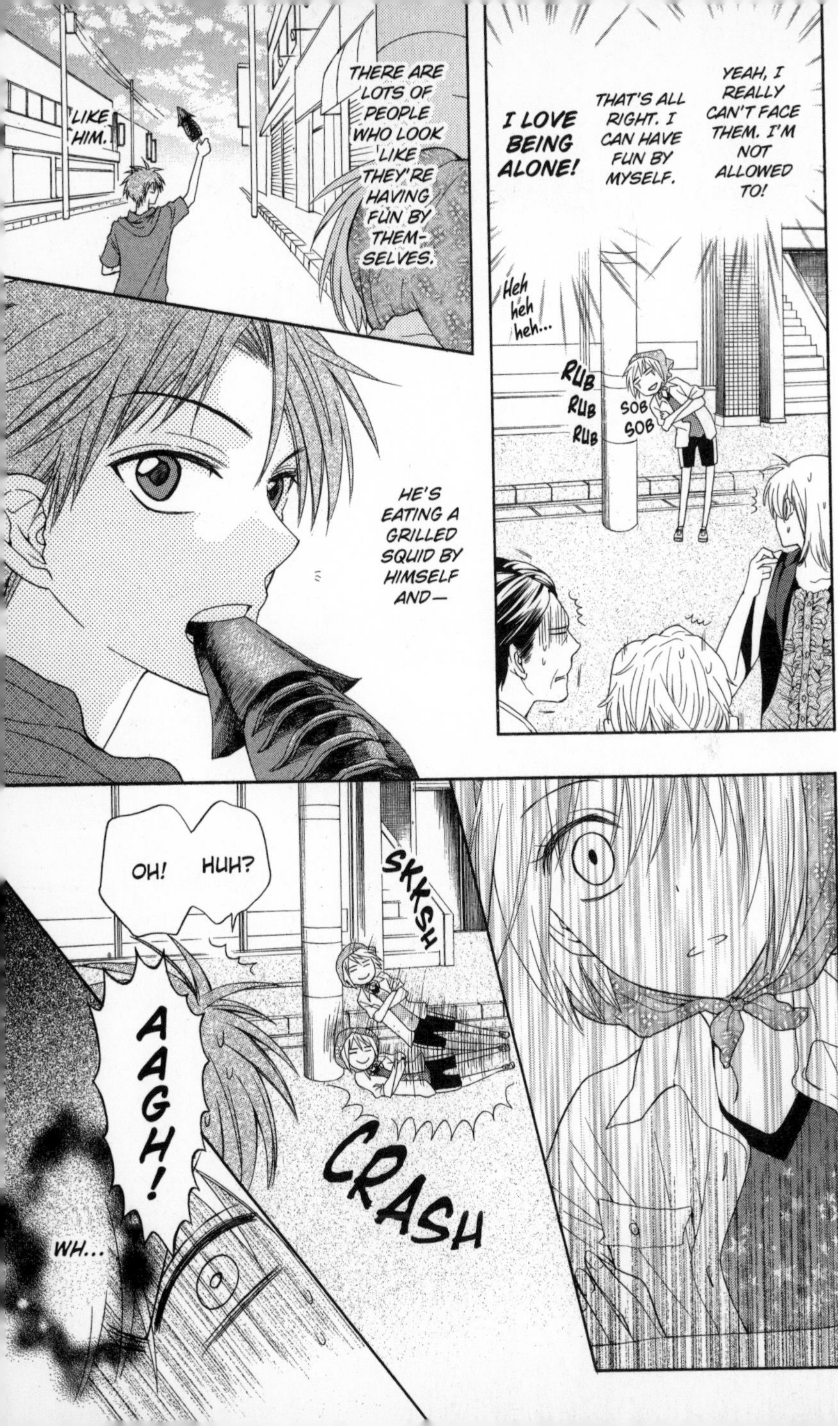

YEAH, I REALLY CAN'T FACE THEM. I'M NOT ALLOWED TO!
THAT'S ALL RIGHT. I CAN HAVE FUN BY MYSELF.
I LOVE BEING ALONE!
Heh heh heh...
SOB SOB
RUB RUB RUB
THERE ARE LOTS OF PEOPLE WHO LOOK LIKE THEY'RE HAVING FUN BY THEM-SELVES.
LIKE HIM.
HE'S EATING A GRILLED SQUID BY HIMSELF AND—
SKKSH
HUH?
OH!
AAGH!
CRASH
WH...

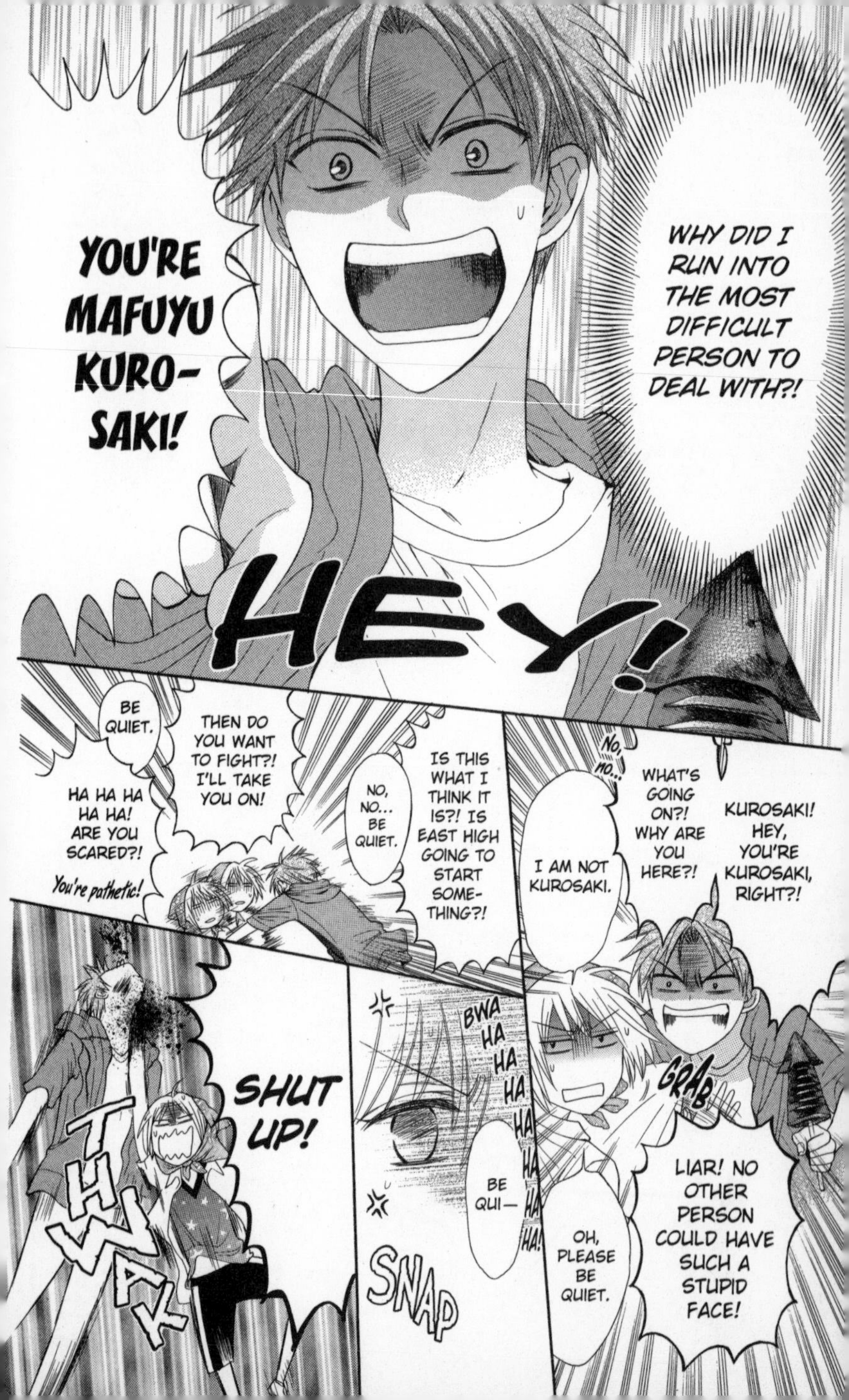

WHY DID I RUN INTO THE MOST DIFFICULT PERSON TO DEAL WITH?!
YOU'RE MAFUYU KURO-SAKI!
HEY!
No, no...
KUROSAKI! HEY, YOU'RE KUROSAKI, RIGHT?!
WHAT'S GOING ON?! WHY ARE YOU HERE?!
I AM NOT KUROSAKI.
IS THIS WHAT I THINK IT IS?! IS EAST HIGH GOING TO START SOME-THING?!
NO, NO... BE QUIET.
THEN DO YOU WANT TO FIGHT?! I'LL TAKE YOU ON!
BE QUIET.
HA HA HA HA HA! ARE YOU SCARED?!
You're pathetic!
GRAB
LIAR! NO OTHER PERSON COULD HAVE SUCH A STUPID FACE!
OH, PLEASE BE QUIET.
BWA HA HA HA HA HA HA HA HA!
BE QUI—
SNAP
SHUT UP!
THWAK

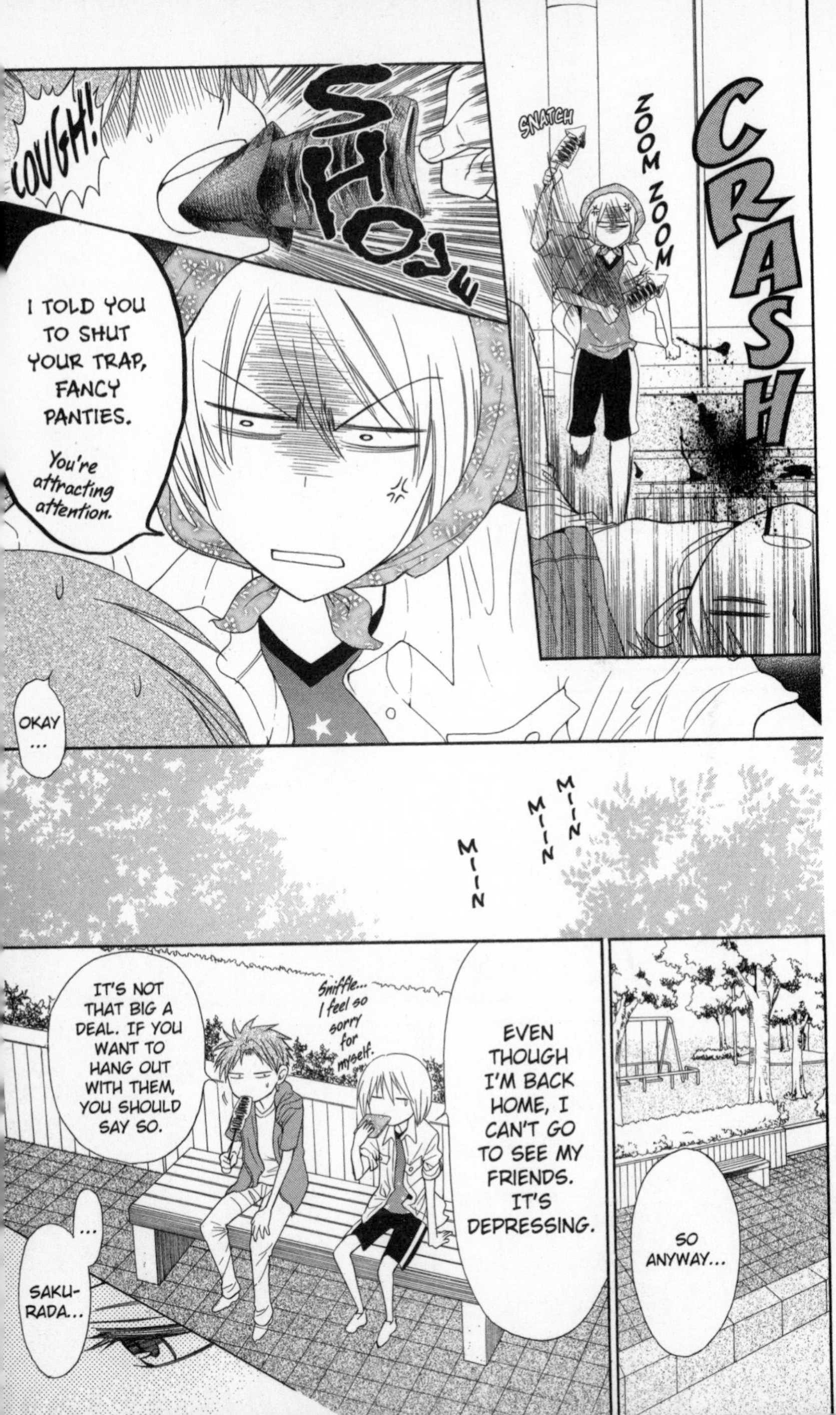

CRASH
ZOOM ZOOM
SNATCH
SHOVE
COUGH!
I TOLD YOU TO SHUT YOUR TRAP, FANCY PANTIES.
You're attracting attention.
OKAY...
MIIN
MIIN
MIIN
SO ANYWAY...
EVEN THOUGH I'M BACK HOME, I CAN'T GO TO SEE MY FRIENDS. IT'S DEPRESSING.
Sniffle... I feel so sorry for myself.
IT'S NOT THAT BIG A DEAL. IF YOU WANT TO HANG OUT WITH THEM, YOU SHOULD SAY SO.
...
SAKURADA...

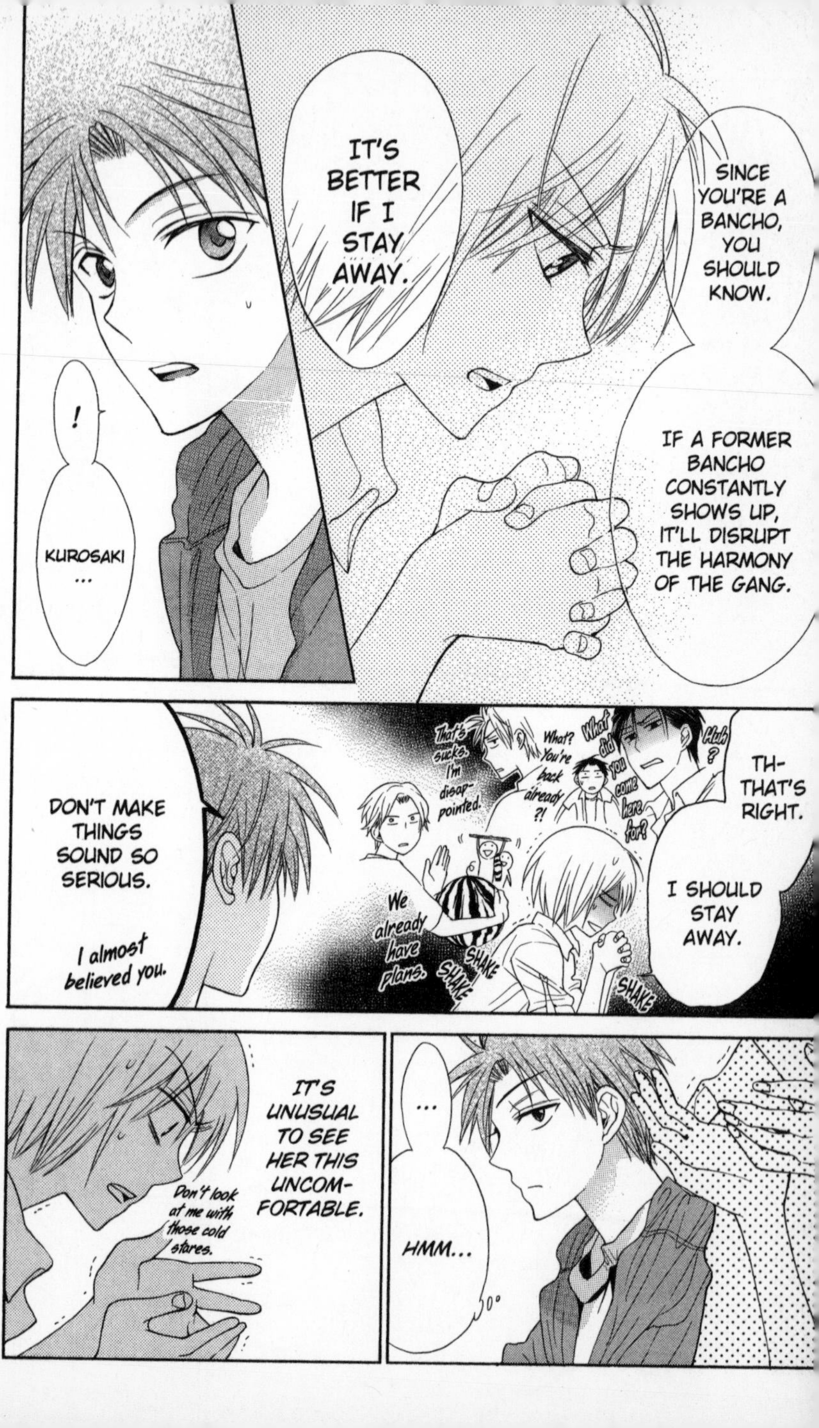
SINCE YOU'RE A BANCHO, YOU SHOULD KNOW.
IF A FORMER BANCHO CONSTANTLY SHOWS UP, IT'LL DISRUPT THE HARMONY OF THE GANG.
IT'S BETTER IF I STAY AWAY.
!
KUROSAKI ...
TH-THAT'S RIGHT.
I SHOULD STAY AWAY.
Huh?
What did you come here for?
What? You're back already?!
That's sucks. I'm disap-pointed.
We already have plans.
SHAKE
SHAKE
SHAKE
DON'T MAKE THINGS SOUND SO SERIOUS.
I almost believed you.
...
HMM...
IT'S UNUSUAL TO SEE HER THIS UNCOM-FORTABLE.
Don't look at me with those cold stares.

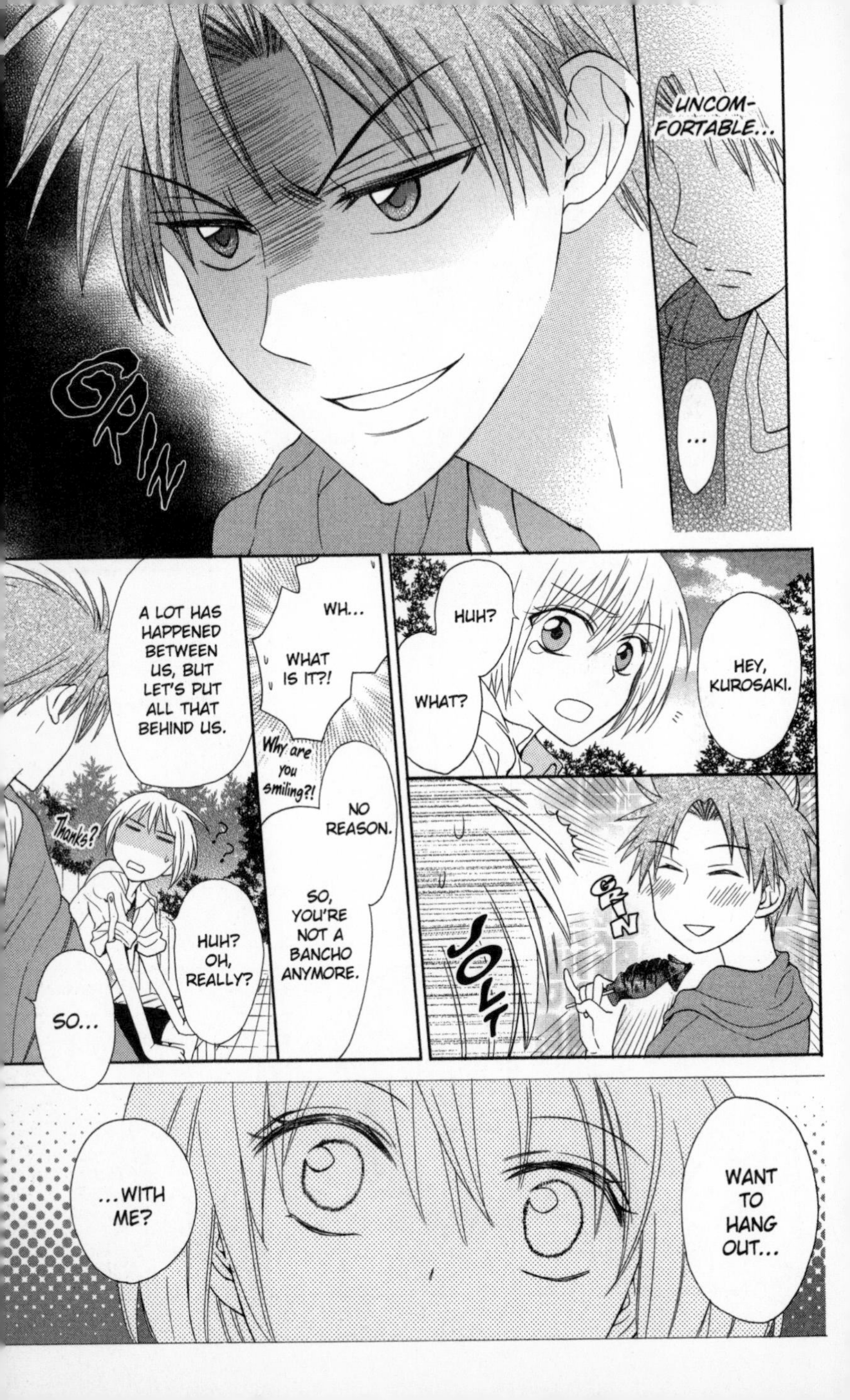
UNCOM-FORTABLE...
...
GRIN
HEY, KUROSAKI.
HUH?
WHAT?
GRIN
JOLT
WH...
WHAT IS IT?!
Why are you smiling?!
NO REASON.
SO, YOU'RE NOT A BANCHO ANYMORE.
A LOT HAS HAPPENED BETWEEN US, BUT LET'S PUT ALL THAT BEHIND US.
Thanks?
HUH? OH, REALLY?
SO...
WANT TO HANG OUT...
...WITH ME?

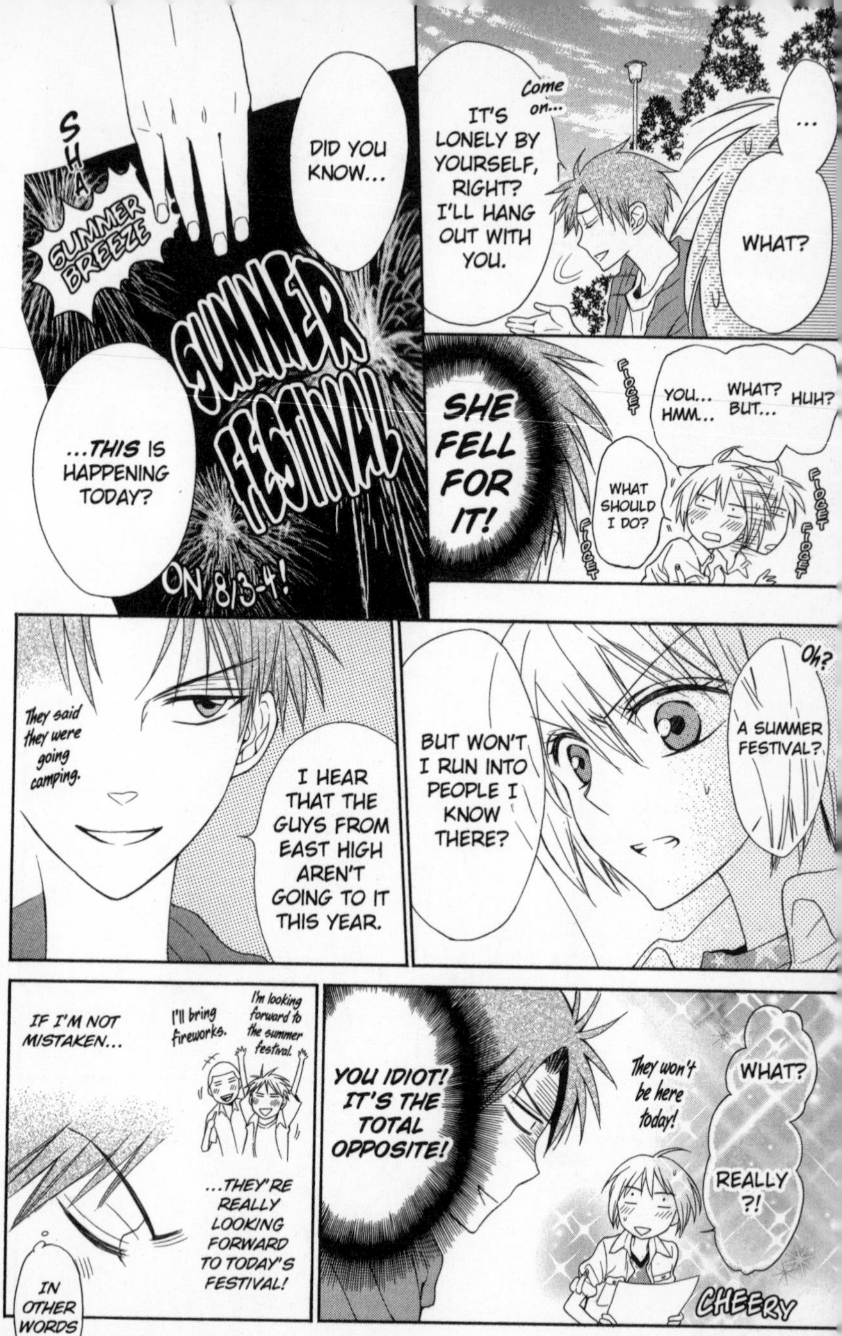
...
WHAT?
Come on...
IT'S LONELY BY YOURSELF, RIGHT? I'LL HANG OUT WITH YOU.
HUH?
WHAT? BUT...
YOU... HMM...
FIDGET
WHAT SHOULD I DO?
FIDGET
FIDGET
FIDGET
SHE FELL FOR IT!
DID YOU KNOW...
SHA
SUMMER BREEZE
SUMMER FESTIVAL
ON 8/3-4!
...THIS IS HAPPENING TODAY?
Oh?
A SUMMER FESTIVAL?
BUT WON'T I RUN INTO PEOPLE I KNOW THERE?
I HEAR THAT THE GUYS FROM EAST HIGH AREN'T GOING TO IT THIS YEAR.
They said they were going camping.
WHAT?
REALLY ?!
They won't be here today!
CHEERY
YOU IDIOT! IT'S THE TOTAL OPPOSITE!
I'm looking forward to the summer festival.
I'll bring fireworks.
IF I'M NOT MISTAKEN...
...THEY'RE REALLY LOOKING FORWARD TO TODAY'S FESTIVAL!
IN OTHER WORDS...

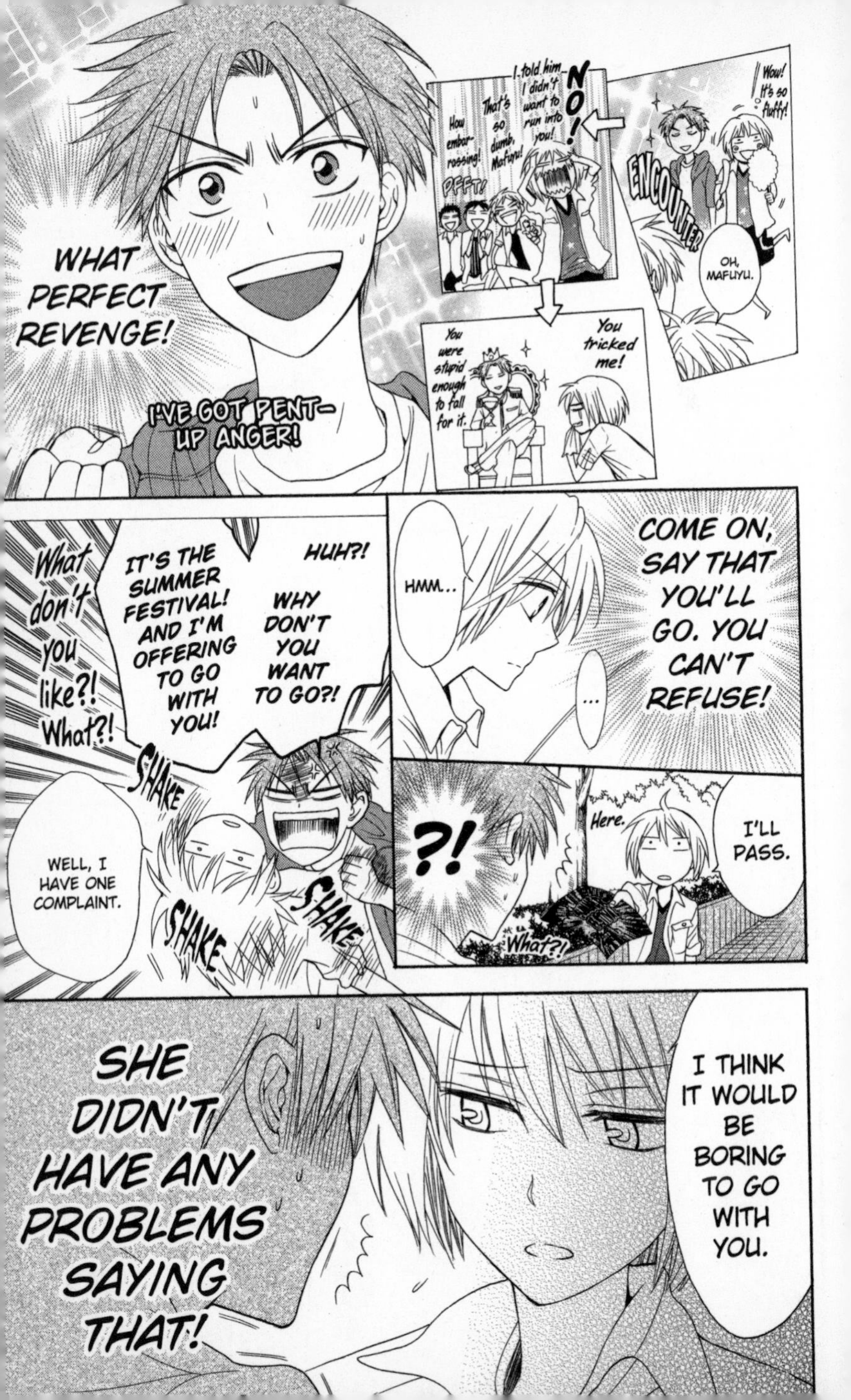
Wow! It's so fluffy!
ENCOUNTER
OH, MAFUYU.
I told him I didn't want to run into you!
NO!
That's so dumb, Mafuyu!
How embarrassing!
PFFT!
You tricked me!
You were stupid enough to fall for it.
WHAT PERFECT REVENGE!
I'VE GOT PENT-UP ANGER!
COME ON, SAY THAT YOU'LL GO. YOU CAN'T REFUSE!
HMM...
...
I'LL PASS.
Here.
?!
What?!
HUH?!
WHY DON'T YOU WANT TO GO?!
IT'S THE SUMMER FESTIVAL! AND I'M OFFERING TO GO WITH YOU!
What don't you like?! What?!
SHAKE
SHAKE
SHAKE
WELL, I HAVE ONE COMPLAINT.
I THINK IT WOULD BE BORING TO GO WITH YOU.
SHE DIDN'T HAVE ANY PROBLEMS SAYING THAT!

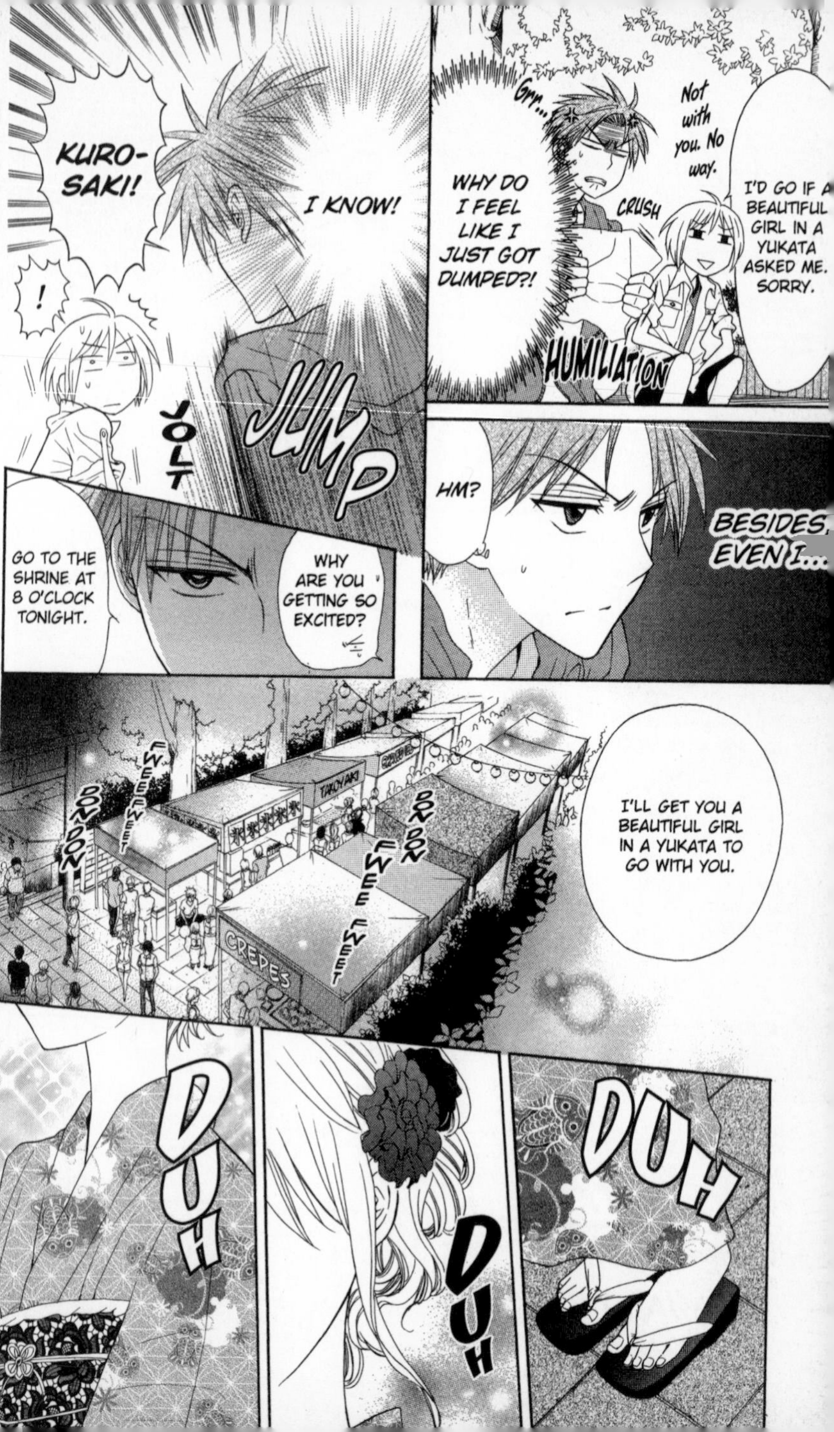
I'D GO IF A BEAUTIFUL GIRL IN A YUKATA ASKED ME. SORRY.
Not with you. No way.
Grr...
CRUSH
WHY DO I FEEL LIKE I JUST GOT DUMPED?!
HUMILIATION
BESIDES, EVEN I...
HM?
KURO-SAKI!
I KNOW!
!
JUMP
JOLT
WHY ARE YOU GETTING SO EXCITED?
GO TO THE SHRINE AT 8 O'CLOCK TONIGHT.
I'LL GET YOU A BEAUTIFUL GIRL IN A YUKATA TO GO WITH YOU.
DON DON
FWEE FWEET
TAKOYAKI
FWEE FWEET
DON DON
CREPES
DUH
DUH
DUH
DUH
DUH
DUH

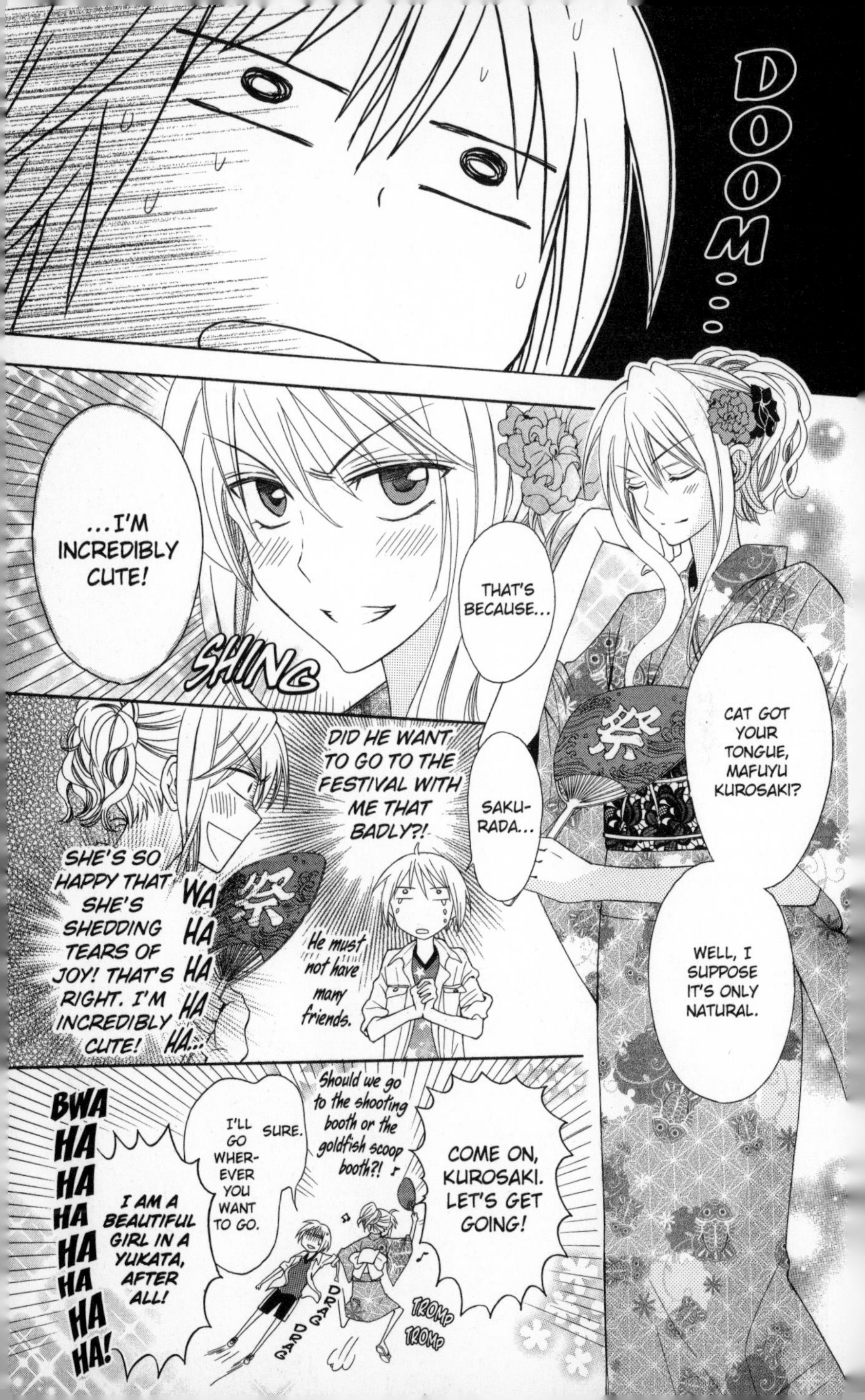
DOOOM...
CAT GOT YOUR TONGUE, MAFUYU KUROSAKI?
SAKU-RADA...
WELL, I SUPPOSE IT'S ONLY NATURAL.
THAT'S BECAUSE...
...I'M INCREDIBLY CUTE!
SHING
DID HE WANT TO GO TO THE FESTIVAL WITH ME THAT BADLY?!
He must not have many friends.
SHE'S SO HAPPY THAT SHE'S SHEDDING TEARS OF JOY! THAT'S RIGHT. I'M INCREDIBLY CUTE!
WA HA HA HA HA HA...
COME ON, KUROSAKI. LET'S GET GOING!
Should we go to the shooting booth or the goldfish scoop booth?!
SURE.
I'LL GO WHER-EVER YOU WANT TO GO.
I AM A BEAUTIFUL GIRL IN A YUKATA, AFTER ALL!
BWA HA HA HA HA HA HA HA HA!
TROMP TROMP
DRAG DRAG DRAG

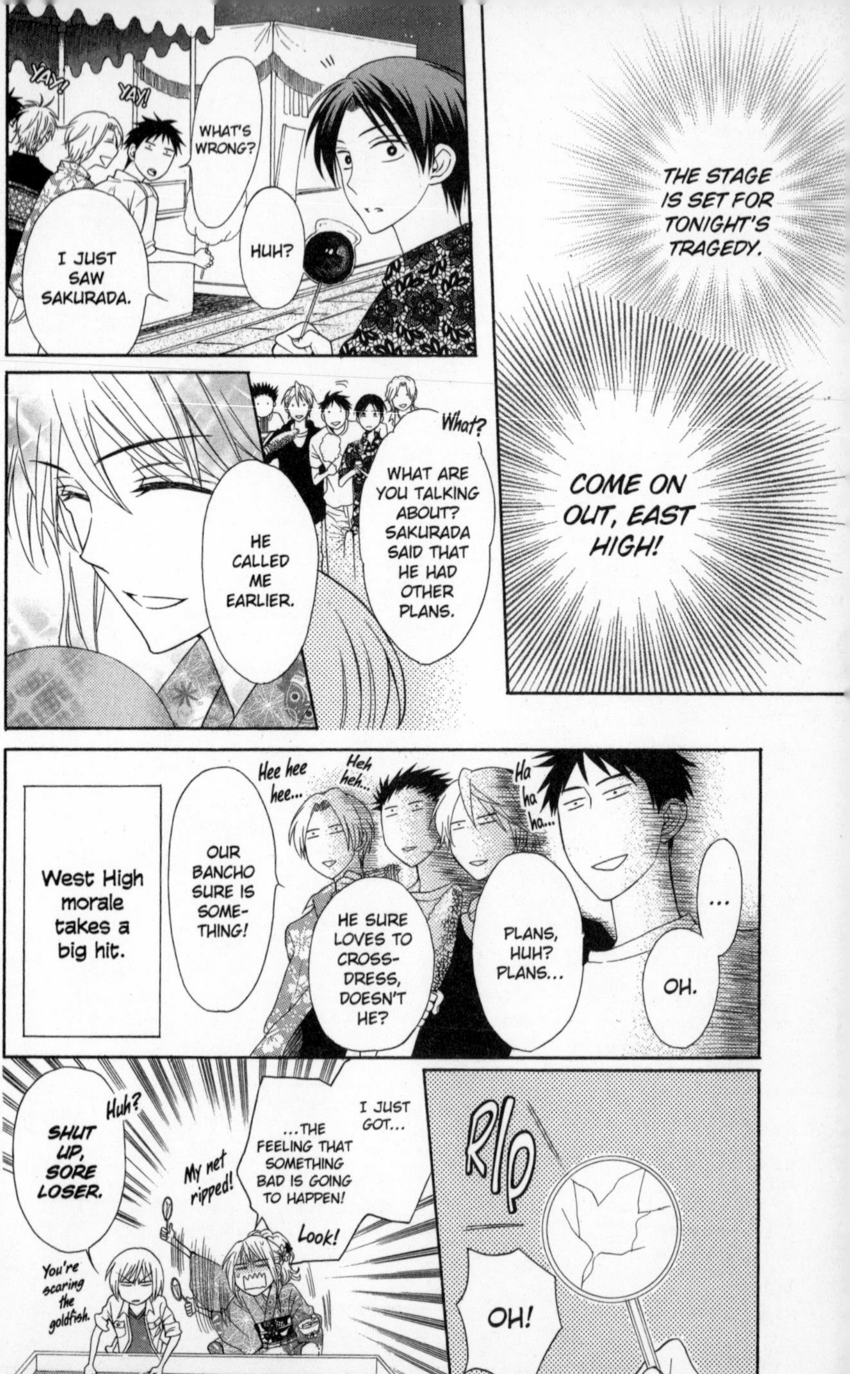
THE STAGE IS SET FOR TONIGHT'S TRAGEDY.
COME ON OUT, EAST HIGH!
YAY!
YAY!
WHAT'S WRONG?
HUH?
I JUST SAW SAKURADA.
What?
WHAT ARE YOU TALKING ABOUT? SAKURADA SAID THAT HE HAD OTHER PLANS.
HE CALLED ME EARLIER.
Ha ha ha...
...
OH.
PLANS, HUH? PLANS...
Heh heh...
HE SURE LOVES TO CROSS-DRESS, DOESN'T HE?
Hee hee hee...
OUR BANCHO SURE IS SOME-THING!
West High morale takes a big hit.
RIP
OH!
I JUST GOT...
...THE FEELING THAT SOMETHING BAD IS GOING TO HAPPEN!
Look!
My net ripped!
Huh?
SHUT UP, SORE LOSER.
You're scaring the goldfish.

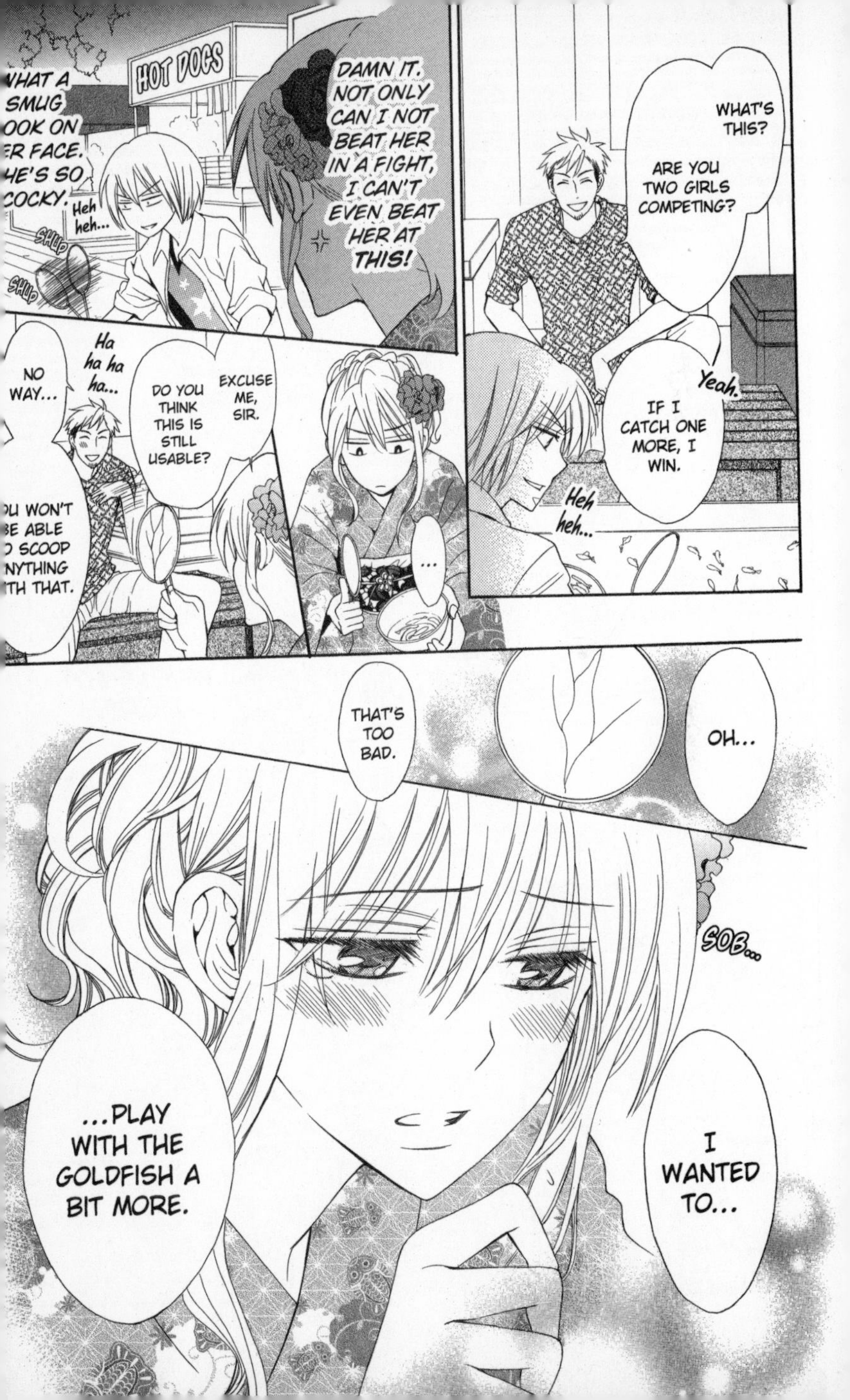
WHAT'S THIS?
ARE YOU TWO GIRLS COMPETING?
DAMN IT. NOT ONLY CAN I NOT BEAT HER IN A FIGHT, I CAN'T EVEN BEAT HER AT THIS!
HOT DOGS
WHAT A SMUG OOK ON ER FACE. HE'S SO COCKY.
Heh heh...
SHUP
SHUP
Yeah.
IF I CATCH ONE MORE, I WIN.
Heh heh...
EXCUSE ME, SIR.
DO YOU THINK THIS IS STILL USABLE?
...
Ha ha ha ha...
NO WAY...
OU WON'T BE ABLE O SCOOP NYTHING TH THAT.
OH...
THAT'S TOO BAD.
SOB...
I WANTED TO...
...PLAY WITH THE GOLDFISH A BIT MORE.

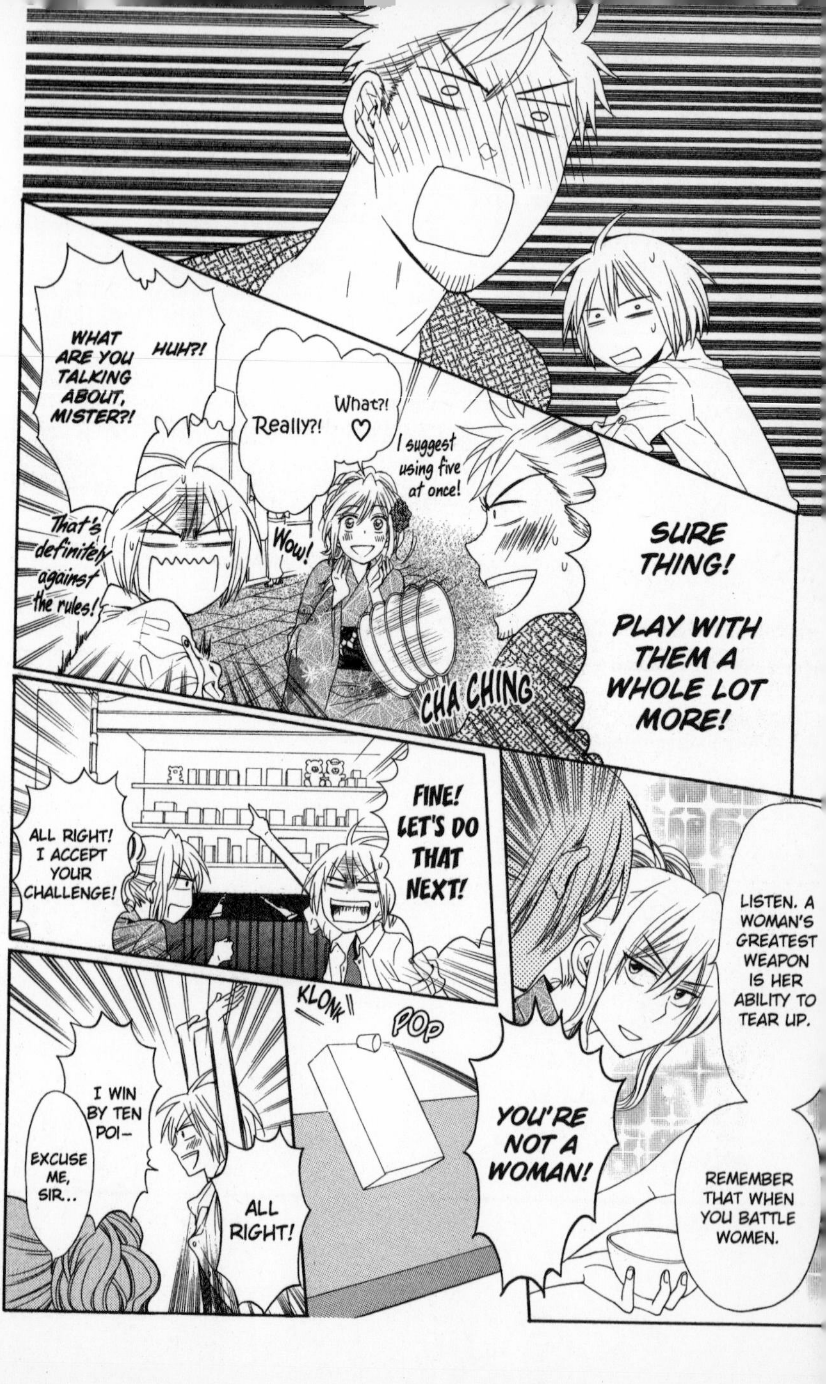
SURE THING!
PLAY WITH THEM A WHOLE LOT MORE!
I suggest using five at once!
Really?!
What?! ♡
Wow!
CHA CHING
HUH?!
WHAT ARE YOU TALKING ABOUT, MISTER?!
That's definitely against the rules!
LISTEN. A WOMAN'S GREATEST WEAPON IS HER ABILITY TO TEAR UP.
REMEMBER THAT WHEN YOU BATTLE WOMEN.
YOU'RE NOT A WOMAN!
FINE! LET'S DO THAT NEXT!
ALL RIGHT! I ACCEPT YOUR CHALLENGE!
POP
KLONK
ALL RIGHT!
I WIN BY TEN POI–
EXCUSE ME, SIR..

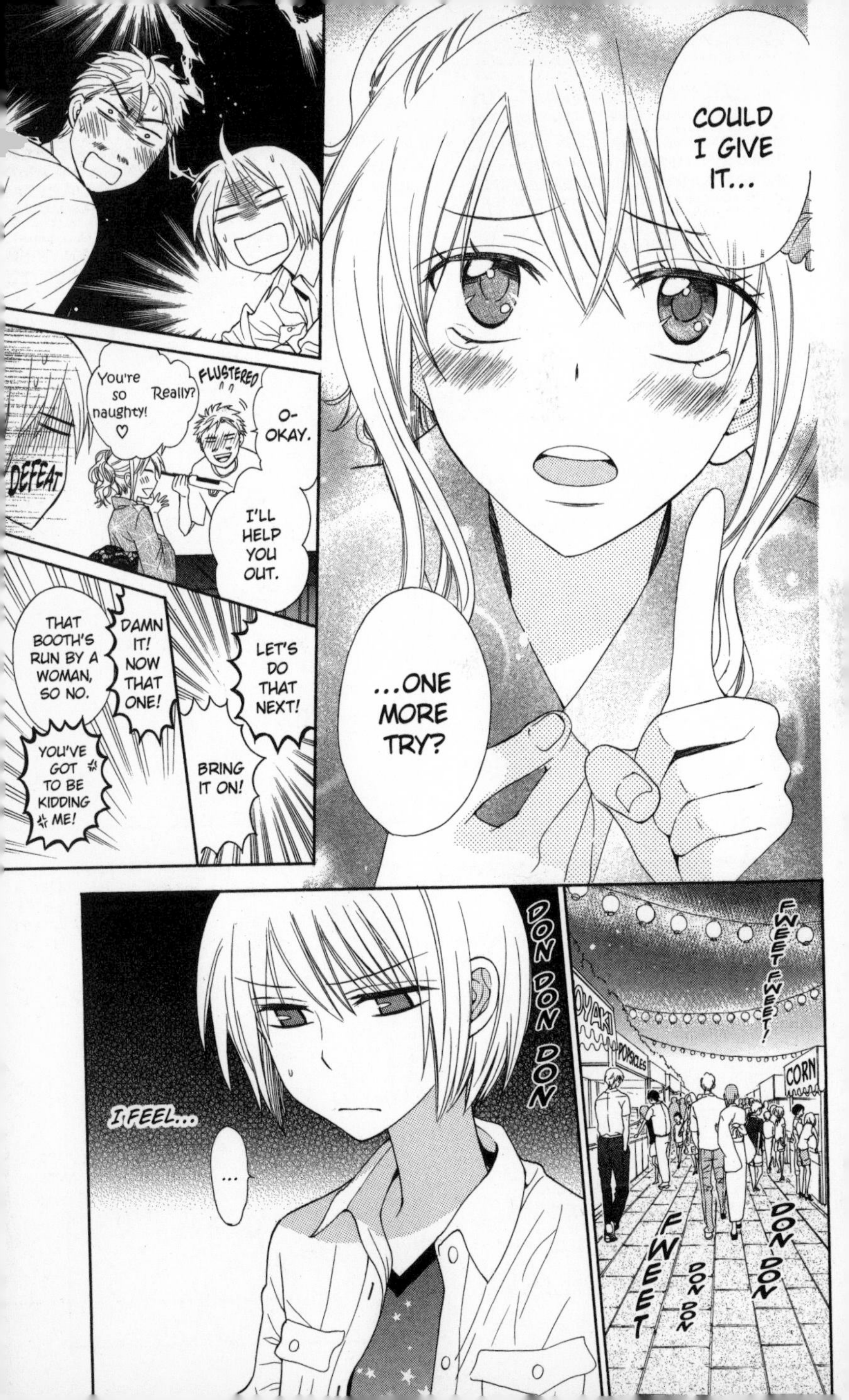
COULD I GIVE IT...
...ONE MORE TRY?
FLUSTERED
O-OKAY.
Really?
You're so naughty! ♡
I'LL HELP YOU OUT.
DEFEAT
LET'S DO THAT NEXT!
BRING IT ON!
DAMN IT! NOW THAT ONE!
THAT BOOTH'S RUN BY A WOMAN, SO NO.
YOU'VE GOT TO BE KIDDING ME!
FWEET FWEET!
OYAKI
POPSICLES
CORN
DON DON
FWEET
DON DON
DON DON DON DON
I FEEL...
...

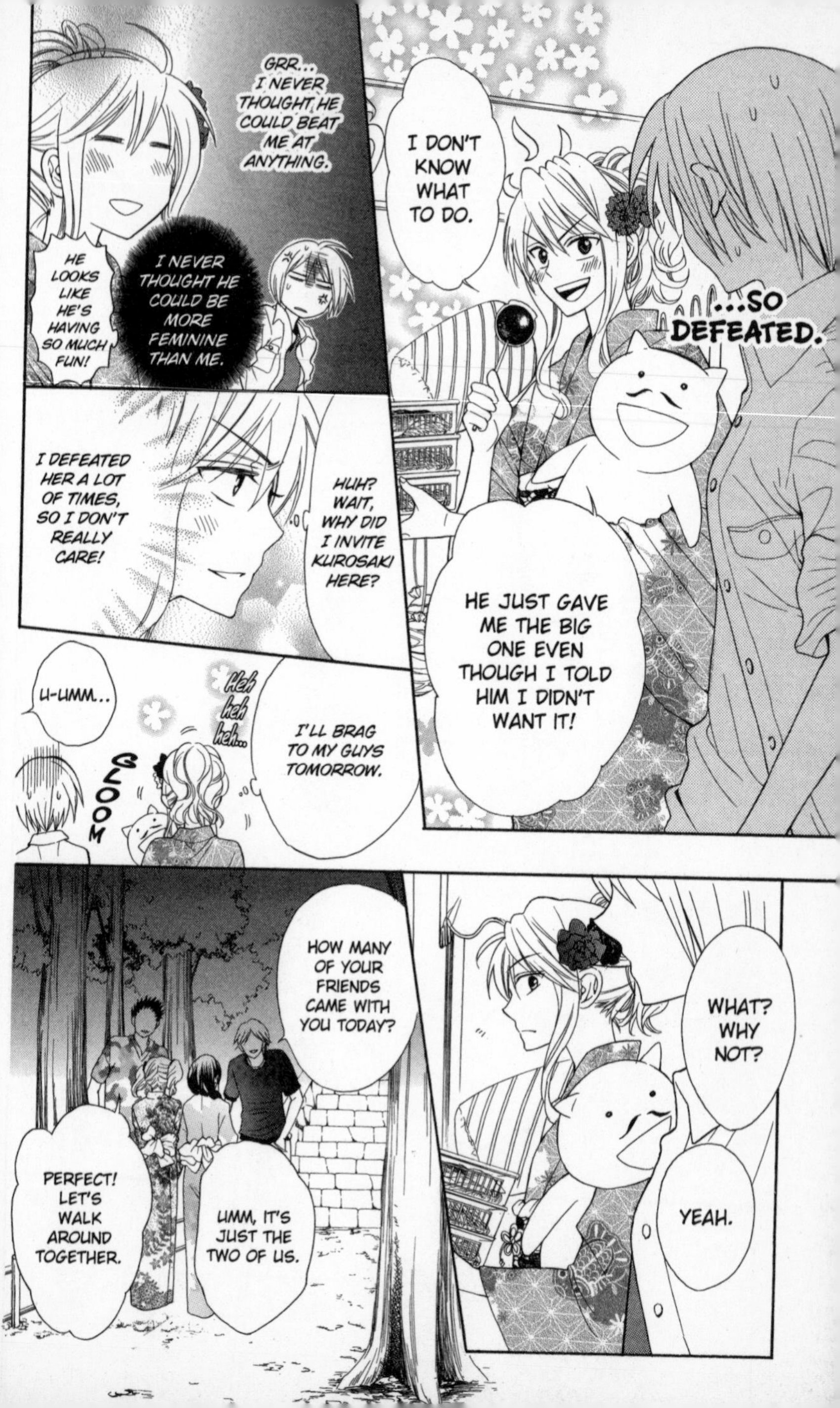
I DON'T KNOW WHAT TO DO.
...SO DEFEATED.
HE JUST GAVE ME THE BIG ONE EVEN THOUGH I TOLD HIM I DIDN'T WANT IT!
GRR... I NEVER THOUGHT HE COULD BEAT ME AT ANYTHING.
HE LOOKS LIKE HE'S HAVING SO MUCH FUN!
I NEVER THOUGHT HE COULD BE MORE FEMININE THAN ME.
HUH? WAIT, WHY DID I INVITE KUROSAKI HERE?
I DEFEATED HER A LOT OF TIMES, SO I DON'T REALLY CARE!
I'LL BRAG TO MY GUYS TOMORROW.
Heh heh heh...
U-UMM...
GLOOM
WHAT? WHY NOT?
YEAH.
HOW MANY OF YOUR FRIENDS CAME WITH YOU TODAY?
UMM, IT'S JUST THE TWO OF US.
PERFECT! LET'S WALK AROUND TOGETHER.

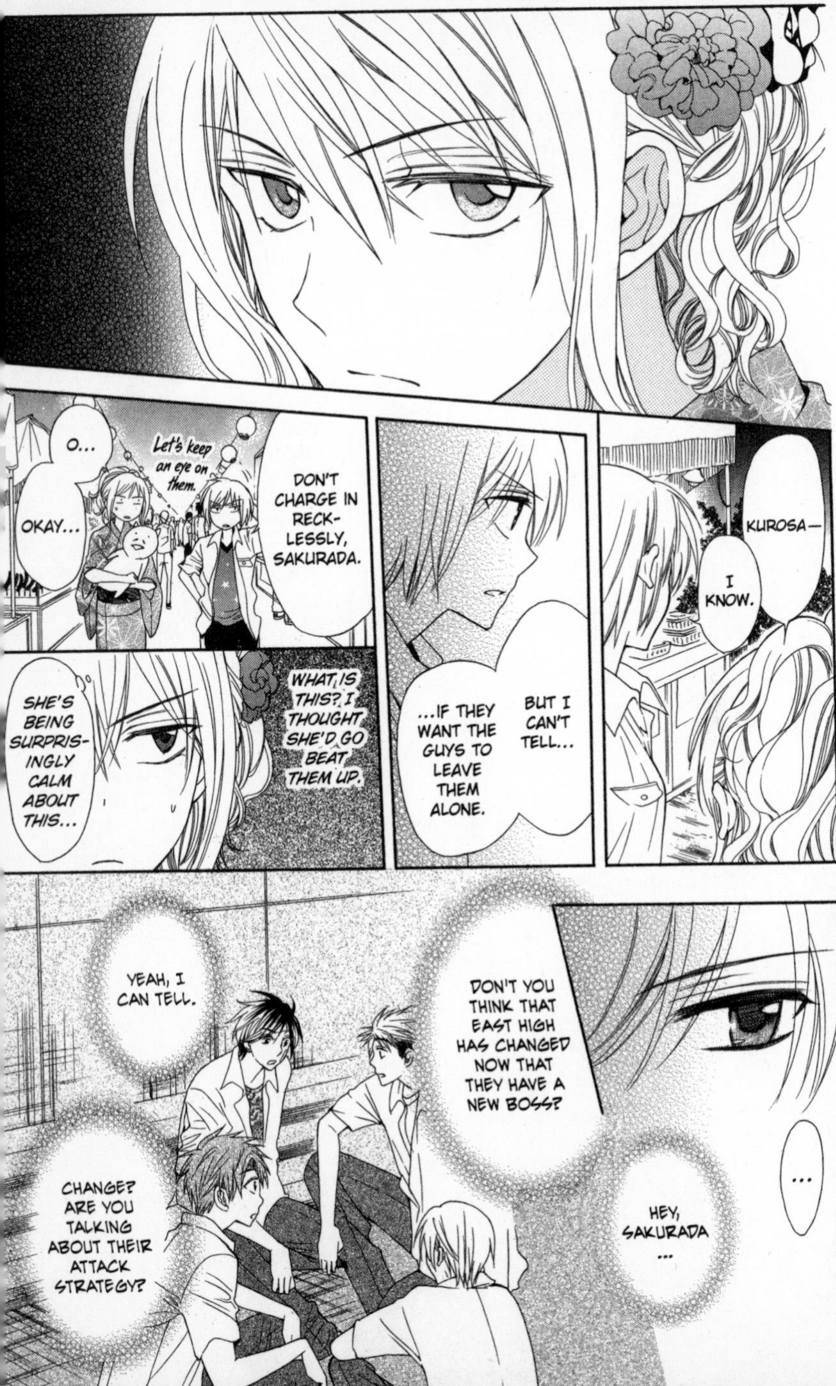
KUROSA—
I KNOW.
BUT I CAN'T TELL...
...IF THEY WANT THE GUYS TO LEAVE THEM ALONE.
DON'T CHARGE IN RECK-LESSLY, SAKURADA.
Let's keep an eye on them.
O...
OKAY...
WHAT IS THIS? I THOUGHT SHE'D GO BEAT THEM UP.
SHE'S BEING SURPRIS-INGLY CALM ABOUT THIS...
DON'T YOU THINK THAT EAST HIGH HAS CHANGED NOW THAT THEY HAVE A NEW BOSS?
...
HEY, SAKURADA...
YEAH, I CAN TELL.
CHANGE? ARE YOU TALKING ABOUT THEIR ATTACK STRATEGY?

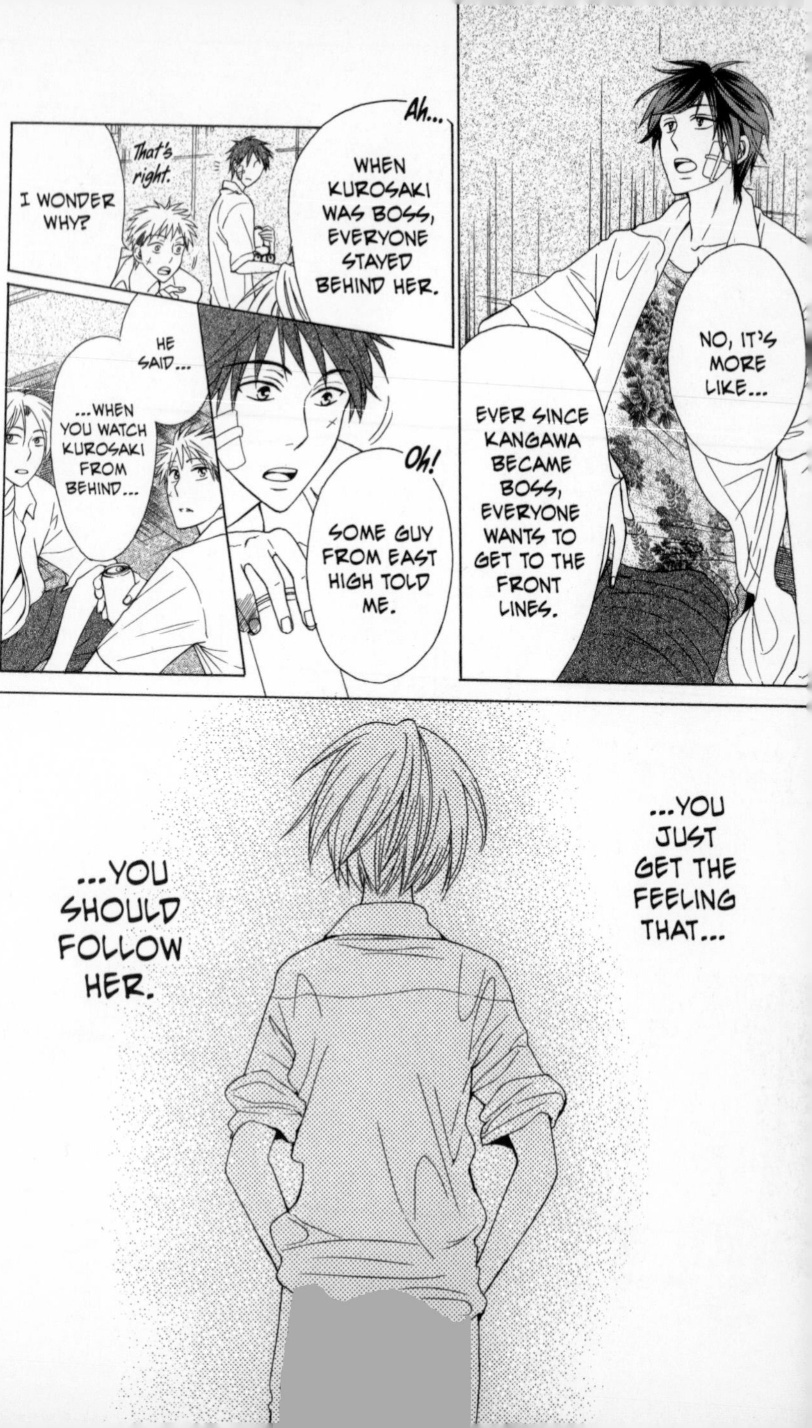
NO, IT'S MORE LIKE...
EVER SINCE KANGAWA BECAME BOSS, EVERYONE WANTS TO GET TO THE FRONT LINES.
Ah...
WHEN KUROSAKI WAS BOSS, EVERYONE STAYED BEHIND HER.
That's right.
I WONDER WHY?
Oh!
SOME GUY FROM EAST HIGH TOLD ME.
HE SAID...
...WHEN YOU WATCH KUROSAKI FROM BEHIND...
...YOU JUST GET THE FEELING THAT...
...YOU SHOULD FOLLOW HER.

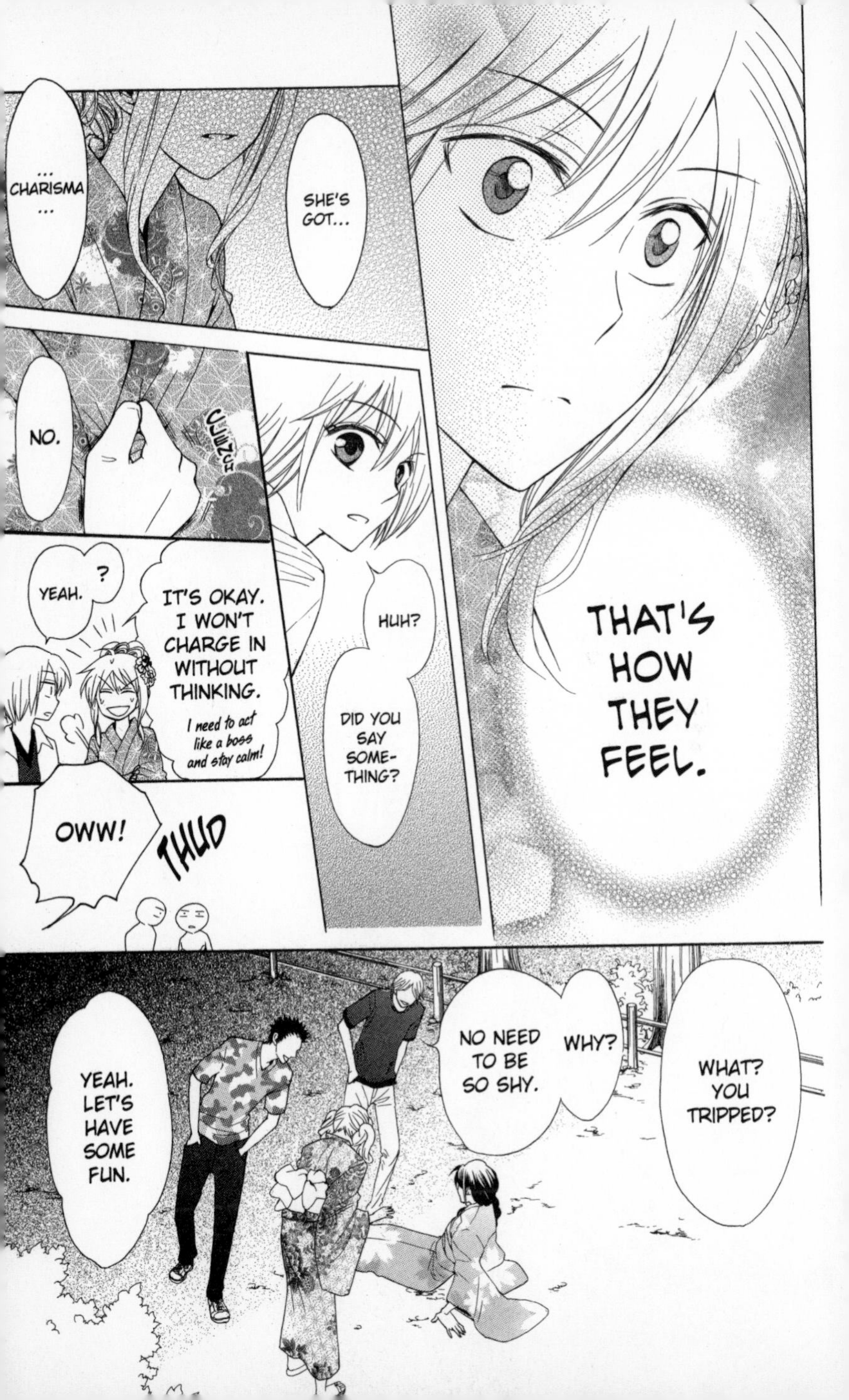
THAT'S HOW THEY FEEL.
SHE'S GOT...
... CHARISMA ...
HUH?
DID YOU SAY SOMETHING?
CLENCH
NO.
IT'S OKAY. I WON'T CHARGE IN WITHOUT THINKING.
I need to act like a boss and stay calm!
?
YEAH.
THUD
OWW!
WHAT? YOU TRIPPED?
WHY?
NO NEED TO BE SO SHY.
YEAH. LET'S HAVE SOME FUN.

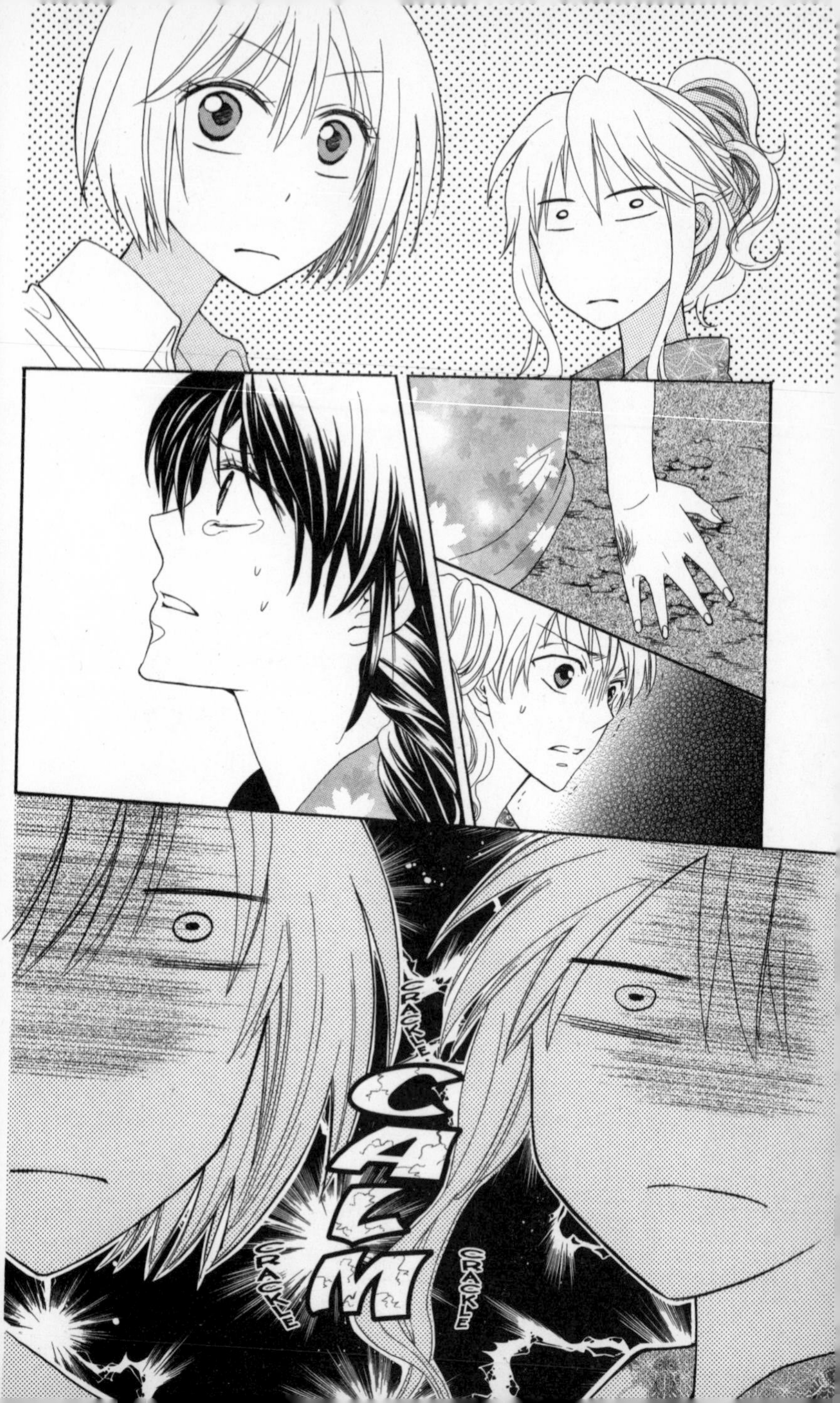
CRACKLE
CALM
CRACKLE
CRACKLE

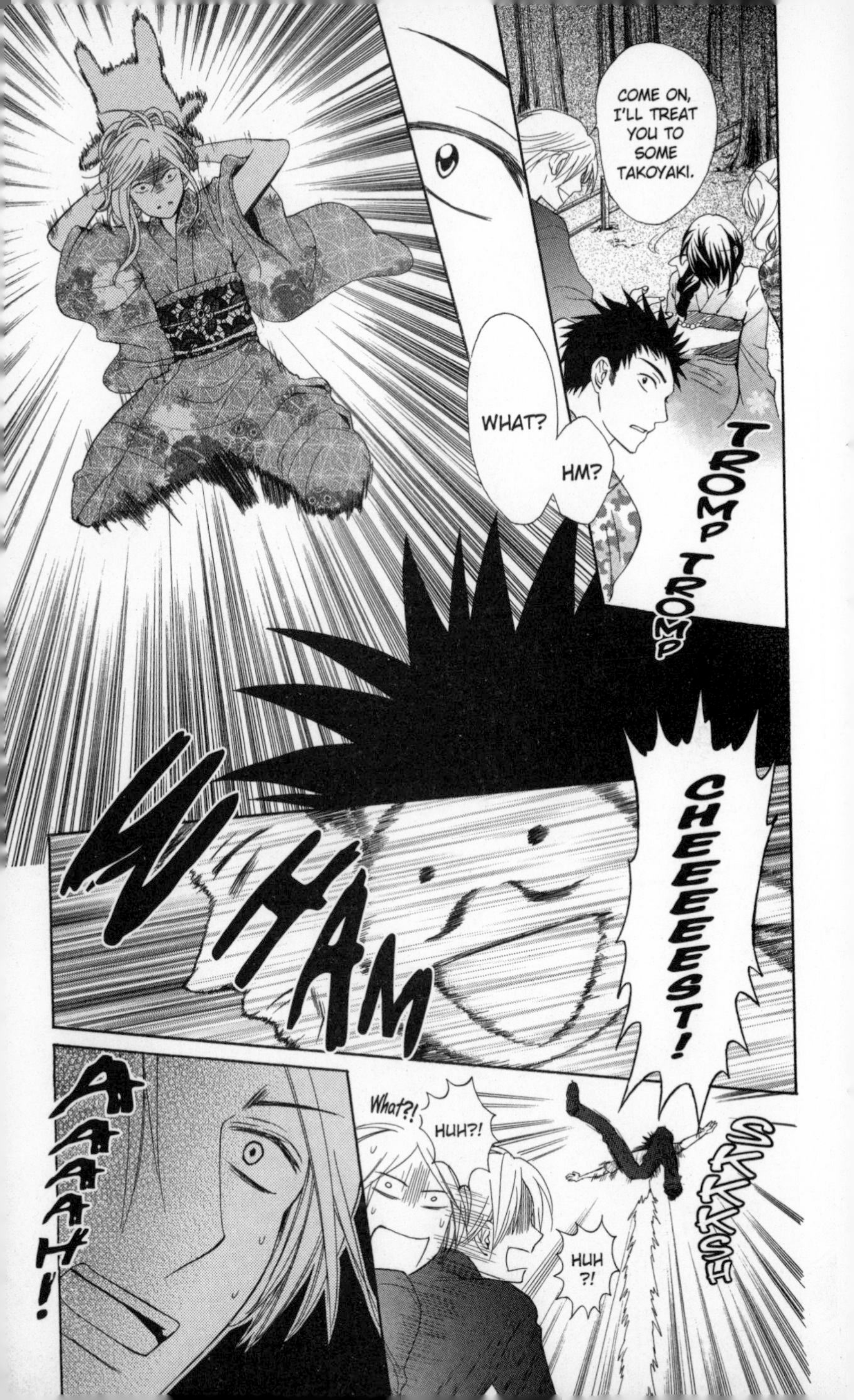
COME ON, I'LL TREAT YOU TO SOME TAKOYAKI.
WHAT?
HM?
TROMP TROMP TROMP
CHEEEEEEST!
WHAM
HUH ?!
What?!
HUH?!
AAAAAAH!

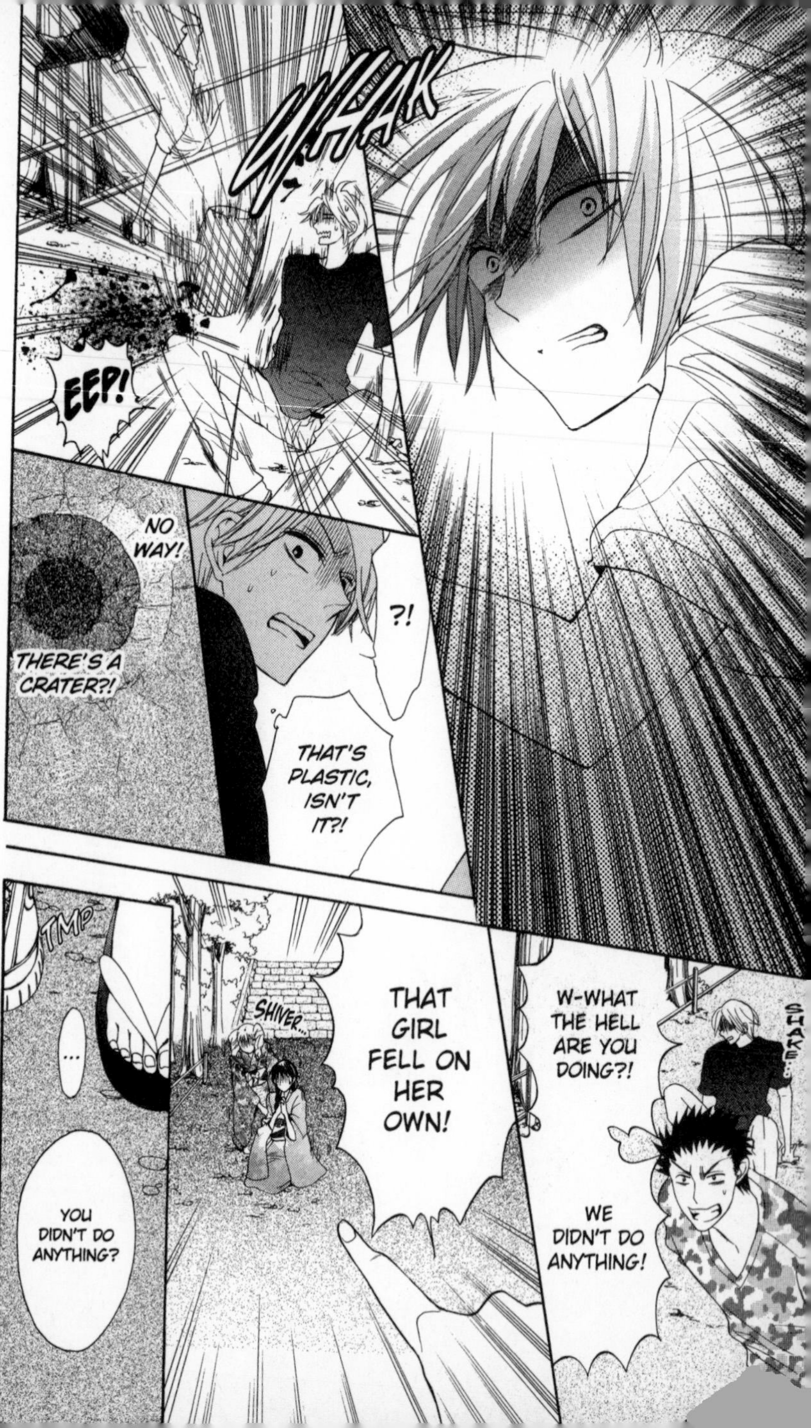
GWHAK
EEP!
?!
THAT'S PLASTIC, ISN'T IT?!
NO WAY!
THERE'S A CRATER?!
SHAKE...
W-WHAT THE HELL ARE YOU DOING?!
WE DIDN'T DO ANYTHING!
THAT GIRL FELL ON HER OWN!
SHIVER...
TMP
...
YOU DIDN'T DO ANYTHING?

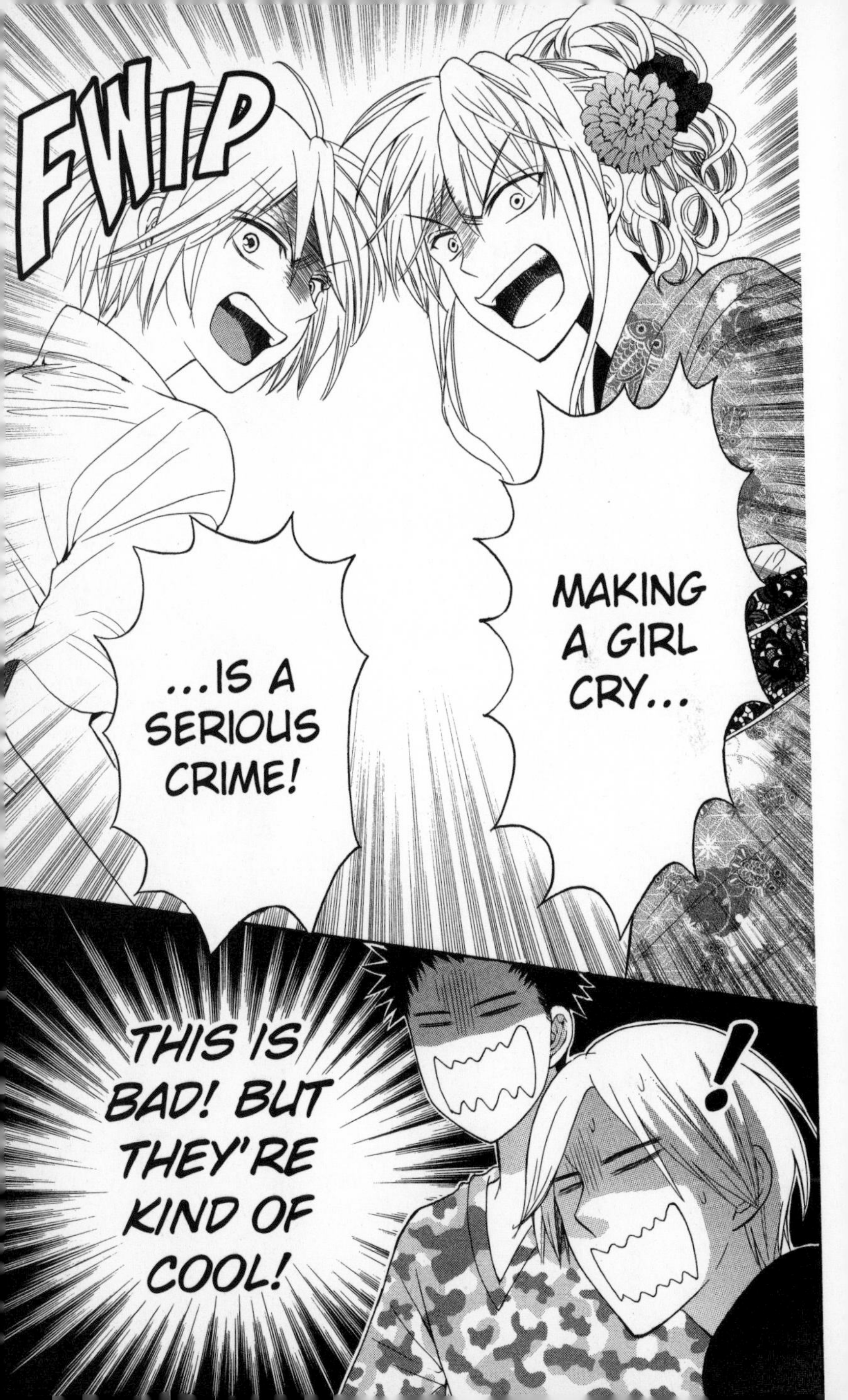
FWIP
MAKING A GIRL CRY...
...IS A SERIOUS CRIME!
THIS IS BAD! BUT THEY'RE KIND OF COOL!
!

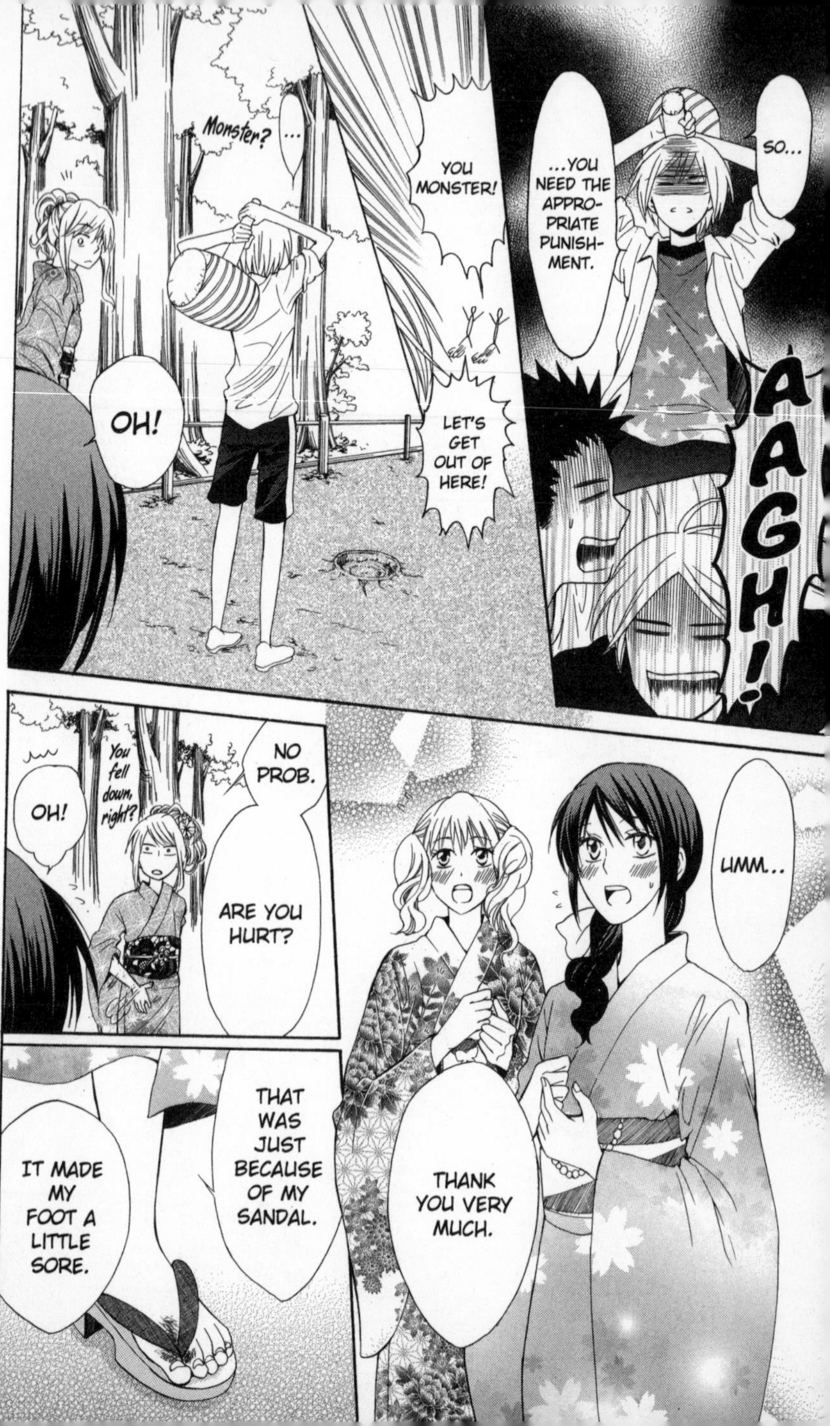
SO...
...YOU NEED THE APPROPRIATE PUNISHMENT.
AAGH!
YOU MONSTER!
Monster? ...
LET'S GET OUT OF HERE!
OH!
UMM...
THANK YOU VERY MUCH.
NO PROB.
ARE YOU HURT?
You fell down, right?
OH!
THAT WAS JUST BECAUSE OF MY SANDAL.
IT MADE MY FOOT A LITTLE SORE.

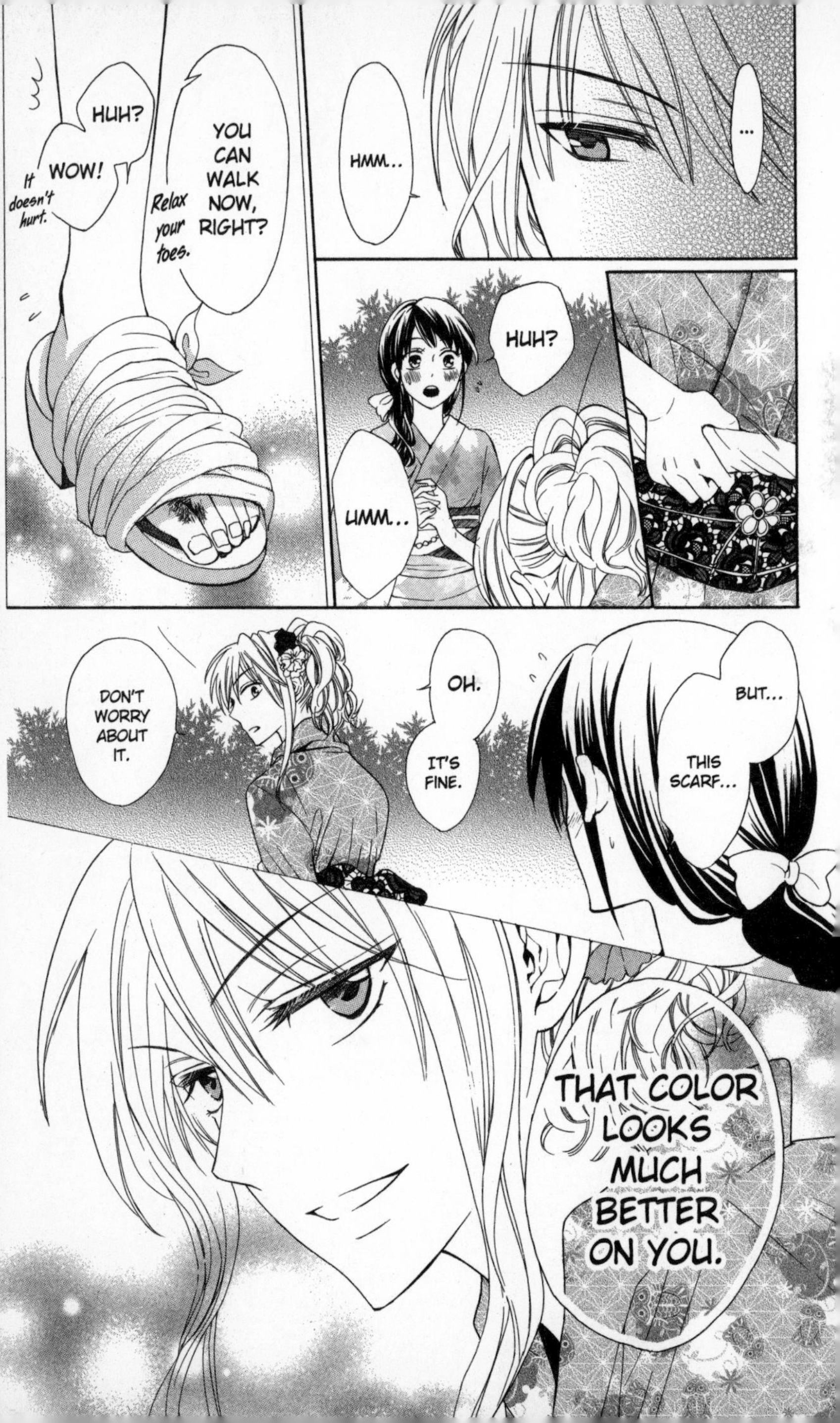
...
HMM...
HUH?
UMM...
YOU CAN WALK NOW, RIGHT?
Relax your toes.
HUH?
WOW!
It doesn't hurt.
BUT...
THIS SCARF...
OH.
IT'S FINE.
DON'T WORRY ABOUT IT.
THAT COLOR LOOKS MUCH BETTER ON YOU.

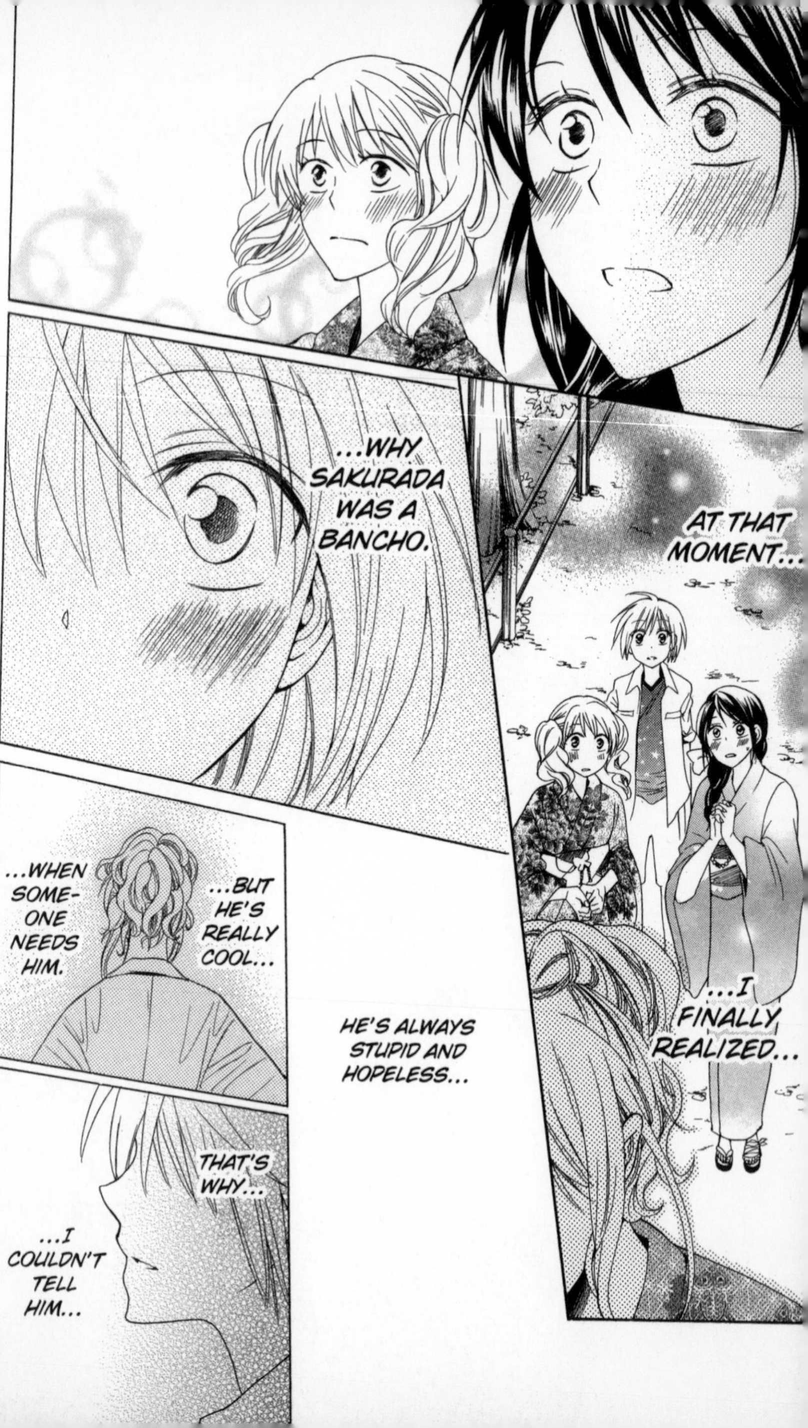
AT THAT MOMENT...
...I FINALLY REALIZED...
...WHY SAKURADA WAS A BANCHO.
HE'S ALWAYS STUPID AND HOPELESS...
...BUT HE'S REALLY COOL...
...WHEN SOME-ONE NEEDS HIM.
THAT'S WHY...
...I COULDN'T TELL HIM...

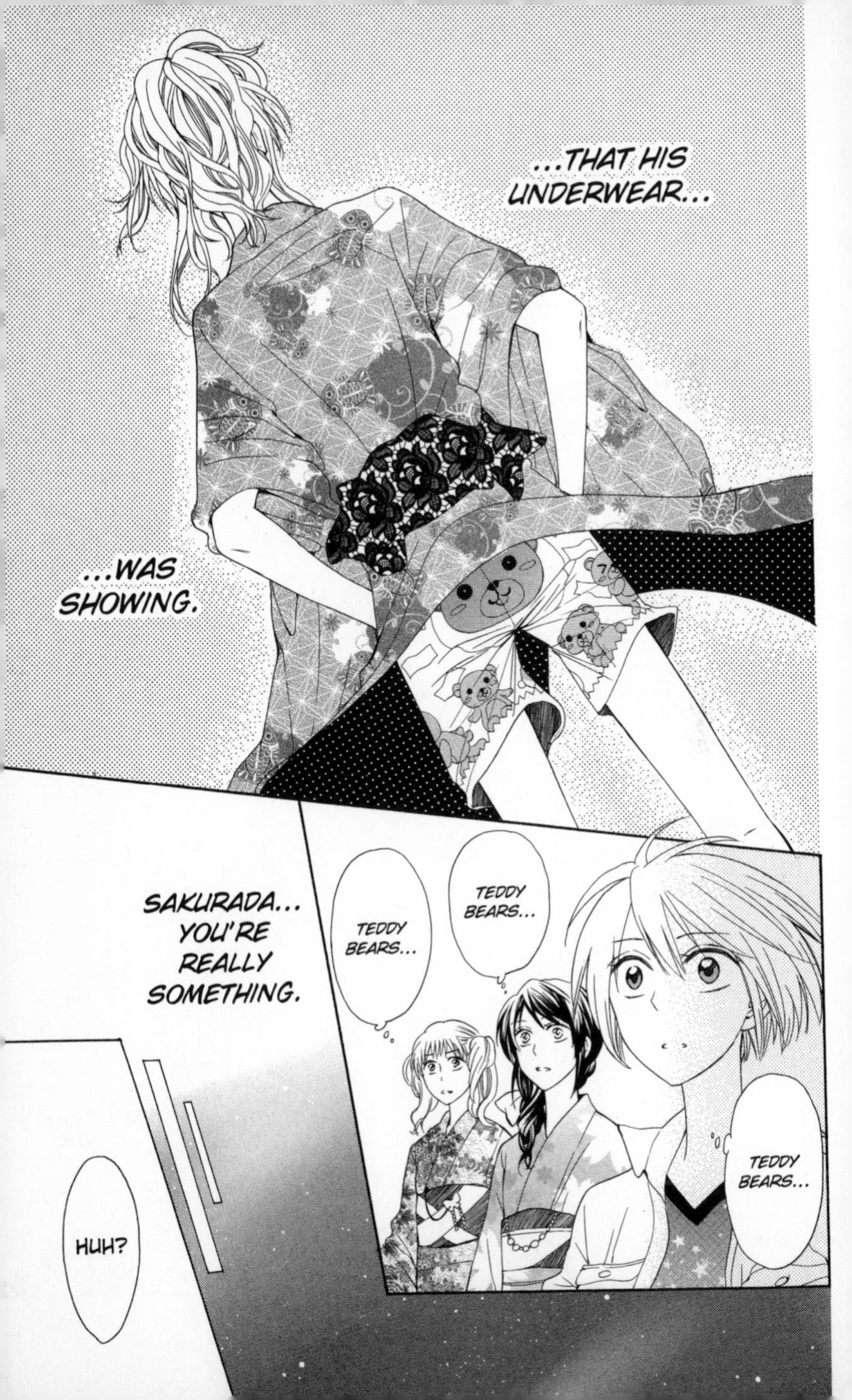
...THAT HIS UNDERWEAR...
...WAS SHOWING.
TEDDY BEARS...
TEDDY BEARS...
TEDDY BEARS...
SAKURADA... YOU'RE REALLY SOMETHING.
HUH?

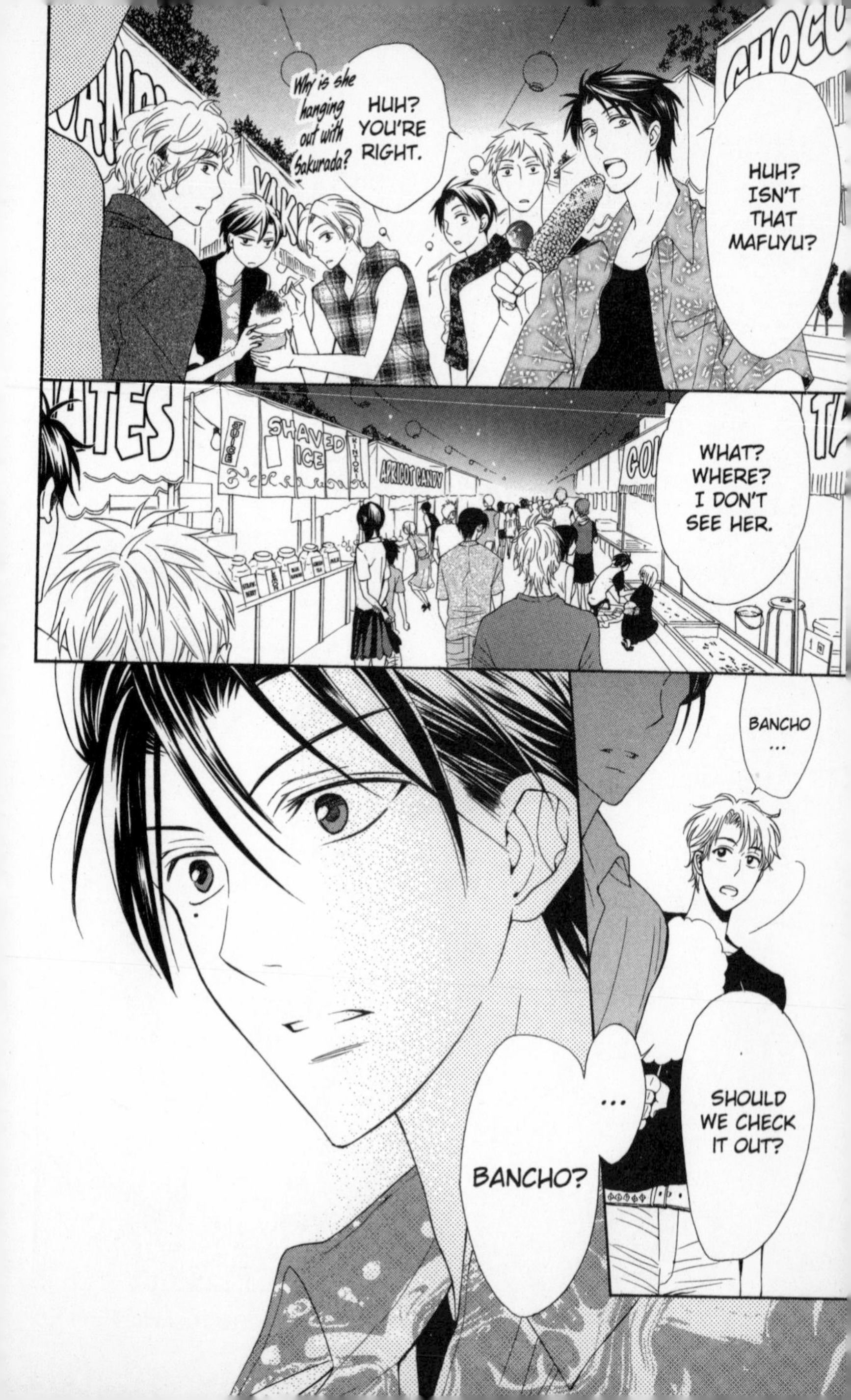
HUH? ISN'T THAT MAFUYU?
HUH? YOU'RE RIGHT.
Why is she hanging out with Sakurada?
WHAT? WHERE? I DON'T SEE HER.
SHAVED ICE
APRICOT CANDY
BANCHO ...
SHOULD WE CHECK IT OUT?
...
BANCHO?

Chapter 38

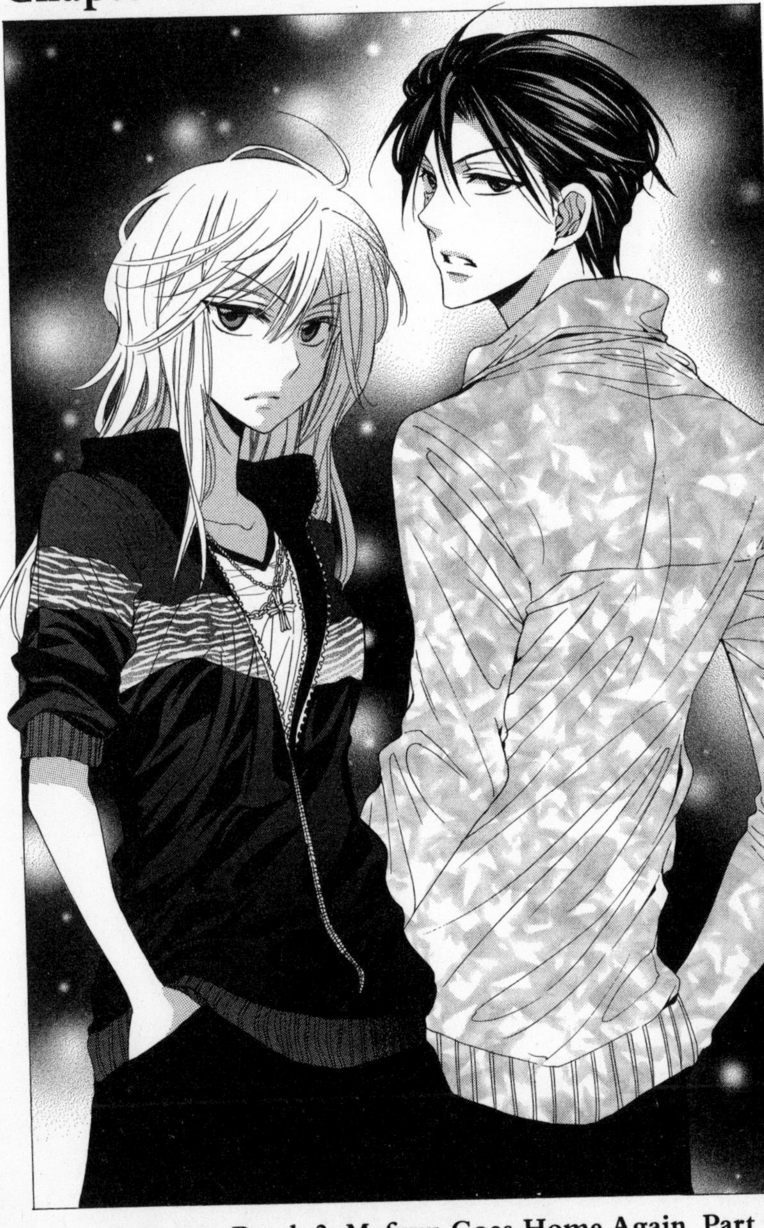

Summer Break 2: Mafuyu Goes Home Again, Part 2

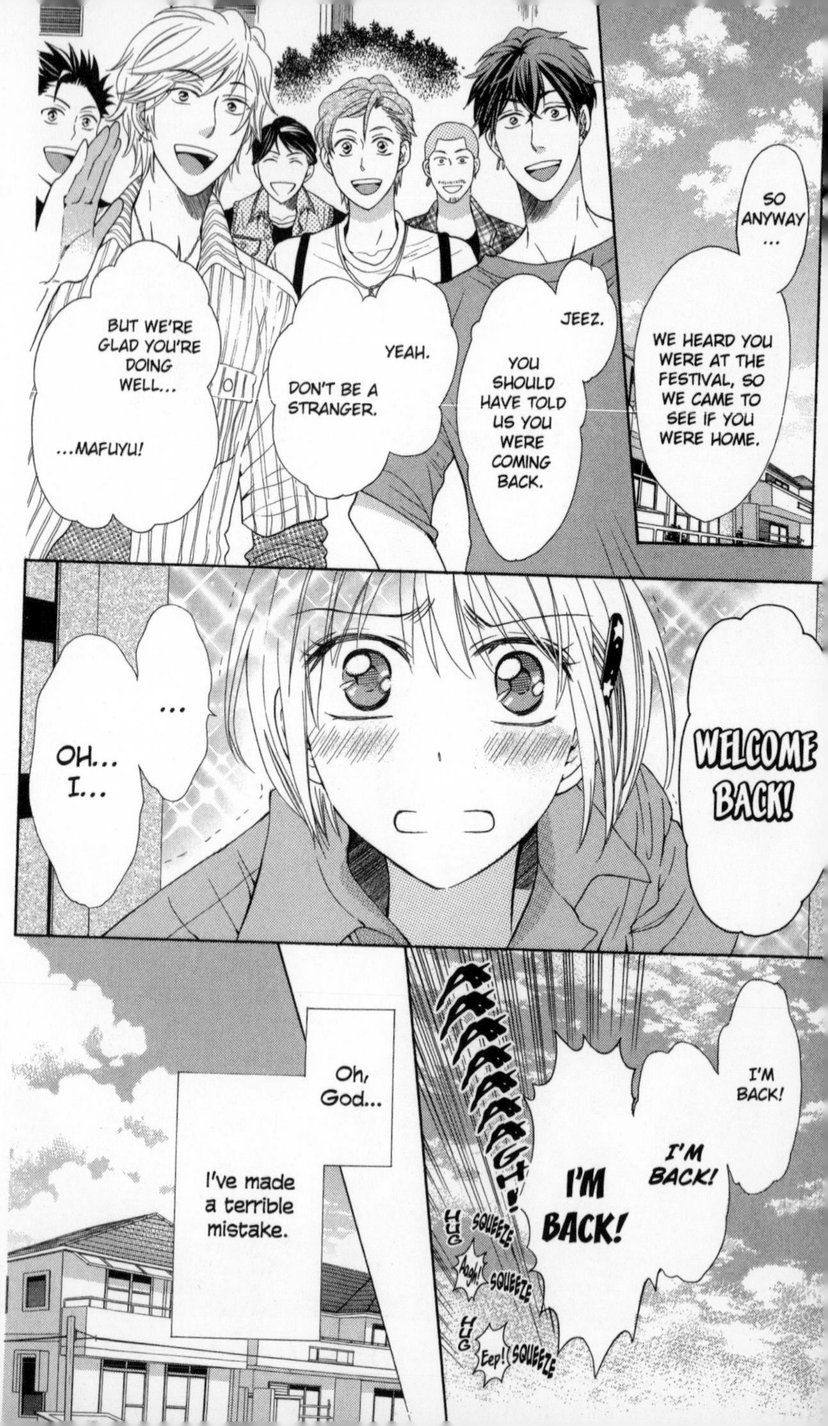
SO ANYWAY...
WE HEARD YOU WERE AT THE FESTIVAL, SO WE CAME TO SEE IF YOU WERE HOME.
JEEZ.
YOU SHOULD HAVE TOLD US YOU WERE COMING BACK.
YEAH.
DON'T BE A STRANGER.
BUT WE'RE GLAD YOU'RE DOING WELL...
...MAFUYU!
WELCOME BACK!
...
OH... I...
I'M BACK!
I'M BACK!
I'M BACK!
AAAAAAAGH!!
HUG
SQUEEZE
Aagh!
SQUEEZE
HUG
Eep!
SQUEEZE
Oh, God...
I've made a terrible mistake.

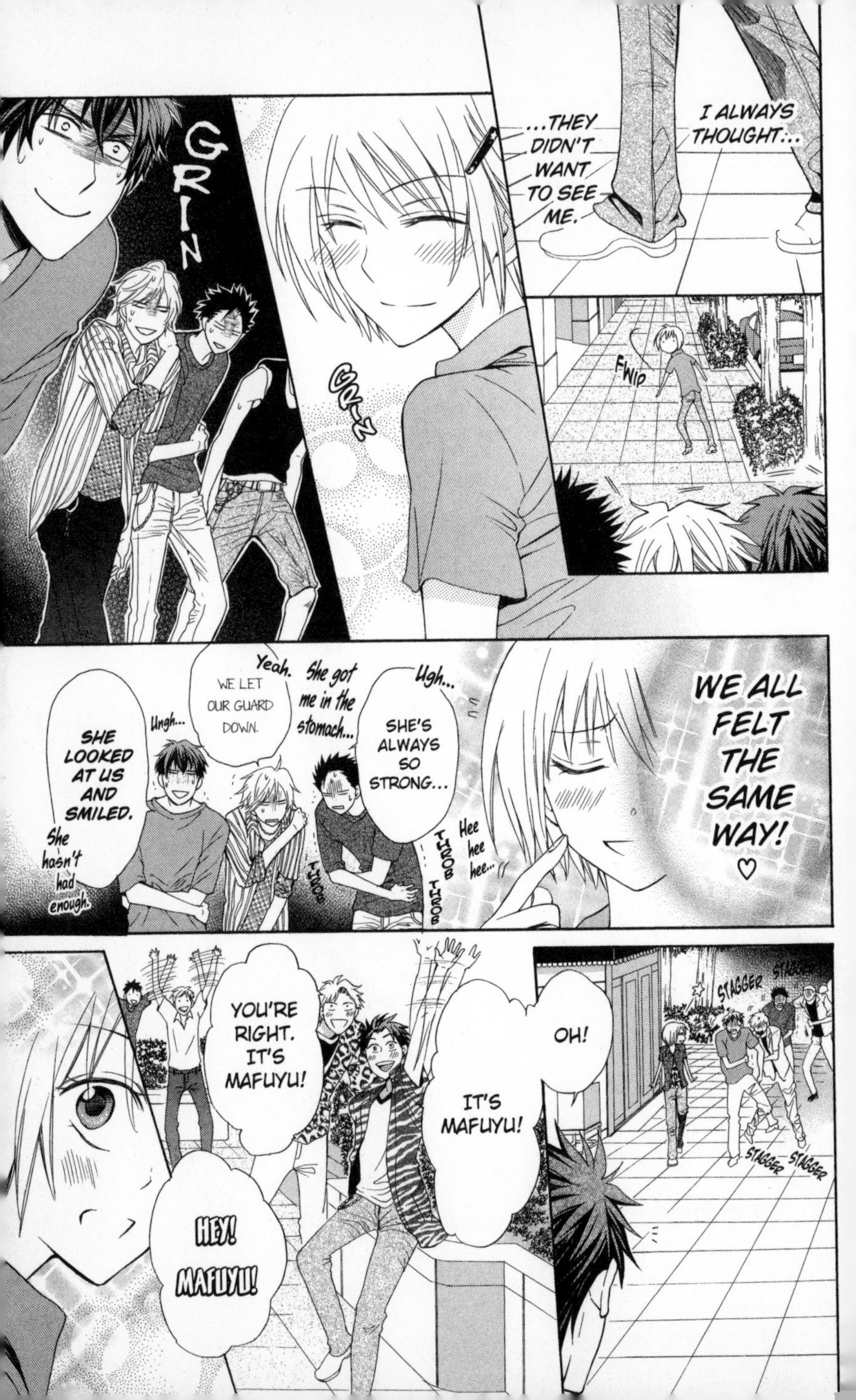
I ALWAYS THOUGHT...
...THEY DIDN'T WANT TO SEE ME.
FWIP
GRIN
WE ALL FELT THE SAME WAY! ♡
Hee hee hee...
THROB THROB
Ugh...
SHE'S ALWAYS SO STRONG...
She got me in the stomach...
Yeah.
WE LET OUR GUARD DOWN.
Ungh...
SHE LOOKED AT US AND SMILED.
She hasn't had enough.
THROB
STAGGER STAGGER
STAGGER STAGGER
OH!
IT'S MAFUYU!
YOU'RE RIGHT. IT'S MAFUYU!
HEY! MAFUYU!

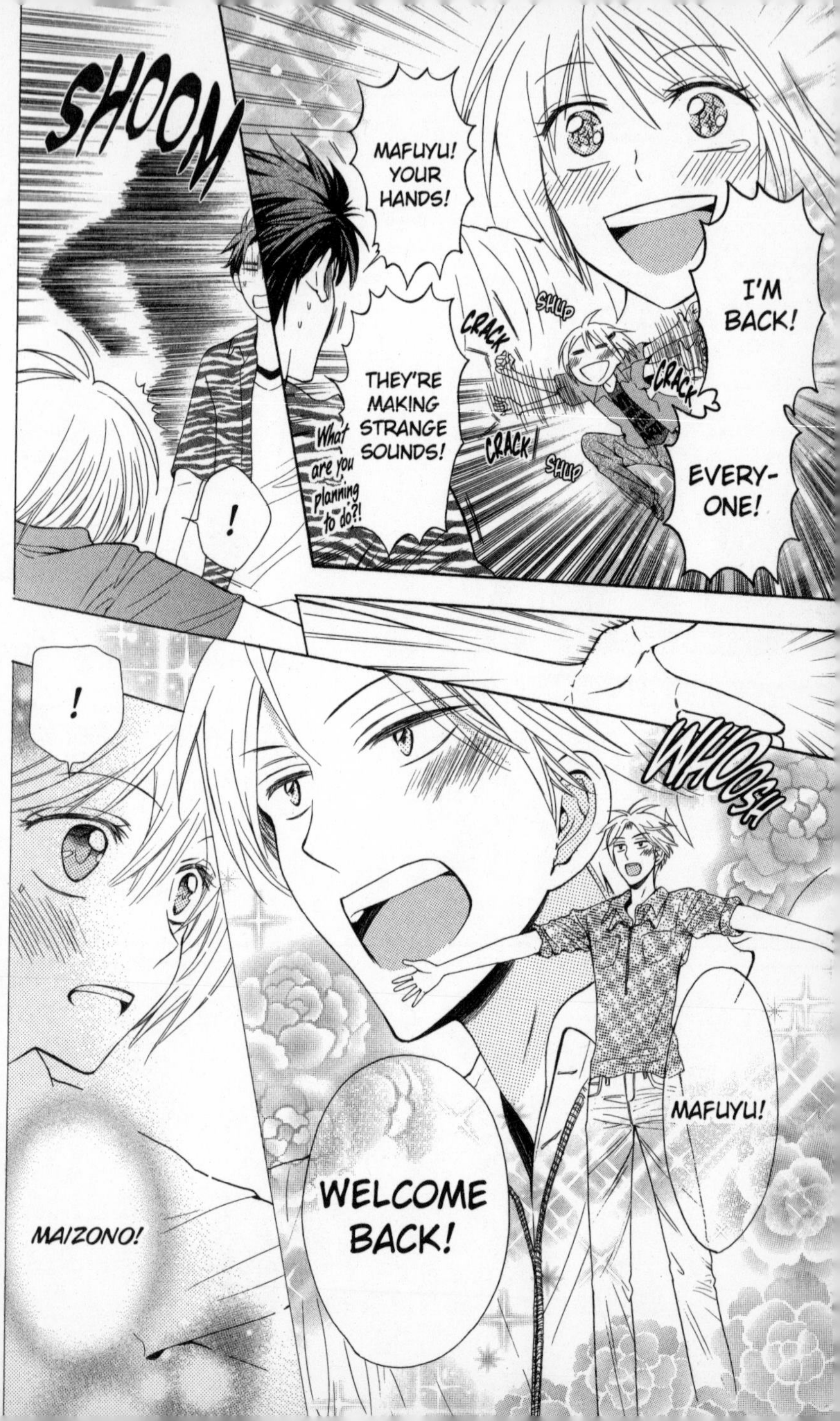

I'M BACK!
EVERY-ONE!
SHUP
CRACK
CRACK
CRACK
SHUP
MAFUYU! YOUR HANDS!
THEY'RE MAKING STRANGE SOUNDS!
What are you planning to do?!
SHOON
!
WHOOSH
MAFUYU!
WELCOME BACK!
!
MAIZONO!

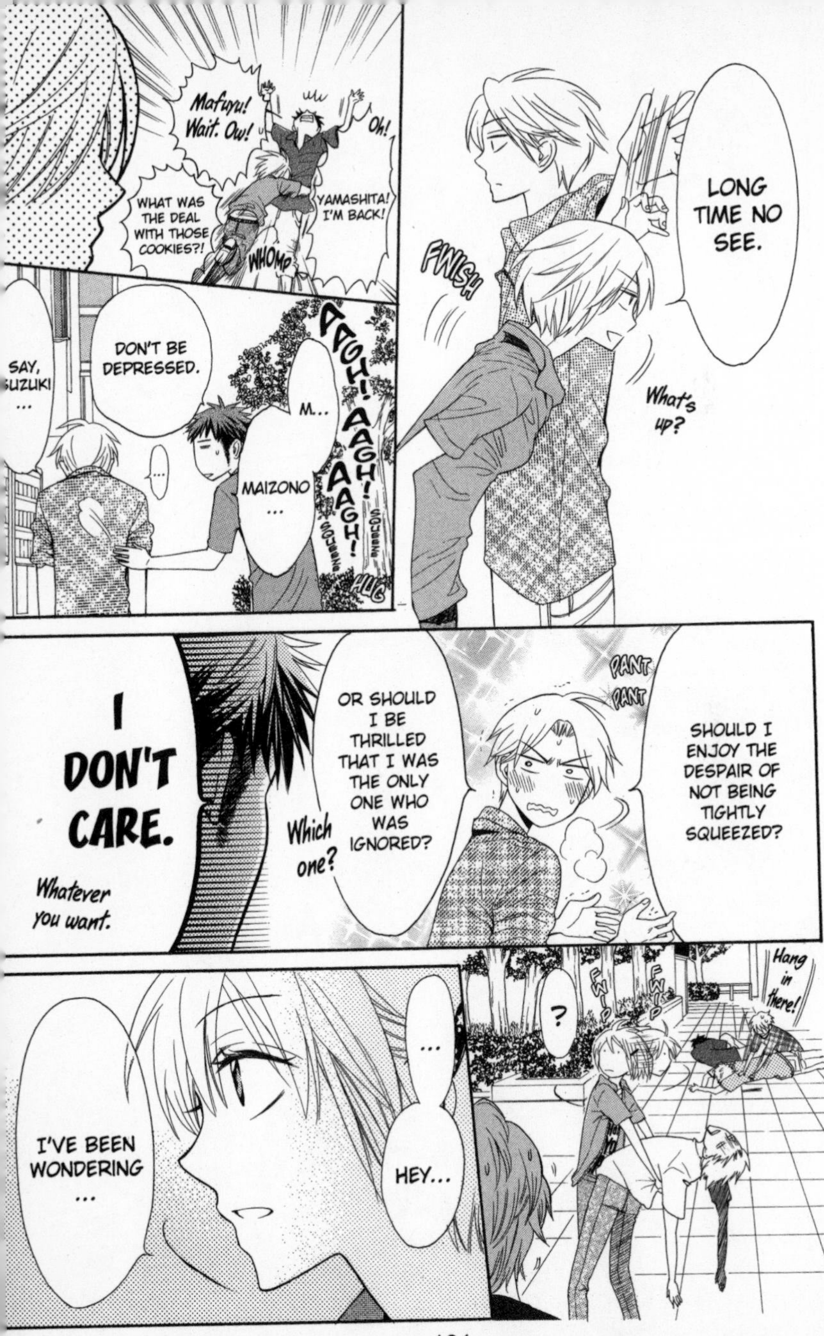
LONG TIME NO SEE.
FWISH
What's up?
Oh!
YAMASHITA! I'M BACK!
Mafuyu! Wait. Ow!
WHAT WAS THE DEAL WITH THOSE COOKIES?!
WHOMP
AAGH! AAGH! AAGH!
SQUEEZE SQUEEZE
HUG
M... MAIZONO ...
...
DON'T BE DEPRESSED.
SAY, UZUKI ...
PANT PANT
SHOULD I ENJOY THE DESPAIR OF NOT BEING TIGHTLY SQUEEZED?
OR SHOULD I BE THRILLED THAT I WAS THE ONLY ONE WHO WAS IGNORED?
Which one?
I DON'T CARE.
Whatever you want.
Hang in there!
FWIP FWIP
?
... HEY...
I'VE BEEN WONDERING ...

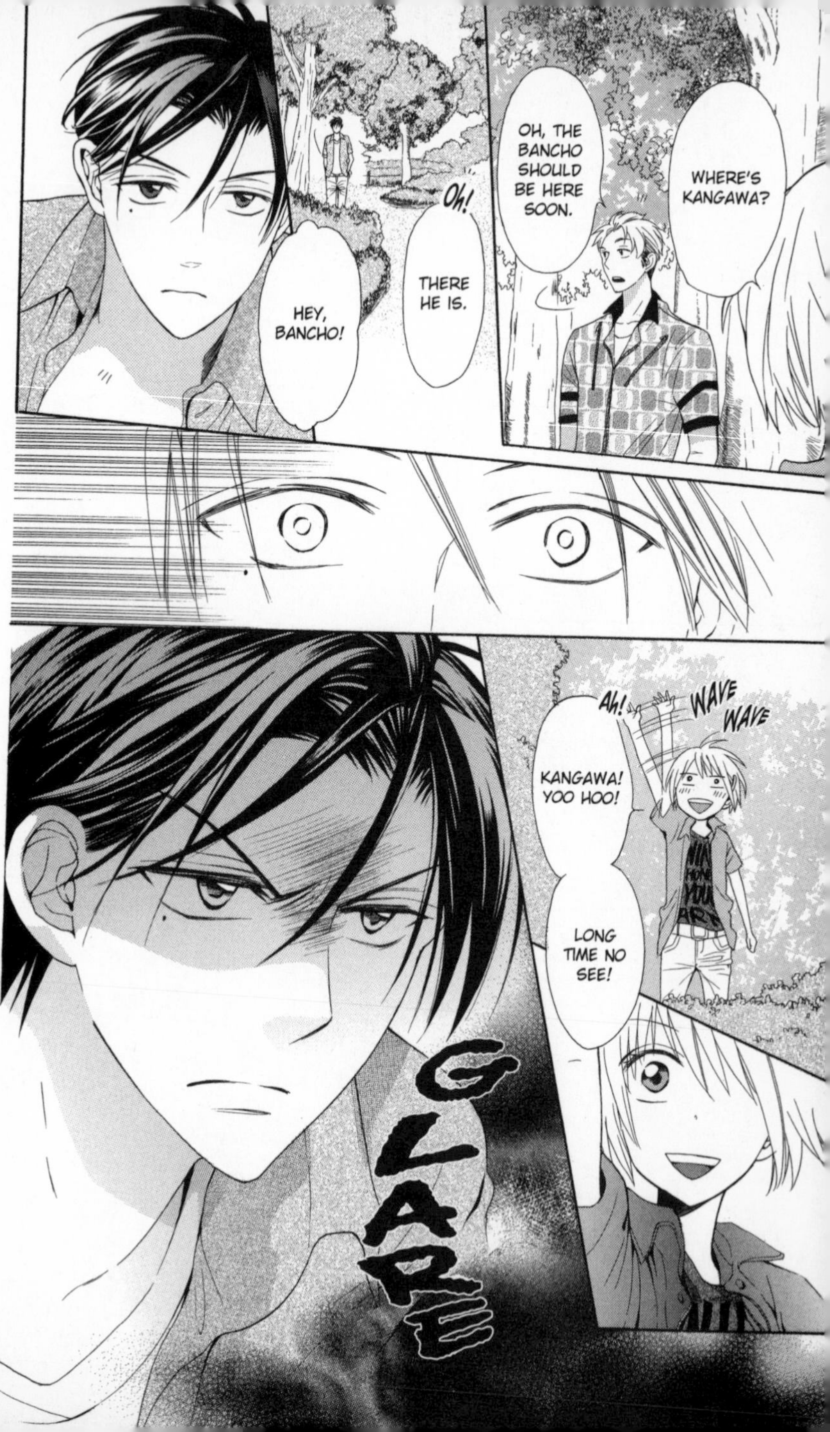
WHERE'S KANGAWA?
OH, THE BANCHO SHOULD BE HERE SOON.
Oh!
THERE HE IS.
HEY, BANCHO!
Ah!
WAVE WAVE
KANGAWA! YOO HOO!
LONG TIME NO SEE!
GLARE

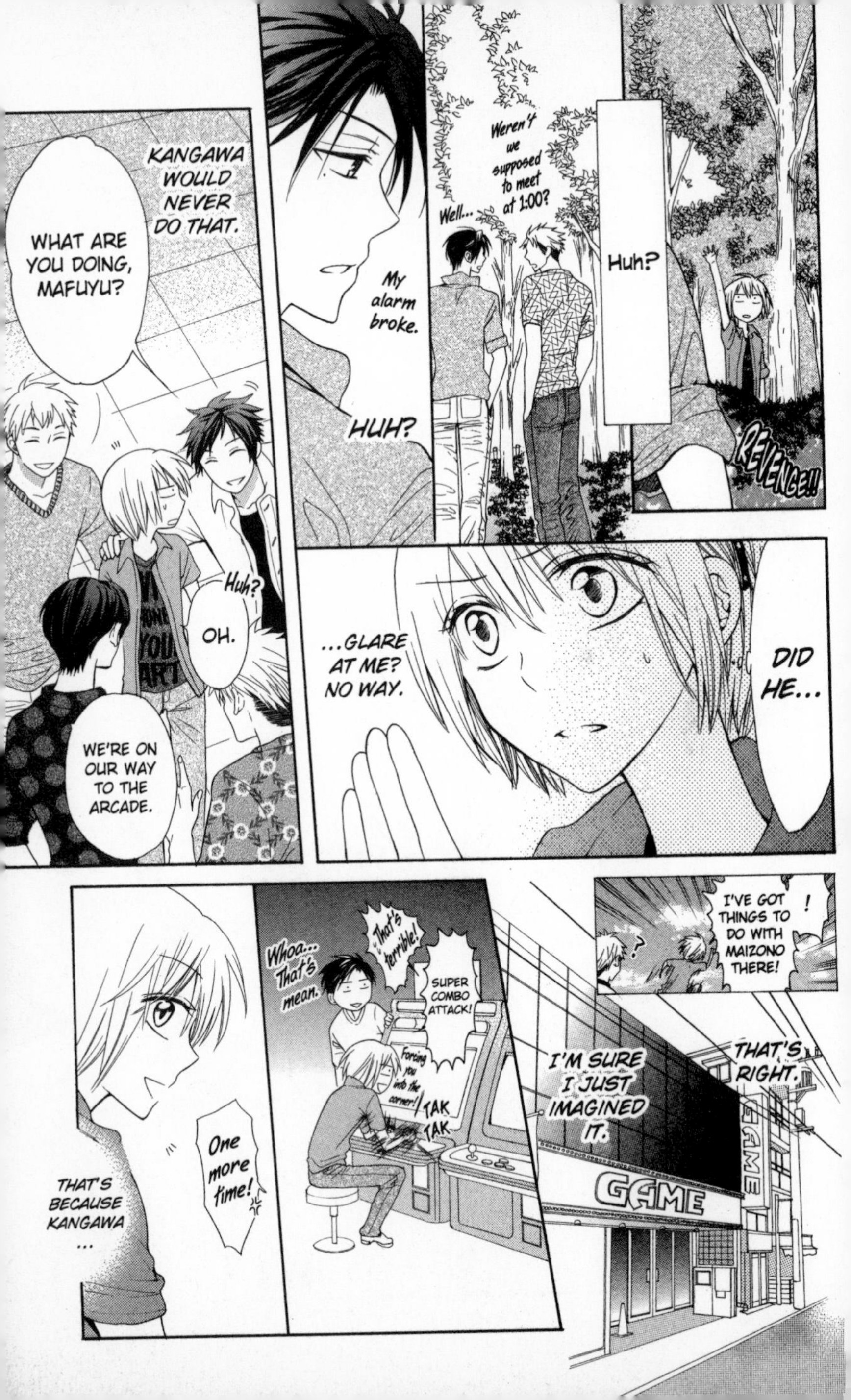
Huh?
REVENGE!!
Weren't we supposed to meet at 1:00?
Well...
My alarm broke.
HUH?
DID HE...
...GLARE AT ME? NO WAY.
KANGAWA WOULD NEVER DO THAT.
WHAT ARE YOU DOING, MAFUYU?
Huh?
OH.
WE'RE ON OUR WAY TO THE ARCADE.
I'VE GOT THINGS TO DO WITH MAIZONO THERE!
THAT'S RIGHT.
I'M SURE I JUST IMAGINED IT.
GAME
GAME
That's terrible!
Whoa... That's mean.
SUPER COMBO ATTACK!
Forcing you into the corner!
TAK TAK
One more time!
THAT'S BECAUSE KANGAWA ...

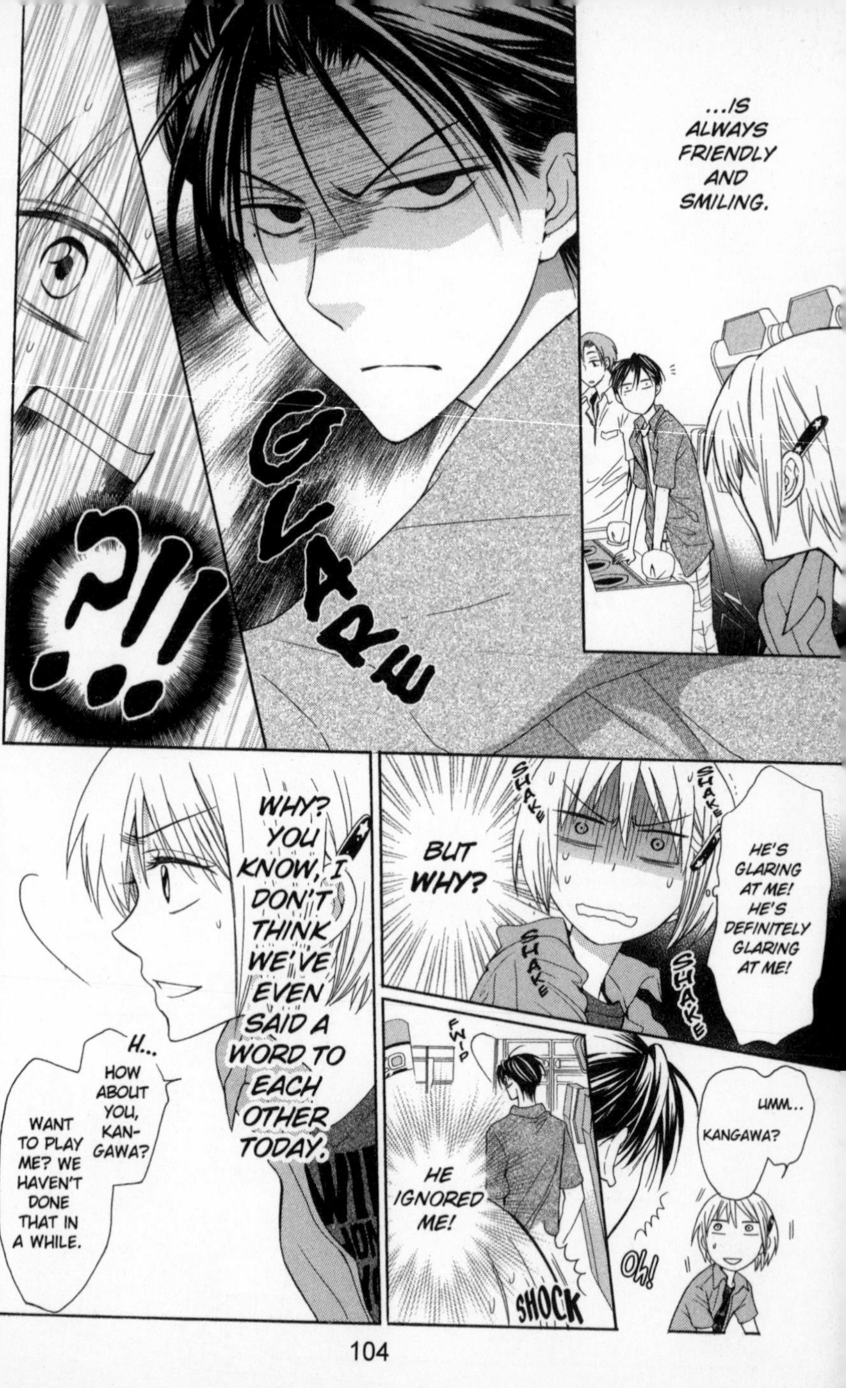
...IS ALWAYS FRIENDLY AND SMILING.
GLARE
?!!
HE'S GLARING AT ME! HE'S DEFINITELY GLARING AT ME!
SHAKE
SHAKE
BUT WHY?
SHAKE
SHAKE
UMM... KANGAWA?
Oh!
FWIP
HE IGNORED ME!
SHOCK
WHY? YOU KNOW, I DON'T THINK WE'VE EVEN SAID A WORD TO EACH OTHER TODAY.
H... HOW ABOUT YOU, KANGAWA?
WANT TO PLAY ME? WE HAVEN'T DONE THAT IN A WHILE.

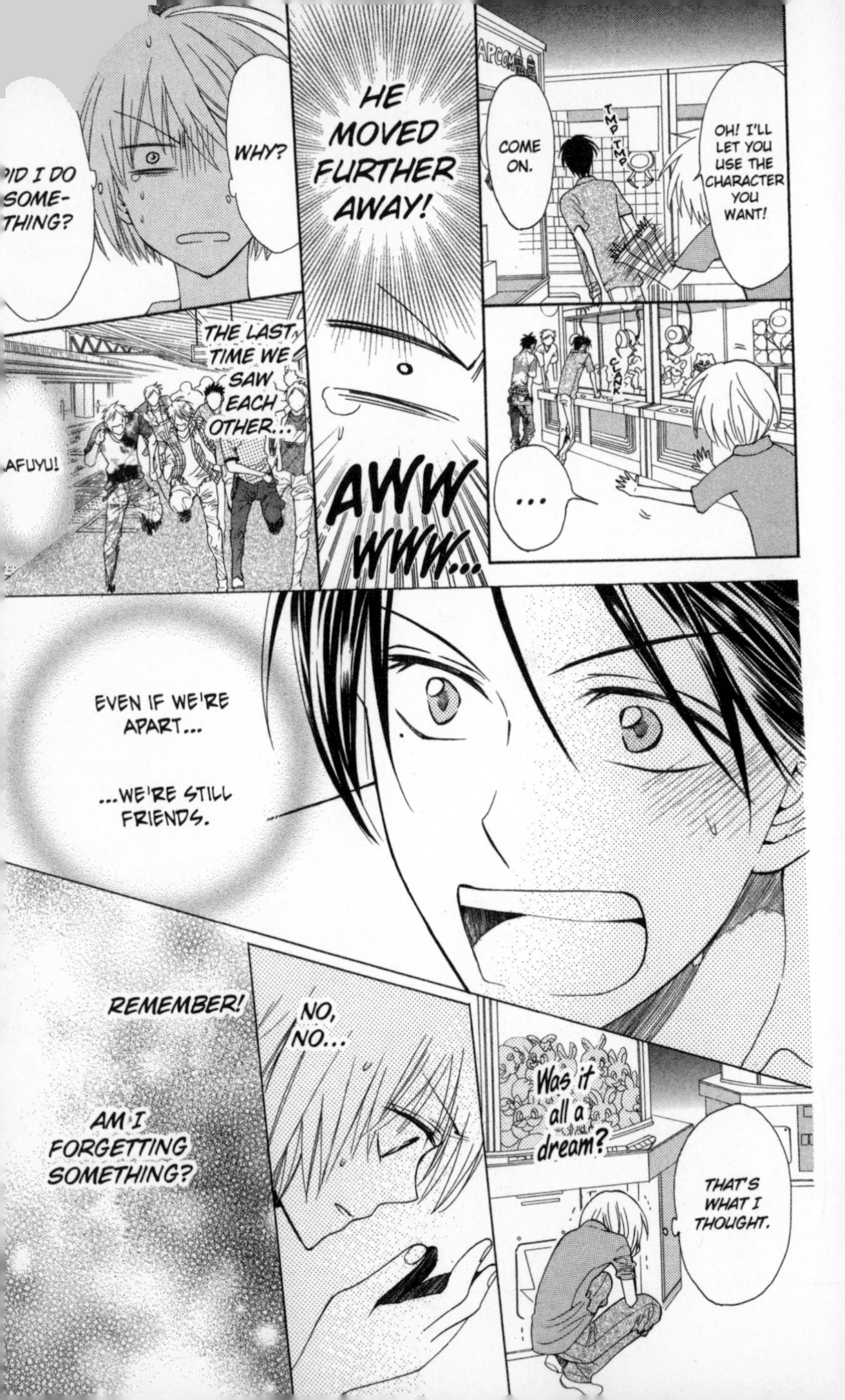

OH! I'LL LET YOU USE THE CHARACTER YOU WANT!
TMP TMP
COME ON.
CLANK
...
HE MOVED FURTHER AWAY!
AWW WWW...
WHY?
DID I DO SOME-THING?
THE LAST TIME WE SAW EACH OTHER...
AFUYU!
EVEN IF WE'RE APART...
...WE'RE STILL FRIENDS.
Was it all a dream?
THAT'S WHAT I THOUGHT.
NO, NO...
REMEMBER!
AM I FORGETTING SOMETHING?

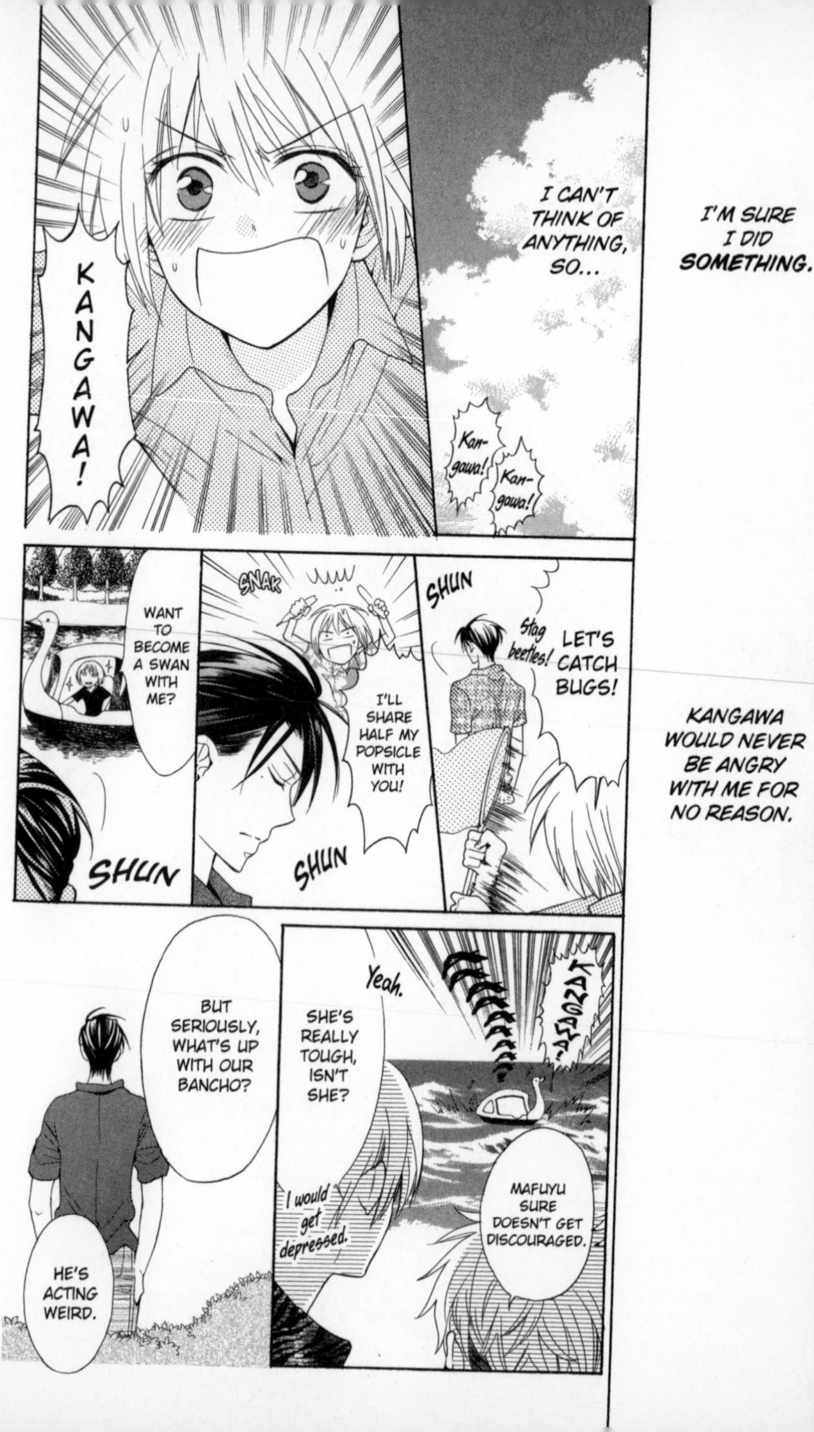
I'M SURE I DID SOMETHING.
I CAN'T THINK OF ANYTHING, SO...
Kan-gawa!
Kan-gawa!
KANGAWA!
KANGAWA WOULD NEVER BE ANGRY WITH ME FOR NO REASON.
SHUN
Stag beetles!
LET'S CATCH BUGS!
SNAK
I'LL SHARE HALF MY POPSICLE WITH YOU!
SHUN
WANT TO BECOME A SWAN WITH ME?
SHUN
KANGAWA!
Yeah.
SHE'S REALLY TOUGH, ISN'T SHE?
MAFUYU SURE DOESN'T GET DISCOURAGED.
I would get depressed.
BUT SERIOUSLY, WHAT'S UP WITH OUR BANCHO?
HE'S ACTING WEIRD.

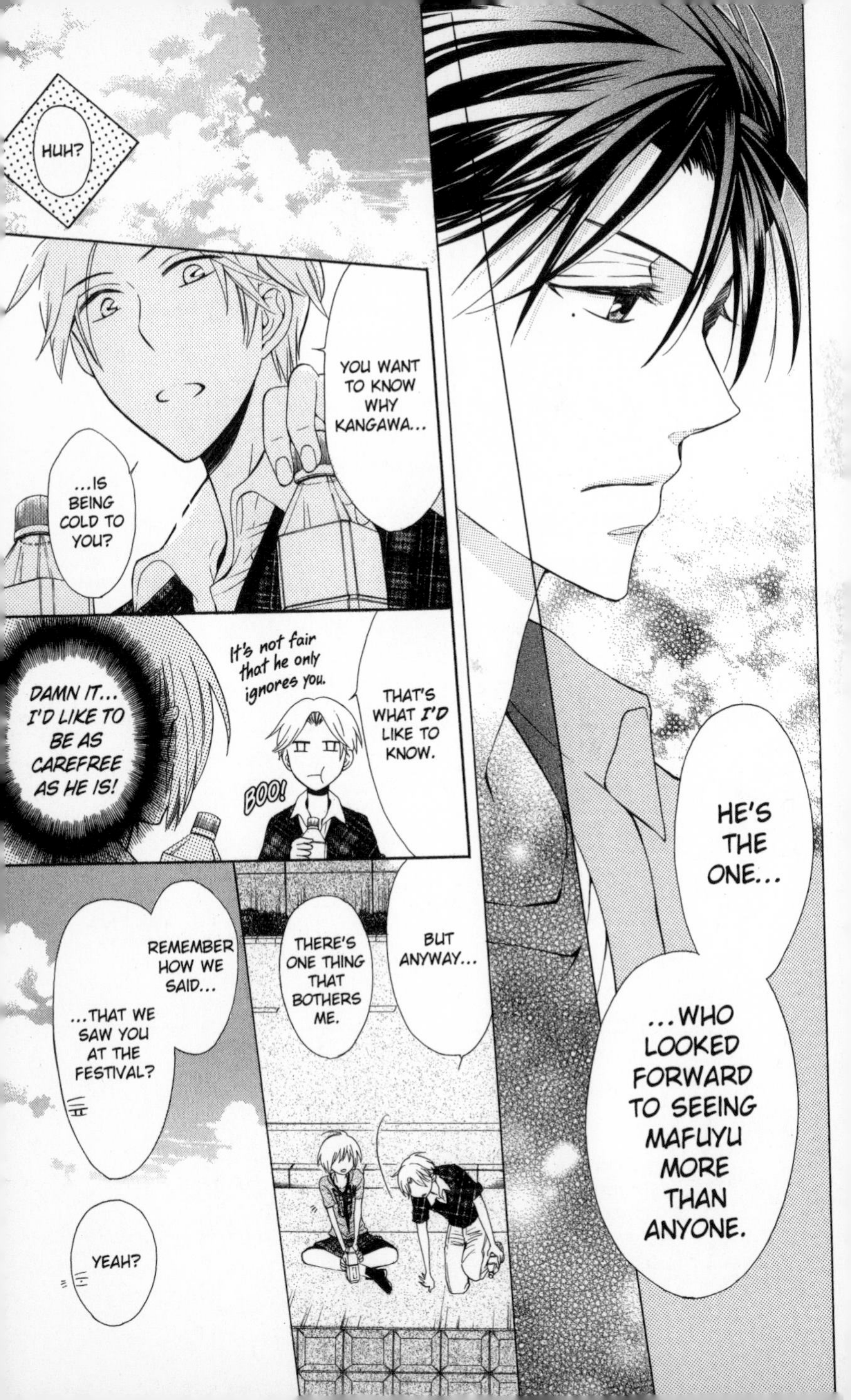
HE'S THE ONE...
...WHO LOOKED FORWARD TO SEEING MAFUYU MORE THAN ANYONE.
HUH?
YOU WANT TO KNOW WHY KANGAWA...
...IS BEING COLD TO YOU?
THAT'S WHAT I'D LIKE TO KNOW.
It's not fair that he only ignores you.
BOO!
DAMN IT... I'D LIKE TO BE AS CAREFREE AS HE IS!
BUT ANYWAY...
THERE'S ONE THING THAT BOTHERS ME.
REMEMBER HOW WE SAID...
...THAT WE SAW YOU AT THE FESTIVAL?
YEAH?

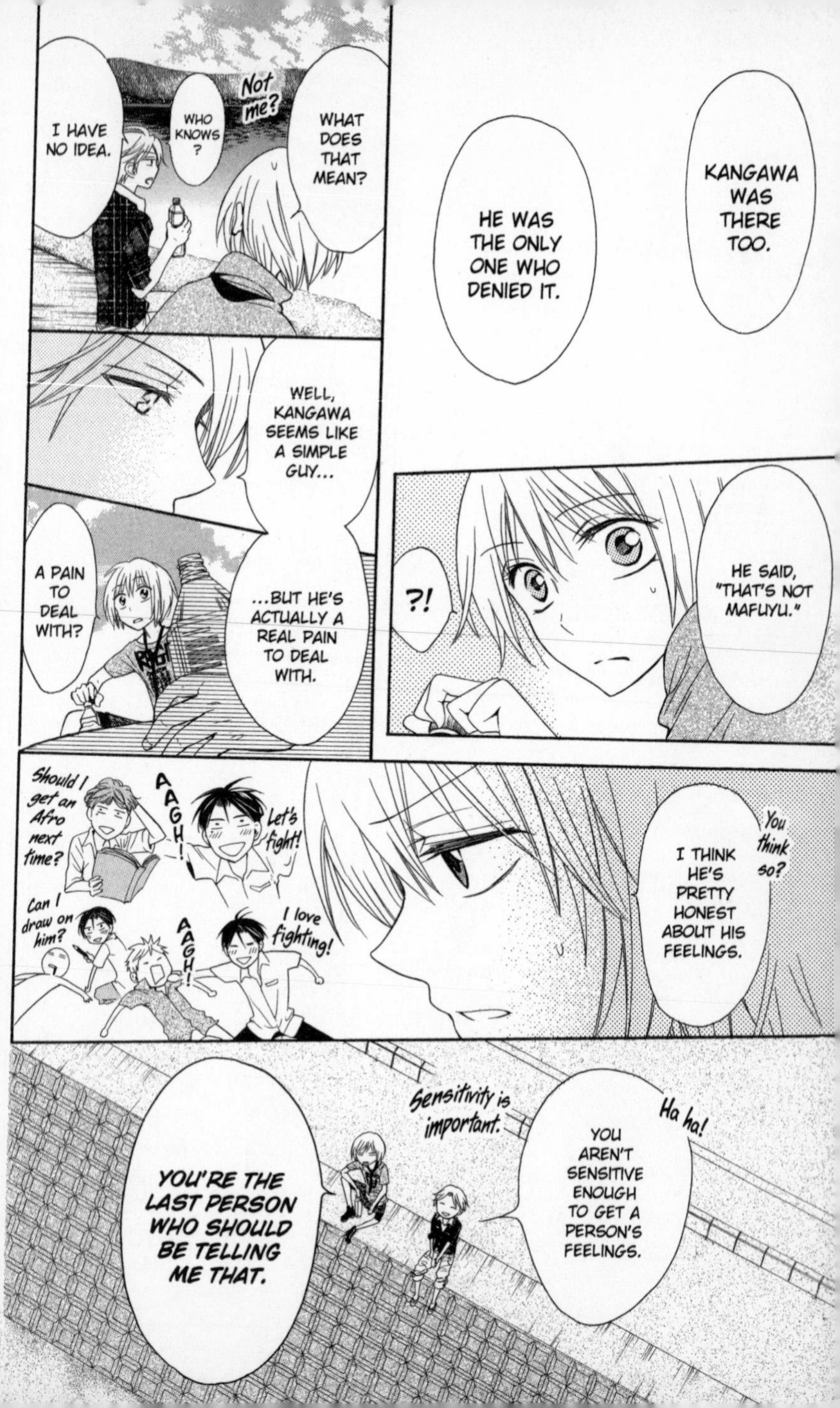
KANGAWA WAS THERE TOO.
HE WAS THE ONLY ONE WHO DENIED IT.
HE SAID, "THAT'S NOT MAFUYU."
?!
WHAT DOES THAT MEAN?
Not me?
WHO KNOWS?
I HAVE NO IDEA.
WELL, KANGAWA SEEMS LIKE A SIMPLE GUY...
...BUT HE'S ACTUALLY A REAL PAIN TO DEAL WITH.
A PAIN TO DEAL WITH?
You think so?
I THINK HE'S PRETTY HONEST ABOUT HIS FEELINGS.
Let's fight!
AAGH!
Should I get an Afro next time?
I love fighting!
AAGH!
Can I draw on him?
Ha ha!
YOU AREN'T SENSITIVE ENOUGH TO GET A PERSON'S FEELINGS.
Sensitivity is important.
YOU'RE THE LAST PERSON WHO SHOULD BE TELLING ME THAT.

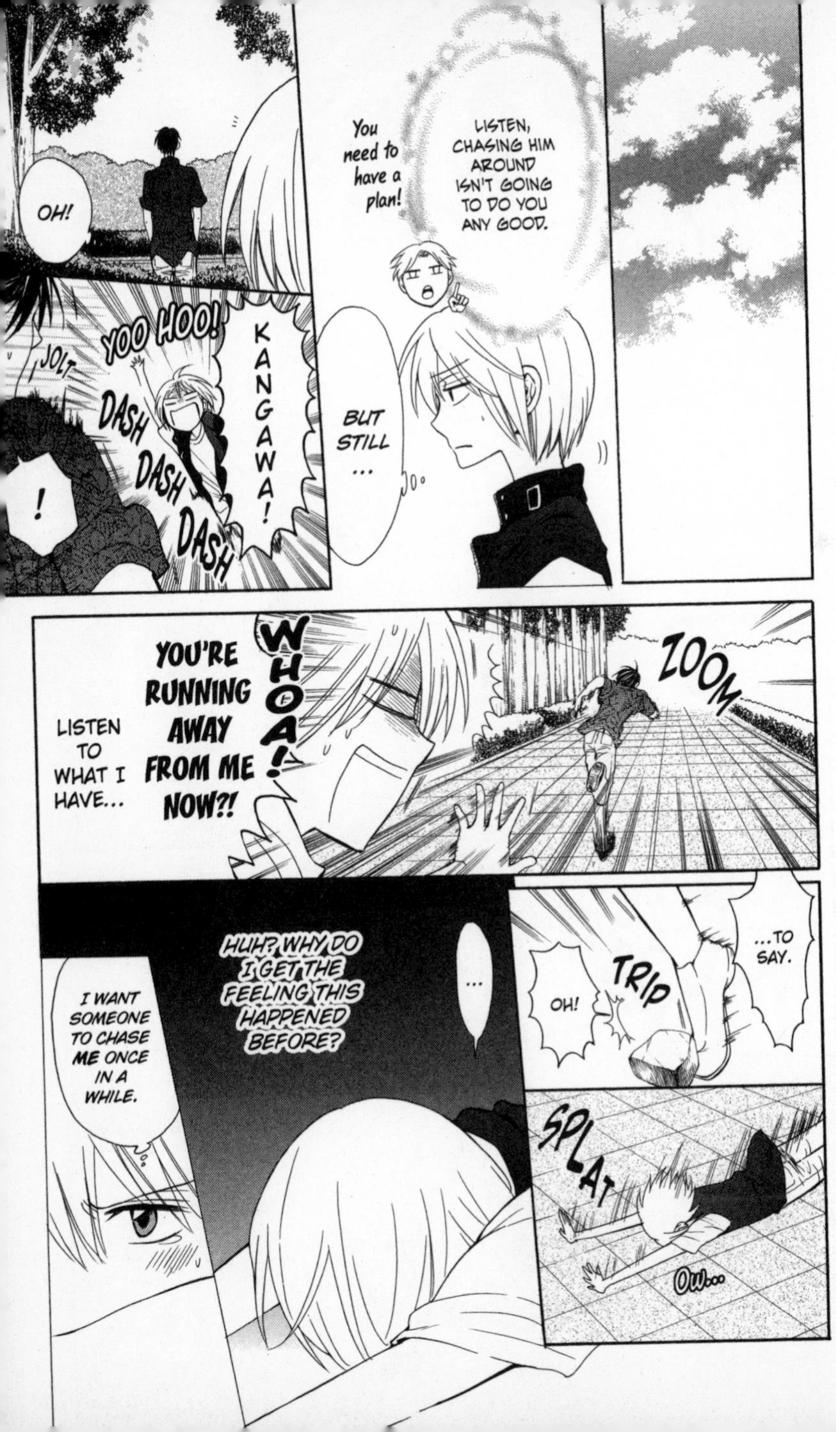
LISTEN, CHASING HIM AROUND ISN'T GOING TO DO YOU ANY GOOD.
You need to have a plan!
BUT STILL...
OH!
KANGAWA!
YOO HOO!
JOLT
DASH
DASH
DASH
DASH
!
ZOOM
WHOA!
YOU'RE RUNNING AWAY FROM ME NOW?!
LISTEN TO WHAT I HAVE...
...TO SAY.
TRIP
OH!
SPLAT
Ow...
...
HUH? WHY DO I GET THE FEELING THIS HAPPENED BEFORE?
I WANT SOMEONE TO CHASE ME ONCE IN A WHILE.

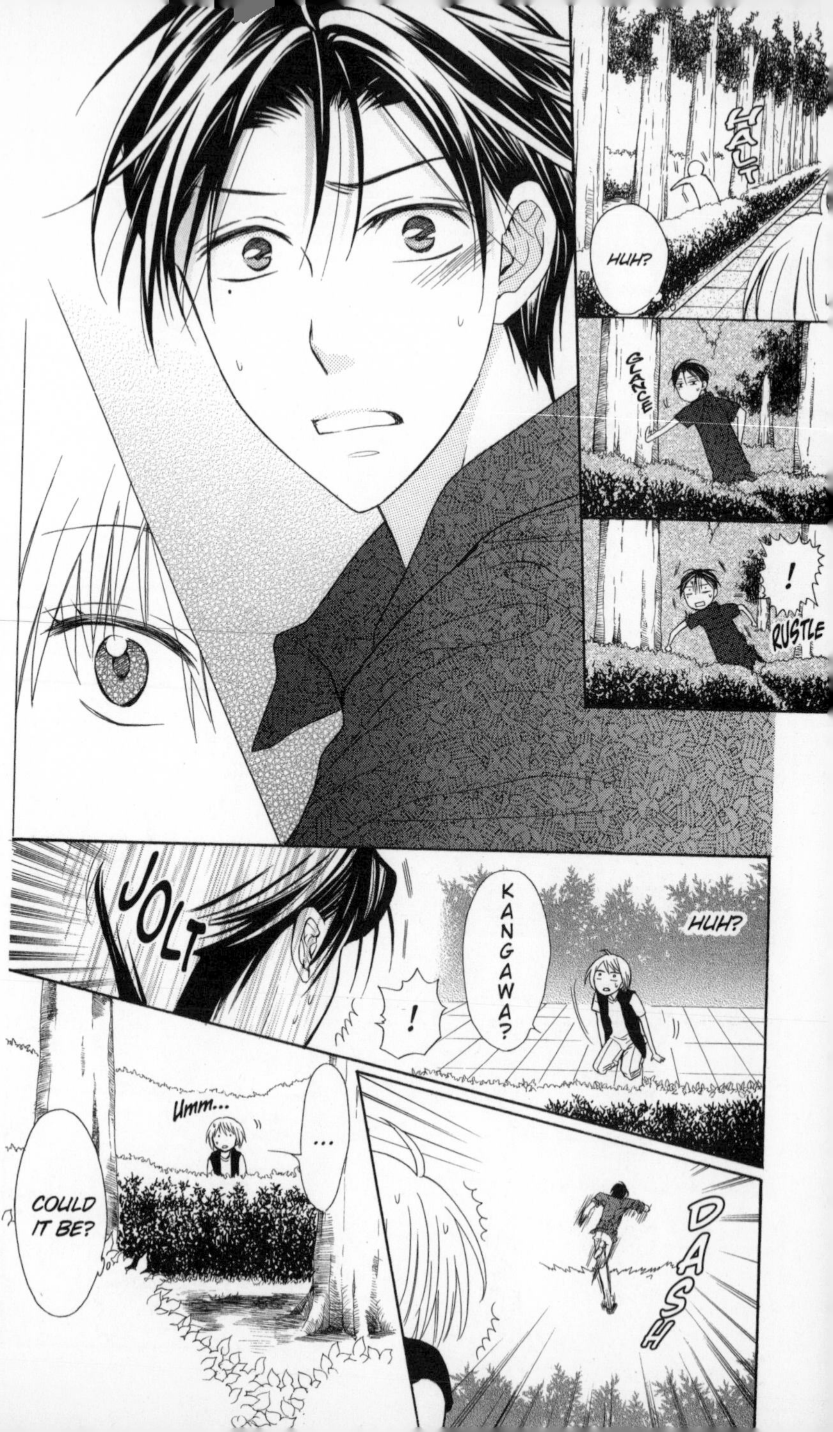
HALT
HUH?
GLANCE
!
RUSTLE
HUH?
KANGAWA?
JOLT
!
DASH
...
Umm...
COULD IT BE?

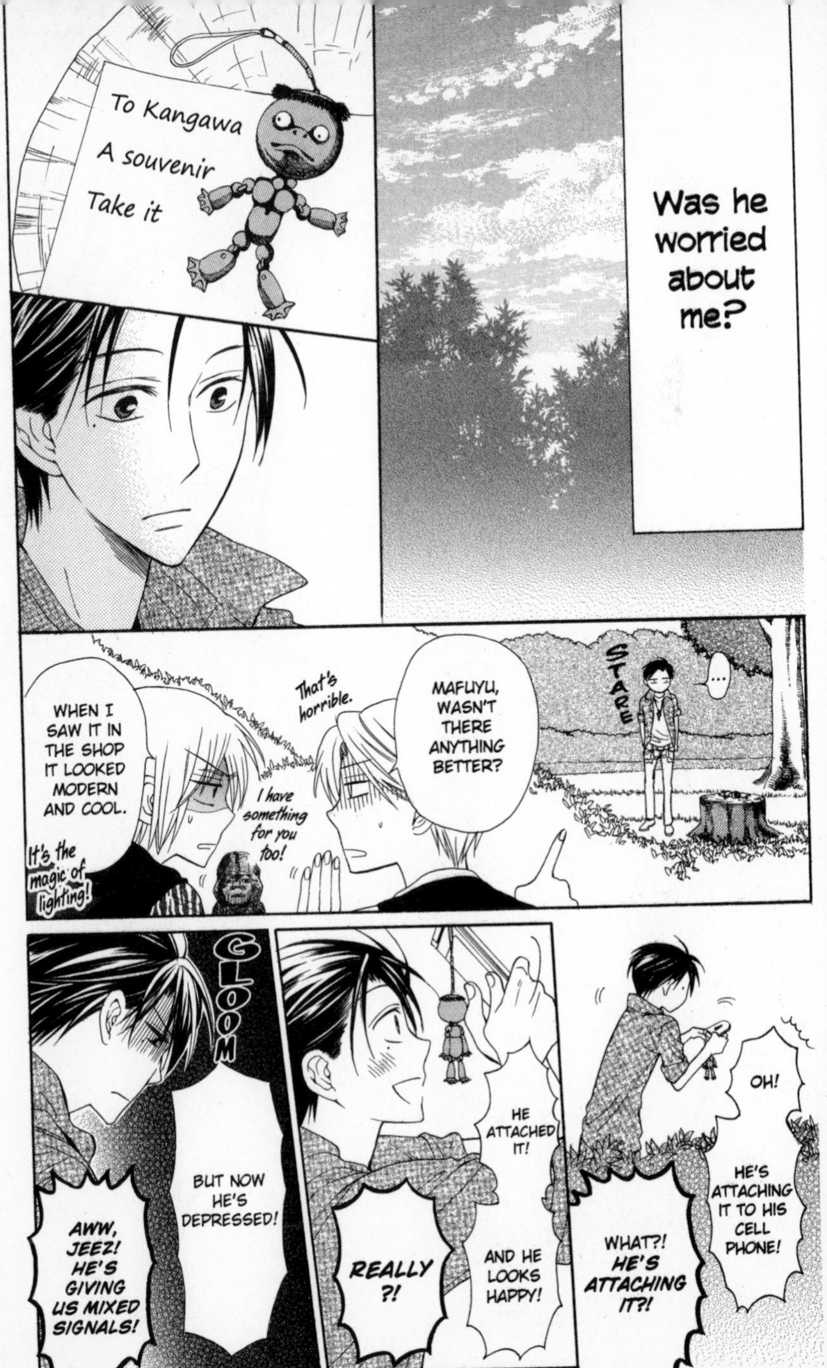
Was he worried about me?
To Kangawa
A souvenir
Take it
STARE
...
MAFUYU, WASN'T THERE ANYTHING BETTER?
That's horrible.
I have something for you too!
WHEN I SAW IT IN THE SHOP IT LOOKED MODERN AND COOL.
It's the magic of lighting!
OH!
HE'S ATTACHING IT TO HIS CELL PHONE!
WHAT?! HE'S ATTACHING IT?!
HE ATTACHED IT!
AND HE LOOKS HAPPY!
REALLY?!
GLOOM
BUT NOW HE'S DEPRESSED!
AWW, JEEZ! HE'S GIVING US MIXED SIGNALS!

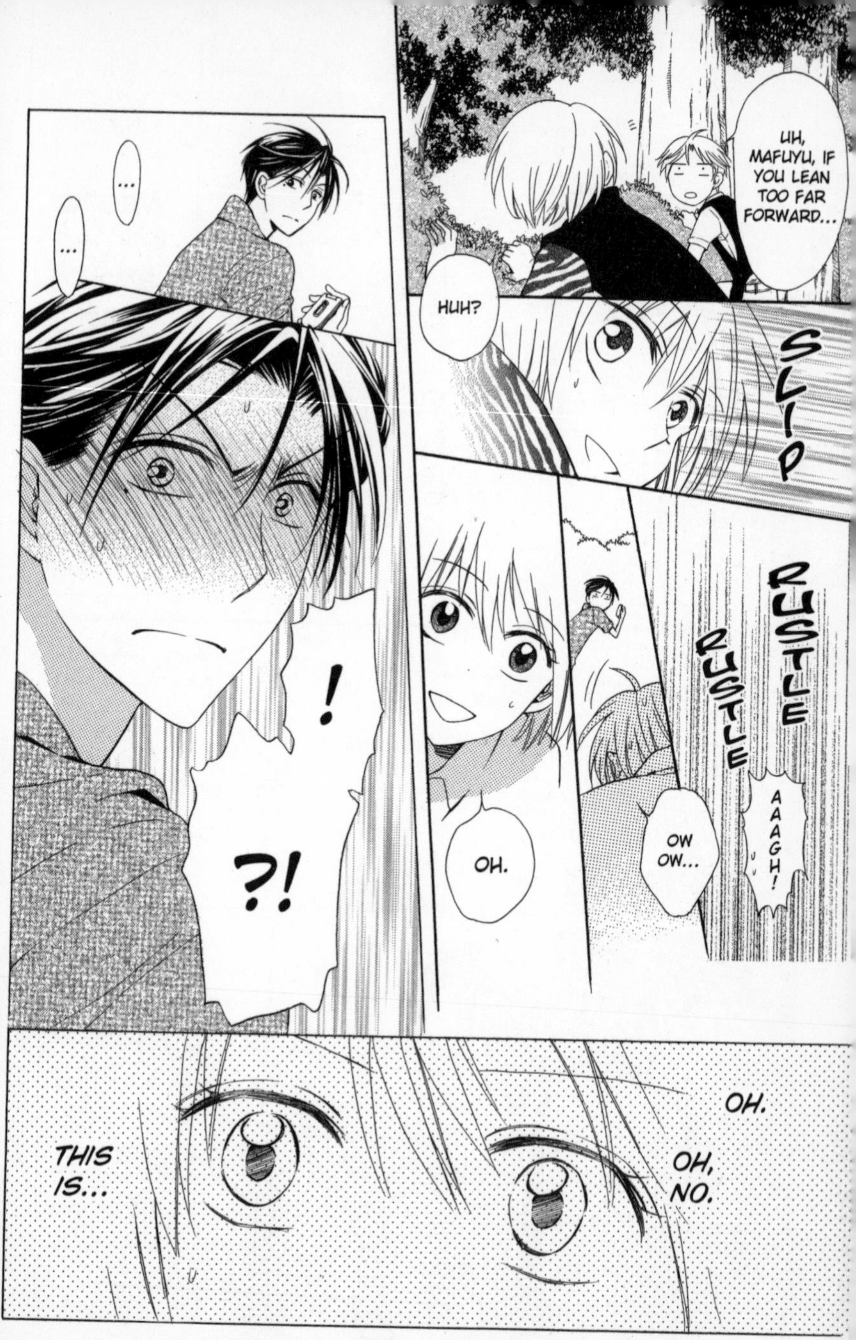
UH, MAFUYU, IF YOU LEAN TOO FAR FORWARD...
HUH?
SLIP
RUSTLE
RUSTLE
AAAGH!
OW OW...
OH.
...
...
!
?!
OH.
OH, NO.
THIS IS...

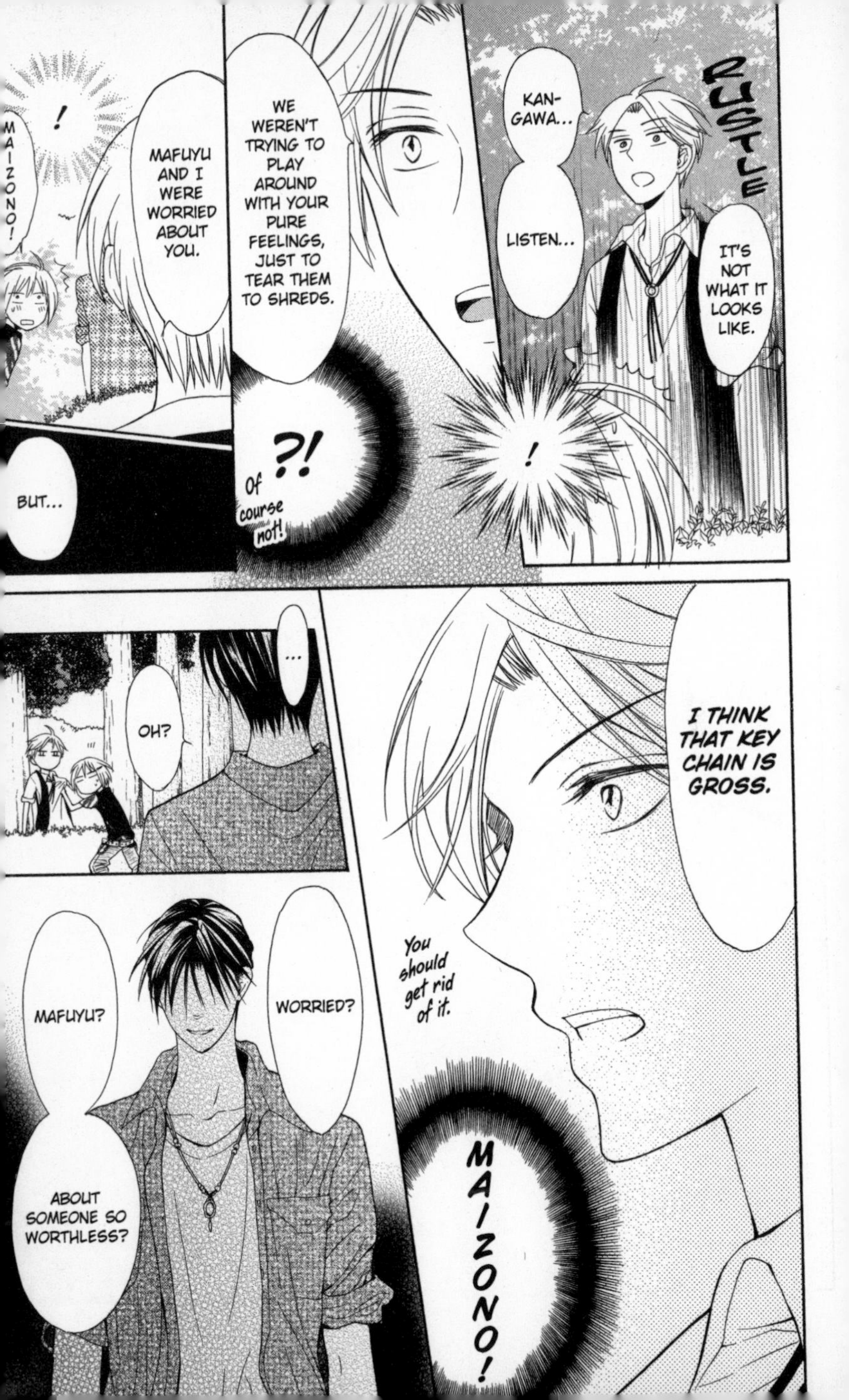
RUSTLE
KAN-GAWA...
LISTEN...
IT'S NOT WHAT IT LOOKS LIKE.
!
WE WEREN'T TRYING TO PLAY AROUND WITH YOUR PURE FEELINGS, JUST TO TEAR THEM TO SHREDS.
?!
Of course not!
MAFUYU AND I WERE WORRIED ABOUT YOU.
!
MAIZONO!
BUT...
I THINK THAT KEY CHAIN IS GROSS.
You should get rid of it.
MAIZONO!
...
OH?
WORRIED?
MAFUYU?
ABOUT SOMEONE SO WORTHLESS?

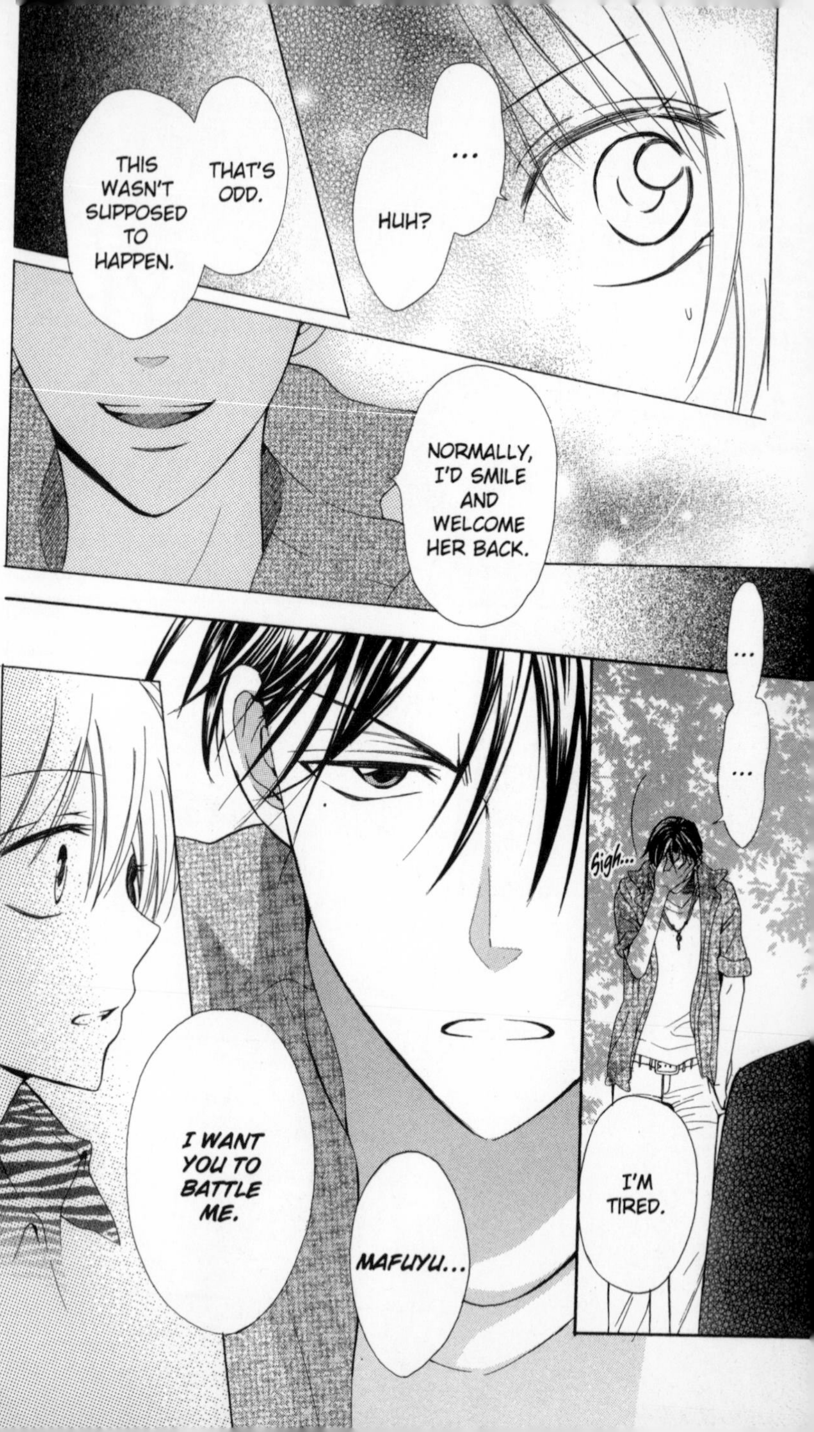
...
HUH?
THAT'S ODD.
THIS WASN'T SUPPOSED TO HAPPEN.
NORMALLY, I'D SMILE AND WELCOME HER BACK.
...
...
Sigh...
I'M TIRED.
MAFUYU...
I WANT YOU TO BATTLE ME.

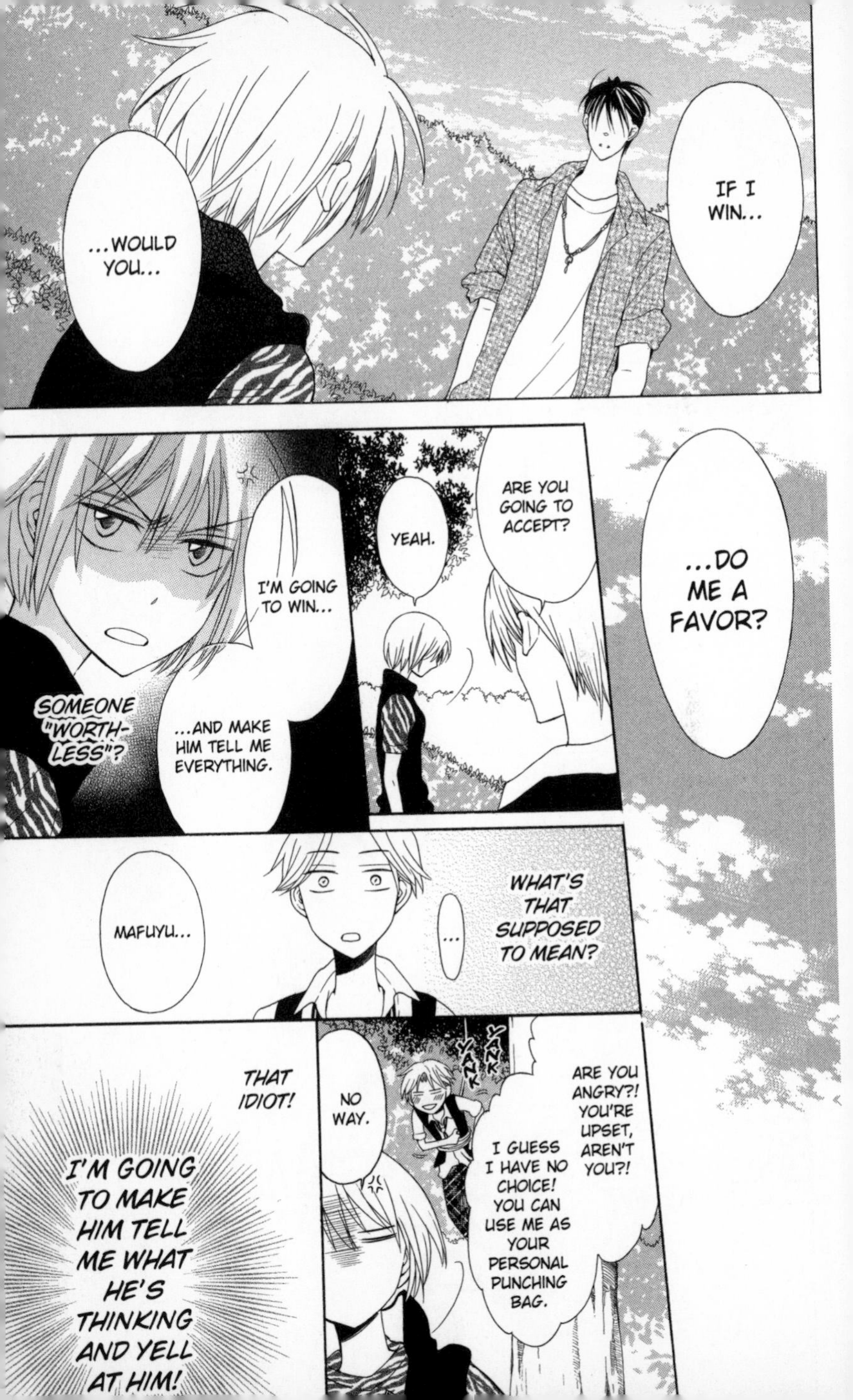
IF I WIN...
...WOULD YOU...
...DO ME A FAVOR?
ARE YOU GOING TO ACCEPT?
YEAH.
I'M GOING TO WIN...
...AND MAKE HIM TELL ME EVERYTHING.
SOMEONE "WORTHLESS"?
WHAT'S THAT SUPPOSED TO MEAN?
...
MAFUYU...
ARE YOU ANGRY?! YOU'RE UPSET, AREN'T YOU?!
YANK YANK
I GUESS I HAVE NO CHOICE! YOU CAN USE ME AS YOUR PERSONAL PUNCHING BAG.
NO WAY.
THAT IDIOT!
I'M GOING TO MAKE HIM TELL ME WHAT HE'S THINKING AND YELL AT HIM!

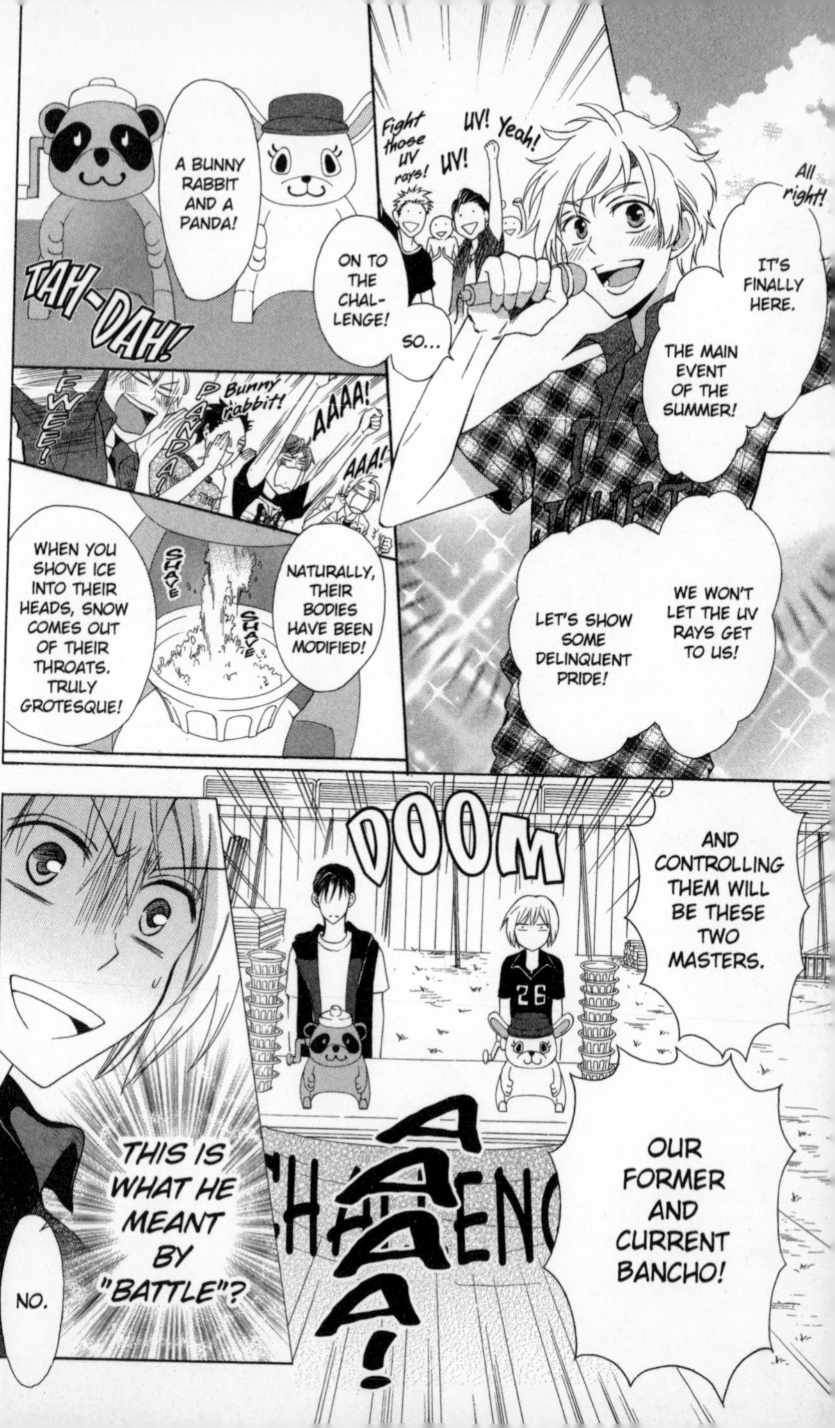
All right!
IT'S FINALLY HERE.
THE MAIN EVENT OF THE SUMMER!
Fight those UV rays!
UV!
UV!
Yeah!
WE WON'T LET THE UV RAYS GET TO US!
LET'S SHOW SOME DELINQUENT PRIDE!
SO...
ON TO THE CHAL-LENGE!
A BUNNY RABBIT AND A PANDA!
TAH-DAH!
AAAA!
Bunny rabbit!
PANDA!
FWEE!
AAA!
NATURALLY, THEIR BODIES HAVE BEEN MODIFIED!
SHAVE
SHAVE
WHEN YOU SHOVE ICE INTO THEIR HEADS, SNOW COMES OUT OF THEIR THROATS. TRULY GROTESQUE!
AND CONTROLLING THEM WILL BE THESE TWO MASTERS.
DOOM
OUR FORMER AND CURRENT BANCHO!
AAAA!
THIS IS WHAT HE MEANT BY "BATTLE"?
NO.

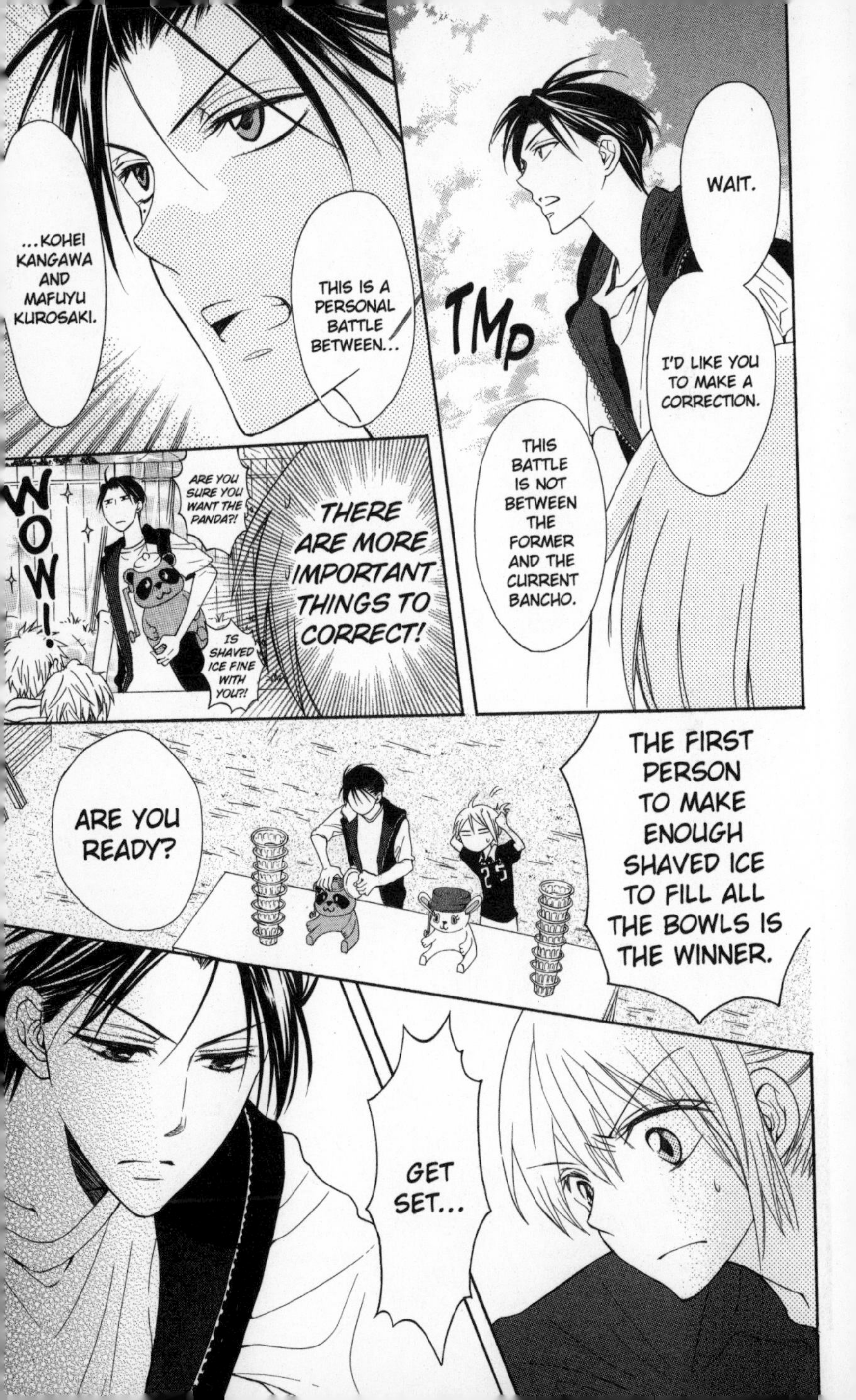
WAIT.
TMP
I'D LIKE YOU TO MAKE A CORRECTION.
THIS BATTLE IS NOT BETWEEN THE FORMER AND THE CURRENT BANCHO.
THIS IS A PERSONAL BATTLE BETWEEN...
...KOHEI KANGAWA AND MAFUYU KUROSAKI.
THERE ARE MORE IMPORTANT THINGS TO CORRECT!
ARE YOU SURE YOU WANT THE PANDA?!
IS SHAVED ICE FINE WITH YOU?!
WOW!
THE FIRST PERSON TO MAKE ENOUGH SHAVED ICE TO FILL ALL THE BOWLS IS THE WINNER.
ARE YOU READY?
GET SET...

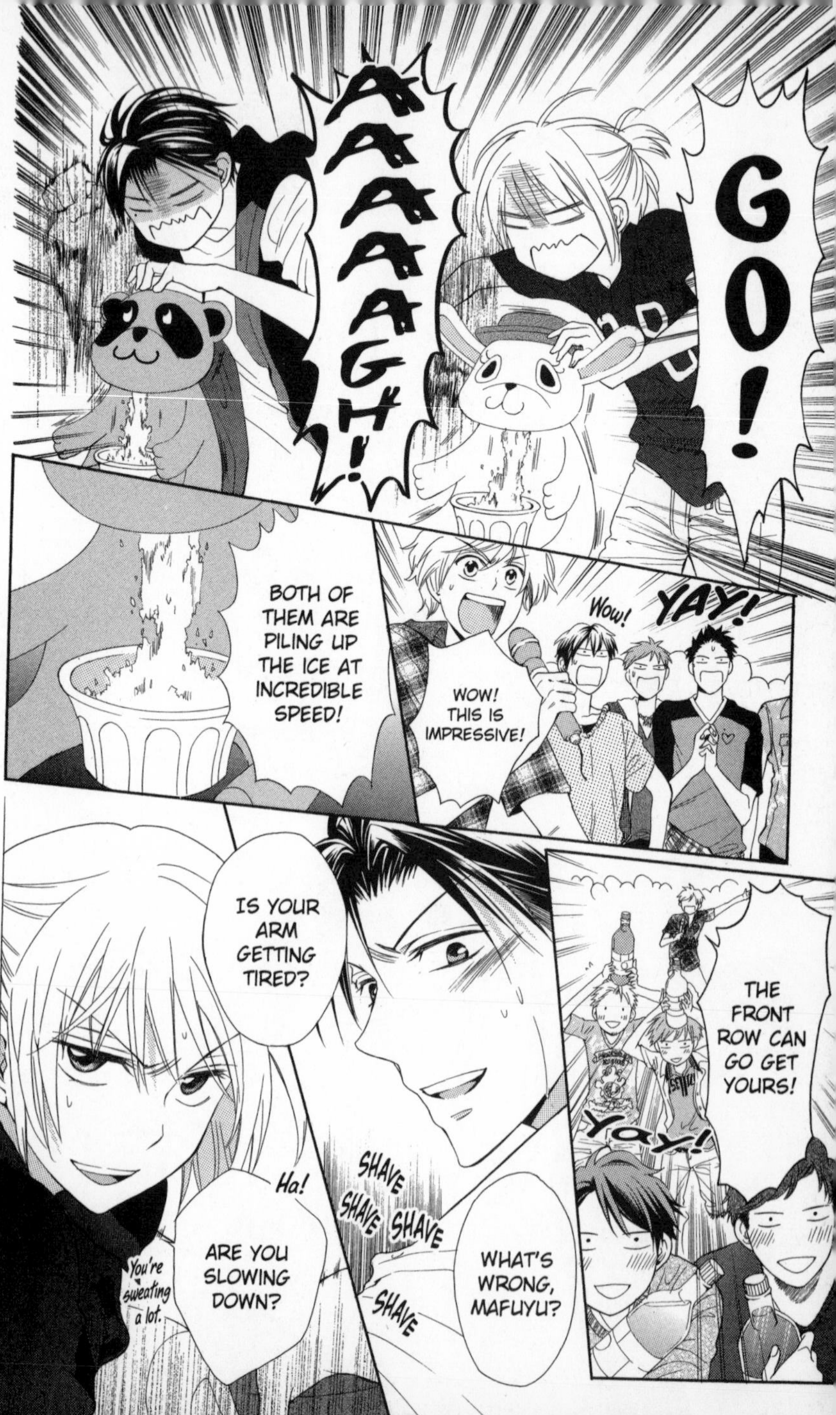
GO!
AAAAAGH!
YAY!
Wow!
WOW! THIS IS IMPRESSIVE!
BOTH OF THEM ARE PILING UP THE ICE AT INCREDIBLE SPEED!
THE FRONT ROW CAN GO GET YOURS!
Yay!
IS YOUR ARM GETTING TIRED?
WHAT'S WRONG, MAFUYU?
SHAVE SHAVE SHAVE
SHAVE
Ha!
ARE YOU SLOWING DOWN?
You're sweating a lot.

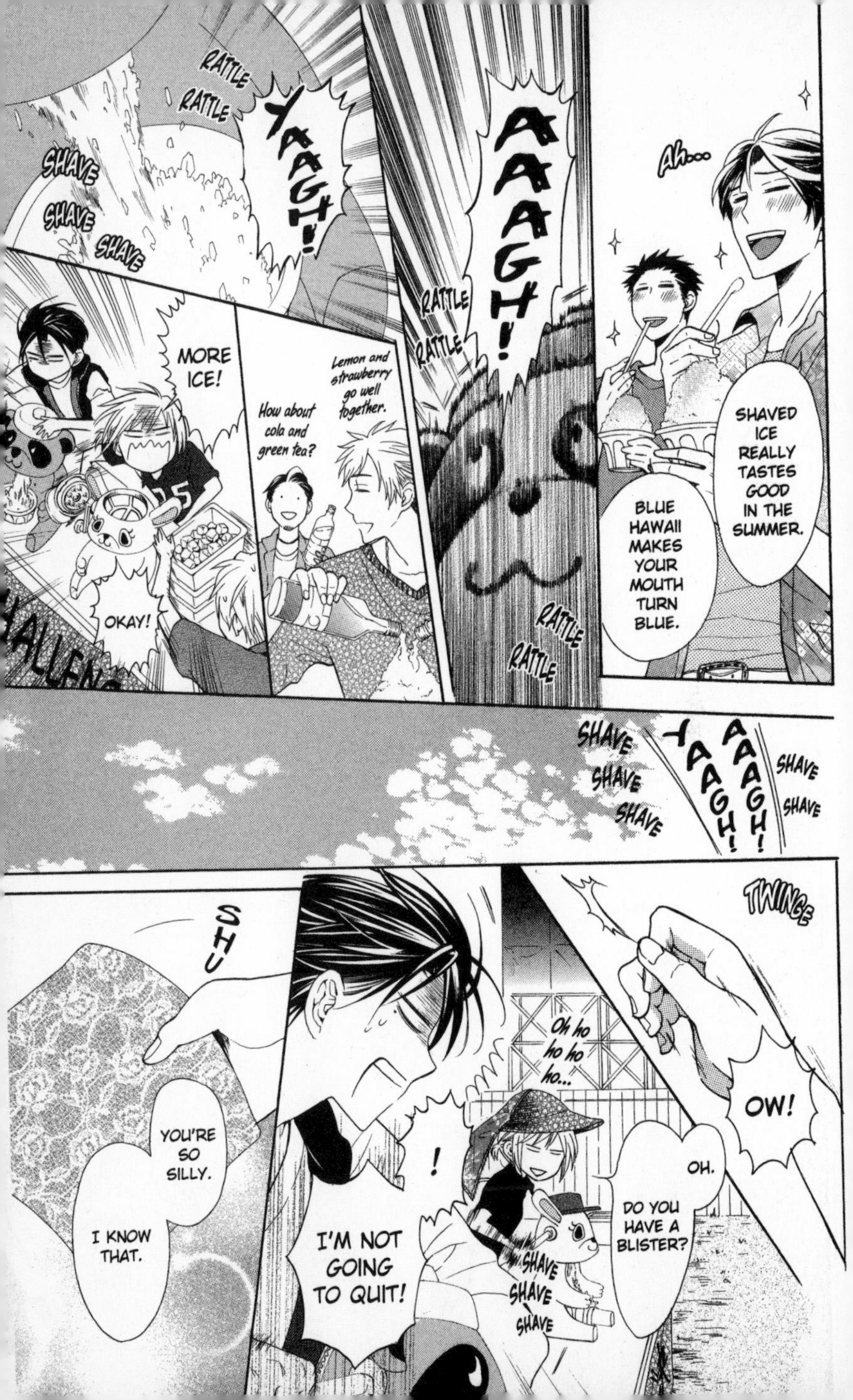
Ah...
SHAVED ICE REALLY TASTES GOOD IN THE SUMMER.
BLUE HAWAII MAKES YOUR MOUTH TURN BLUE.
AAAAGH!
RATTLE RATTLE
RATTLE RATTLE
RATTLE RATTLE
YAAGH!
SHAVE SHAVE SHAVE
Lemon and strawberry go well together.
How about cola and green tea?
MORE ICE!
OKAY!
SHAVE SHAVE
AAAGH!
YAAGH!
SHAVE SHAVE SHAVE
TWINGE
OW!
OH.
DO YOU HAVE A BLISTER?
Oh ho ho ho ho...
SHAVE SHAVE SHAVE
!
I'M NOT GOING TO QUIT!
SHU
YOU'RE SO SILLY.
I KNOW THAT.

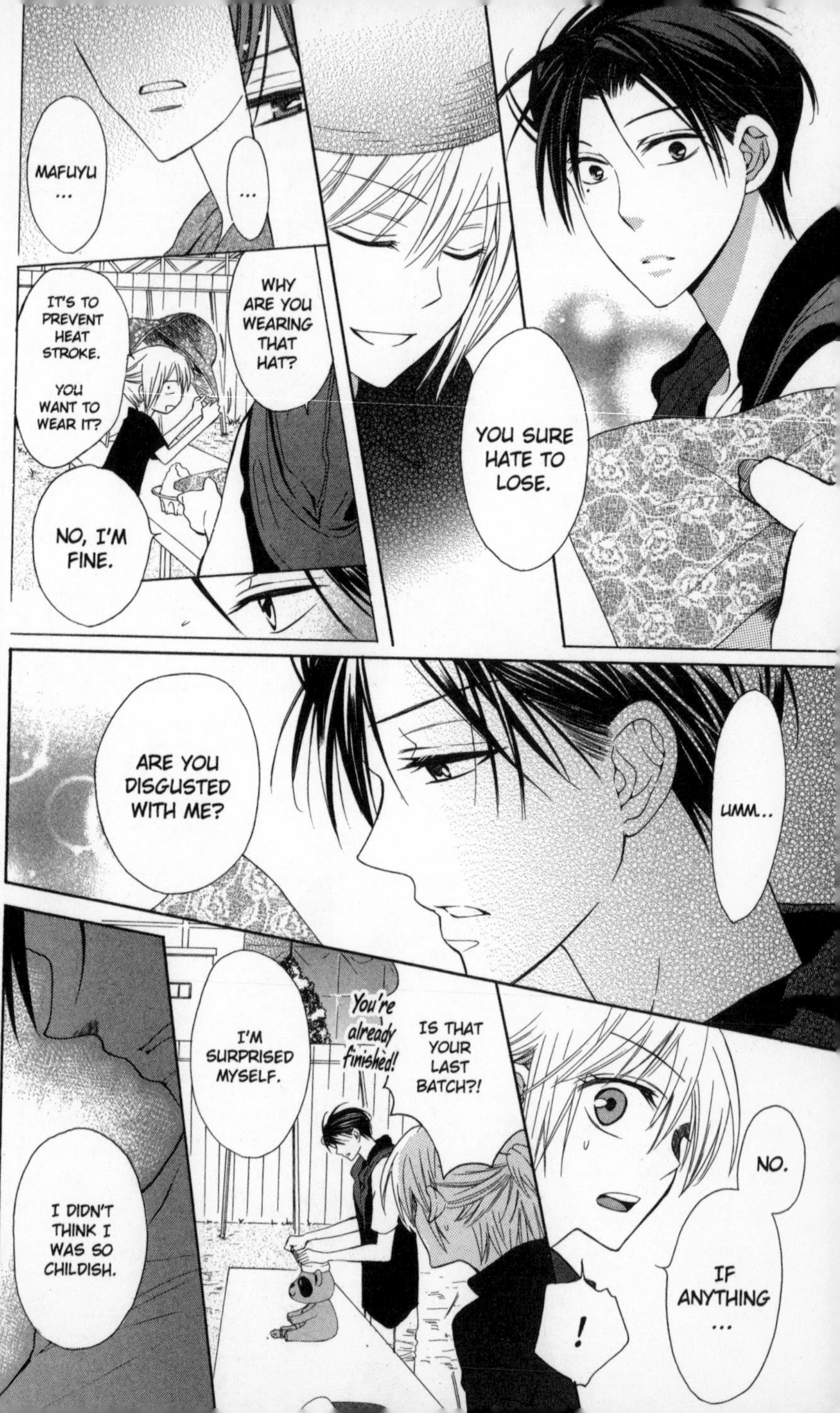
YOU SURE HATE TO LOSE.
...
MAFUYU ...
WHY ARE YOU WEARING THAT HAT?
IT'S TO PREVENT HEAT STROKE.
YOU WANT TO WEAR IT?
NO, I'M FINE.
UMM...
ARE YOU DISGUSTED WITH ME?
NO.
IF ANYTHING ...
!
IS THAT YOUR LAST BATCH?!
You're already finished!
I'M SURPRISED MYSELF.
I DIDN'T THINK I WAS SO CHILDISH.

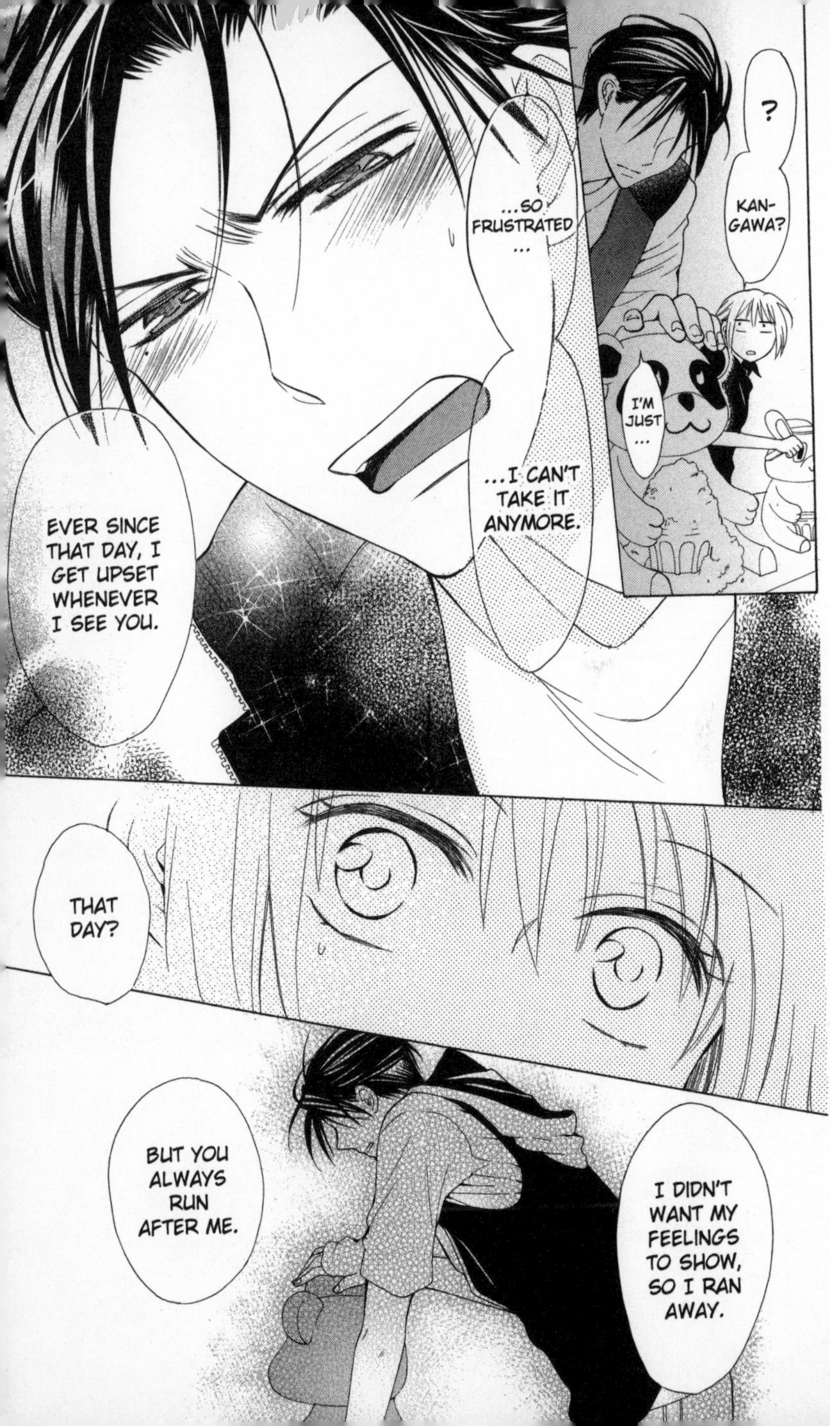
?
KAN-GAWA?
I'M JUST...
...SO FRUSTRATED...
...I CAN'T TAKE IT ANYMORE.
EVER SINCE THAT DAY, I GET UPSET WHENEVER I SEE YOU.
THAT DAY?
I DIDN'T WANT MY FEELINGS TO SHOW, SO I RAN AWAY.
BUT YOU ALWAYS RUN AFTER ME.

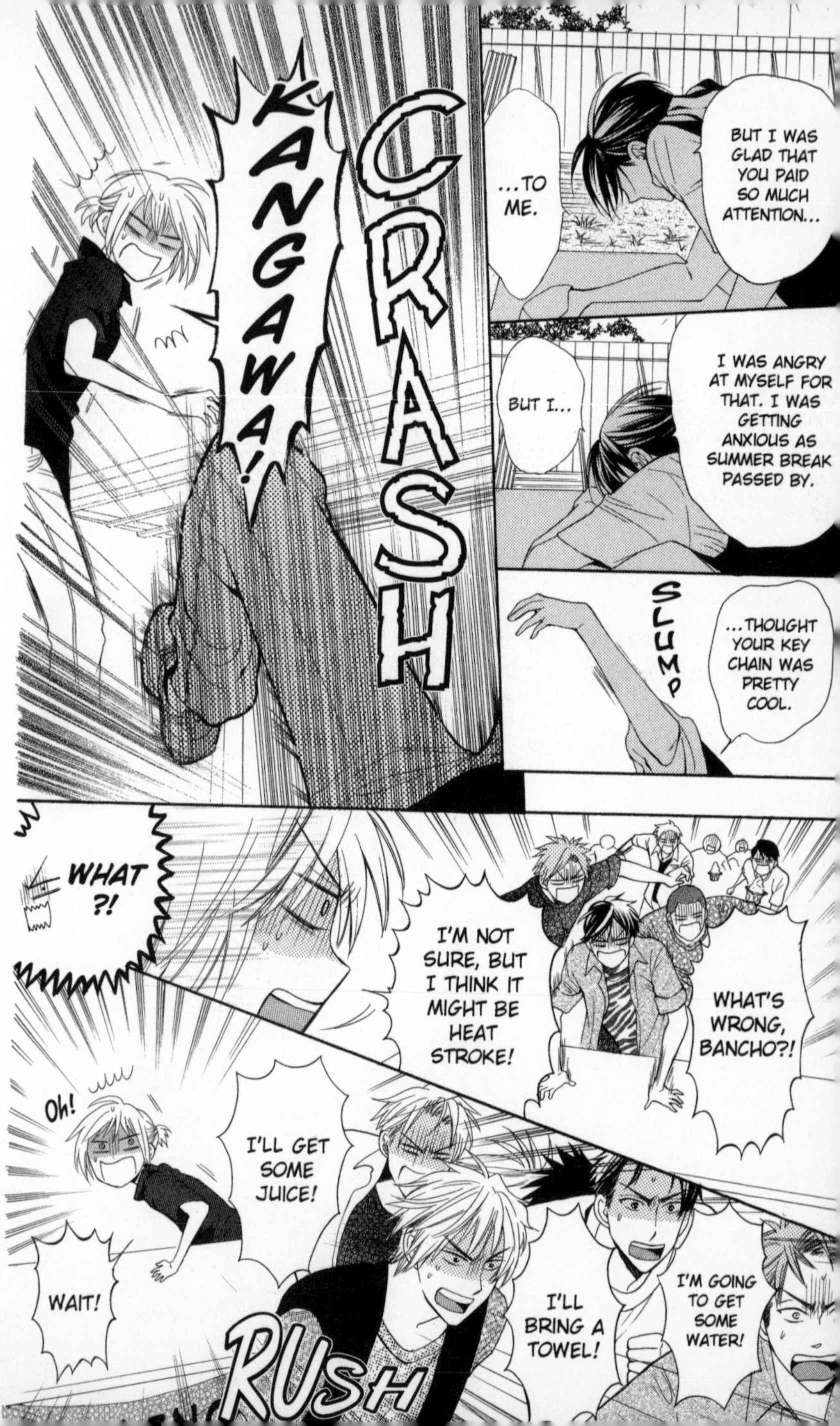
BUT I WAS GLAD THAT YOU PAID SO MUCH ATTENTION...
...TO ME.
I WAS ANGRY AT MYSELF FOR THAT. I WAS GETTING ANXIOUS AS SUMMER BREAK PASSED BY.
BUT I...
...THOUGHT YOUR KEY CHAIN WAS PRETTY COOL.
SLUMP
CRASH
KANGAWAA!
WHAT'S WRONG, BANCHO?!
I'M NOT SURE, BUT I THINK IT MIGHT BE HEAT STROKE!
WHAT?!
I'M GOING TO GET SOME WATER!
I'LL BRING A TOWEL!
I'LL GET SOME JUICE!
RUSH
Oh!
WAIT!

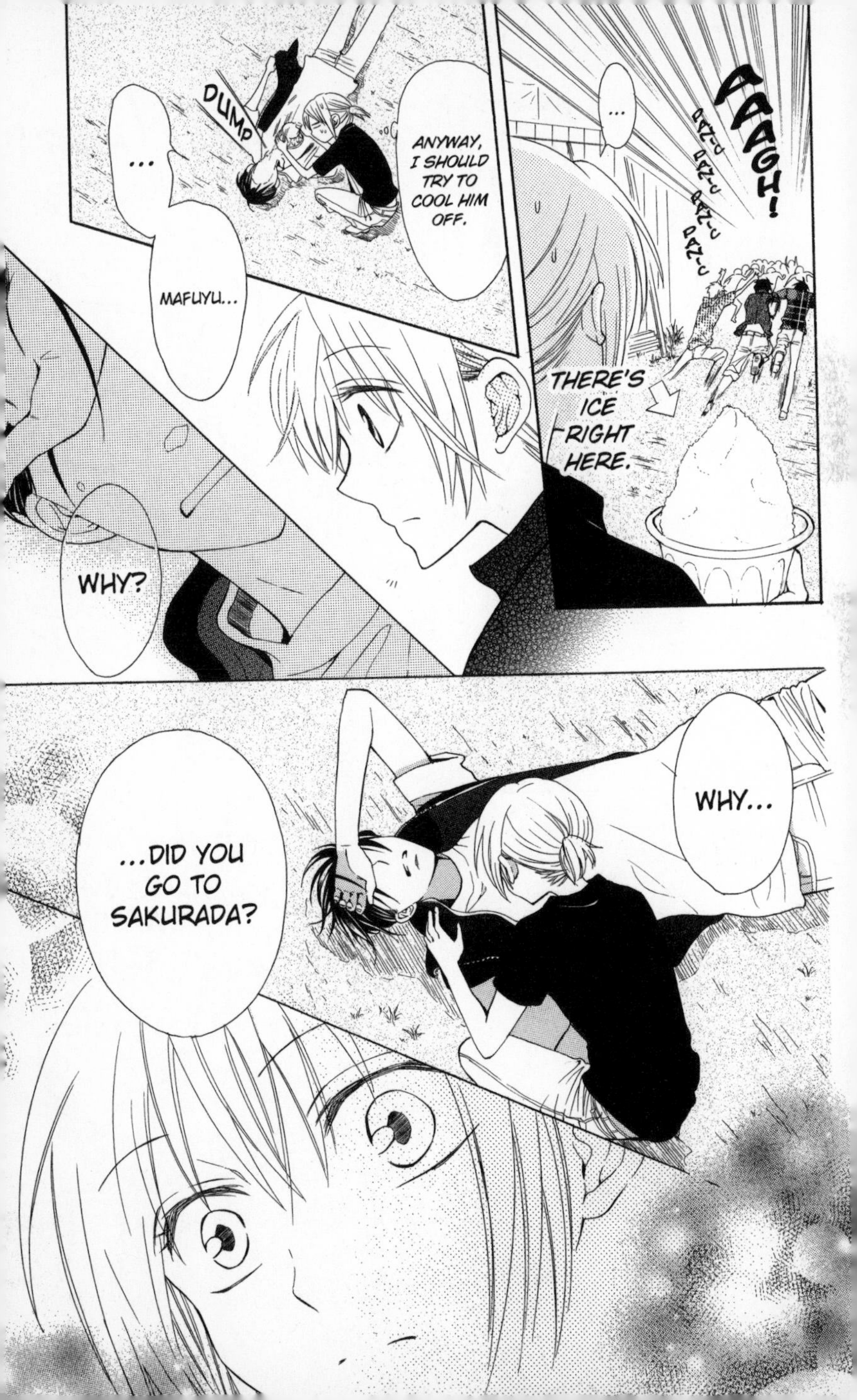
AAAGH!
DAZ-U
DAZ-U
DAZ-U
DAZ-U
...
THERE'S ICE RIGHT HERE.
ANYWAY, I SHOULD TRY TO COOL HIM OFF.
DUMP
...
MAFUYU...
WHY?
WHY...
...DID YOU GO TO SAKURADA?

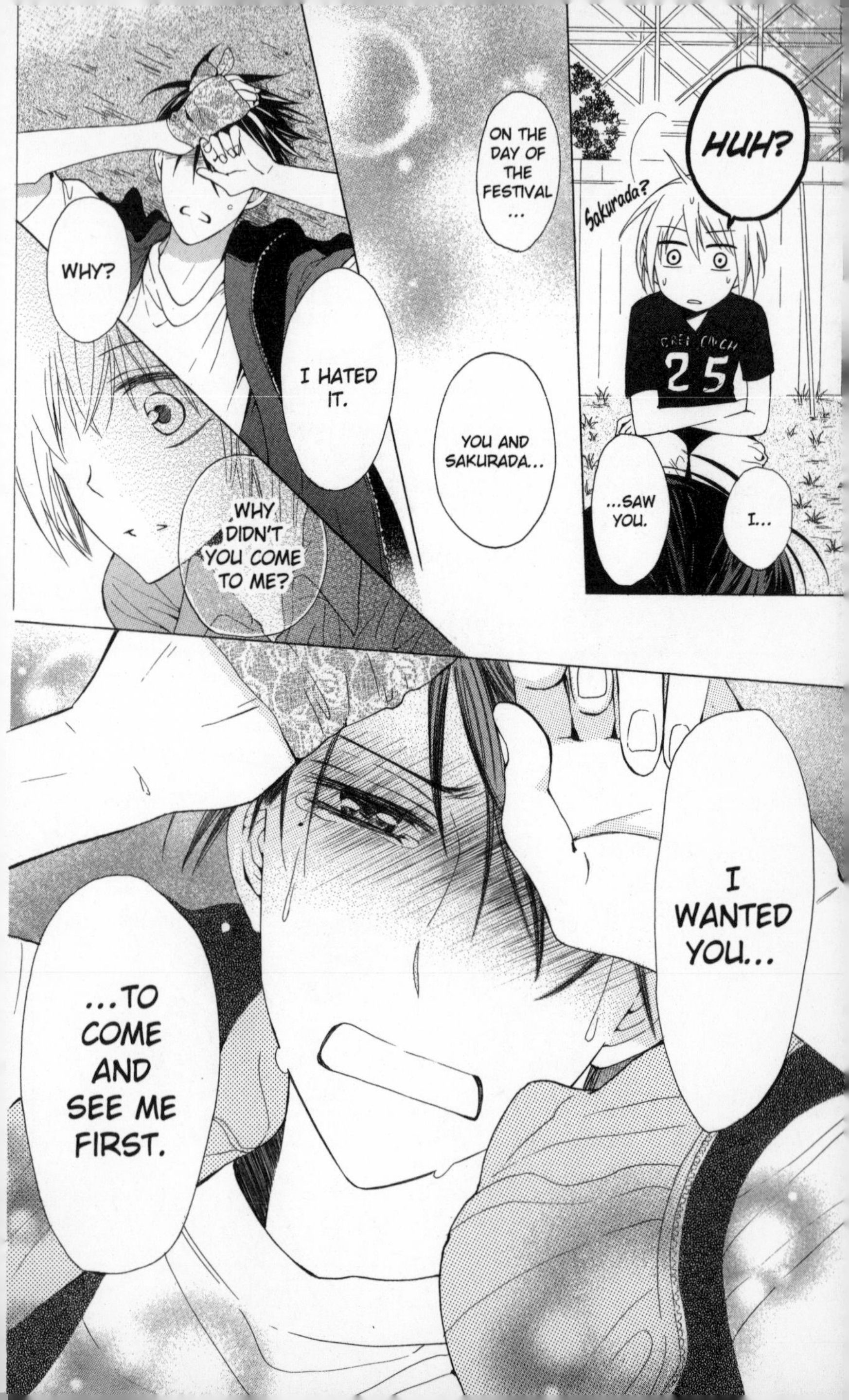
HUH?
Sakurada?
I...
...SAW YOU.
ON THE DAY OF THE FESTIVAL...
YOU AND SAKURADA...
I HATED IT.
WHY?
WHY DIDN'T YOU COME TO ME?
I WANTED YOU...
...TO COME AND SEE ME FIRST.

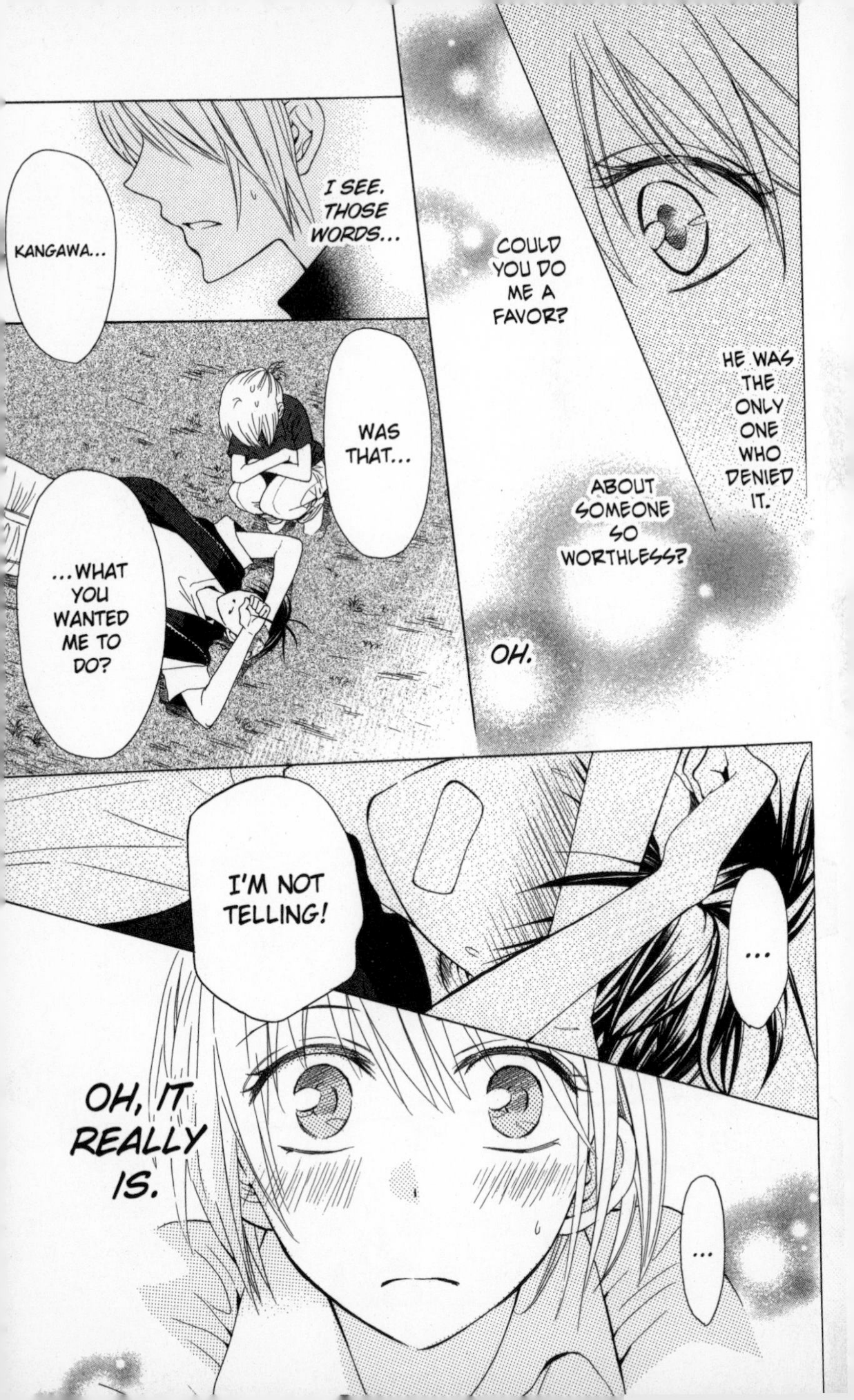
COULD YOU DO ME A FAVOR?
HE WAS THE ONLY ONE WHO DENIED IT.
ABOUT SOMEONE SO WORTHLESS?
OH.
I SEE. THOSE WORDS...
KANGAWA...
WAS THAT...
...WHAT YOU WANTED ME TO DO?
...
I'M NOT TELLING!
...
OH, IT REALLY IS.

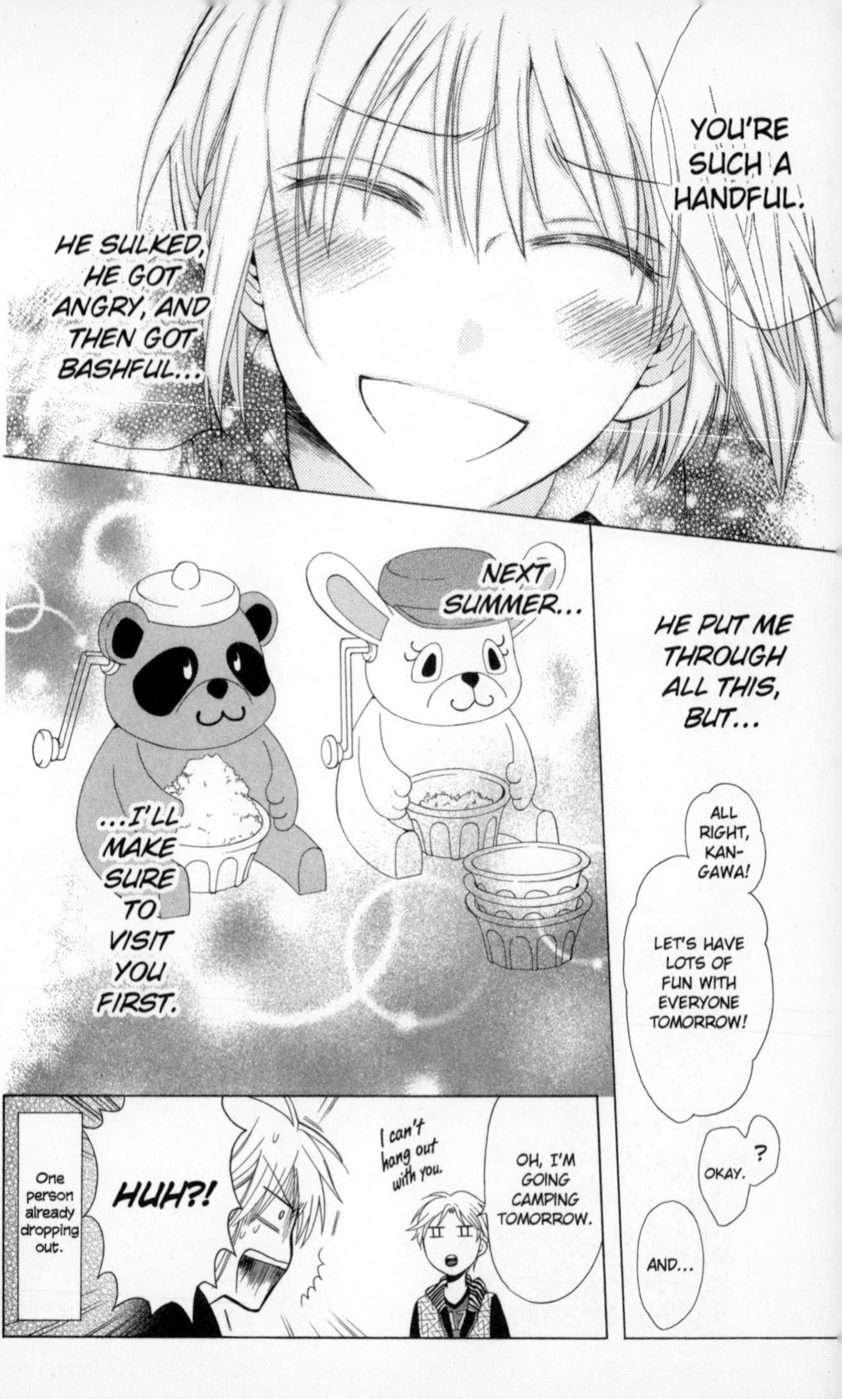
YOU'RE SUCH A HANDFUL.
HE SULKED, HE GOT ANGRY, AND THEN GOT BASHFUL...
HE PUT ME THROUGH ALL THIS, BUT...
ALL RIGHT, KAN-GAWA!
LET'S HAVE LOTS OF FUN WITH EVERYONE TOMORROW!
?
OKAY.
AND...
NEXT SUMMER...
...I'LL MAKE SURE TO VISIT YOU FIRST.
OH, I'M GOING CAMPING TOMORROW.
I can't hang out with you.
HUH?!
One person already dropping out.

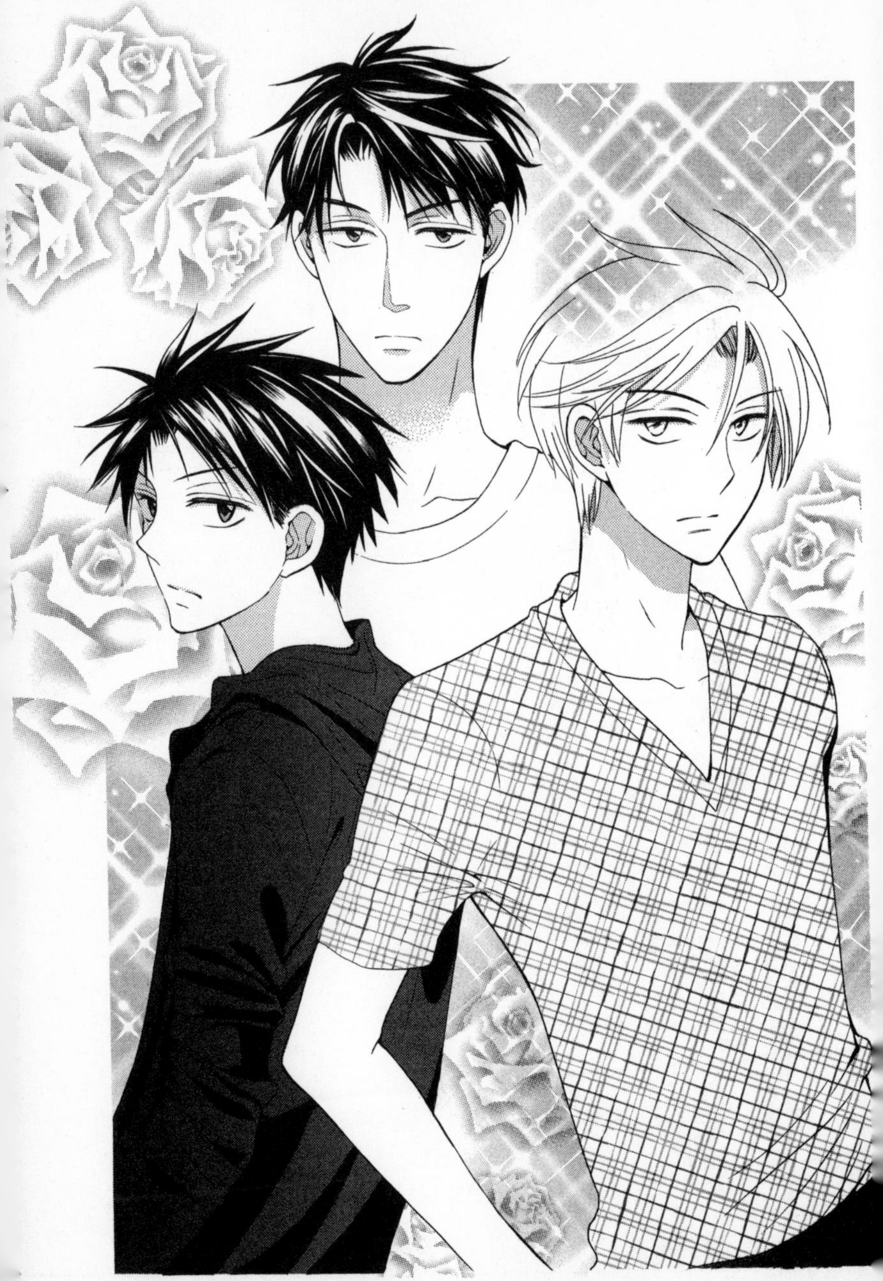

Chapter 39 Summer Break 3: Maizono Returns

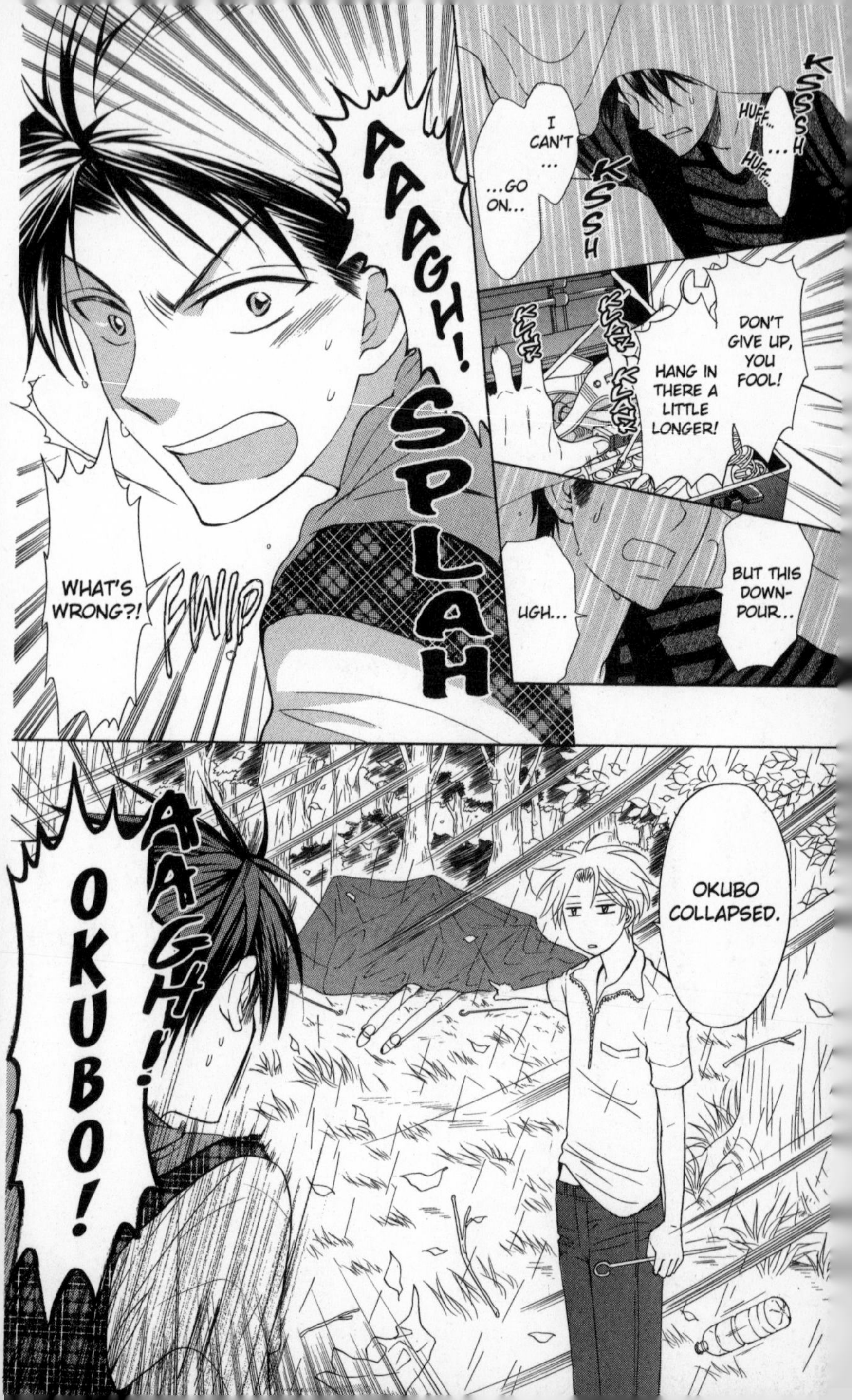
KSSSH
HUFF... ...HUFF...
KSSH
I CAN'T ...
...GO ON...
DON'T GIVE UP, YOU FOOL!
HANG IN THERE A LITTLE LONGER!
KLAK KLAK KLAK
BUT THIS DOWN-POUR...
UGH...
AAAGH!
SPLASH
FWIP
WHAT'S WRONG?!
OKUBO COLLAPSED.
AAAGH!!
OKUBO!

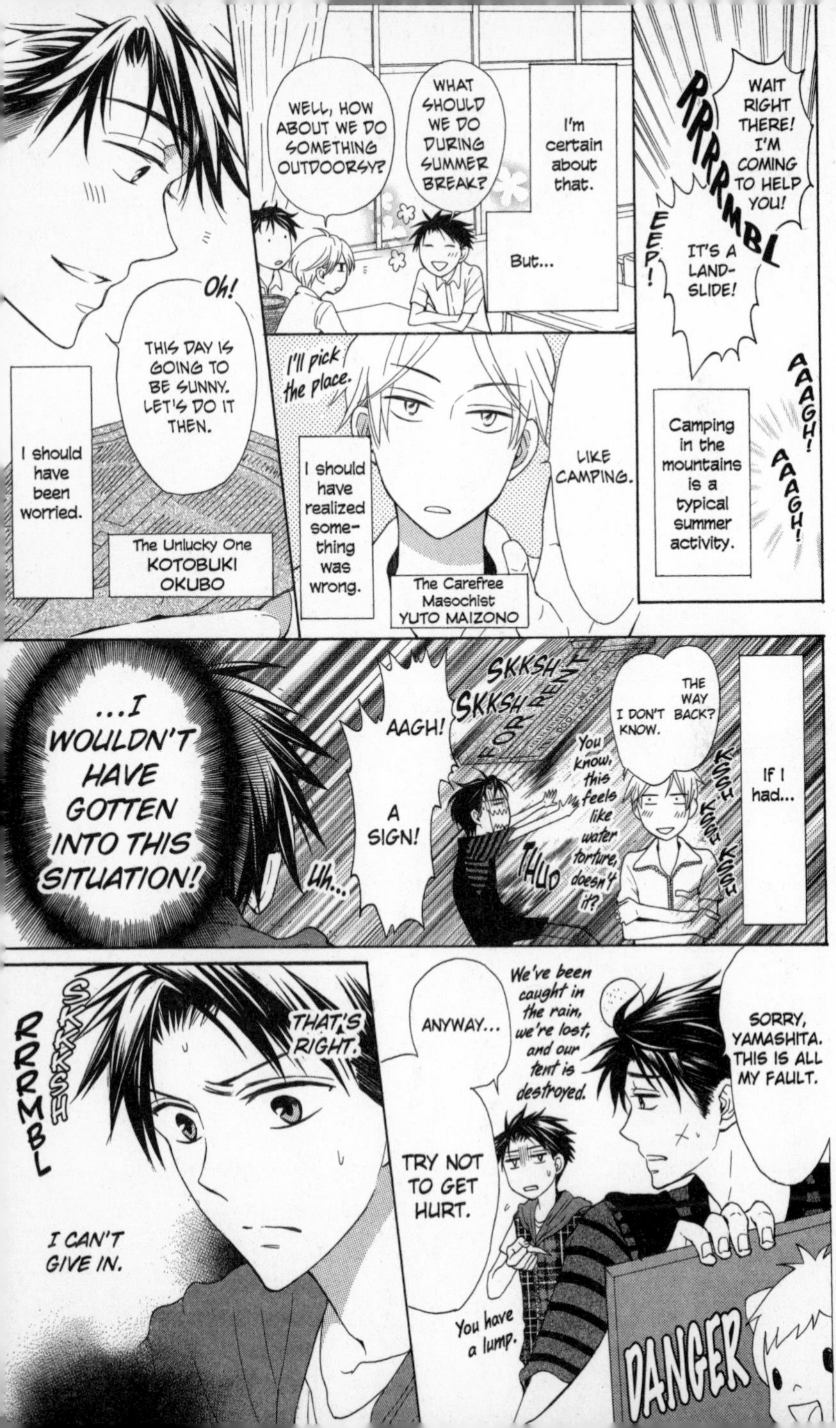
WAIT RIGHT THERE! I'M COMING TO HELP YOU!
RRRRRMBL
EEP!
IT'S A LANDSLIDE!
AAAGH!
AAAGH!
Camping in the mountains is a typical summer activity.
I'm certain about that.
But...
WHAT SHOULD WE DO DURING SUMMER BREAK?
WELL, HOW ABOUT WE DO SOMETHING OUTDOORSY?
LIKE CAMPING.
I'll pick the place.
I should have realized some-thing was wrong.
The Carefree Masochist YUTO MAIZONO
Oh!
THIS DAY IS GOING TO BE SUNNY. LET'S DO IT THEN.
I should have been worried.
The Unlucky One KOTOBUKI OKUBO
If I had...
THE WAY BACK?
I DON'T KNOW.
KSSH KSSH KSSH
You know, this feels like water torture, doesn't it?
SKKSH SKKSH
FOR RENT
AAGH!
A SIGN!
THUD
Uh...
...I WOULDN'T HAVE GOTTEN INTO THIS SITUATION!
SORRY, YAMASHITA. THIS IS ALL MY FAULT.
We've been caught in the rain, we're lost, and our tent is destroyed.
ANYWAY...
TRY NOT TO GET HURT.
You have a lump.
DANGER
SKKSH
RRRMBL
THAT'S RIGHT.
I CAN'T GIVE IN.

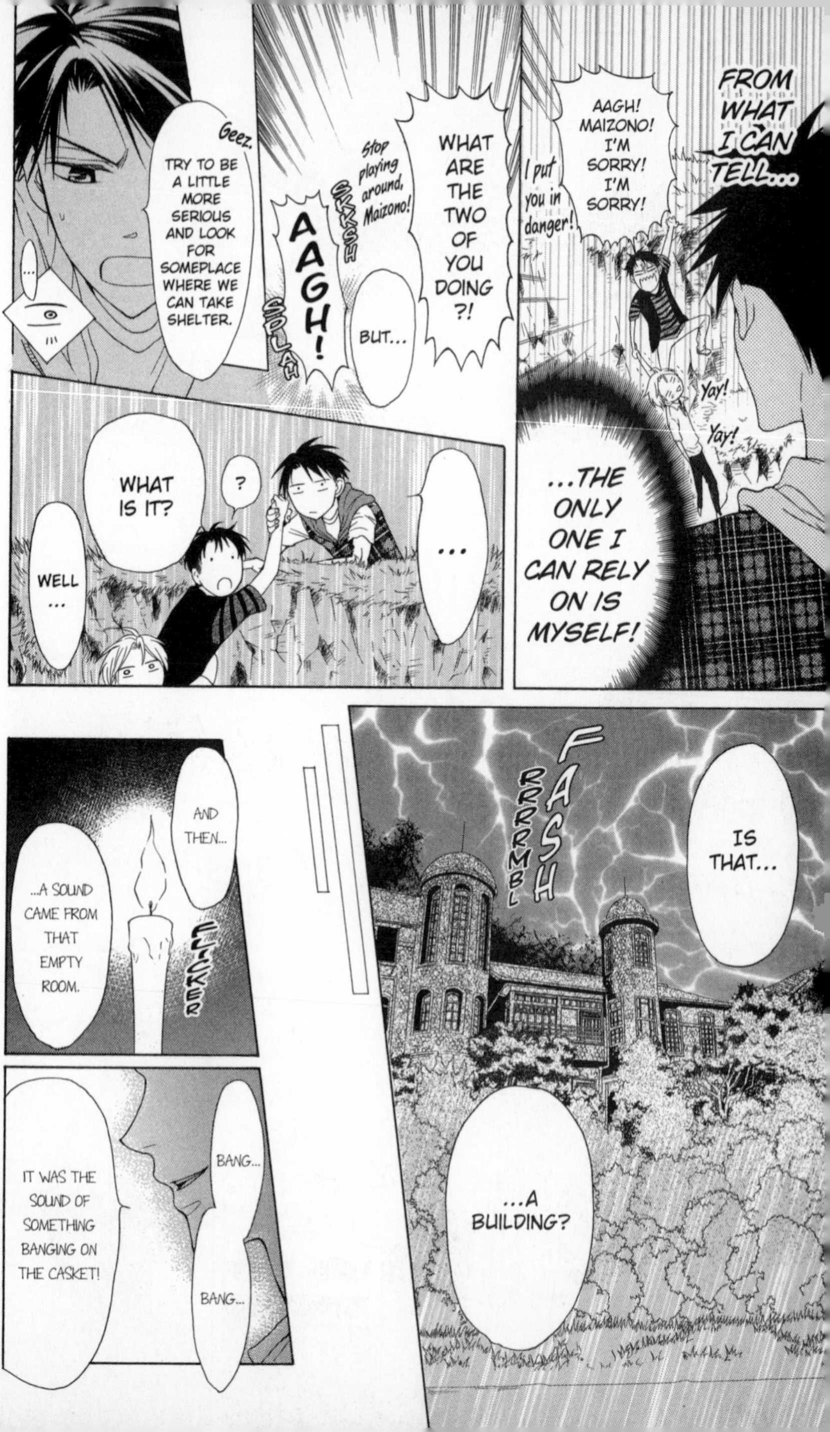
FROM WHAT I CAN TELL...
AAGH! MAIZONO! I'M SORRY! I'M SORRY!
I put you in danger!
Yay!
Yay!
...THE ONLY ONE I CAN RELY ON IS MYSELF!
WHAT ARE THE TWO OF YOU DOING?!
Stop playing around, Maizono!
SKKSH
AAGH!
SPLAH
BUT...
Geez.
TRY TO BE A LITTLE MORE SERIOUS AND LOOK FOR SOMEPLACE WHERE WE CAN TAKE SHELTER.
...
...
?
WHAT IS IT?
WELL...
FASH
RRRRMBL
IS THAT...
...A BUILDING?
AND THEN...
...A SOUND CAME FROM THAT EMPTY ROOM.
FLICKER
BANG...
IT WAS THE SOUND OF SOMETHING BANGING ON THE CASKET!
BANG...

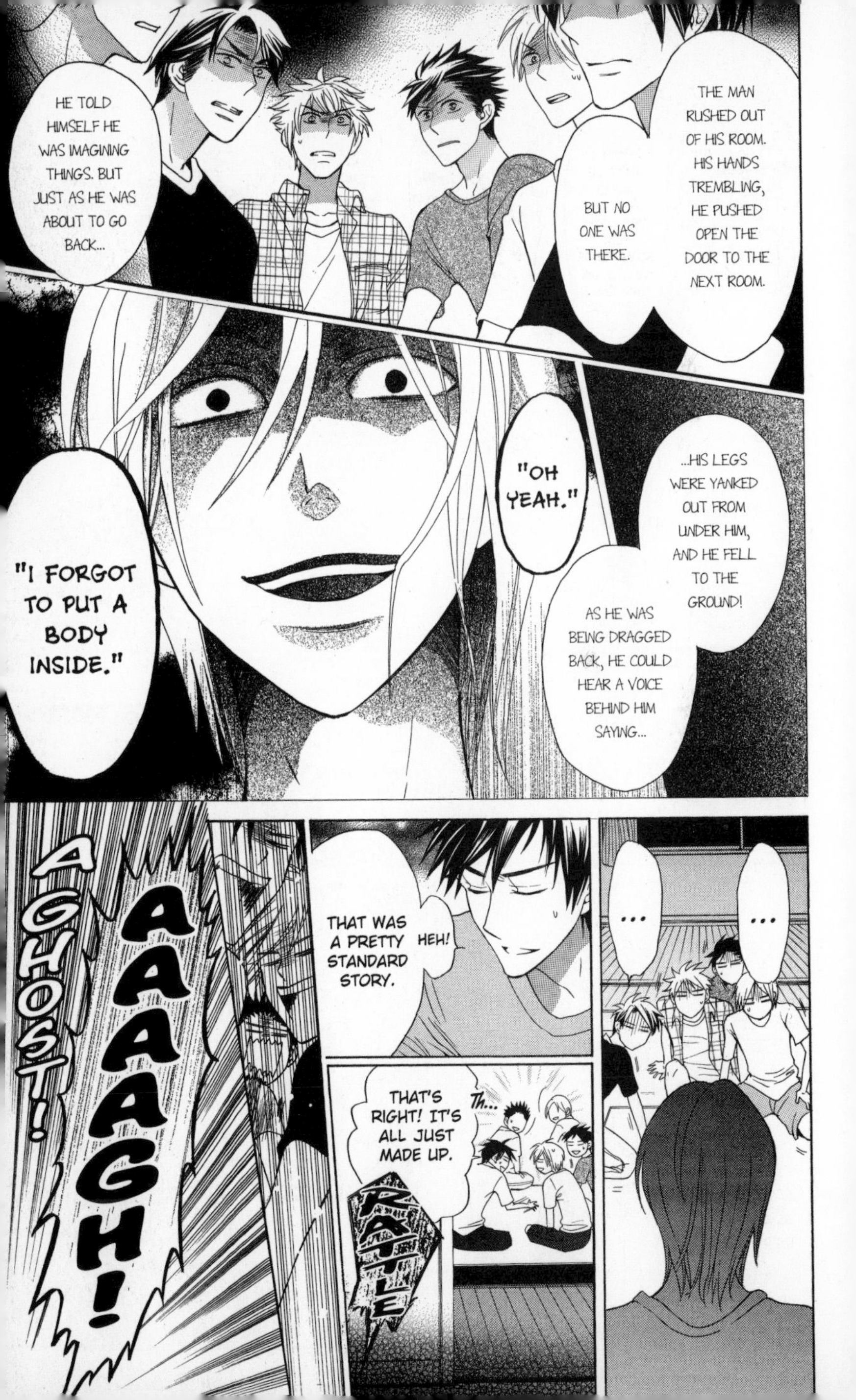
THE MAN RUSHED OUT OF HIS ROOM. HIS HANDS TREMBLING, HE PUSHED OPEN THE DOOR TO THE NEXT ROOM.
BUT NO ONE WAS THERE.
HE TOLD HIMSELF HE WAS IMAGINING THINGS. BUT JUST AS HE WAS ABOUT TO GO BACK...
...HIS LEGS WERE YANKED OUT FROM UNDER HIM, AND HE FELL TO THE GROUND!
AS HE WAS BEING DRAGGED BACK, HE COULD HEAR A VOICE BEHIND HIM SAYING...
"OH YEAH."
"I FORGOT TO PUT A BODY INSIDE."
...
...
THAT WAS A PRETTY STANDARD STORY.
HEH!
Th...
THAT'S RIGHT! IT'S ALL JUST MADE UP.
RATTLE
AAAAGH!
A GHOST!

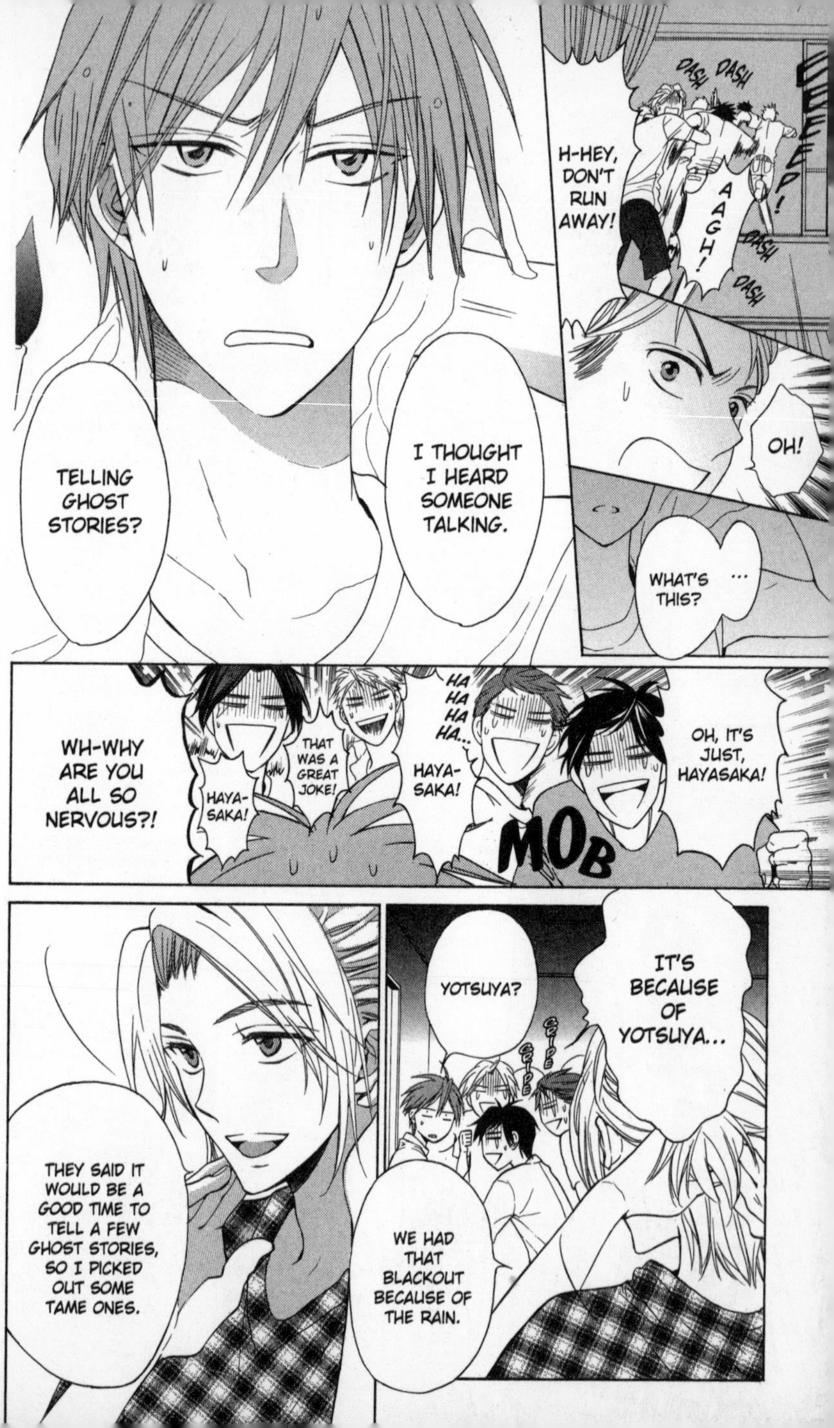
DASH DASH
AAGH!
H-HEY, DON'T RUN AWAY!
DASH
DASH
OH!
WHAT'S THIS? ...
I THOUGHT I HEARD SOMEONE TALKING.
TELLING GHOST STORIES?
OH, IT'S JUST, HAYASAKA!
MOB
HA HA HA HA...
HAYA-SAKA!
THAT WAS A GREAT JOKE!
HAYA-SAKA!
WH-WHY ARE YOU ALL SO NERVOUS?!
IT'S BECAUSE OF YOTSUYA...
YOTSUYA?
GRIPE GRIPE
WE HAD THAT BLACKOUT BECAUSE OF THE RAIN.
THEY SAID IT WOULD BE A GOOD TIME TO TELL A FEW GHOST STORIES, SO I PICKED OUT SOME TAME ONES.

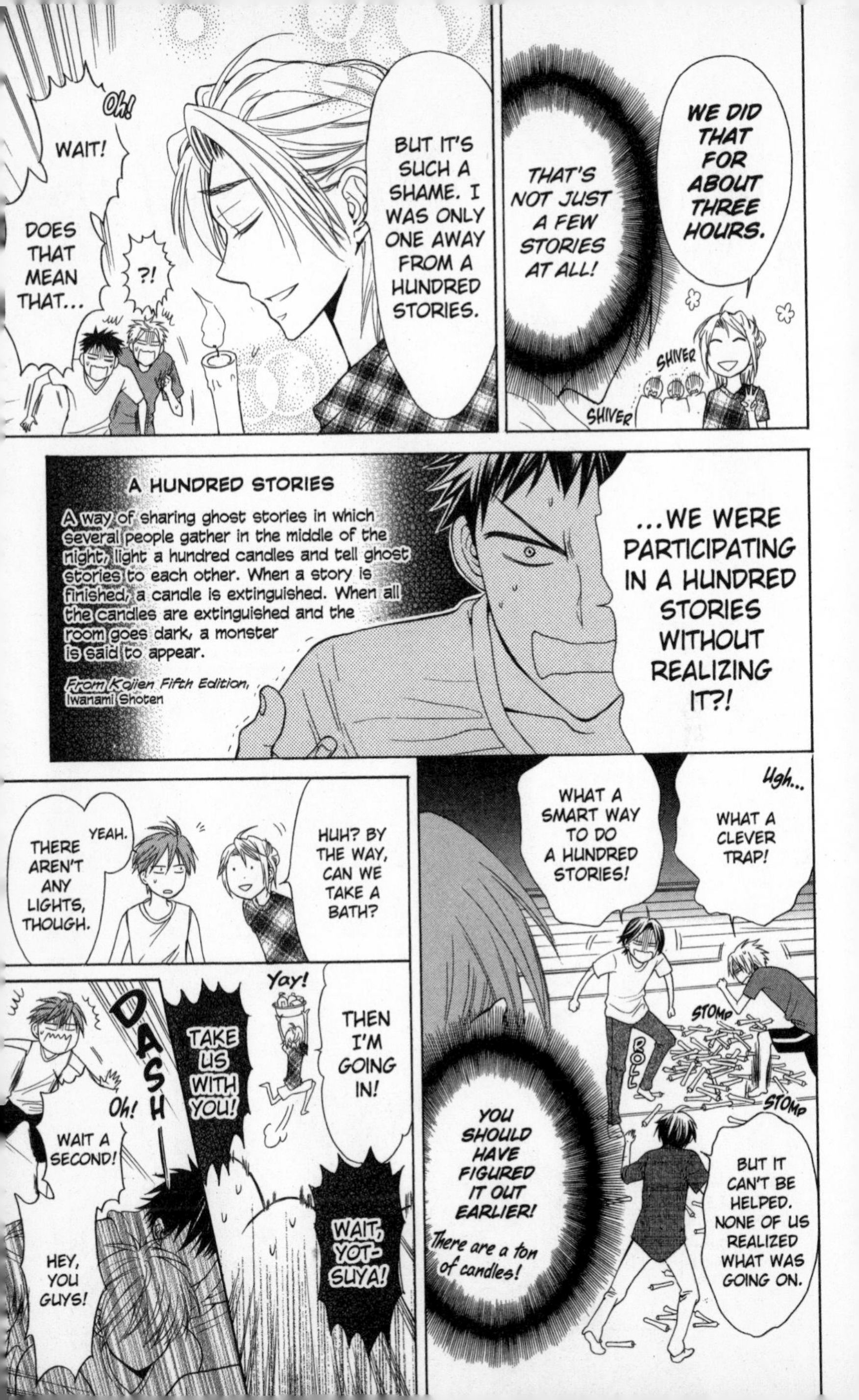
WE DID THAT FOR ABOUT THREE HOURS.
THAT'S NOT JUST A FEW STORIES AT ALL!
SHIVER
SHIVER
BUT IT'S SUCH A SHAME. I WAS ONLY ONE AWAY FROM A HUNDRED STORIES.
Oh!
WAIT!
?!
DOES THAT MEAN THAT...
...WE WERE PARTICIPATING IN A HUNDRED STORIES WITHOUT REALIZING IT?!
A HUNDRED STORIES
A way of sharing ghost stories in which several people gather in the middle of the night, light a hundred candles and tell ghost stories to each other. When a story is finished, a candle is extinguished. When all the candles are extinguished and the room goes dark, a monster is said to appear.
From Kojien Fifth Edition, Iwanami Shoten
Ugh...
WHAT A CLEVER TRAP!
WHAT A SMART WAY TO DO A HUNDRED STORIES!
STOMP
ROLL
STOMP
BUT IT CAN'T BE HELPED. NONE OF US REALIZED WHAT WAS GOING ON.
YOU SHOULD HAVE FIGURED IT OUT EARLIER!
There are a ton of candles!
HUH? BY THE WAY, CAN WE TAKE A BATH?
YEAH.
THERE AREN'T ANY LIGHTS, THOUGH.
THEN I'M GOING IN!
Yay!
TAKE US WITH YOU!
DASH
WAIT, YOT-SUYA!
Oh!
WAIT A SECOND!
HEY, YOU GUYS!

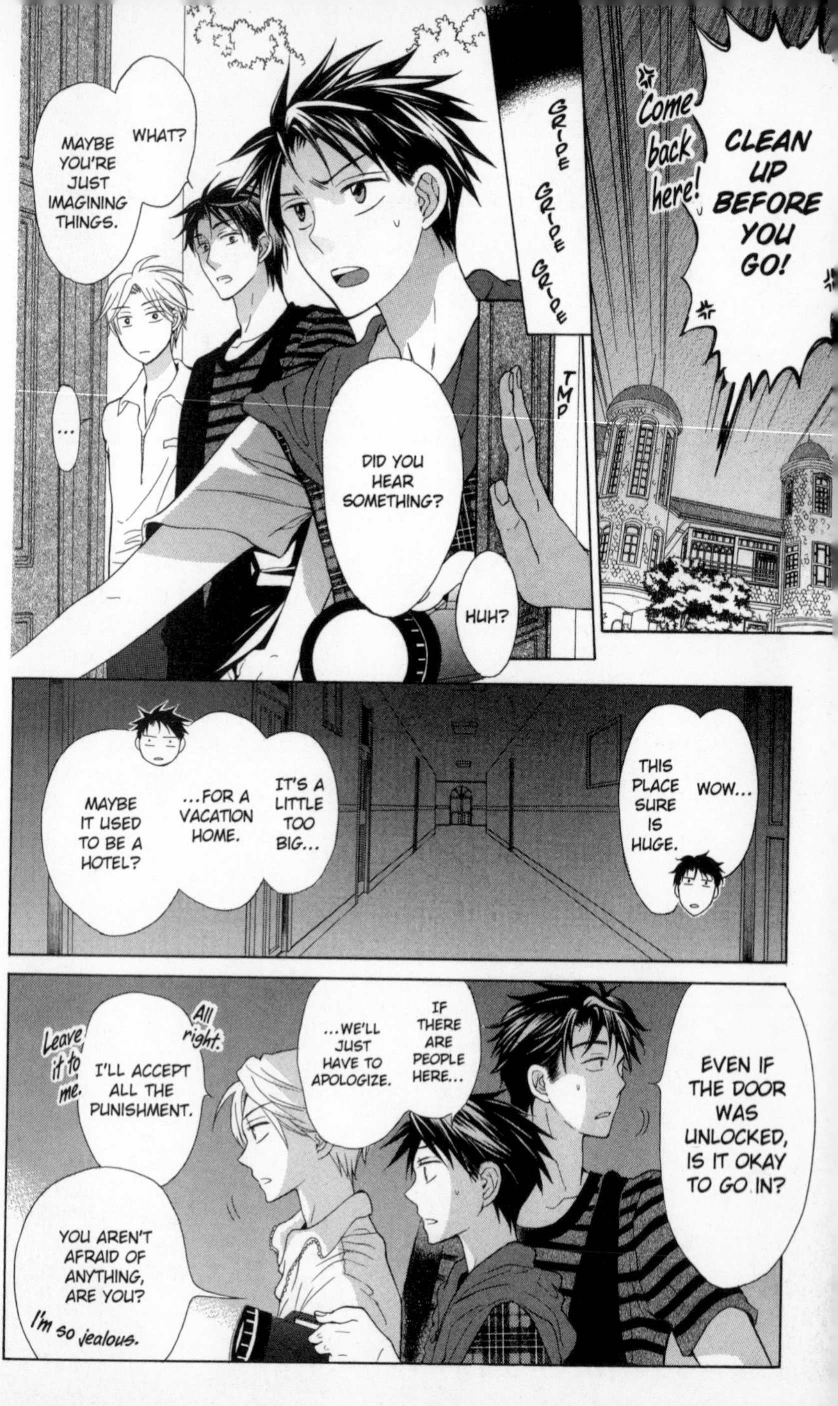
Come back here!
CLEAN UP BEFORE YOU GO!
GRIPE GRIPE GRIPE
TMP
DID YOU HEAR SOMETHING?
HUH?
WHAT?
MAYBE YOU'RE JUST IMAGINING THINGS.
...
WOW...
THIS PLACE SURE IS HUGE.
IT'S A LITTLE TOO BIG...
...FOR A VACATION HOME.
MAYBE IT USED TO BE A HOTEL?
EVEN IF THE DOOR WAS UNLOCKED, IS IT OKAY TO GO IN?
IF THERE ARE PEOPLE HERE...
...WE'LL JUST HAVE TO APOLOGIZE.
All right.
I'LL ACCEPT ALL THE PUNISHMENT.
Leave it to me.
YOU AREN'T AFRAID OF ANYTHING, ARE YOU?
I'm so jealous.

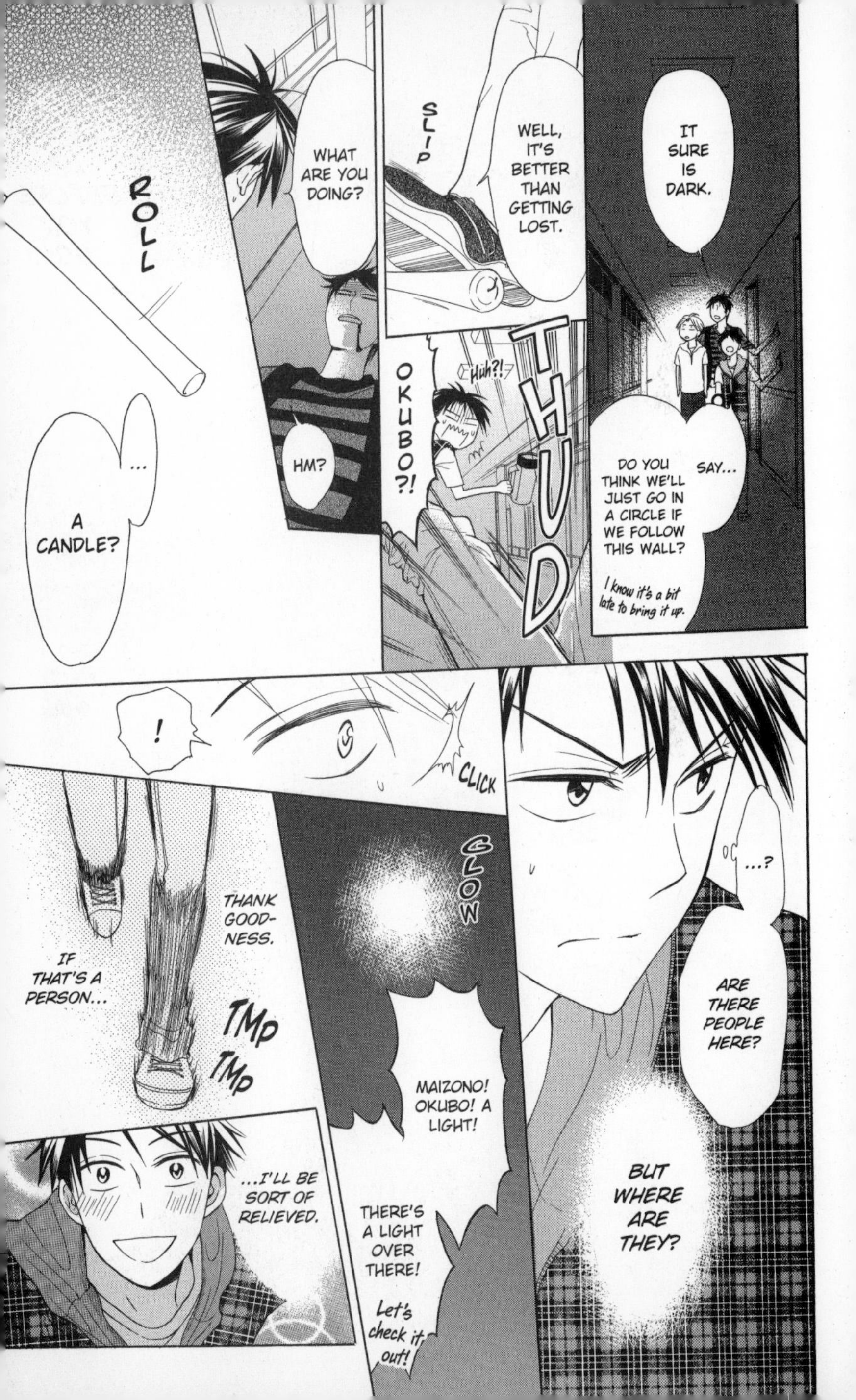
IT SURE IS DARK.
SAY...
DO YOU THINK WE'LL JUST GO IN A CIRCLE IF WE FOLLOW THIS WALL?
I know it's a bit late to bring it up.
WELL, IT'S BETTER THAN GETTING LOST.
SLIP
THUD
Huh?!
OKUBO?!
WHAT ARE YOU DOING?
HM?
ROLL
...
A CANDLE?
...?
ARE THERE PEOPLE HERE?
BUT WHERE ARE THEY?
!
CLICK
GLOW
MAIZONO! OKUBO! A LIGHT!
THERE'S A LIGHT OVER THERE!
Let's check it out!
THANK GOODNESS.
IF THAT'S A PERSON...
TMP
TMP
...I'LL BE SORT OF RELIEVED.

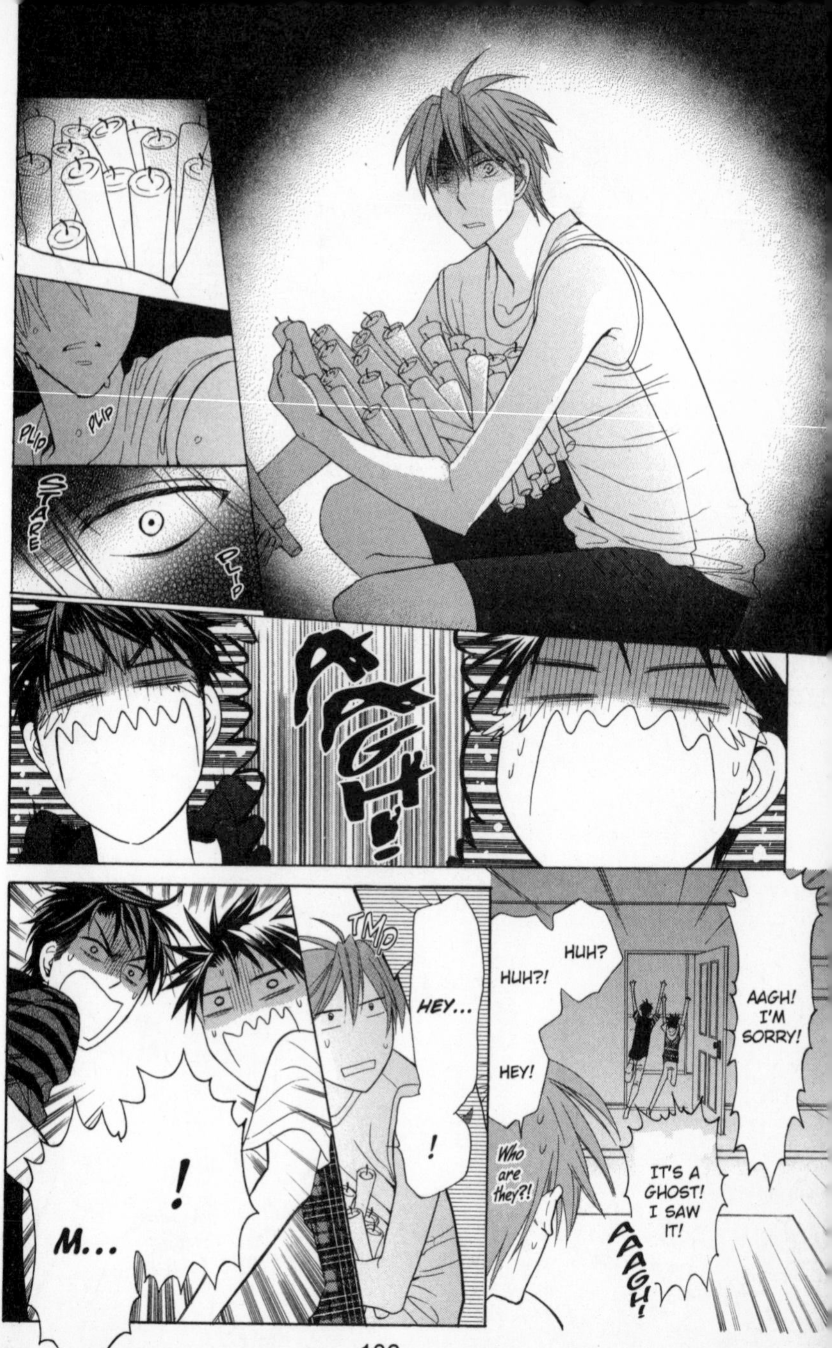
PLIP
PLIP
STARE
PLIP
AAGH!!
AAGH! I'M SORRY!
HUH?
HUH?!
HEY!
IT'S A GHOST! I SAW IT!
AAAGH!
Who are they?!
TMP
HEY...
!
!
M...

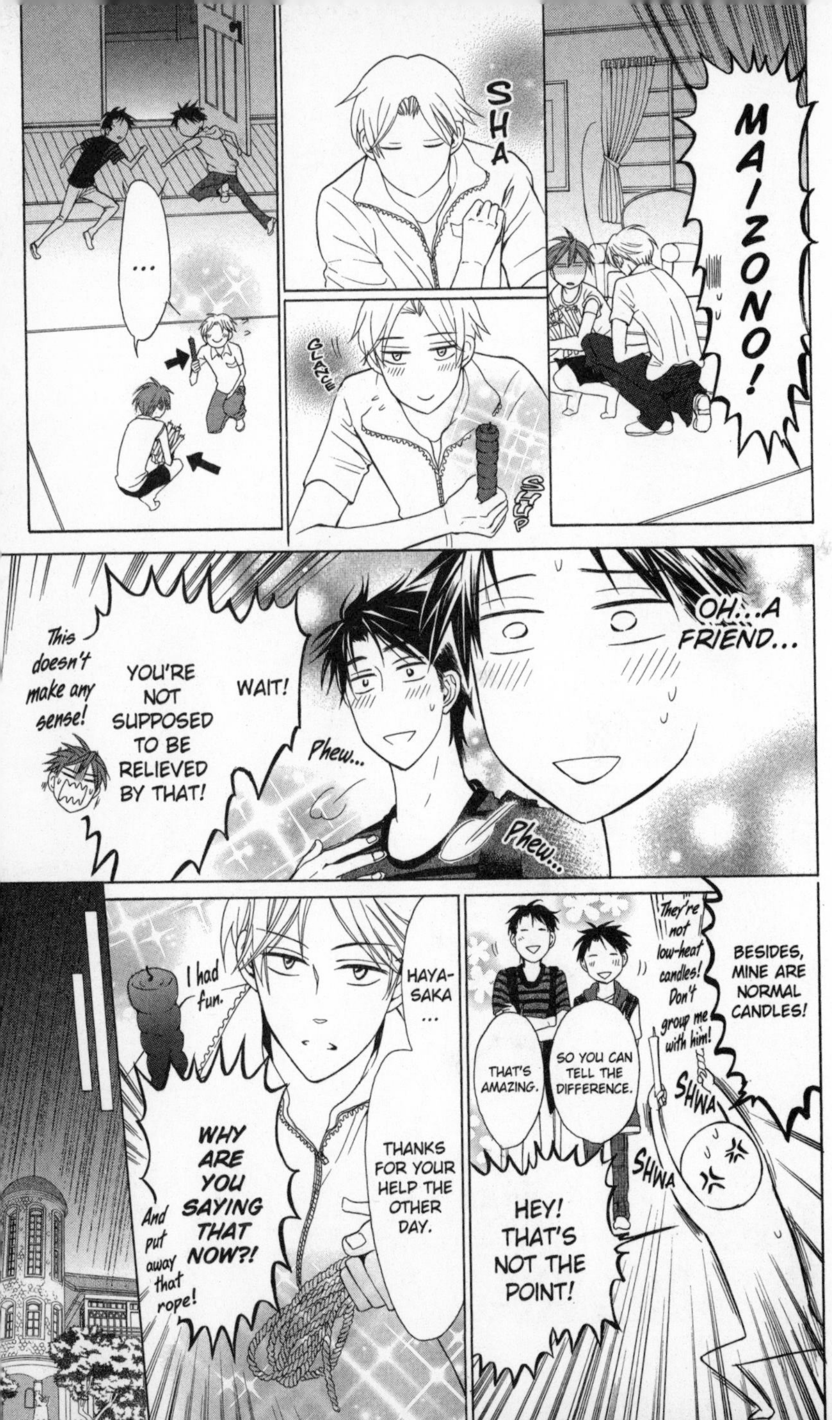
MAIZONO!
SHA
GLANCE
SHUP
...
OH...A FRIEND...
Phew...
Phew...
WAIT!
YOU'RE NOT SUPPOSED TO BE RELIEVED BY THAT!
This doesn't make any sense!
BESIDES, MINE ARE NORMAL CANDLES!
They're not low-heat candles! Don't group me with him!
SO YOU CAN TELL THE DIFFERENCE.
THAT'S AMAZING.
SHWA
SHWA
HEY! THAT'S NOT THE POINT!
HAYA-SAKA...
I had fun.
THANKS FOR YOUR HELP THE OTHER DAY.
WHY ARE YOU SAYING THAT NOW?!
And put away that rope!

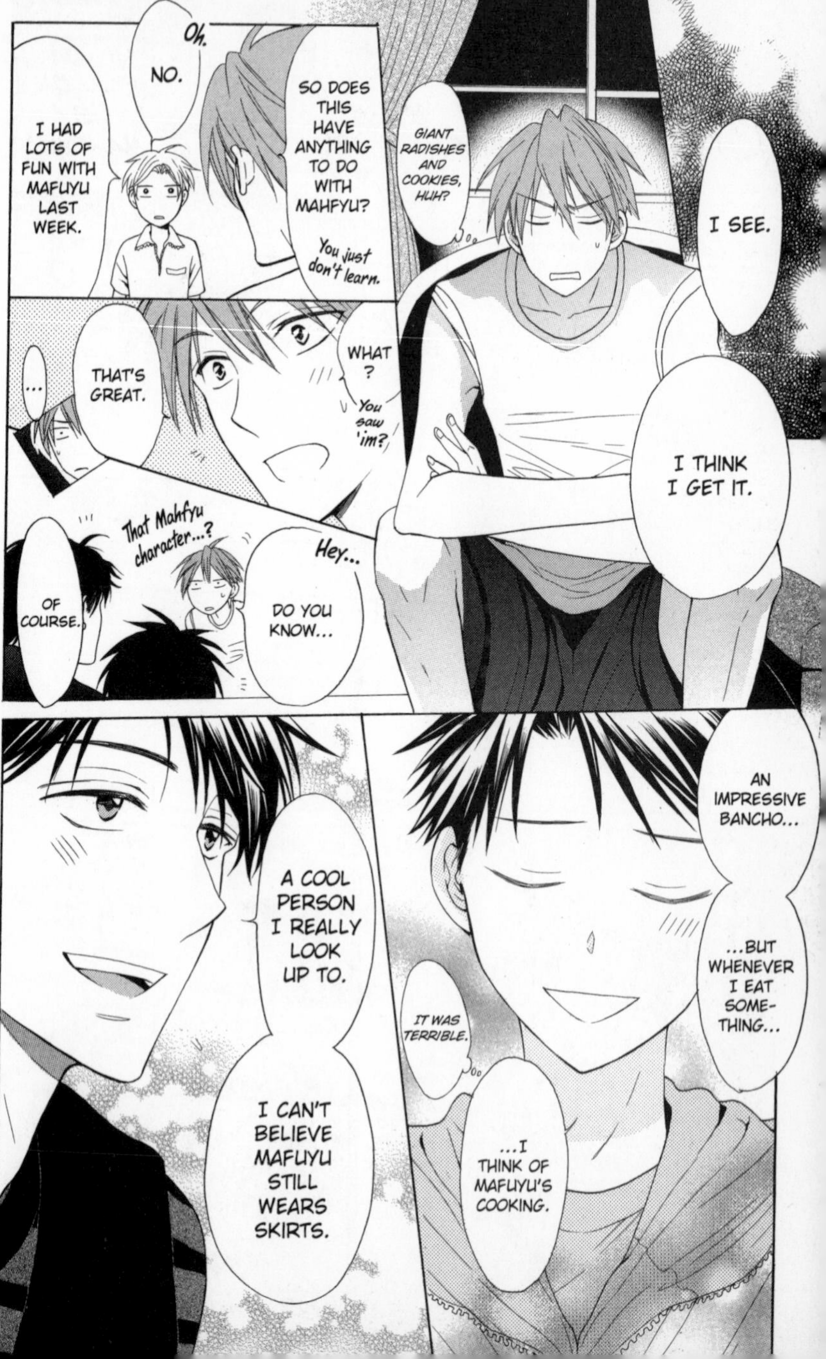
I SEE.
GIANT RADISHES AND COOKIES, HUH?
I THINK I GET IT.
SO DOES THIS HAVE ANYTHING TO DO WITH MAHFYU?
You just don't learn.
Oh.
NO.
I HAD LOTS OF FUN WITH MAFUYU LAST WEEK.
WHAT?
You saw 'im?
THAT'S GREAT.
...
Hey...
DO YOU KNOW...
That Mahfyu character...?
OF COURSE.
AN IMPRESSIVE BANCHO...
...BUT WHENEVER I EAT SOME-THING...
IT WAS TERRIBLE.
...I THINK OF MAFUYU'S COOKING.
A COOL PERSON I REALLY LOOK UP TO.
I CAN'T BELIEVE MAFUYU STILL WEARS SKIRTS.

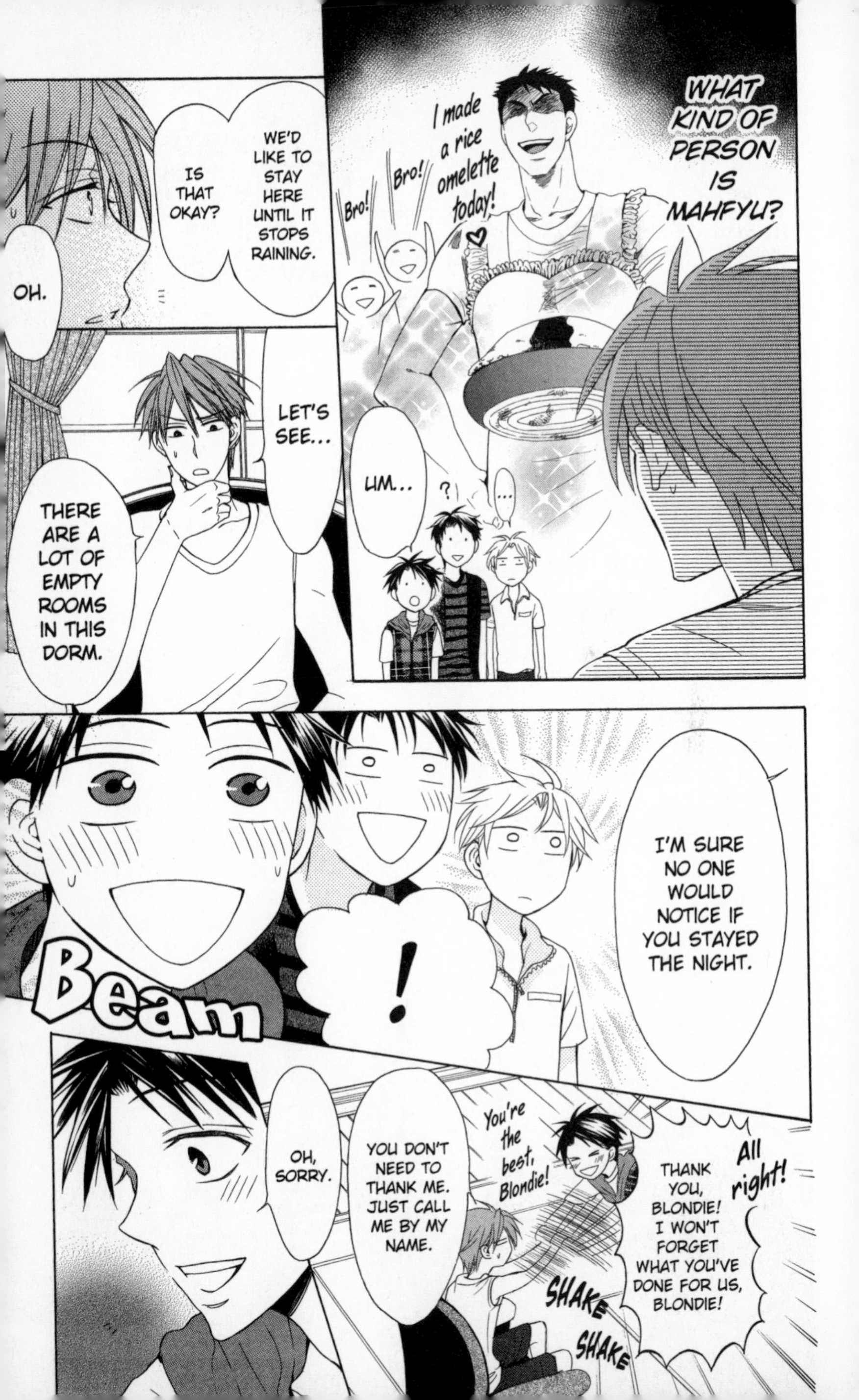
WHAT KIND OF PERSON IS MAHFYU?
I made a rice omelette today! ♥
Bro!
Bro!
UM...
?
...
WE'D LIKE TO STAY HERE UNTIL IT STOPS RAINING.
IS THAT OKAY?
OH.
LET'S SEE...
THERE ARE A LOT OF EMPTY ROOMS IN THIS DORM.
I'M SURE NO ONE WOULD NOTICE IF YOU STAYED THE NIGHT.
!
Beam
All right!
THANK YOU, BLONDIE! I WON'T FORGET WHAT YOU'VE DONE FOR US, BLONDIE!
You're the best, Blondie!
SHAKE
SHAKE
YOU DON'T NEED TO THANK ME. JUST CALL ME BY MY NAME.
OH, SORRY.

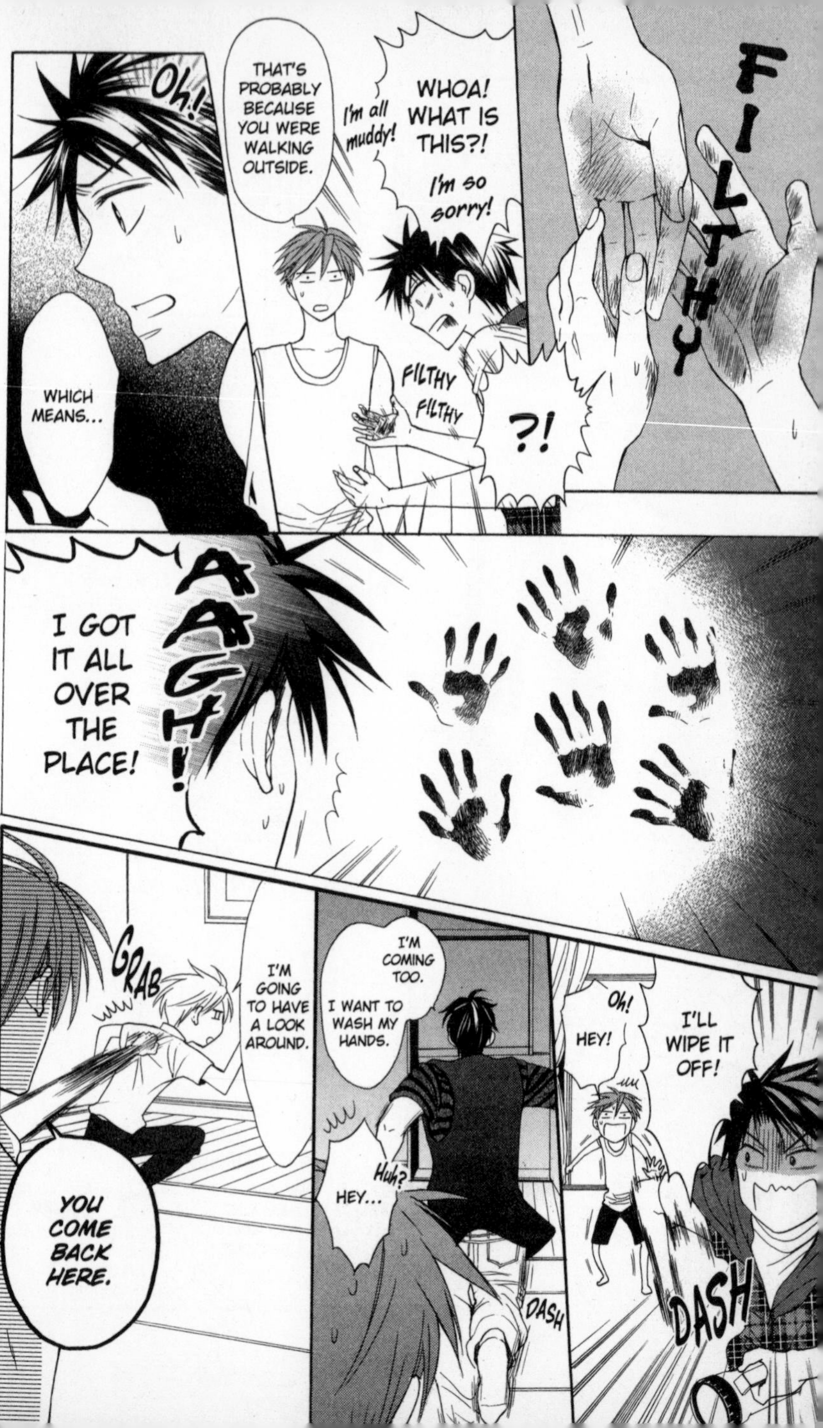
FILTHY
?!
WHOA! WHAT IS THIS?!
I'm all muddy!
I'm so sorry!
THAT'S PROBABLY BECAUSE YOU WERE WALKING OUTSIDE.
FILTHY FILTHY
OH!
WHICH MEANS...
AAGH!!
I GOT IT ALL OVER THE PLACE!
I'LL WIPE IT OFF!
Oh!
HEY!
DASH
I'M COMING TOO.
I WANT TO WASH MY HANDS.
Huh?
HEY...
DASH
I'M GOING TO HAVE A LOOK AROUND.
GRAB
YOU COME BACK HERE.

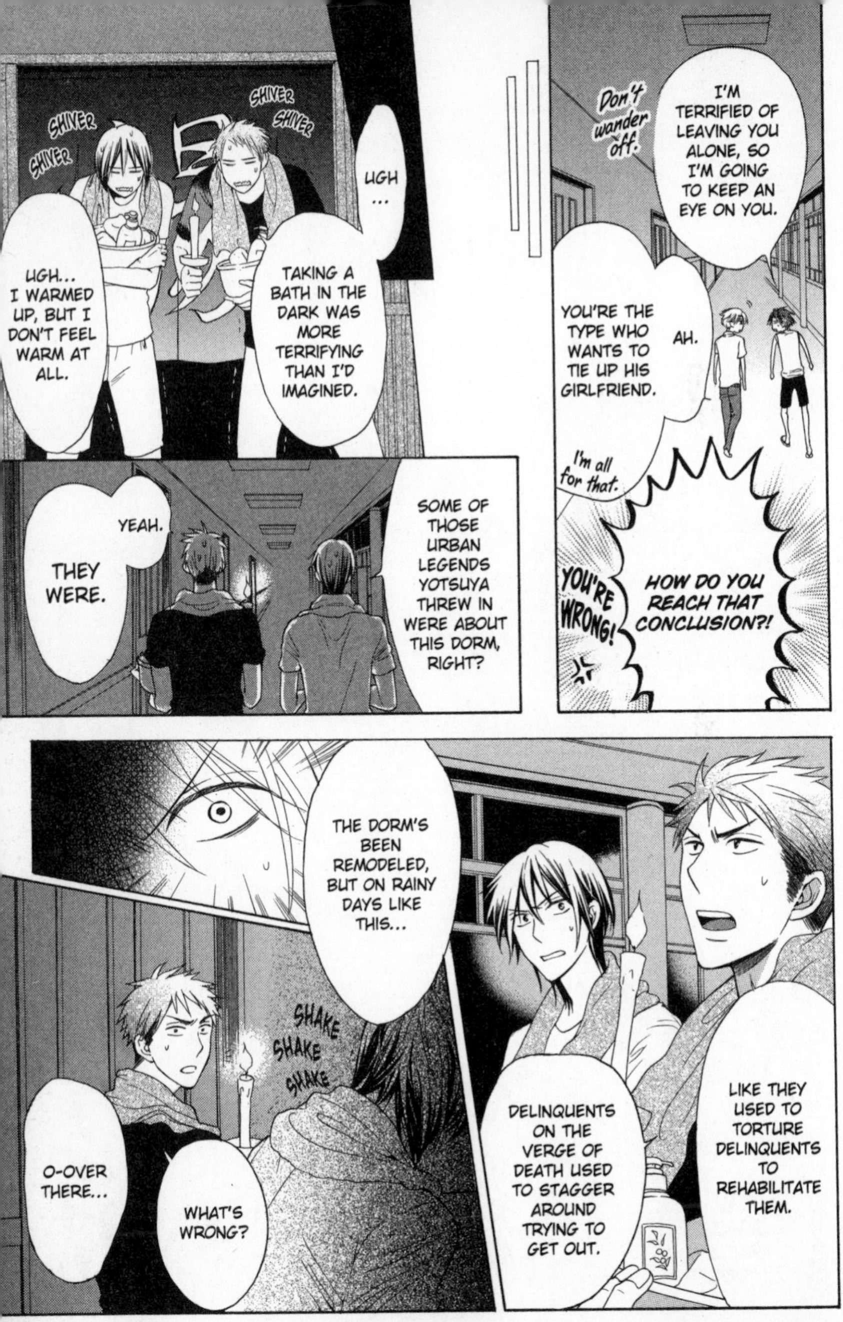
I'M TERRIFIED OF LEAVING YOU ALONE, SO I'M GOING TO KEEP AN EYE ON YOU.
Don't wander off.
AH.
YOU'RE THE TYPE WHO WANTS TO TIE UP HIS GIRLFRIEND.
I'm all for that.
HOW DO YOU REACH THAT CONCLUSION?!
YOU'RE WRONG!
UGH ...
TAKING A BATH IN THE DARK WAS MORE TERRIFYING THAN I'D IMAGINED.
SHIVER SHIVER
SHIVER SHIVER
UGH... I WARMED UP, BUT I DON'T FEEL WARM AT ALL.
SOME OF THOSE URBAN LEGENDS YOTSUYA THREW IN WERE ABOUT THIS DORM, RIGHT?
YEAH.
THEY WERE.
LIKE THEY USED TO TORTURE DELINQUENTS TO REHABILITATE THEM.
DELINQUENTS ON THE VERGE OF DEATH USED TO STAGGER AROUND TRYING TO GET OUT.
THE DORM'S BEEN REMODELED, BUT ON RAINY DAYS LIKE THIS...
SHAKE SHAKE SHAKE
WHAT'S WRONG?
O-OVER THERE...

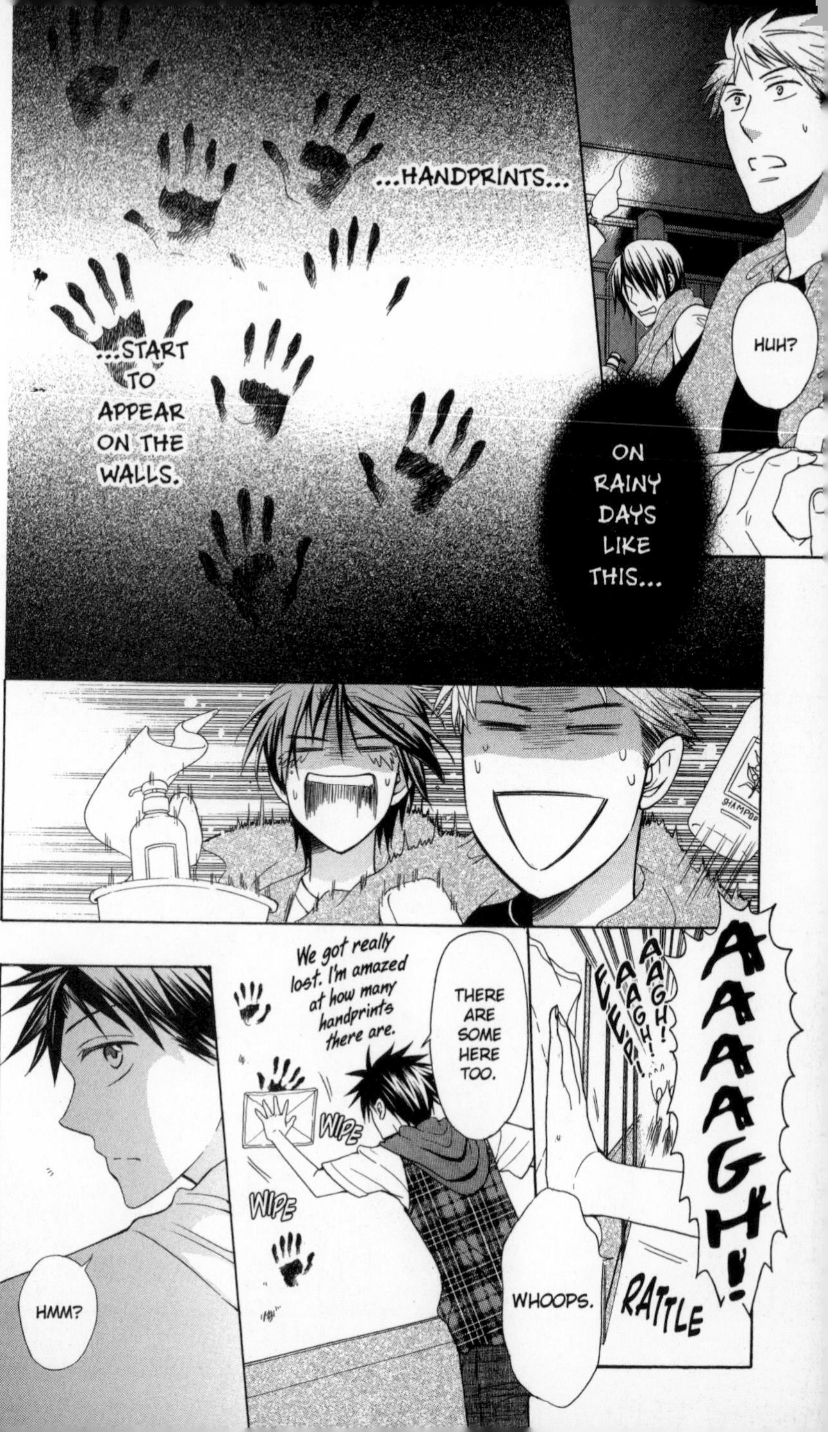
HUH?
ON RAINY DAYS LIKE THIS...
...HANDPRINTS...
...START TO APPEAR ON THE WALLS.
AAAAAGH!
AAGH!
AAAGH!
EEEP!
RATTLE
THERE ARE SOME HERE TOO.
WHOOPS.
We got really lost. I'm amazed at how many handprints there are.
WIPE
WIPE
HMM?

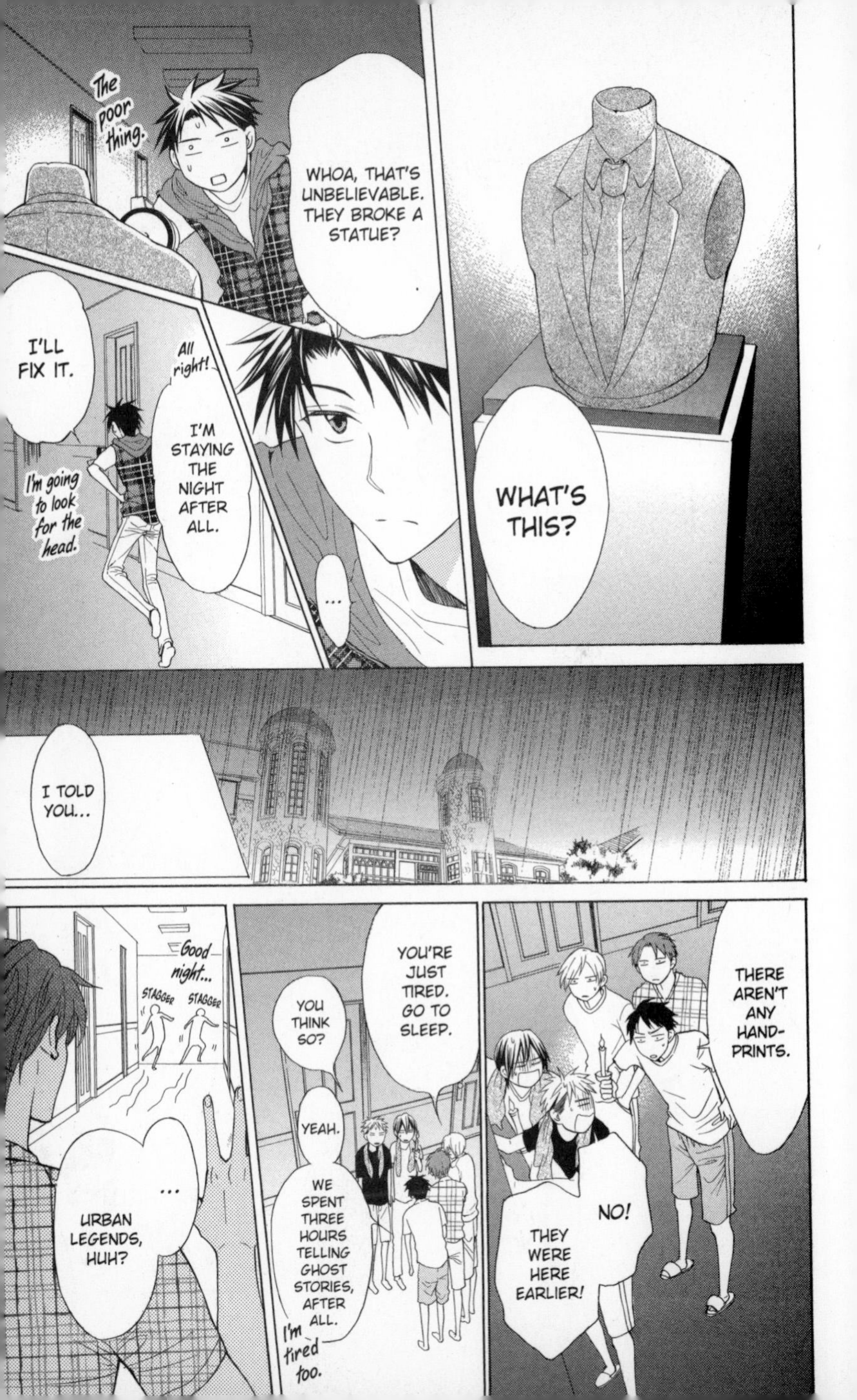
WHAT'S THIS?
WHOA, THAT'S UNBELIEVABLE. THEY BROKE A STATUE?
The poor thing.
...
All right!
I'M STAYING THE NIGHT AFTER ALL.
I'LL FIX IT.
I'm going to look for the head.
I TOLD YOU...
THERE AREN'T ANY HAND-PRINTS.
NO!
THEY WERE HERE EARLIER!
YOU'RE JUST TIRED. GO TO SLEEP.
YOU THINK SO?
YEAH.
WE SPENT THREE HOURS TELLING GHOST STORIES, AFTER ALL.
I'm tired too.
Good night...
STAGGER
STAGGER
...
URBAN LEGENDS, HUH?

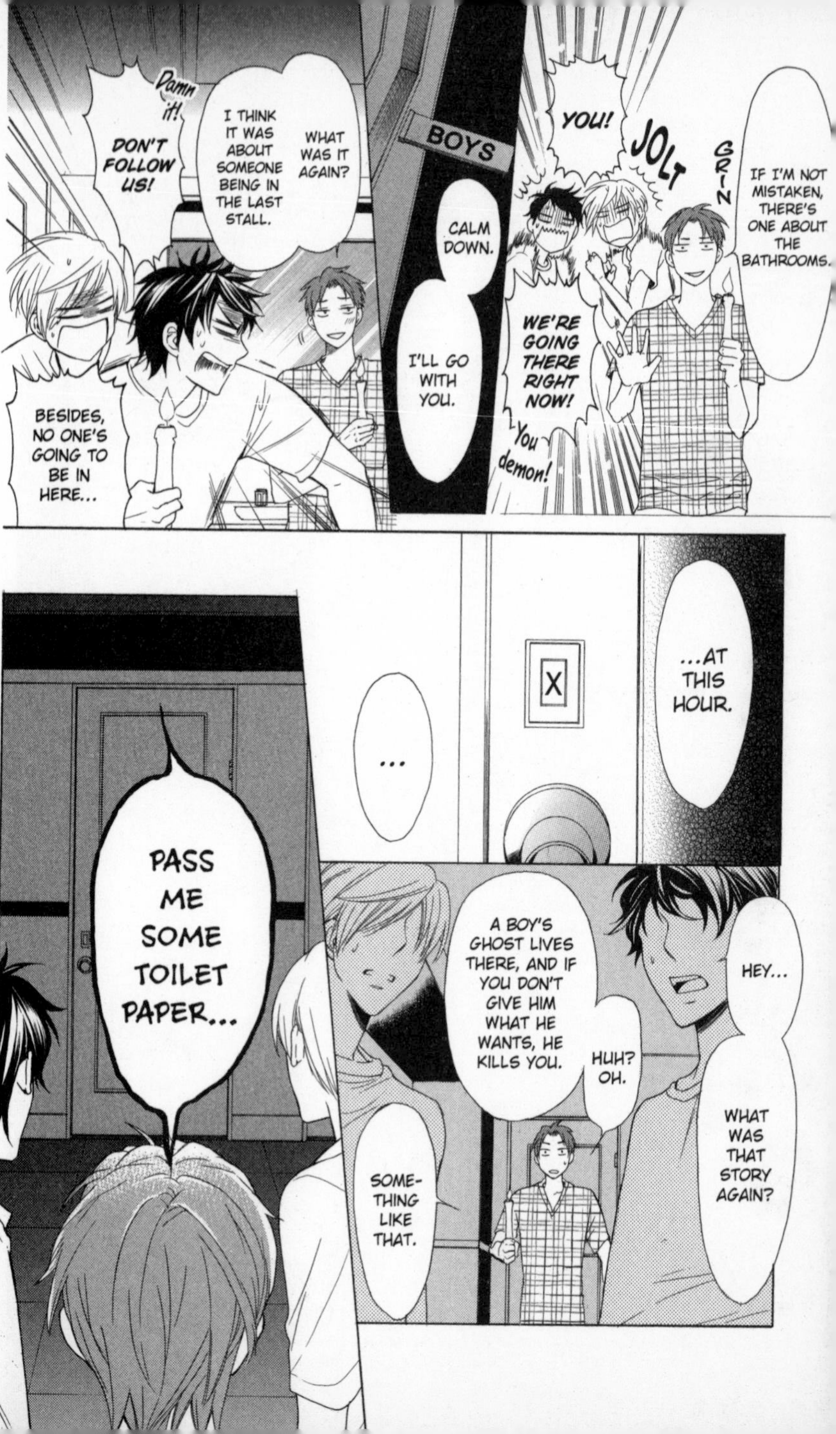

IF I'M NOT MISTAKEN, THERE'S ONE ABOUT THE BATHROOMS.
GRIN
JOLT
YOU!
WE'RE GOING THERE RIGHT NOW!
You demon!
BOYS
CALM DOWN.
I'LL GO WITH YOU.
Damn it!
DON'T FOLLOW US!
WHAT WAS IT AGAIN?
I THINK IT WAS ABOUT SOMEONE BEING IN THE LAST STALL.
BESIDES, NO ONE'S GOING TO BE IN HERE...
...AT THIS HOUR.
...
X
HEY...
WHAT WAS THAT STORY AGAIN?
HUH? OH.
A BOY'S GHOST LIVES THERE, AND IF YOU DON'T GIVE HIM WHAT HE WANTS, HE KILLS YOU.
SOME-THING LIKE THAT.
PASS ME SOME TOILET PAPER...

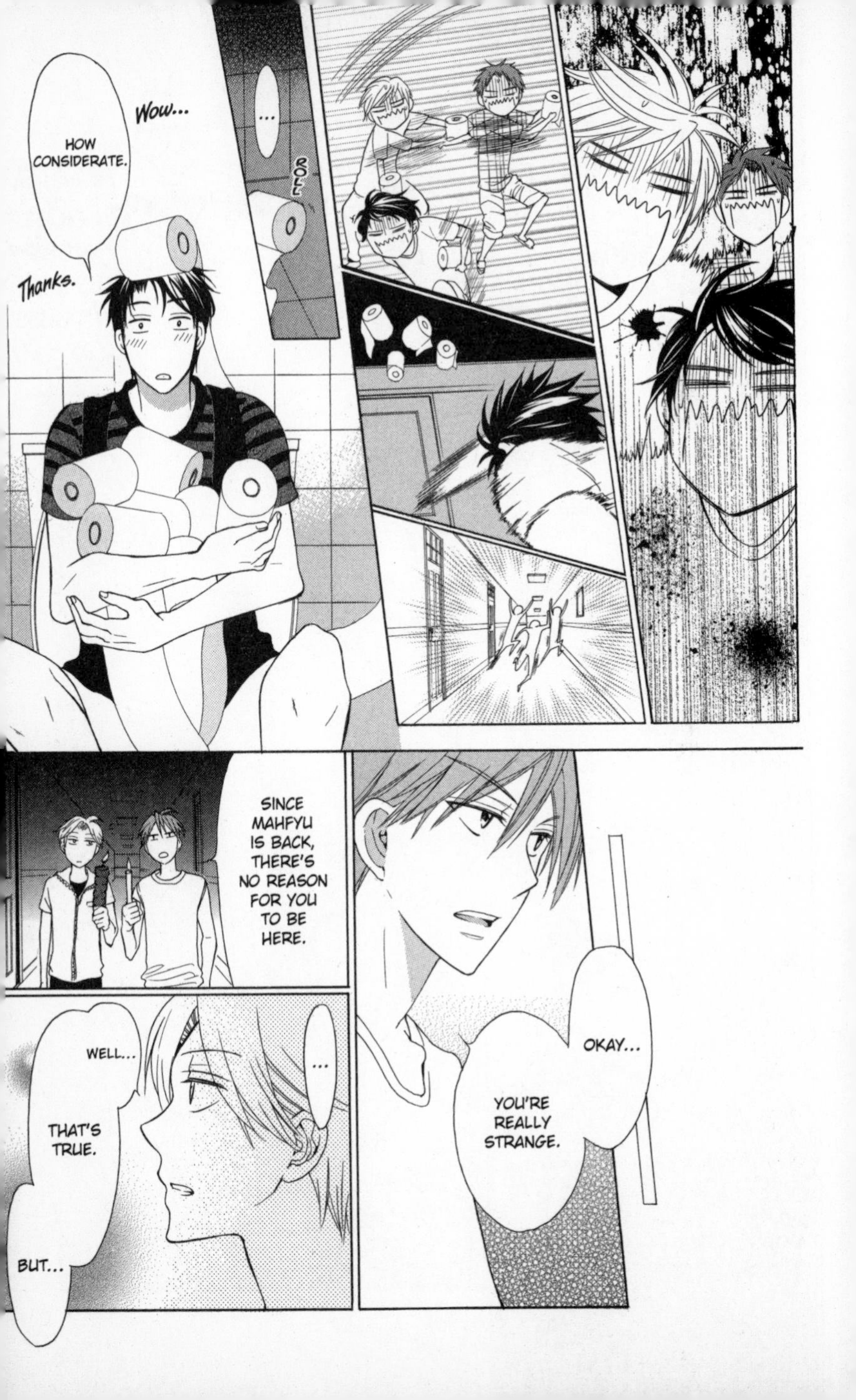
...
ROLL
Wow...
HOW CONSIDERATE.
Thanks.
OKAY...
YOU'RE REALLY STRANGE.
SINCE MAHFYU IS BACK, THERE'S NO REASON FOR YOU TO BE HERE.
...
WELL...
THAT'S TRUE.
BUT...

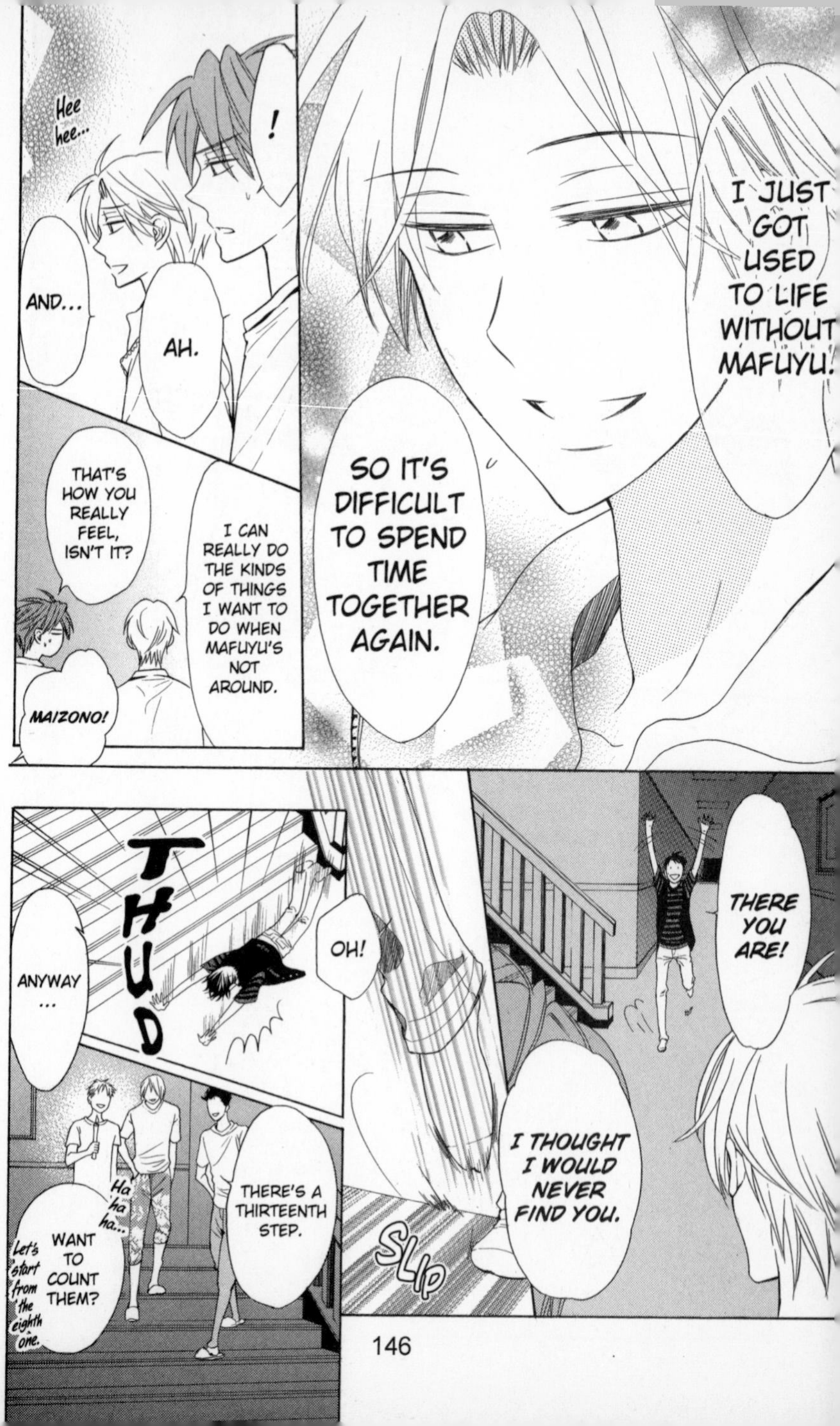
I JUST GOT USED TO LIFE WITHOUT MAFUYU!
SO IT'S DIFFICULT TO SPEND TIME TOGETHER AGAIN.
!
Hee hee...
AH.
AND...
I CAN REALLY DO THE KINDS OF THINGS I WANT TO DO WHEN MAFUYU'S NOT AROUND.
THAT'S HOW YOU REALLY FEEL, ISN'T IT?
MAIZONO!
THERE YOU ARE!
I THOUGHT I WOULD NEVER FIND YOU.
SLIP
OH!
THUD
ANYWAY...
THERE'S A THIRTEENTH STEP.
Ha ha ha...
WANT TO COUNT THEM?
Let's start from the eighth one.

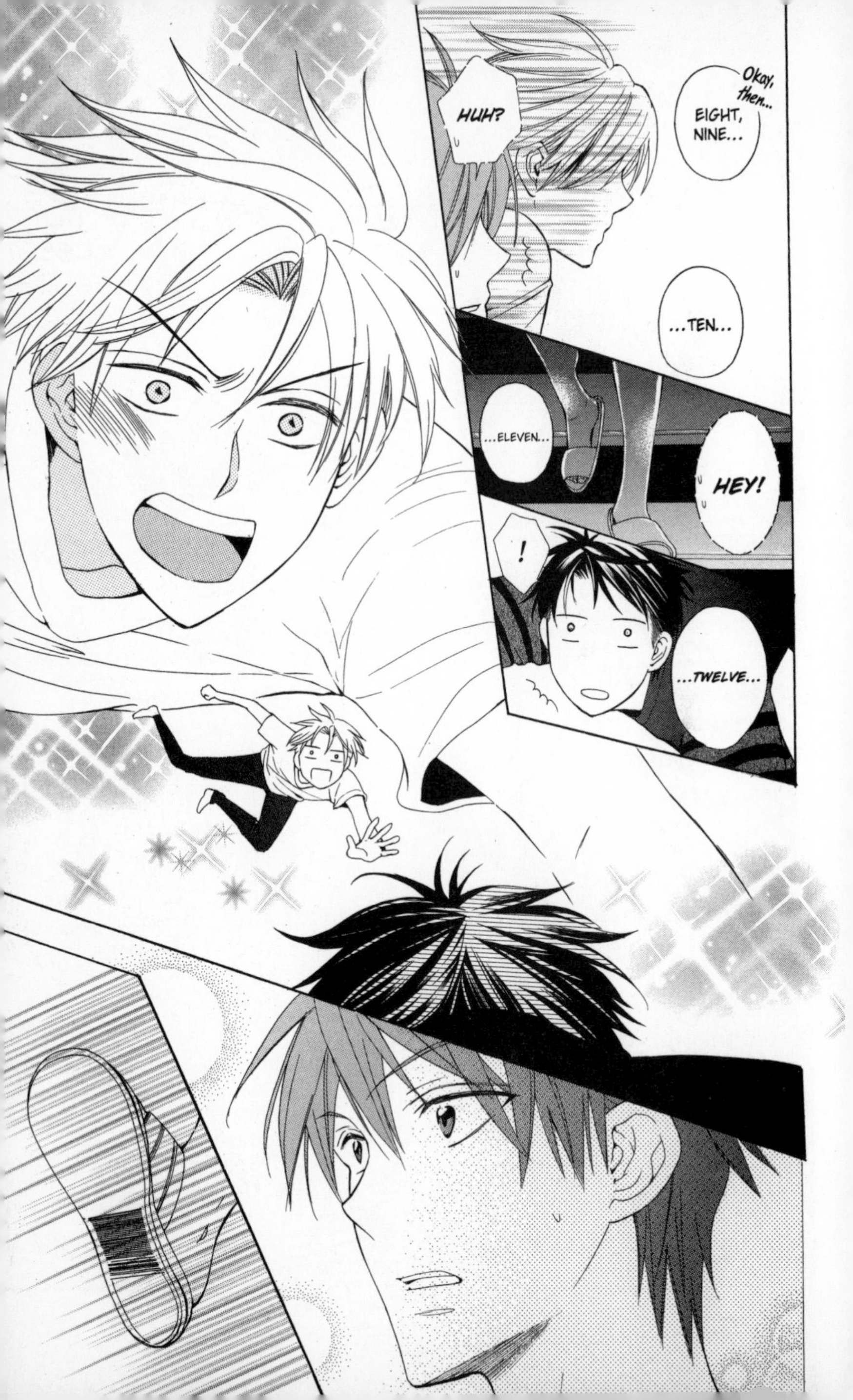
Okay, then...
EIGHT, NINE...
HUH?
...TEN...
HEY!
...ELEVEN...
...TWELVE...
!

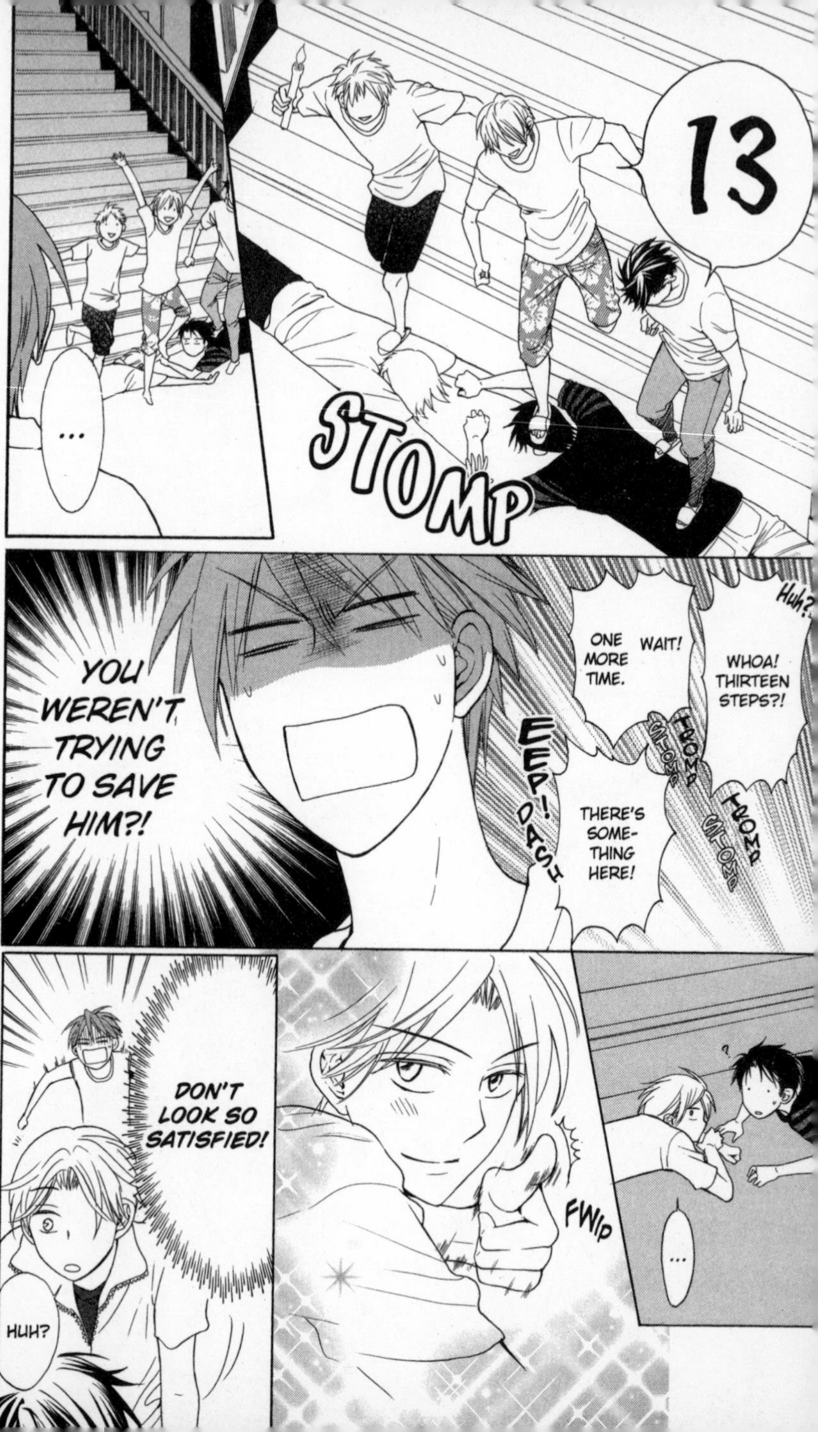
13
STOMP
...
Huh?!
WHOA! THIRTEEN STEPS?!
WAIT!
ONE MORE TIME.
TROMP STOMP
TROMP STOMP
THERE'S SOME-THING HERE!
EEP! DASH
YOU WEREN'T TRYING TO SAVE HIM?!
...
FWIP
DON'T LOOK SO SATISFIED!
HUH?

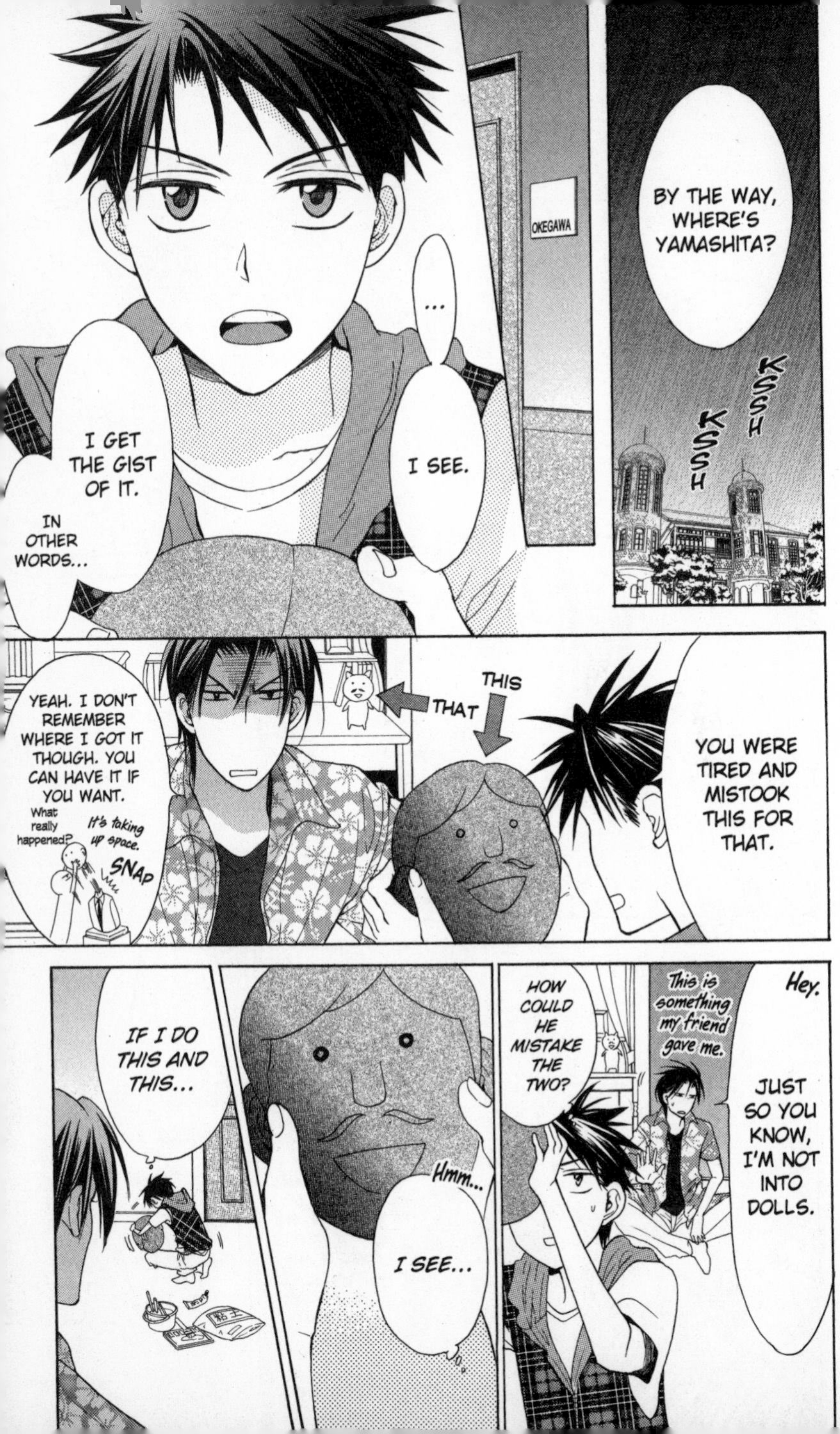
OKEGAWA
BY THE WAY, WHERE'S YAMASHITA?
KSSH
KSSH
...
I SEE.
I GET THE GIST OF IT.
IN OTHER WORDS...
YOU WERE TIRED AND MISTOOK THIS FOR THAT.
THIS
THAT
YEAH. I DON'T REMEMBER WHERE I GOT IT THOUGH. YOU CAN HAVE IT IF YOU WANT.
It's taking up space.
What really happened?
SNAP
Hey.
JUST SO YOU KNOW, I'M NOT INTO DOLLS.
This is something my friend gave me.
HOW COULD HE MISTAKE THE TWO?
Hmm...
I SEE...
IF I DO THIS AND THIS...

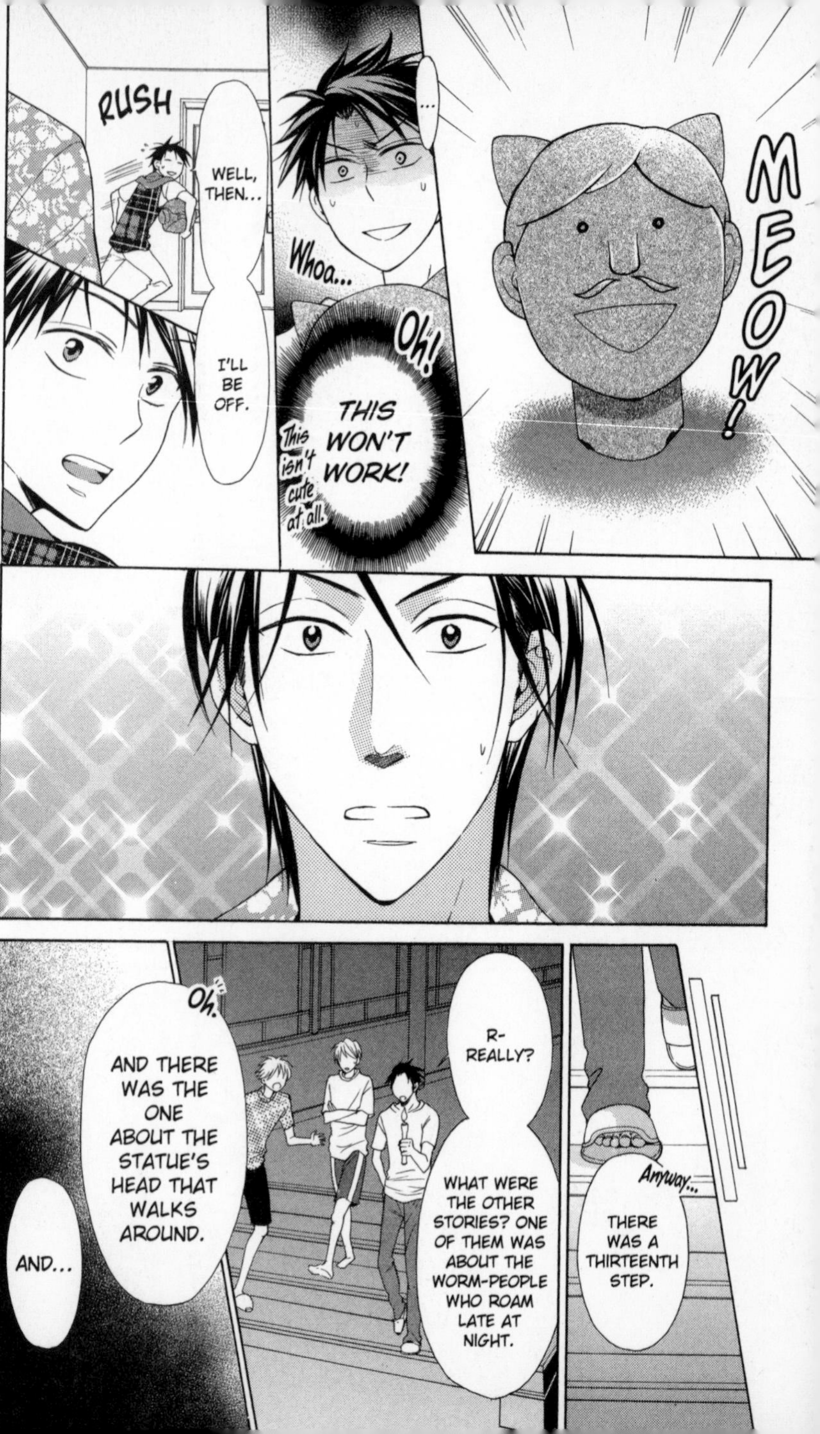
MEOW!
...
Whoa...
Oh!
THIS WON'T WORK!
This isn't cute at all.
RUSH
WELL, THEN...
I'LL BE OFF.
Anyway...
THERE WAS A THIRTEENTH STEP.
R-REALLY?
WHAT WERE THE OTHER STORIES? ONE OF THEM WAS ABOUT THE WORM-PEOPLE WHO ROAM LATE AT NIGHT.
Oh.
AND THERE WAS THE ONE ABOUT THE STATUE'S HEAD THAT WALKS AROUND.
AND...

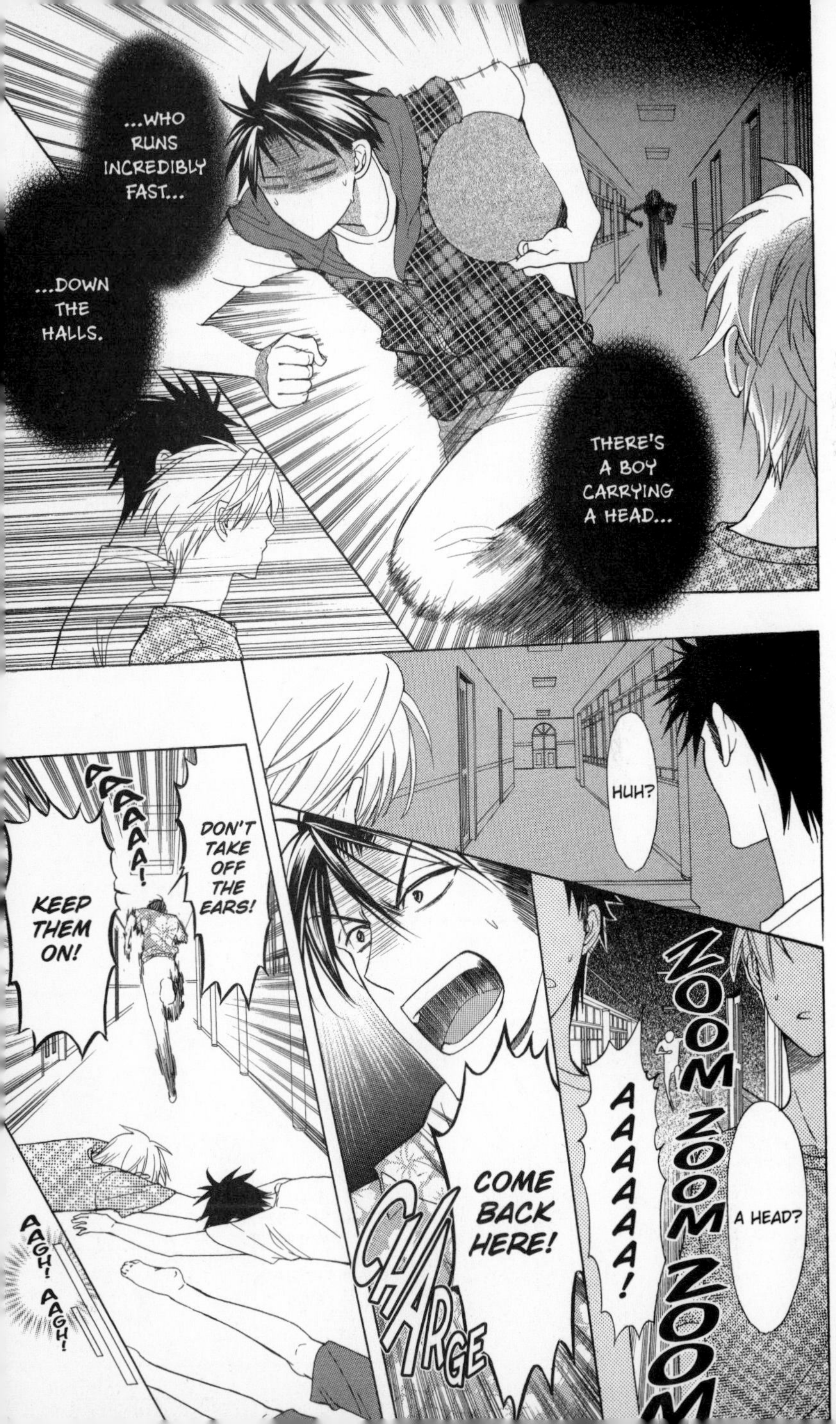
THERE'S A BOY CARRYING A HEAD...
...WHO RUNS INCREDIBLY FAST...
...DOWN THE HALLS.
HUH?
A HEAD?
ZOOM ZOOM ZOOM
AAAAAAA!
COME BACK HERE!
CHARGE
AAAAAA!
DON'T TAKE OFF THE EARS!
KEEP THEM ON!
AAGH! AAGH!

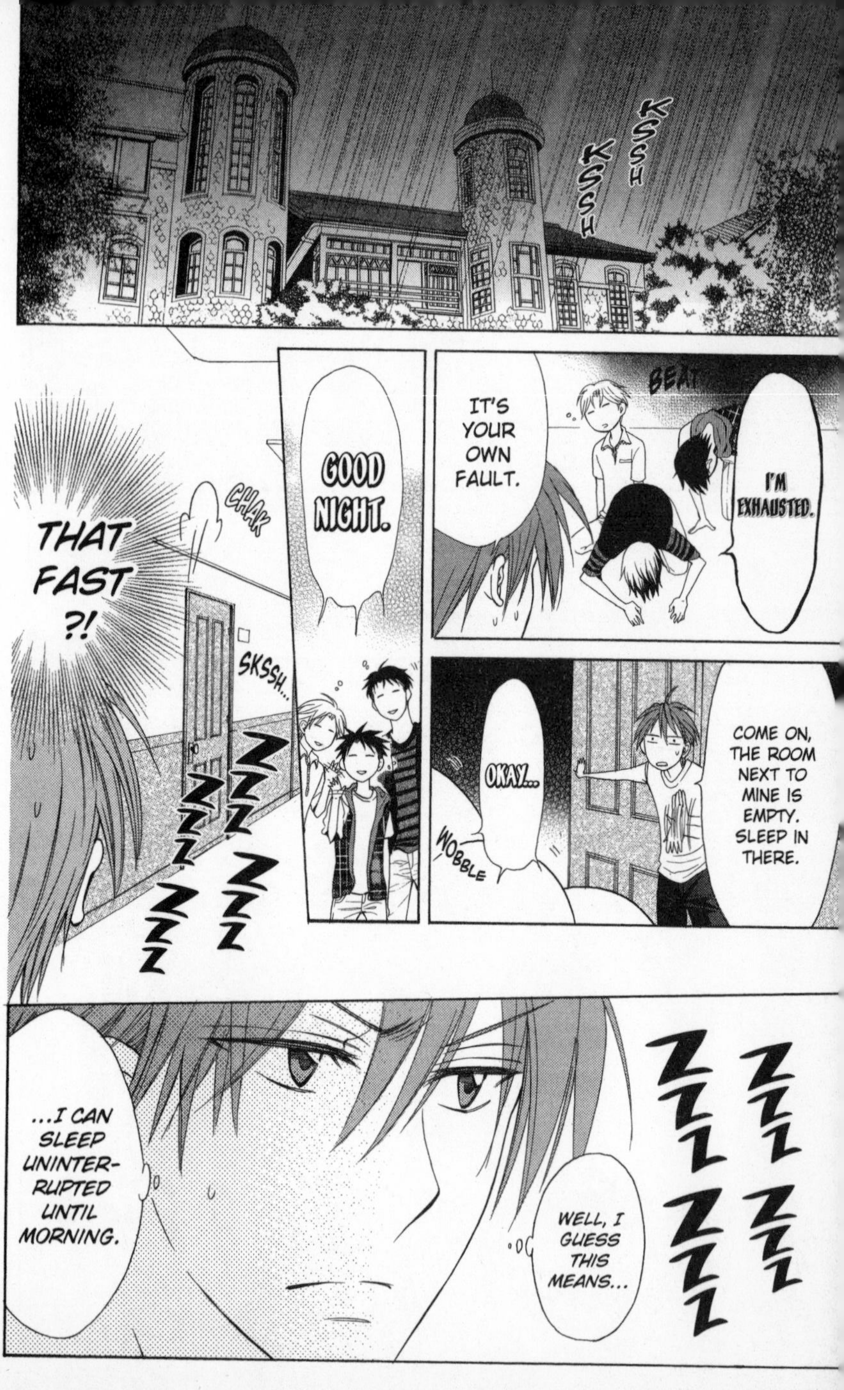
KSSH
KSSH
BEAT
I'M EXHAUSTED.
IT'S YOUR OWN FAULT.
COME ON, THE ROOM NEXT TO MINE IS EMPTY. SLEEP IN THERE.
OKAY...
WOBBLE
GOOD NIGHT.
CHAK
SKSSH...
ZZZ
ZZZ
ZZZ
ZZZ
THAT FAST?!
ZZZ
ZZZ
ZZZ
ZZZ
WELL, I GUESS THIS MEANS...
...I CAN SLEEP UNINTER-RUPTED UNTIL MORNING.

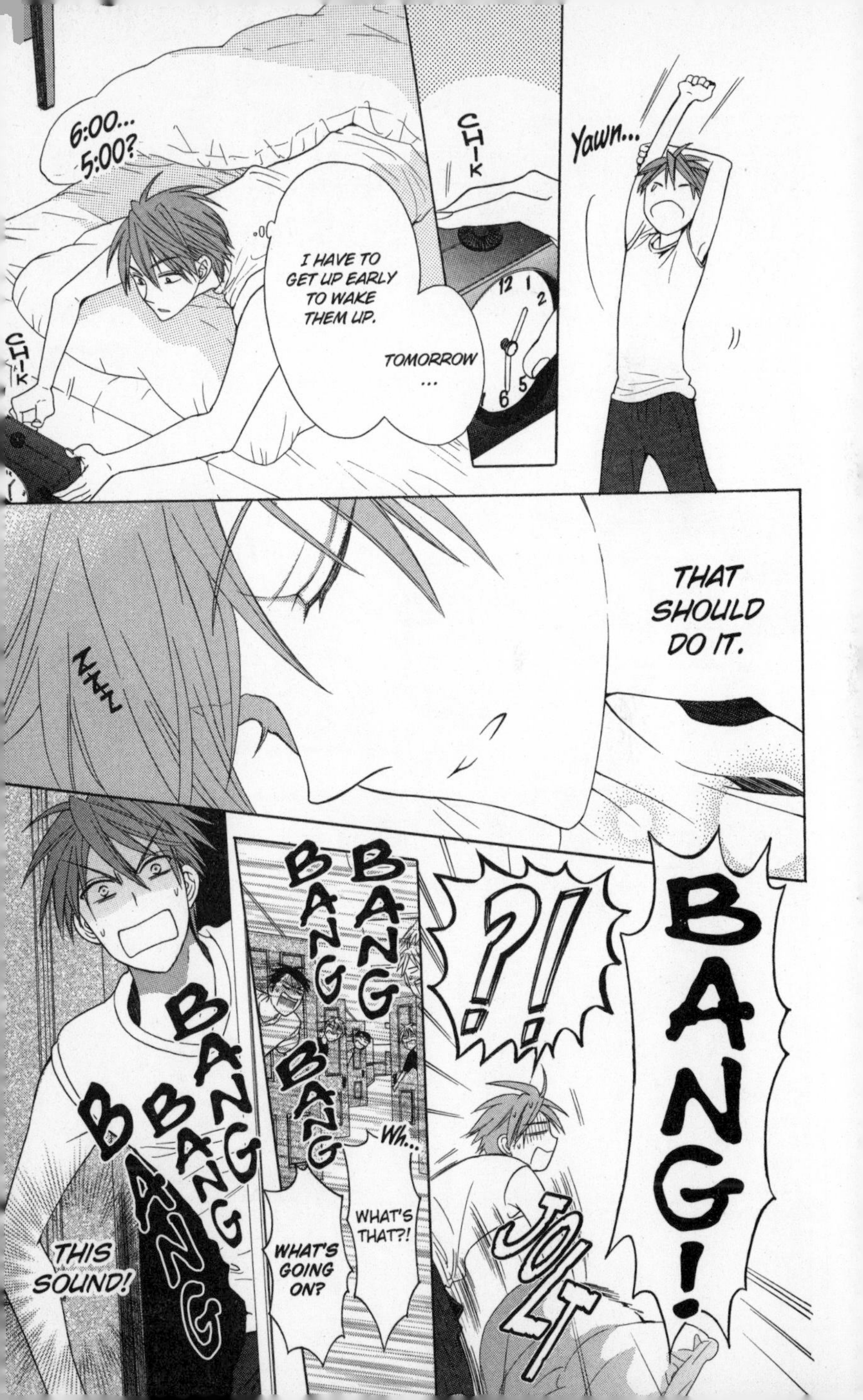
Yawn...
CHIK
TOMORROW ...
I HAVE TO GET UP EARLY TO WAKE THEM UP.
6:00... 5:00?
CHIK
THAT SHOULD DO IT.
NNN
BANG!
?!
JOLT
BANG BANG
BANG
Wh...
WHAT'S THAT?!
WHAT'S GOING ON?
BANG BANG
BANG BANG
THIS SOUND!

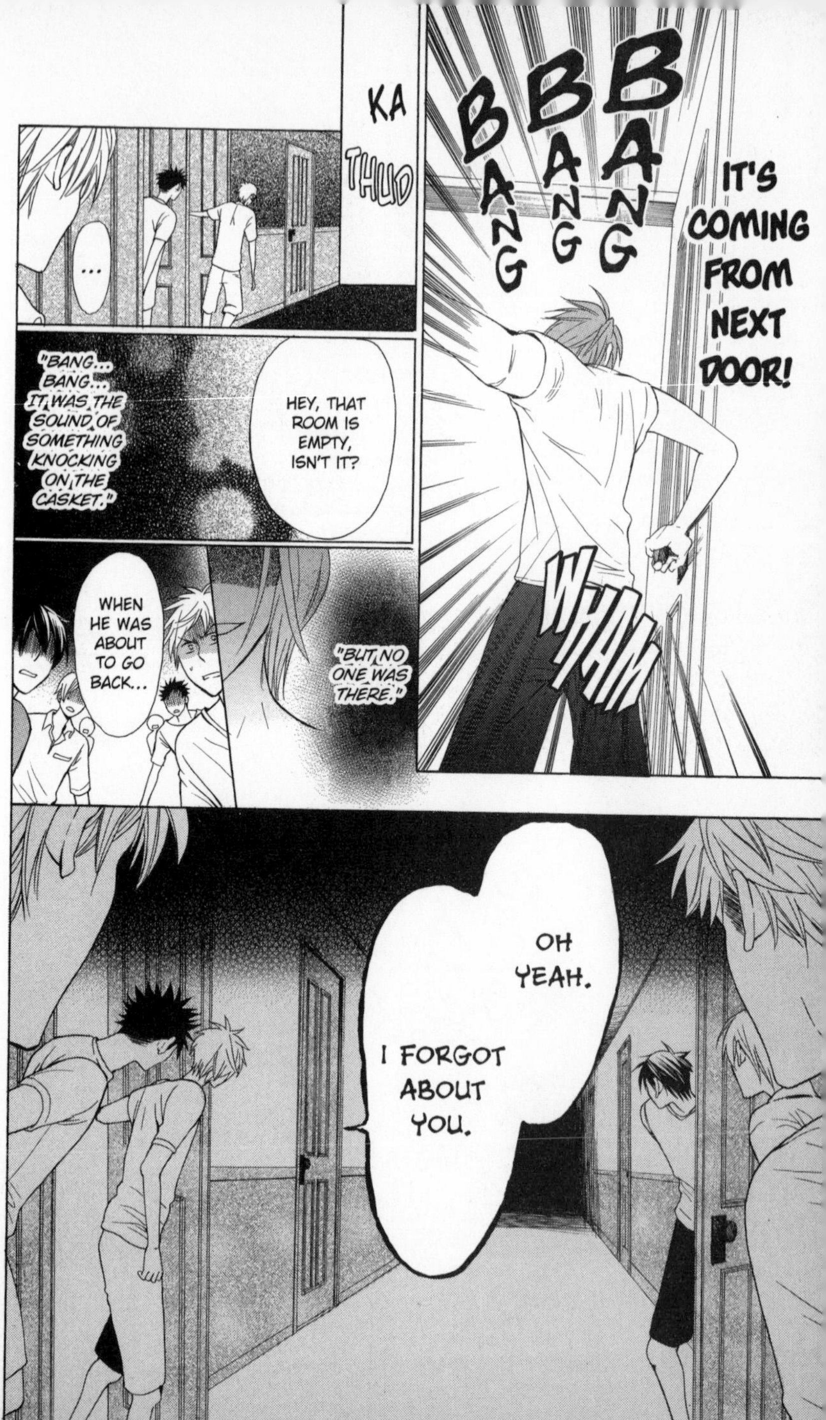
BANG BANG BANG
IT'S COMING FROM NEXT DOOR!
WHAM
KA
THUD
...
HEY, THAT ROOM IS EMPTY, ISN'T IT?
"BANG... BANG... IT WAS THE SOUND OF SOMETHING KNOCKING ON THE CASKET."
"BUT NO ONE WAS THERE."
WHEN HE WAS ABOUT TO GO BACK...
OH YEAH.
I FORGOT ABOUT YOU.

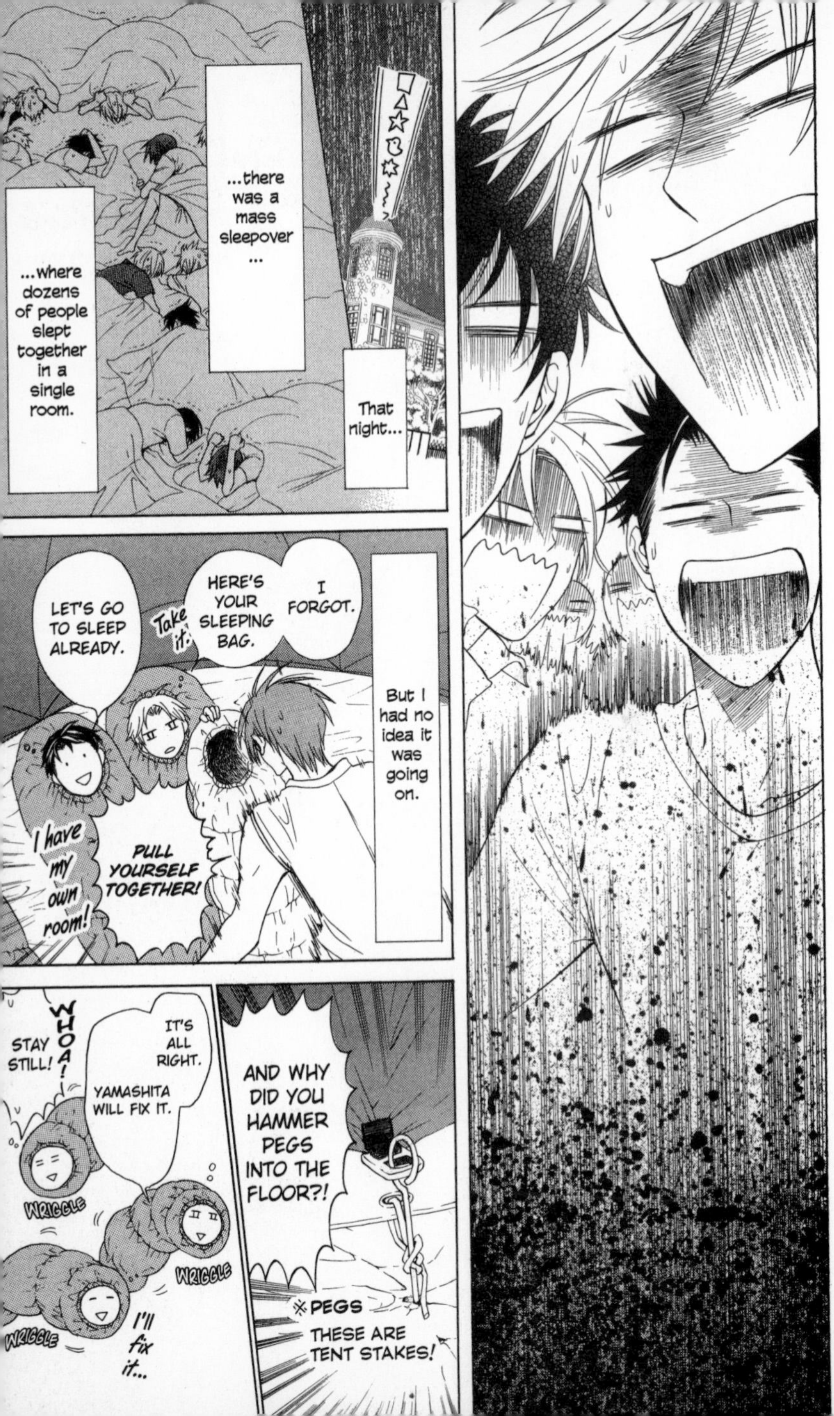
That night...
...there was a mass sleepover...
...where dozens of people slept together in a single room.
But I had no idea it was going on.
I FORGOT.
HERE'S YOUR SLEEPING BAG.
Take it.
LET'S GO TO SLEEP ALREADY.
PULL YOURSELF TOGETHER!
I have my own room!
AND WHY DID YOU HAMMER PEGS INTO THE FLOOR?!
※PEGS
THESE ARE TENT STAKES!
IT'S ALL RIGHT.
YAMASHITA WILL FIX IT.
WHOA!
STAY STILL!
WRIGGLE
WRIGGLE
WRIGGLE
I'll fix it...

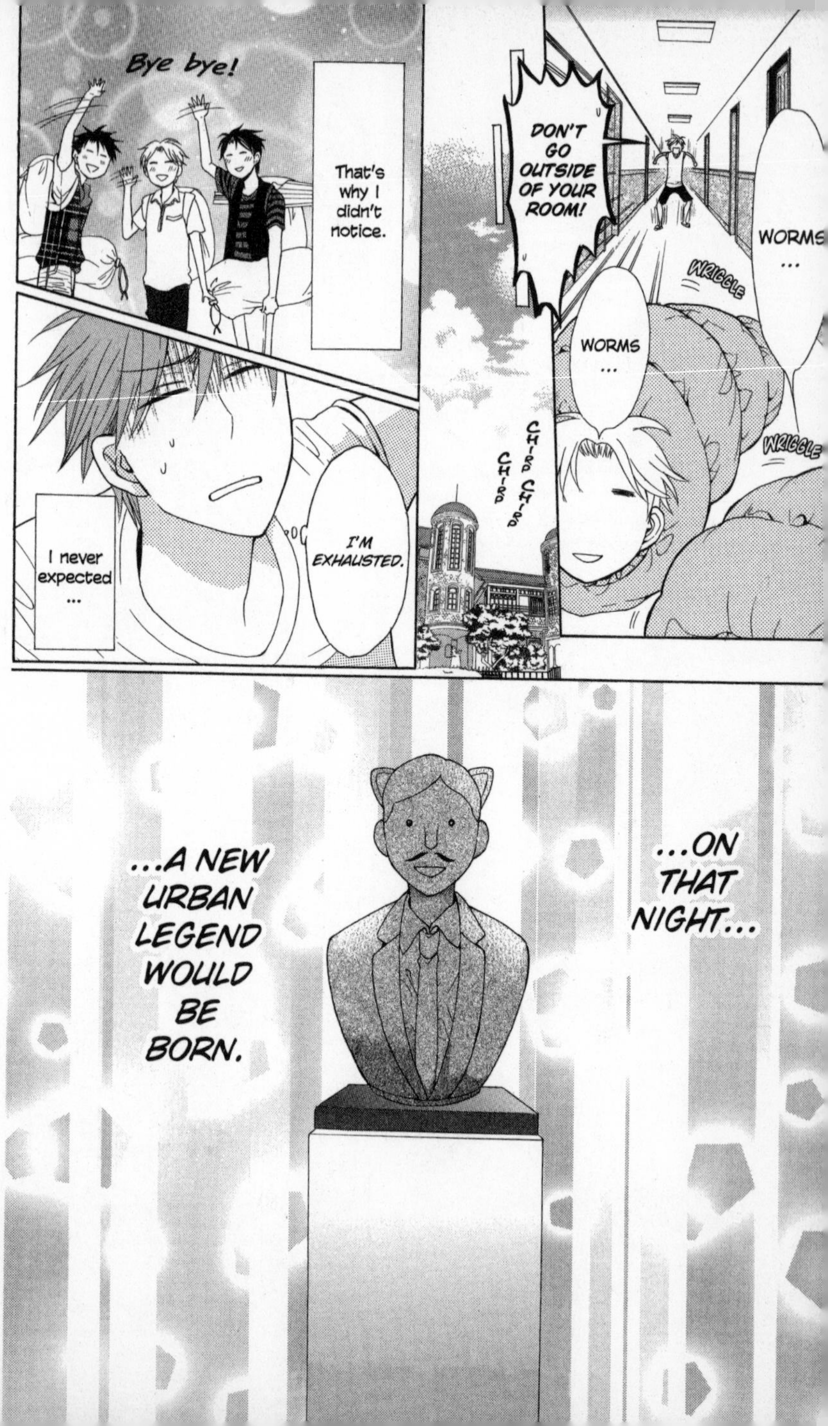
DON'T GO OUTSIDE OF YOUR ROOM!
WORMS ...
WRIGGLE
WORMS ...
WRIGGLE
CHIRP CHIRP CHIRP
Bye bye!
That's why I didn't notice.
I'M EXHAUSTED.
I never expected ...
...ON THAT NIGHT...
...A NEW URBAN LEGEND WOULD BE BORN.

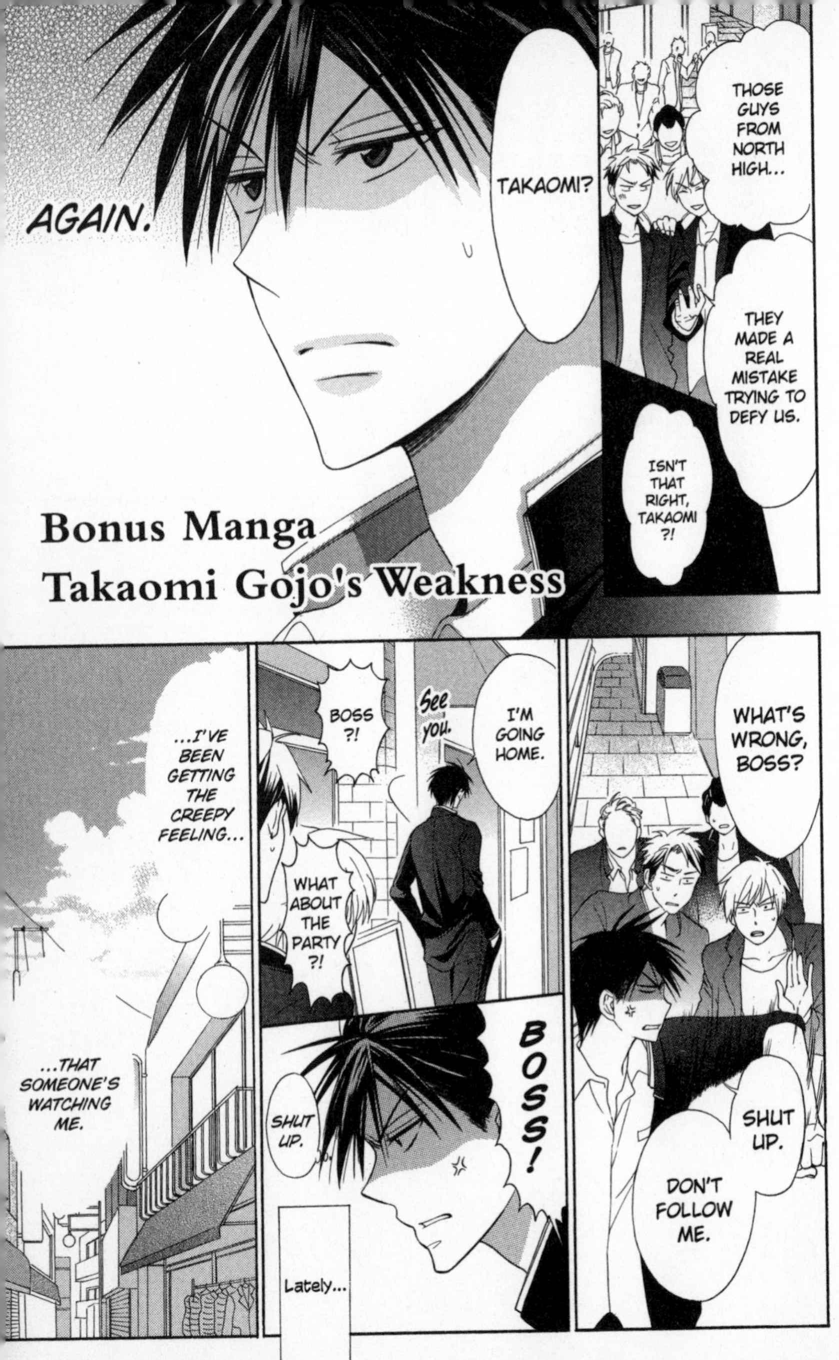
THOSE GUYS FROM NORTH HIGH...
THEY MADE A REAL MISTAKE TRYING TO DEFY US.
ISN'T THAT RIGHT, TAKAOMI?!
TAKAOMI?
AGAIN.
Bonus Manga
Takaomi Gojo's Weakness
WHAT'S WRONG, BOSS?
SHUT UP.
DON'T FOLLOW ME.
I'M GOING HOME.
See you.
BOSS?!
WHAT ABOUT THE PARTY?!
BOSS!
SHUT UP.
Lately...
...I'VE BEEN GETTING THE CREEPY FEELING...
...THAT SOMEONE'S WATCHING ME.

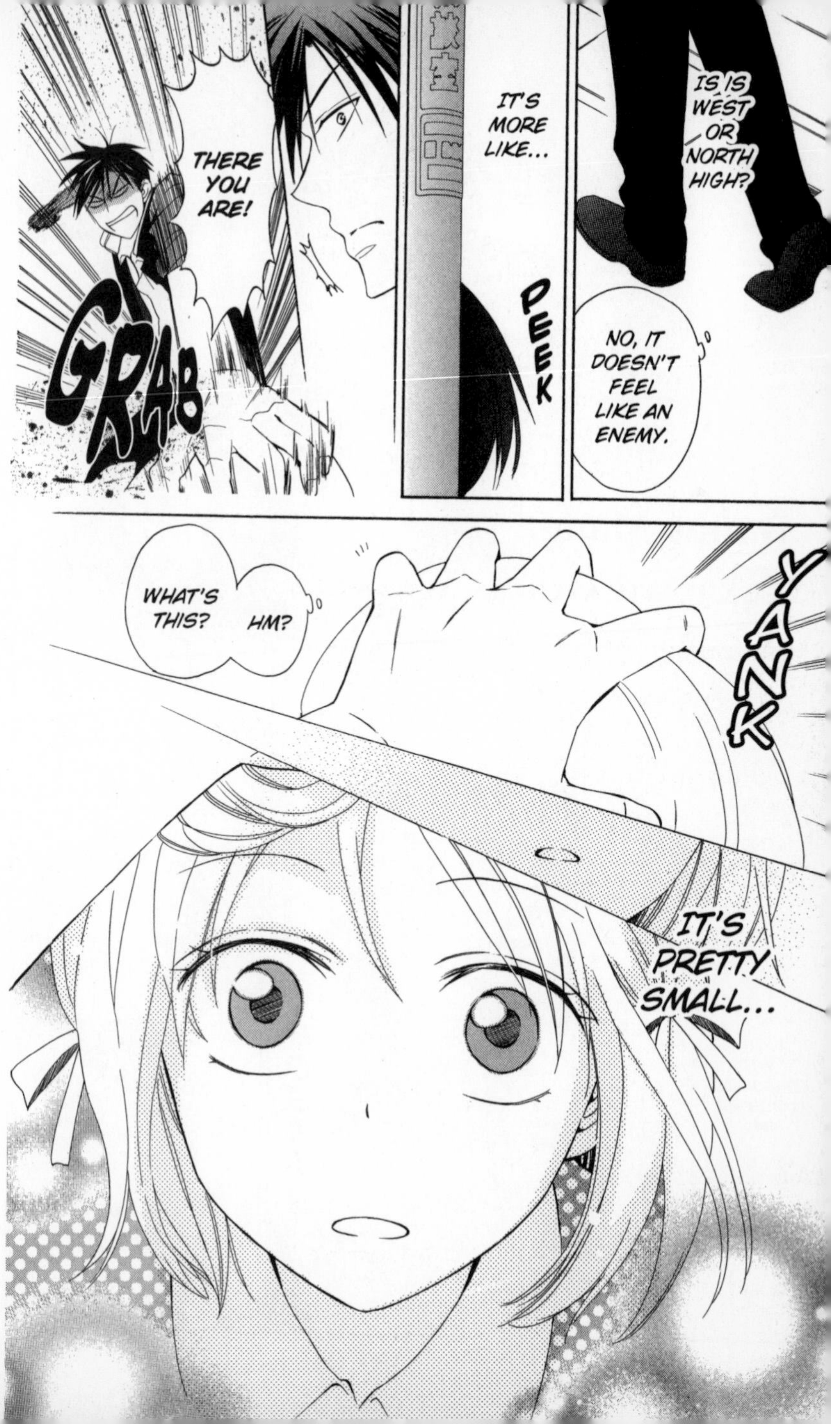
IS IS WEST OR NORTH HIGH?
NO, IT DOESN'T FEEL LIKE AN ENEMY.
IT'S MORE LIKE...
PEEK
THERE YOU ARE!
GRAB
YANK
HM?
WHAT'S THIS?
IT'S PRETTY SMALL...

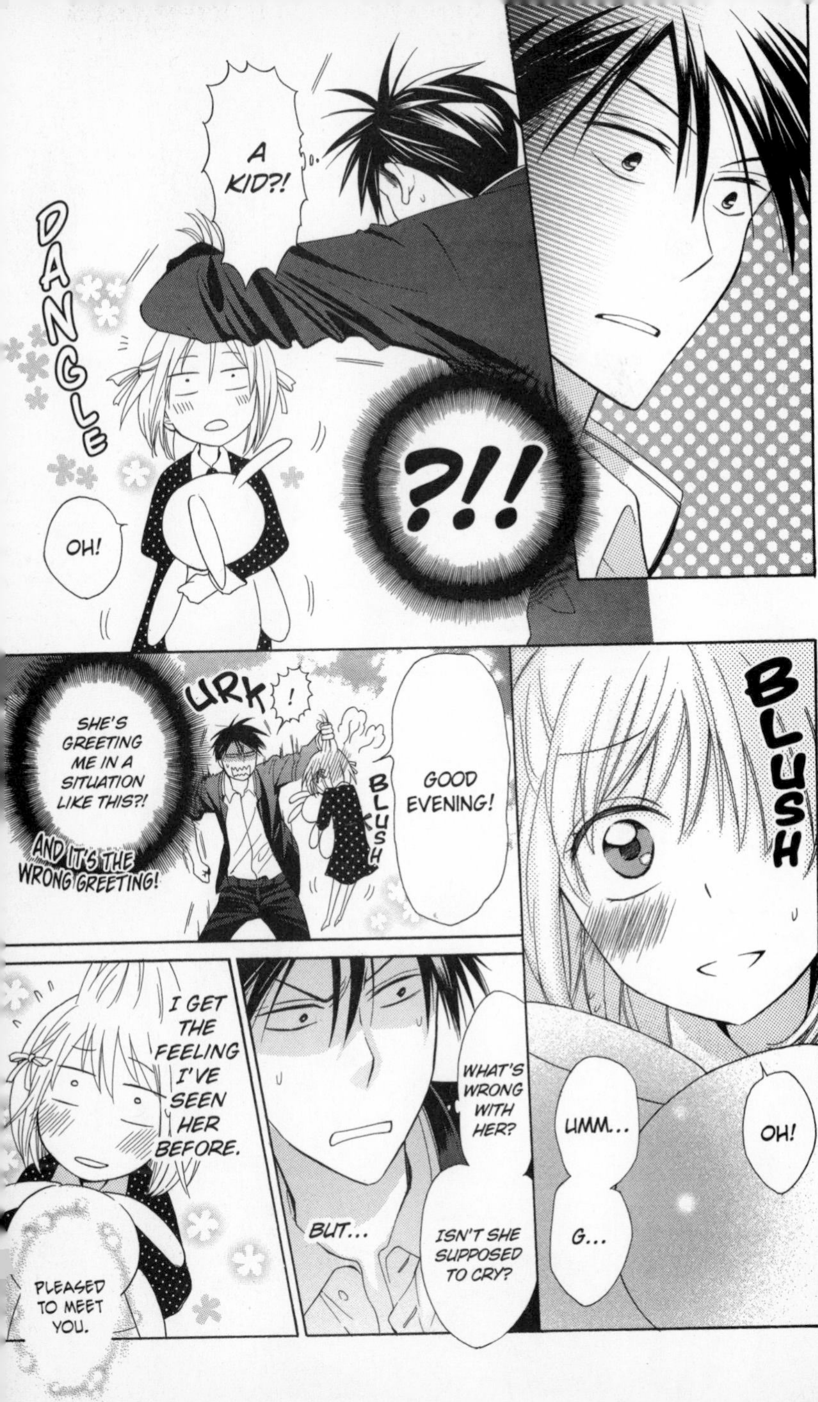
A KID?!
?!!
DANGLE
OH!
BLUSH
OH!
UMM...
G...
GOOD EVENING!
BLUSH
URK !
SHE'S GREETING ME IN A SITUATION LIKE THIS?!
AND IT'S THE WRONG GREETING!
WHAT'S WRONG WITH HER?
ISN'T SHE SUPPOSED TO CRY?
BUT...
I GET THE FEELING I'VE SEEN HER BEFORE.
PLEASED TO MEET YOU.

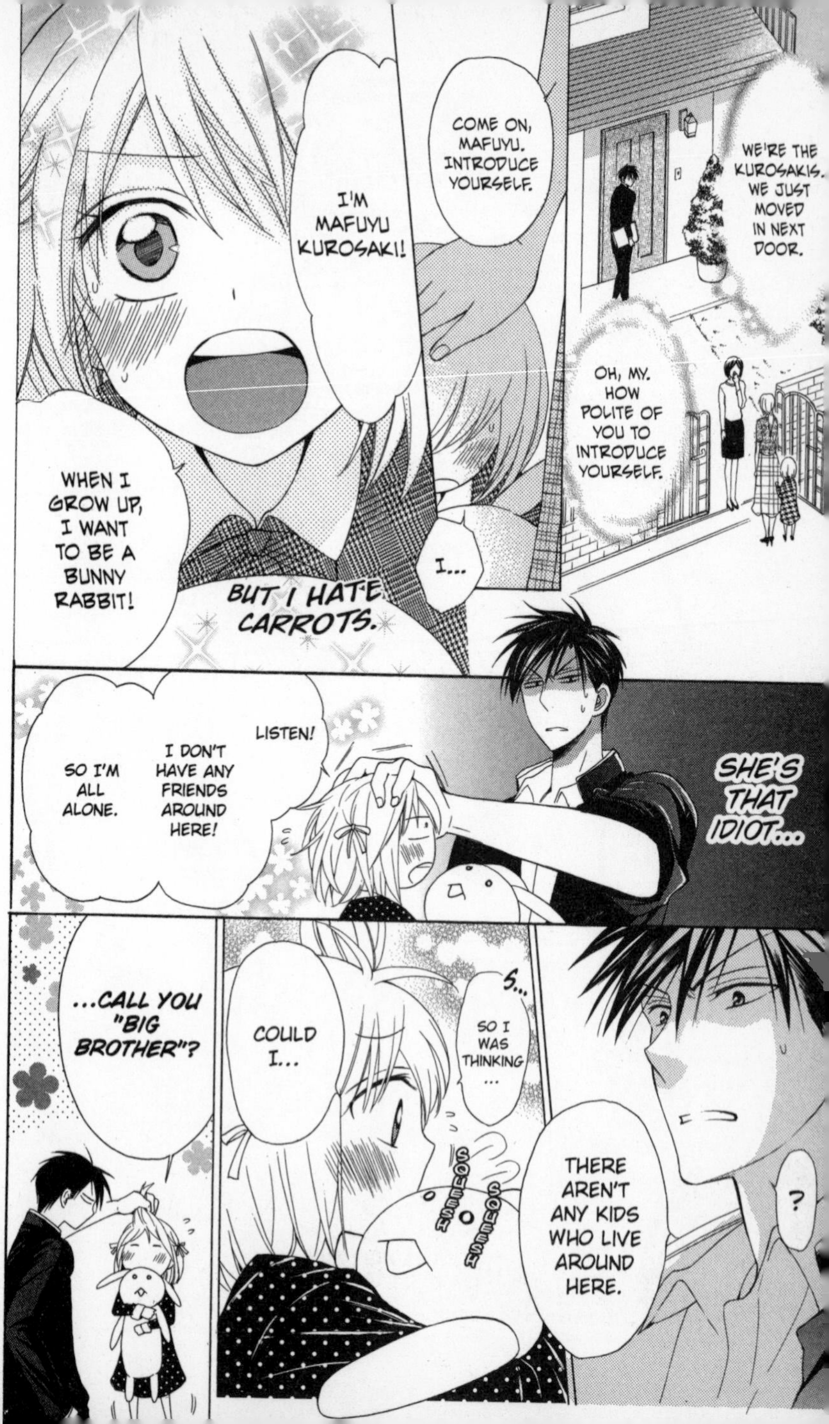
WE'RE THE KUROSAKIS. WE JUST MOVED IN NEXT DOOR.
OH, MY. HOW POLITE OF YOU TO INTRODUCE YOURSELF.
COME ON, MAFUYU. INTRODUCE YOURSELF.
I'M MAFUYU KUROSAKI!
I...
WHEN I GROW UP, I WANT TO BE A BUNNY RABBIT!
BUT I HATE CARROTS.
SHE'S THAT IDIOT...
LISTEN!
I DON'T HAVE ANY FRIENDS AROUND HERE!
SO I'M ALL ALONE.
?
THERE AREN'T ANY KIDS WHO LIVE AROUND HERE.
S...
SO I WAS THINKING...
SQUEESH
SQUEESH
COULD I...
...CALL YOU "BIG BROTHER"?

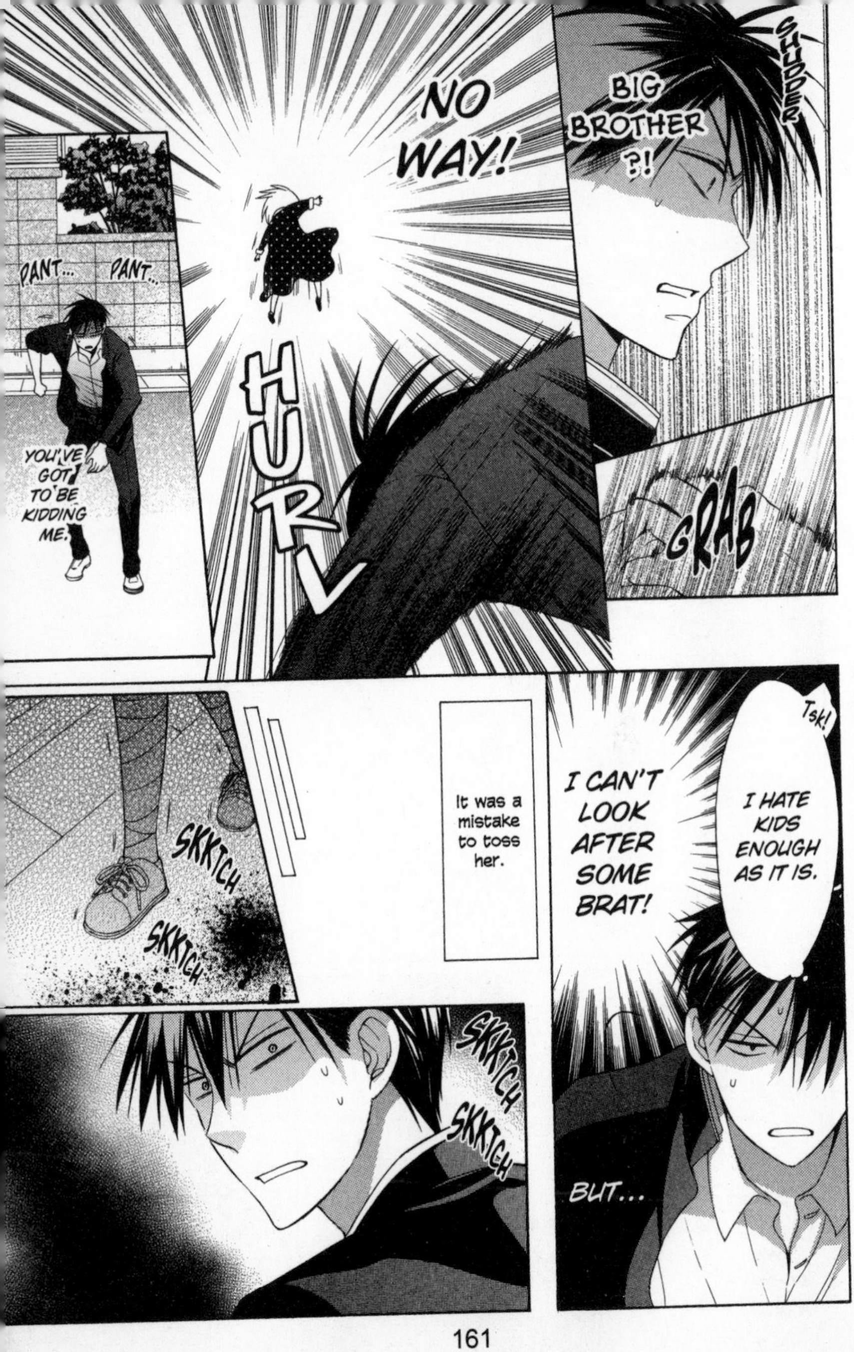
SHUDDER
BIG BROTHER ?!
GRAB
NO WAY!
HURL
PANT... PANT...
YOU'VE GOT TO BE KIDDING ME.
Tsk!
I HATE KIDS ENOUGH AS IT IS.
I CAN'T LOOK AFTER SOME BRAT!
BUT...
It was a mistake to toss her.
SKKTCH
SKKTCH
SKKTCH
SKKTCH

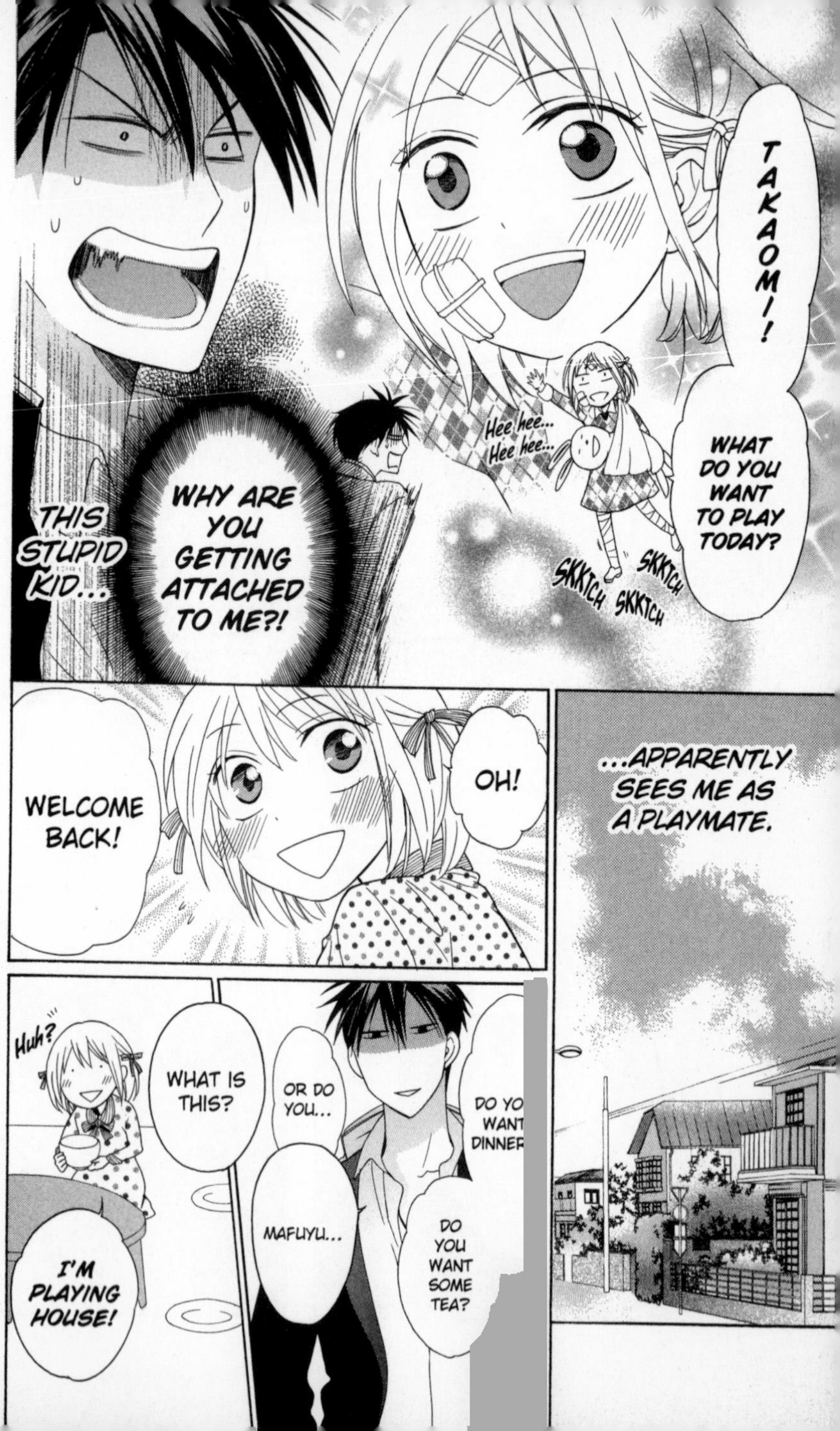
TAKAOMI!
WHAT DO YOU WANT TO PLAY TODAY?
Hee hee... Hee hee...
SKKITCH SKKITCH SKKITCH
WHY ARE YOU GETTING ATTACHED TO ME?!
THIS STUPID KID...
...APPARENTLY SEES ME AS A PLAYMATE.
OH!
WELCOME BACK!
DO YO WANT DINNER
OR DO YOU...
DO YOU WANT SOME TEA?
MAFUYU...
WHAT IS THIS?
Huh?
I'M PLAYING HOUSE!

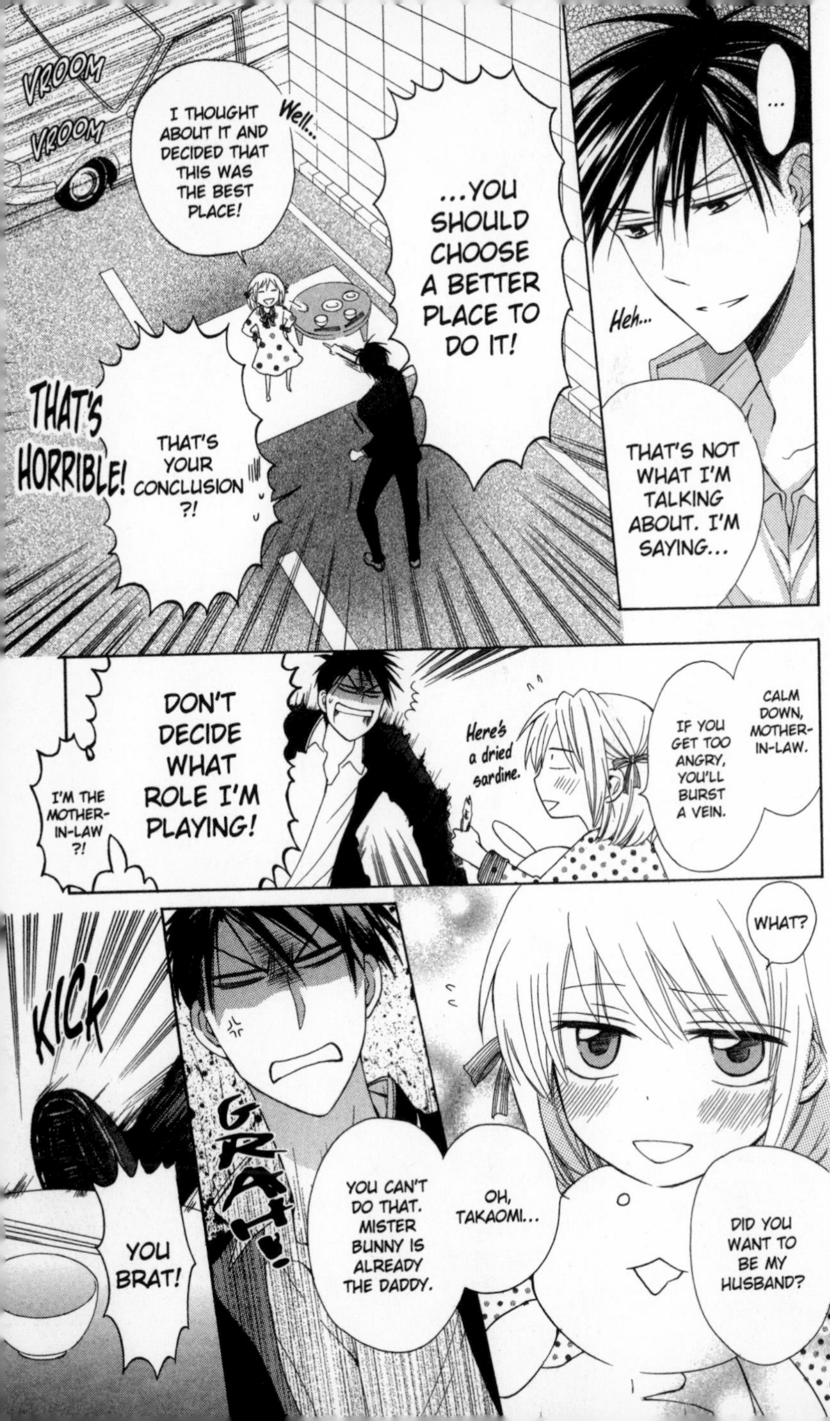
...
Heh...
THAT'S NOT WHAT I'M TALKING ABOUT. I'M SAYING...
...YOU SHOULD CHOOSE A BETTER PLACE TO DO IT!
Well...
I THOUGHT ABOUT IT AND DECIDED THAT THIS WAS THE BEST PLACE!
VROOM
VROOM
THAT'S YOUR CONCLUSION?!
THAT'S HORRIBLE!
CALM DOWN, MOTHER-IN-LAW.
IF YOU GET TOO ANGRY, YOU'LL BURST A VEIN.
Here's a dried sardine.
DON'T DECIDE WHAT ROLE I'M PLAYING!
I'M THE MOTHER-IN-LAW?!
WHAT?
DID YOU WANT TO BE MY HUSBAND?
OH, TAKAOMI...
YOU CAN'T DO THAT. MISTER BUNNY IS ALREADY THE DADDY.
GRAH!
KICK
YOU BRAT!

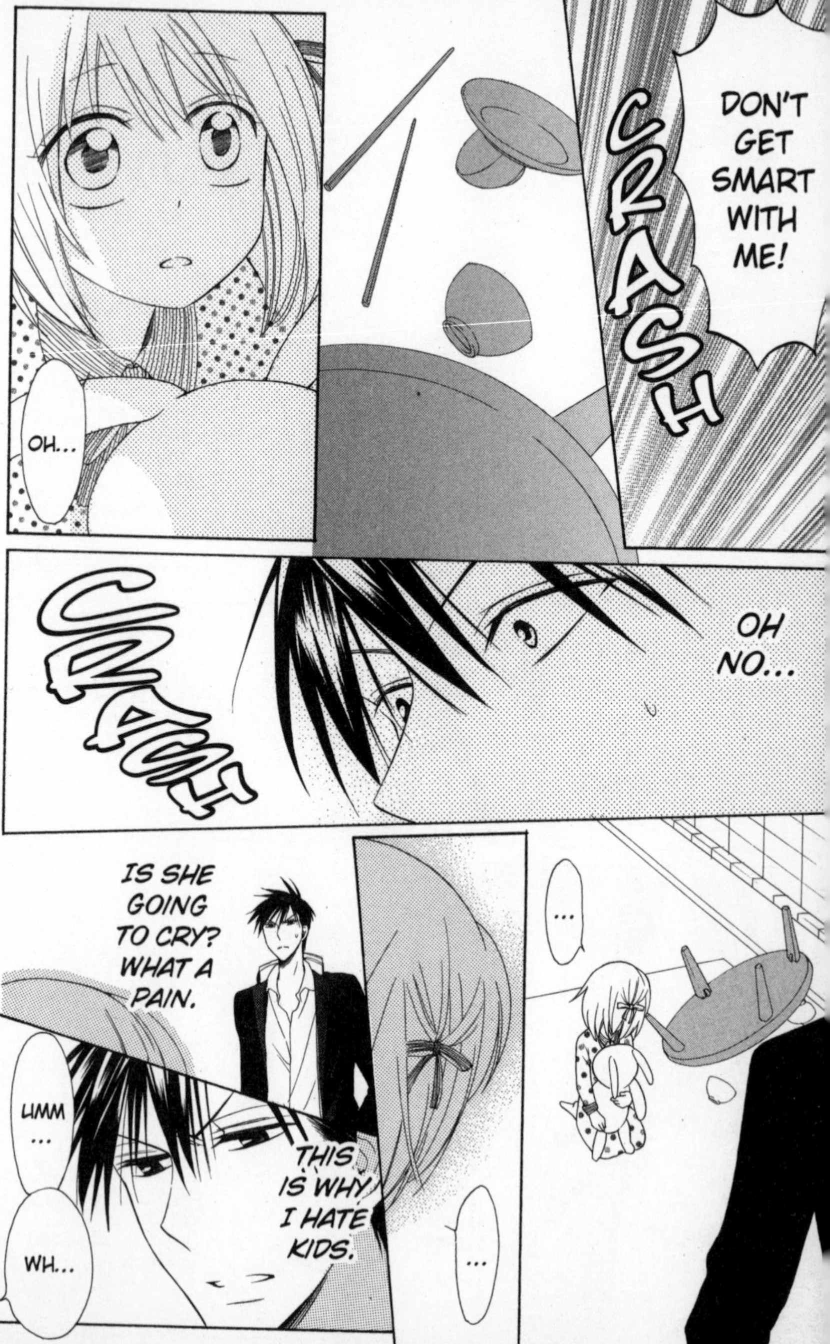
CRASH
DON'T GET SMART WITH ME!
OH...
OH NO...
...
...
IS SHE GOING TO CRY? WHAT A PAIN.
THIS IS WHY I HATE KIDS.
UMM...
WH...

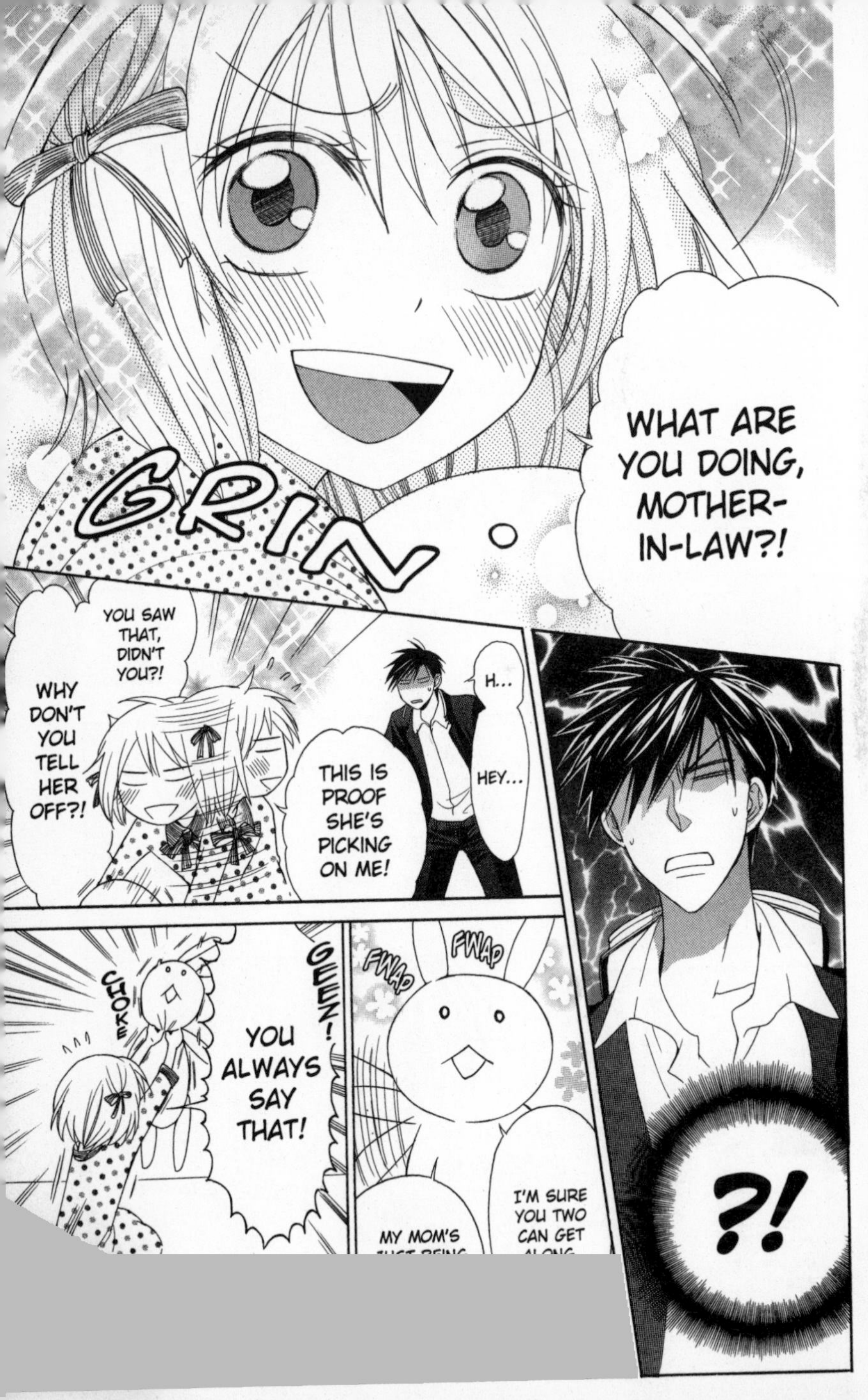
WHAT ARE YOU DOING, MOTHER-IN-LAW?!
GRIN
?!
H...
HEY...
THIS IS PROOF SHE'S PICKING ON ME!
YOU SAW THAT, DIDN'T YOU?!
WHY DON'T YOU TELL HER OFF?!
FWAP
FWAP
I'M SURE YOU TWO CAN GET
MY MOM'S
GEEZ!
YOU ALWAYS SAY THAT!
CHOKE

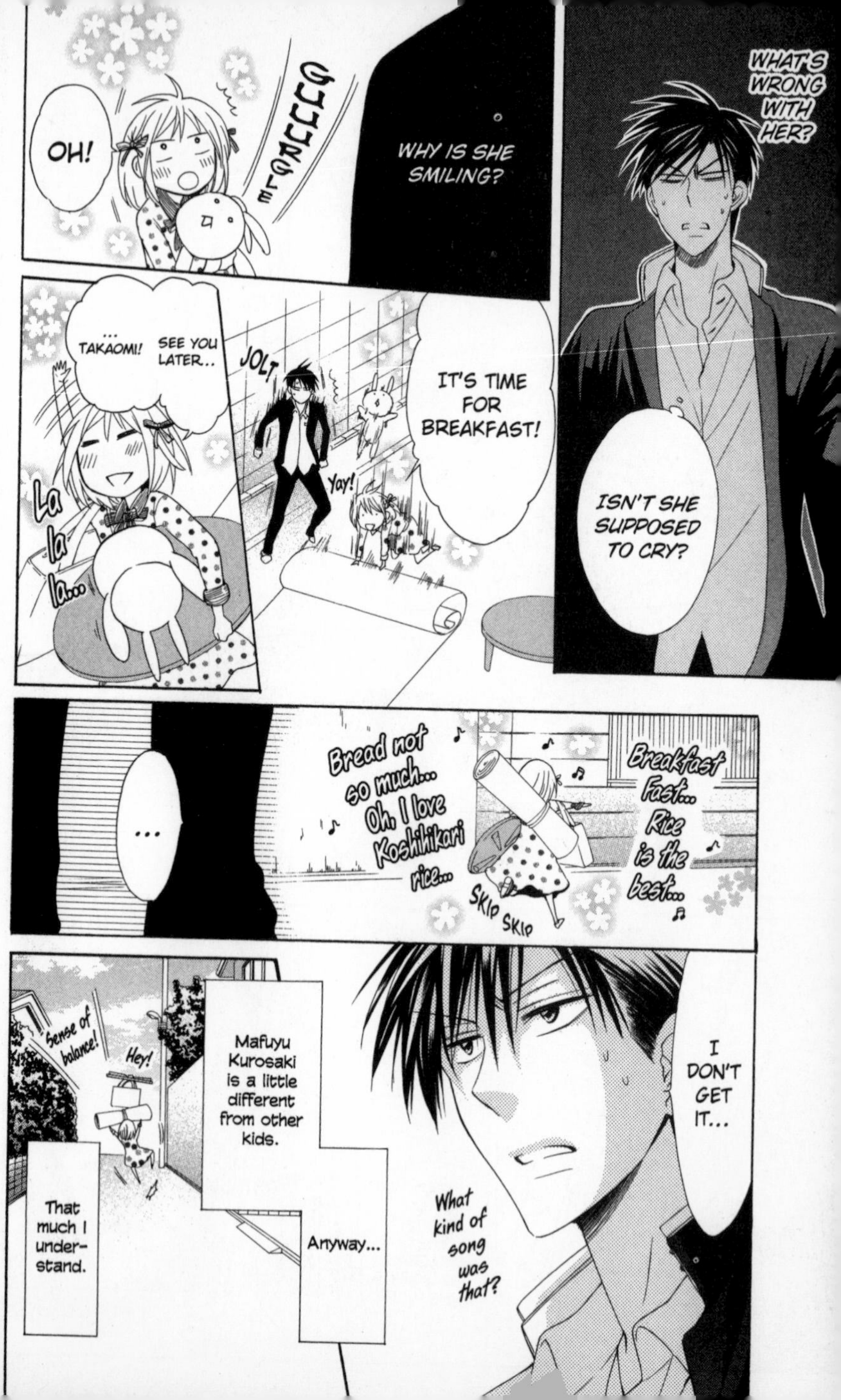
WHAT'S WRONG WITH HER?
ISN'T SHE SUPPOSED TO CRY?
WHY IS SHE SMILING?
GUURGLE
OH!
IT'S TIME FOR BREAKFAST!
JOLT
Yay!
... TAKAOMI! SEE YOU LATER...
La la la...
Breakfast Fast... Rice is the best...
Bread not so much... Oh, I love Koshihikari rice...
SKIP SKIP
...
I DON'T GET IT...
What kind of song was that?
Mafuyu Kurosaki is a little different from other kids.
Anyway...
That much I understand.
Sense of balance!
Hey!

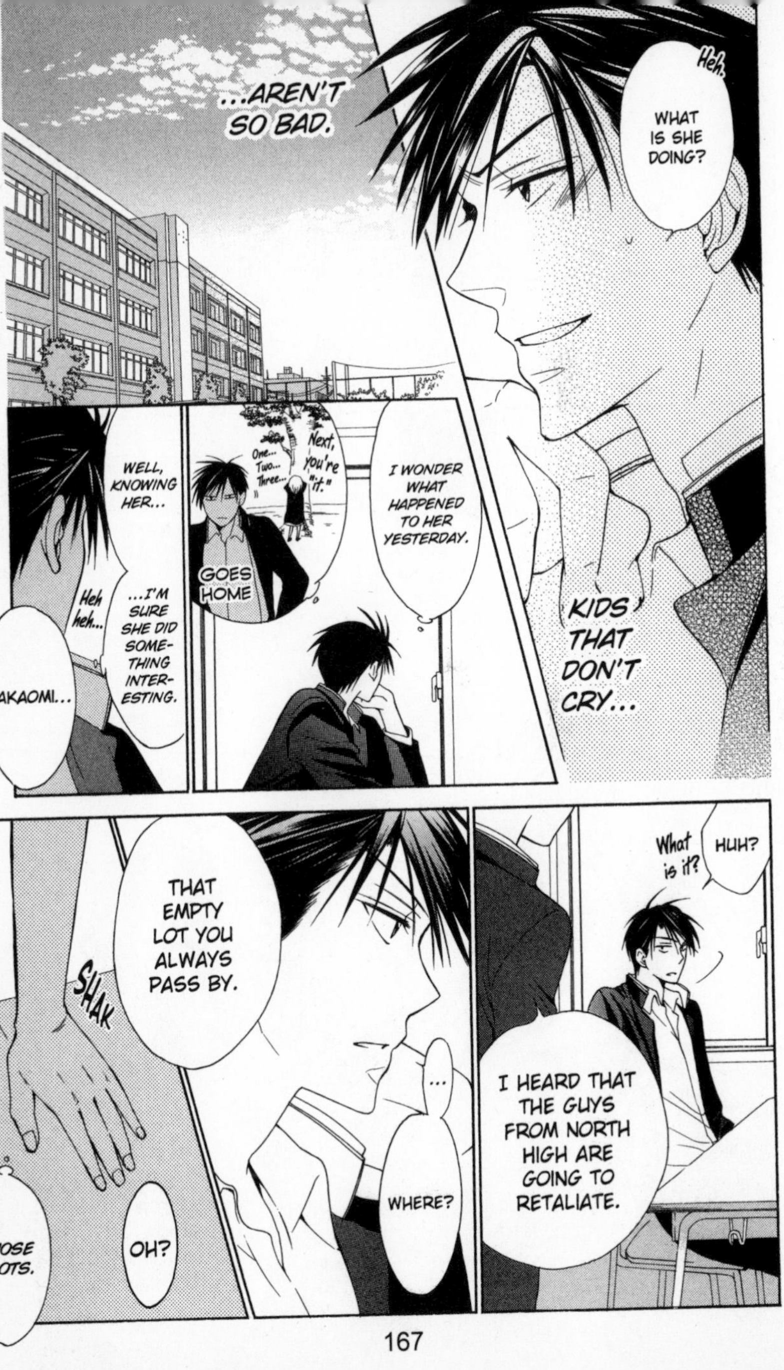
Heh.
WHAT IS SHE DOING?
KIDS THAT DON'T CRY...
...AREN'T SO BAD.
I WONDER WHAT HAPPENED TO HER YESTERDAY.
Next, you're "it."
One... Two... Three...
GOES HOME
WELL, KNOWING HER...
...I'M SURE SHE DID SOME-THING INTER-ESTING.
Heh heh...
TAKAOMI...
HUH?
What is it?
I HEARD THAT THE GUYS FROM NORTH HIGH ARE GOING TO RETALIATE.
...
WHERE?
THAT EMPTY LOT YOU ALWAYS PASS BY.
SHAK
OH?
THOSE IDIOTS.

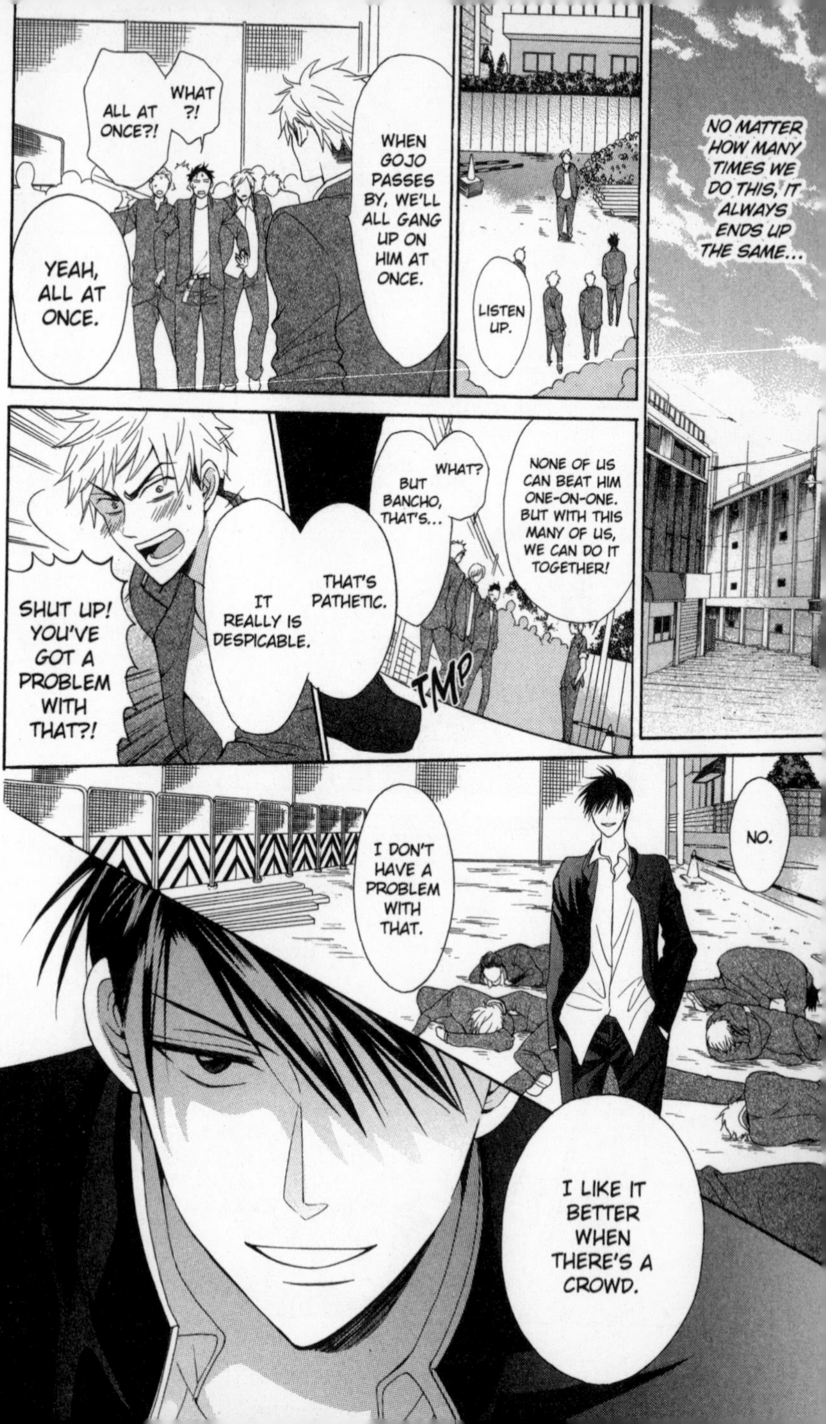
NO MATTER HOW MANY TIMES WE DO THIS, IT ALWAYS ENDS UP THE SAME...
LISTEN UP.
WHEN GOJO PASSES BY, WE'LL ALL GANG UP ON HIM AT ONCE.
WHAT ?!
ALL AT ONCE?!
YEAH, ALL AT ONCE.
NONE OF US CAN BEAT HIM ONE-ON-ONE. BUT WITH THIS MANY OF US, WE CAN DO IT TOGETHER!
WHAT?
BUT BANCHO, THAT'S...
THAT'S PATHETIC.
IT REALLY IS DESPICABLE.
SHUT UP! YOU'VE GOT A PROBLEM WITH THAT?!
TMP
NO.
I DON'T HAVE A PROBLEM WITH THAT.
I LIKE IT BETTER WHEN THERE'S A CROWD.

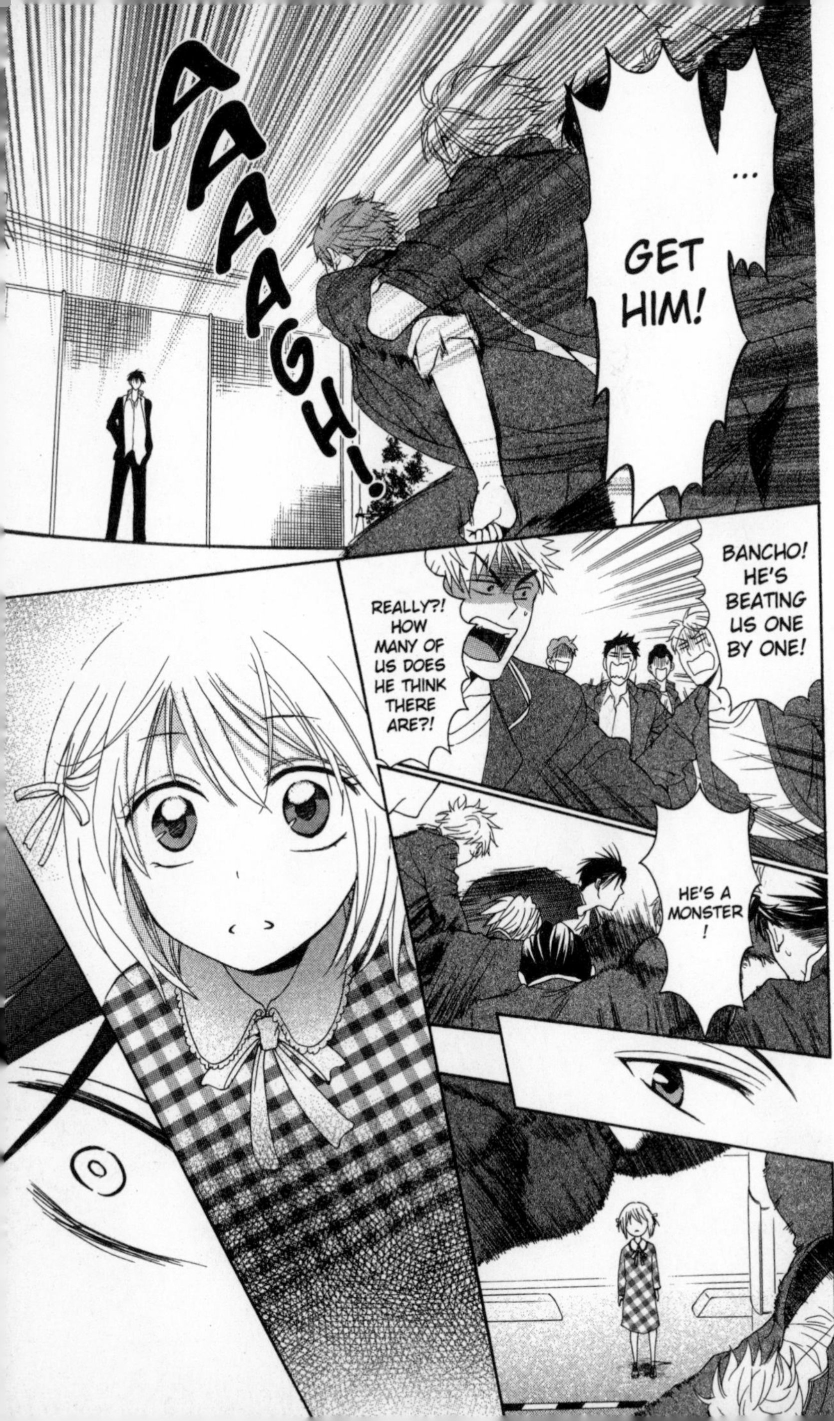
...
GET HIM!
AAAAGH!
BANCHO! HE'S BEATING US ONE BY ONE!
REALLY?! HOW MANY OF US DOES HE THINK THERE ARE?!
HE'S A MONSTER!

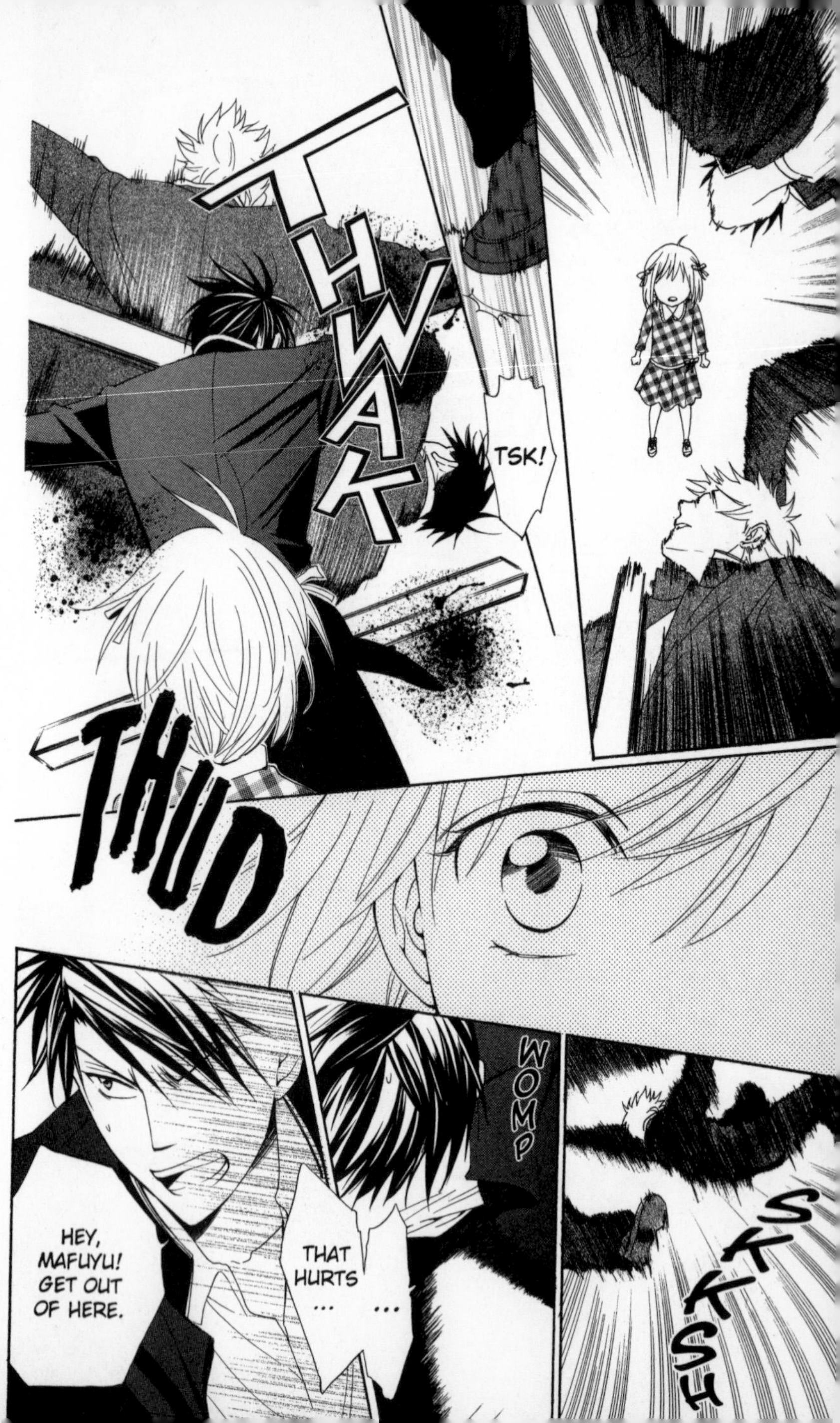
THWAK
TSK!
THUD
WOMP
SKKSH
THAT HURTS ... ...
HEY, MAFUYU! GET OUT OF HERE.

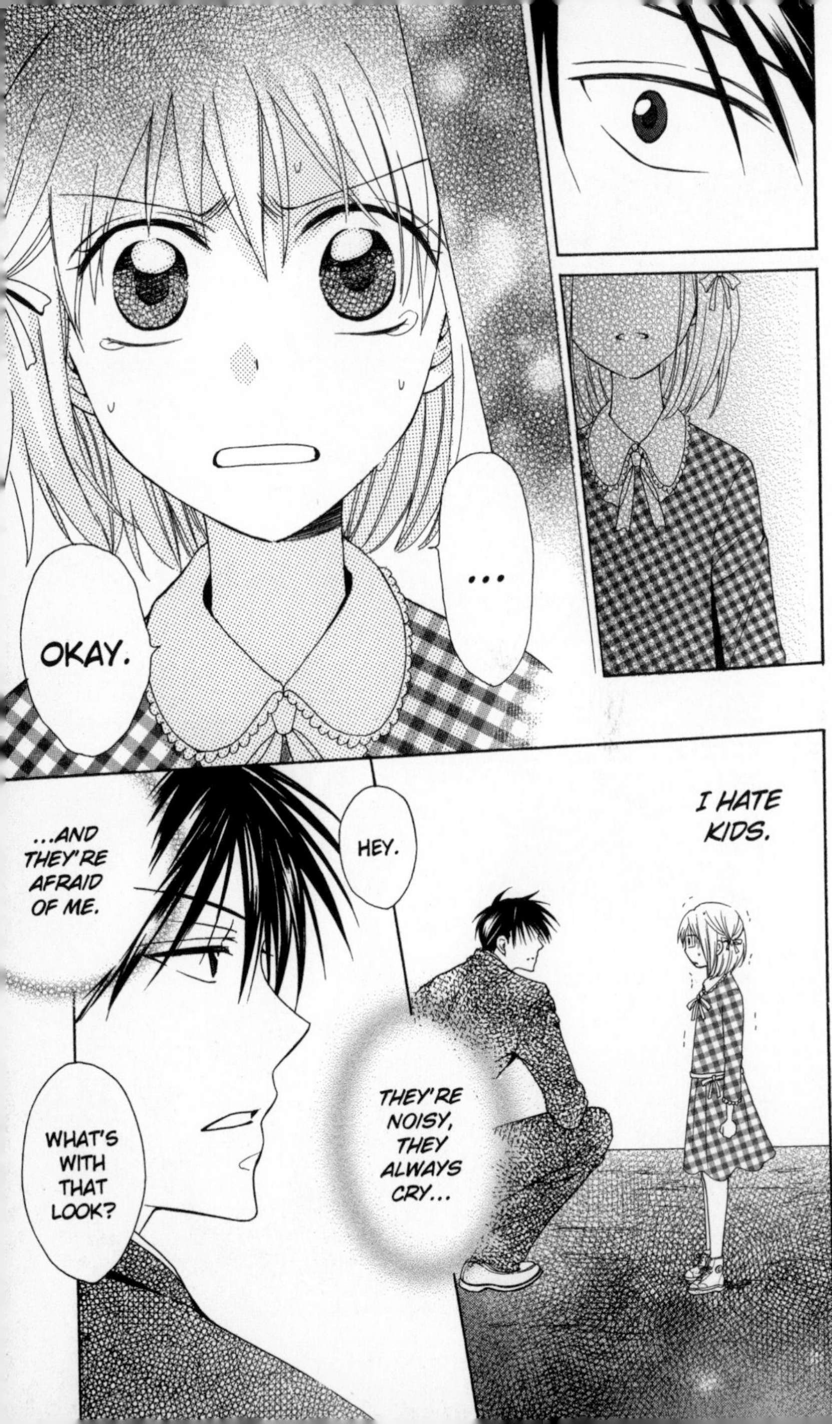
...
OKAY.
I HATE KIDS.
THEY'RE NOISY, THEY ALWAYS CRY...
HEY.
...AND THEY'RE AFRAID OF ME.
WHAT'S WITH THAT LOOK?

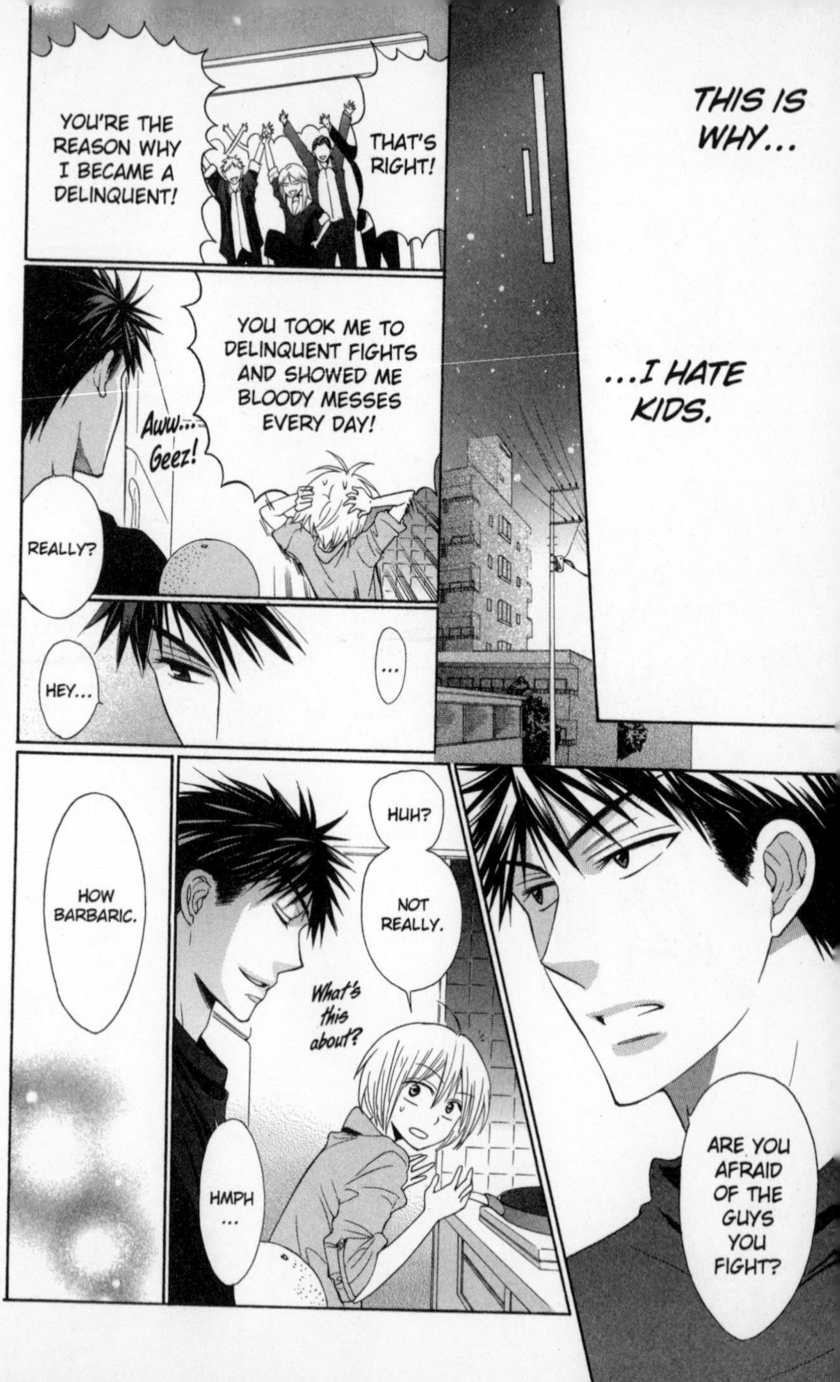
THIS IS WHY...
...I HATE KIDS.
YOU'RE THE REASON WHY I BECAME A DELINQUENT!
THAT'S RIGHT!
YOU TOOK ME TO DELINQUENT FIGHTS AND SHOWED ME BLOODY MESSES EVERY DAY!
Aww... Geez!
REALLY?
...
HEY...
ARE YOU AFRAID OF THE GUYS YOU FIGHT?
HUH?
NOT REALLY.
What's this about?
HMPH ...
HOW BARBARIC.

North South
East West

North South East West

SUMMER FESTIVAL

A YOUNGER SISTER'S DUTY

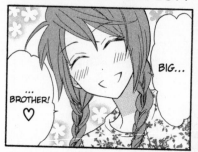

BIG...
... BROTHER! ♡
Hey...
THE FESTIVAL IS TODAY, ISN'T IT?
O-OKUBO AND YOUR OTHER FRIENDS ARE GOING TO IT, RIGHT?
YEAH.
YEAH.
I WANT TO GO WITH—
NO WAY.
...
BUT WHY?! IT'S NO BIG DEAL! I WON'T CAUSE TROUBLE!
I'LL THANK EVERYONE FOR BEING NICE TO YOU!
I DON'T WANT YOU DOING THAT.
I'm a good sister.

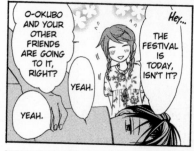

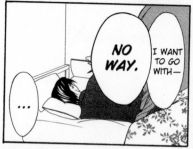

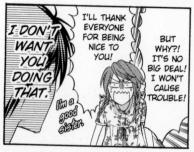

SEPARATE ACTIVITIES

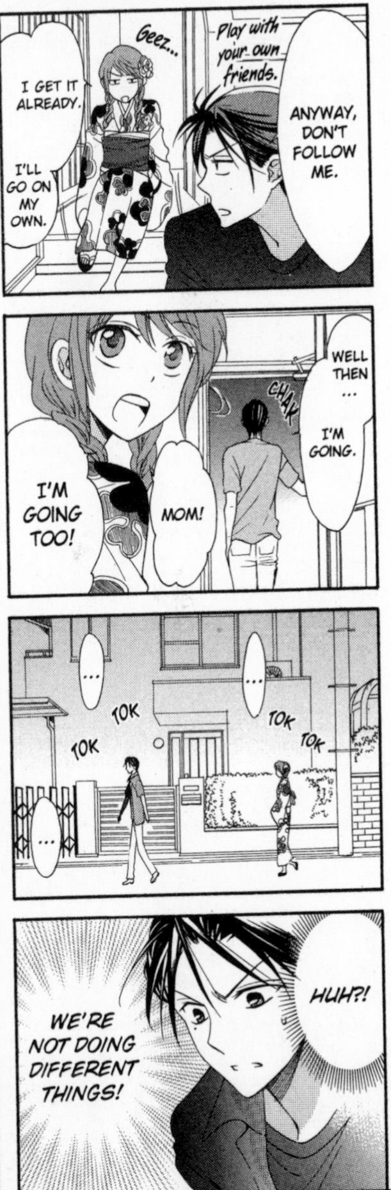
Play with your own friends.
ANYWAY, DON'T FOLLOW ME.
Geez...
I GET IT ALREADY.
I'LL GO ON MY OWN.
WELL THEN ... I'M GOING.
CHAK
MOM!
I'M GOING TOO!
...
TOK
TOK
...
TOK
TOK
...
HUH?!
WE'RE NOT DOING DIFFERENT THINGS!

They're headed to the same place

SIBLING STRATEGY

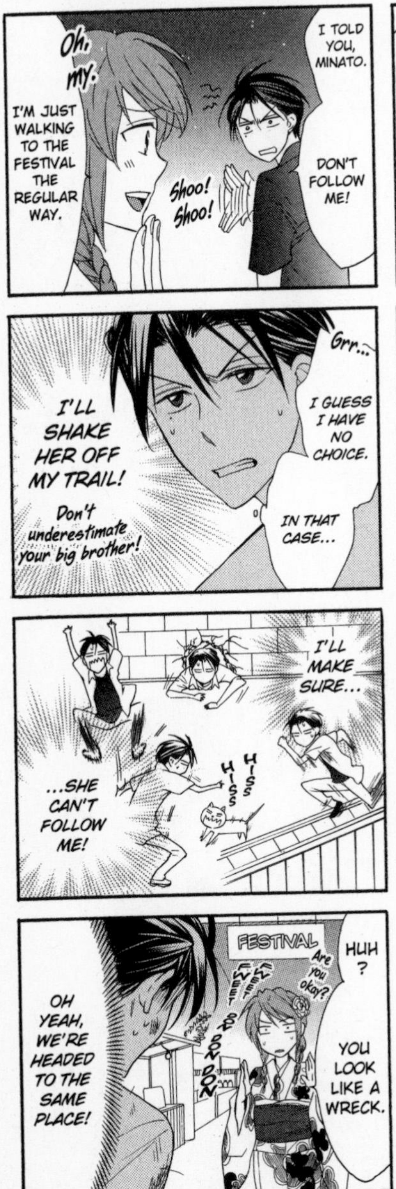
I TOLD YOU, MINATO.
DON'T FOLLOW ME!
Shoo! Shoo!
Oh, my.
I'M JUST WALKING TO THE FESTIVAL THE REGULAR WAY.
Grr...
I GUESS I HAVE NO CHOICE.
IN THAT CASE...
I'LL SHAKE HER OFF MY TRAIL!
Don't underestimate your big brother!
I'LL MAKE SURE...
HISS HISS
...SHE CAN'T FOLLOW ME!
HUH?
Are you okay?
FESTIVAL
FWEET FWEET
DON DON
YOU LOOK LIKE A WRECK.
OH YEAH, WE'RE HEADED TO THE SAME PLACE!

HIS WAY OF PLAYING ALONG

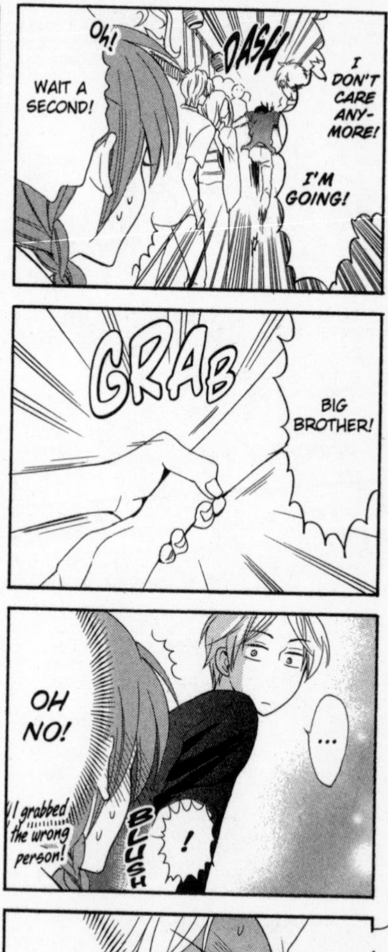
I DON'T CARE ANYMORE!
DASH
Oh!
I'M GOING!
WAIT A SECOND!
GRAB
BIG BROTHER!
...
BLUSH
!
OH NO!
I grabbed the wrong person!
A...
ARE YOU MY LONG-LOST SISTER?!
You're alive?!
YOU DON'T NEED TO PLAY ALONG!
What kind of story is that?!

EXPECTATIONS

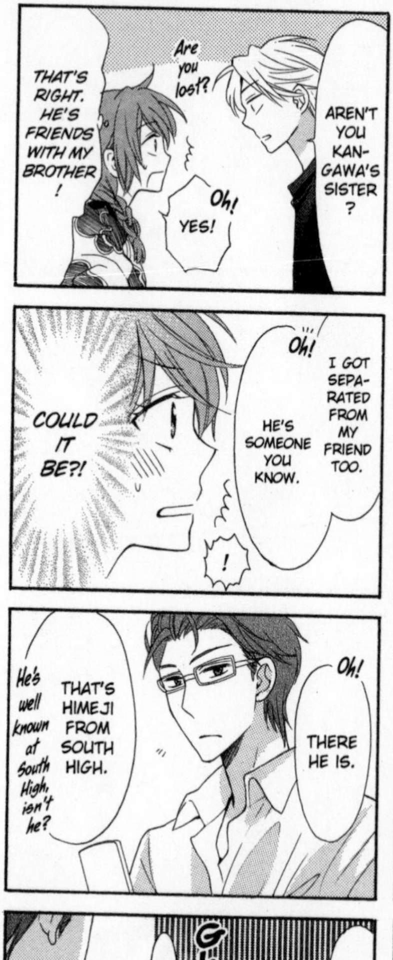
AREN'T YOU KAN-GAWA'S SISTER?
Are you lost?
Oh! YES!
THAT'S RIGHT. HE'S FRIENDS WITH MY BROTHER!
I GOT SEPARATED FROM MY FRIEND TOO.
Oh!
HE'S SOMEONE YOU KNOW.
!
COULD IT BE?!
Oh!
THERE HE IS.
THAT'S HIMEJI FROM SOUTH HIGH.
He's well known at South High, isn't he?
OH...
IT'S JUST OUR STUDENT COUNCIL PRESIDENT.
GLOOM...
...
YOU'RE NOT VERY POPULAR, ARE YOU?
...

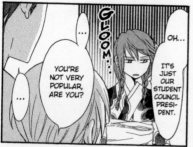

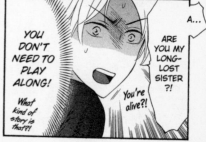

CHARACTERISTICS

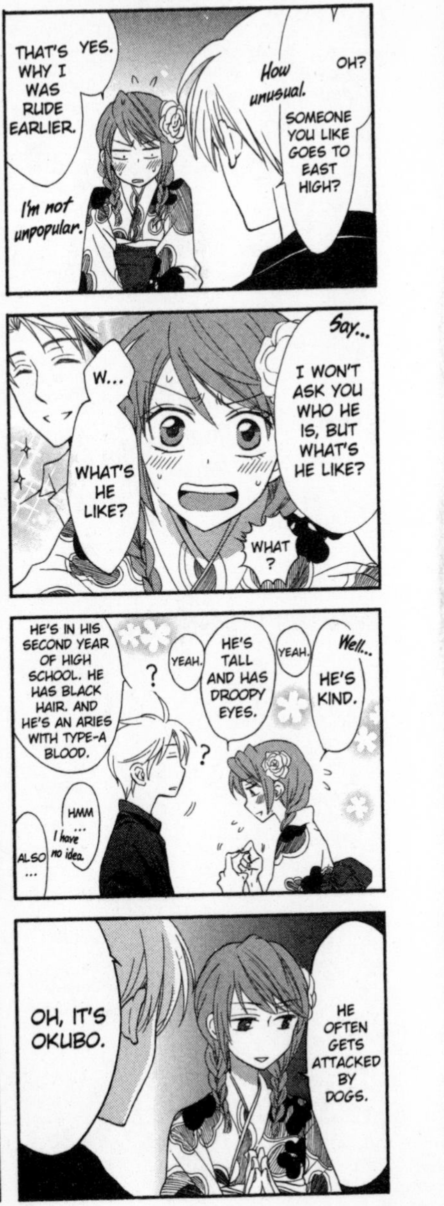
OH?
How unusual.
SOMEONE YOU LIKE GOES TO EAST HIGH?
YES.
THAT'S WHY I WAS RUDE EARLIER.
I'm not unpopular.
Say...
I WON'T ASK YOU WHO HE IS, BUT WHAT'S HE LIKE?
WHAT?
W...
WHAT'S HE LIKE?
Well...
HE'S KIND.
YEAH.
HE'S TALL AND HAS DROOPY EYES.
YEAH.
HE'S IN HIS SECOND YEAR OF HIGH SCHOOL. HE HAS BLACK HAIR. AND HE'S AN ARIES WITH TYPE-A BLOOD.
?
?
HMM... I have no idea.
ALSO...
HE OFTEN GETS ATTACKED BY DOGS.
OH, IT'S OKUBO.

RIVALRY

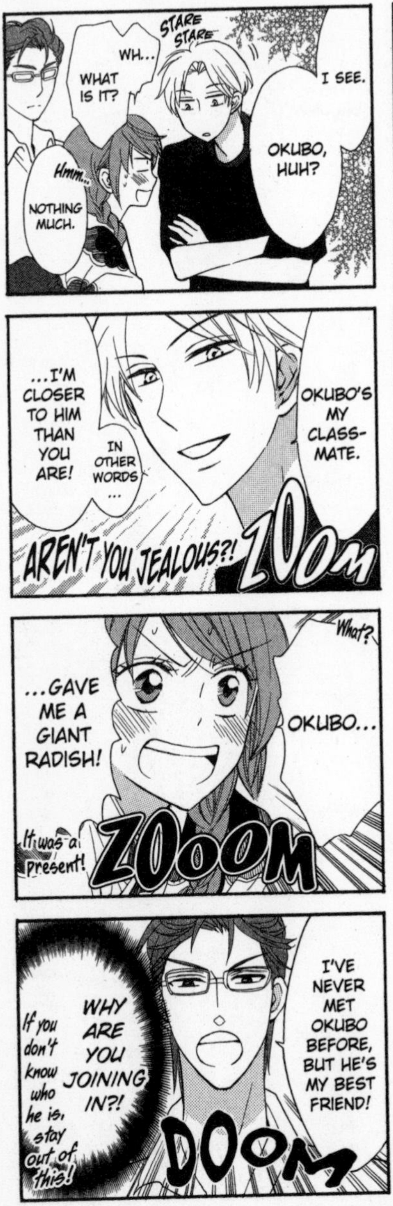
STARE STARE
I SEE.
OKUBO, HUH?
WH... WHAT IS IT?
Hmm...
NOTHING MUCH.
OKUBO'S MY CLASSMATE.
IN OTHER WORDS...
...I'M CLOSER TO HIM THAN YOU ARE!
AREN'T YOU JEALOUS?!
ZOOM
What?
OKUBO...
...GAVE ME A GIANT RADISH!
ZOOOM
It was a present!
I'VE NEVER MET OKUBO BEFORE, BUT HE'S MY BEST FRIEND!
WHY ARE YOU JOINING IN?!
If you don't know who he is, stay out of this!
DOOM

MODE OF COMMUNICATION

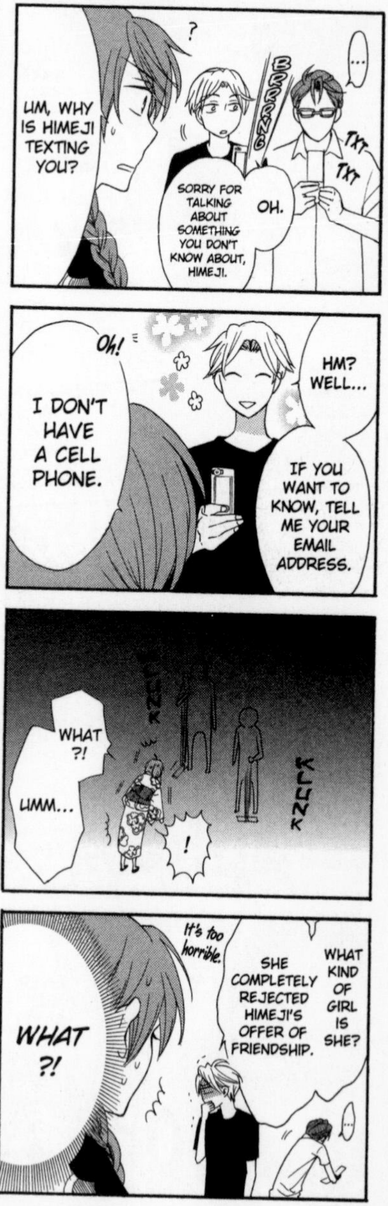
...
TXT
TXT
BRRRING
?
UM, WHY IS HIMEJI TEXTING YOU?
OH.
SORRY FOR TALKING ABOUT SOMETHING YOU DON'T KNOW ABOUT, HIMEJI.
HM? WELL...
IF YOU WANT TO KNOW, TELL ME YOUR EMAIL ADDRESS.
Oh!
I DON'T HAVE A CELL PHONE.
KLUNK
KLUNK
WHAT ?!
UMM...
!
WHAT KIND OF GIRL IS SHE?
SHE COMPLETELY REJECTED HIMEJI'S OFFER OF FRIENDSHIP.
It's too horrible.
...
WHAT ?!

UNABLE TO UNDERSTAND EACH OTHER

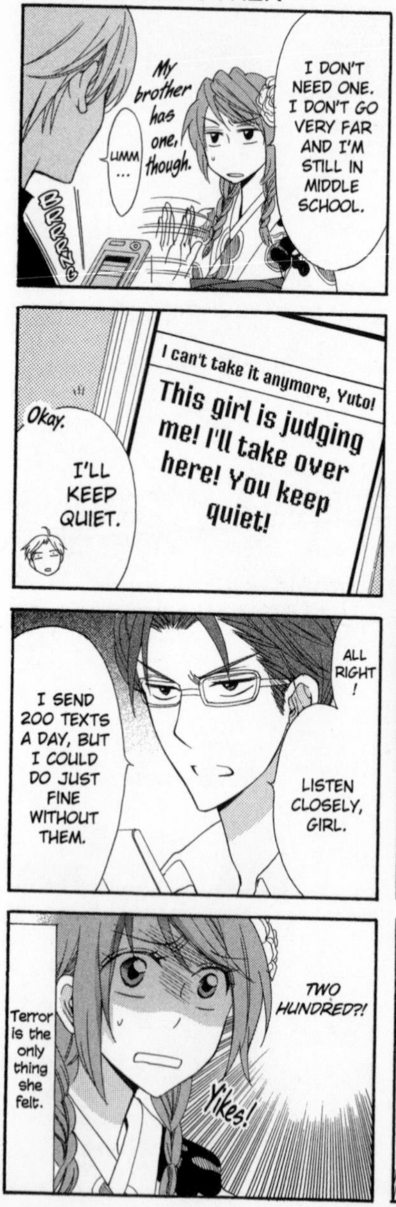
I DON'T NEED ONE. I DON'T GO VERY FAR AND I'M STILL IN MIDDLE SCHOOL.
My brother has one, though.
UMM ...
BRRRING
I can't take it anymore, Yuto!
This girl is judging me! I'll take over here! You keep quiet!
Okay.
I'LL KEEP QUIET.
ALL RIGHT!
LISTEN CLOSELY, GIRL.
I SEND 200 TEXTS A DAY, BUT I COULD DO JUST FINE WITHOUT THEM.
TWO HUNDRED?!
Yikes!
Terror is the only thing she felt.

EVIL ITEM

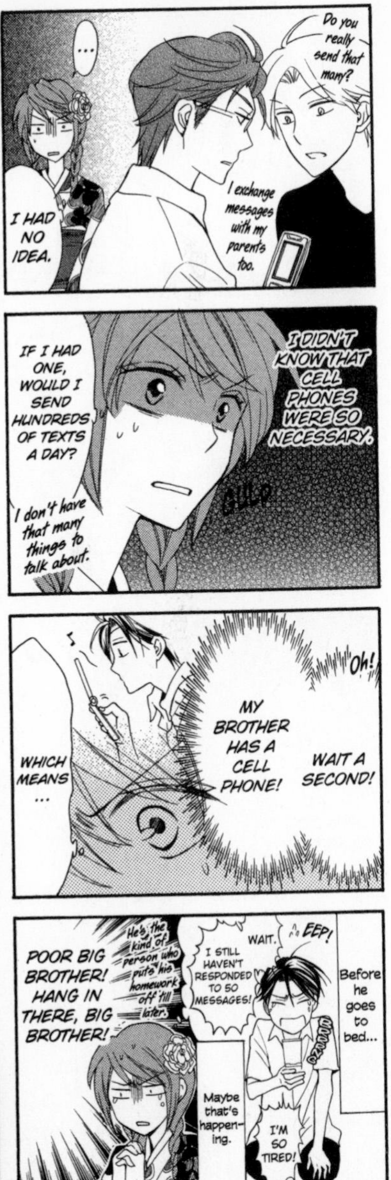
Do you really send that many?
I exchange messages with my parents too.
...
I HAD NO IDEA.
I DIDN'T KNOW THAT CELL PHONES WERE SO NECESSARY.
GULP
IF I HAD ONE, WOULD I SEND HUNDREDS OF TEXTS A DAY?
I don't have that many things to talk about.
Oh!
WAIT A SECOND!
MY BROTHER HAS A CELL PHONE!
WHICH MEANS ...
Before he goes to bed...
EEP!
WAIT.
I'M SO TIRED!
I STILL HAVEN'T RESPONDED TO 50 MESSAGES!
Maybe that's happening.
He's the kind of person who puts his homework off till later.
POOR BIG BROTHER! HANG IN THERE, BIG BROTHER!

CONFUSING LINEUP

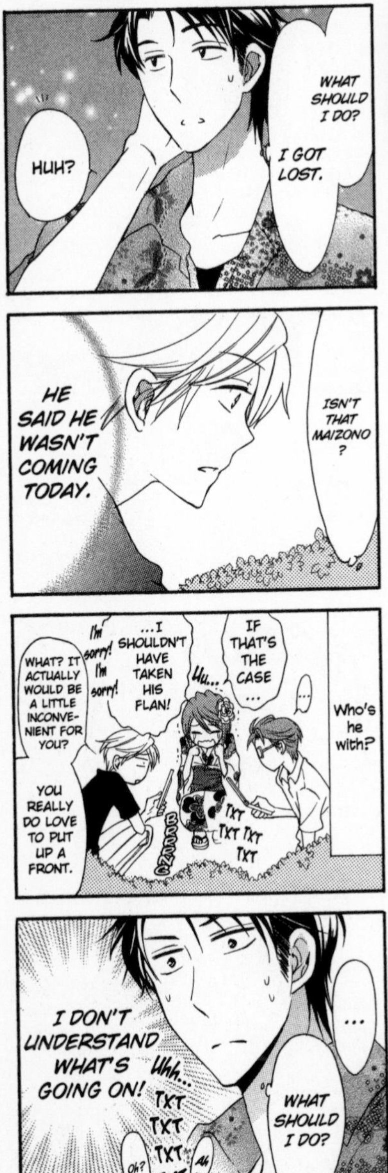
WHAT SHOULD I DO?
I GOT LOST.
HUH?
ISN'T THAT MAIZONO?
HE SAID HE WASN'T COMING TODAY.
Who's he with?
...
IF THAT'S THE CASE ...
Uu...
...I SHOULDN'T HAVE TAKEN HIS FLAN!
I'm sorry! I'm sorry!
WHAT? IT ACTUALLY WOULD BE A LITTLE INCONVENIENT FOR YOU?
YOU REALLY DO LOVE TO PUT UP A FRONT.
TXT TXT TXT TXT
...
WHAT SHOULD I DO?
Uhh...
I DON'T UNDERSTAND WHAT'S GOING ON!
TXT TXT TXT TXT
Ah~
Oh?

Naturally!

NOT THE TIME FOR A TOUCHING REUNION

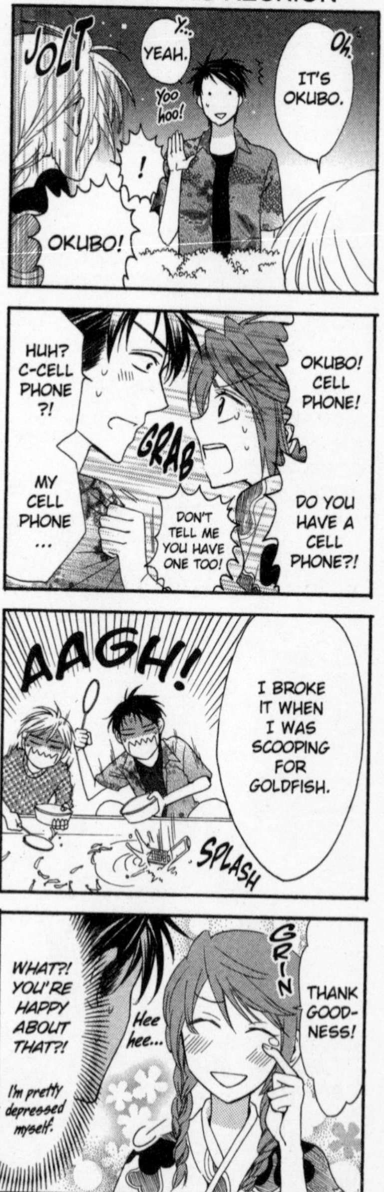
Oh.
IT'S OKUBO.
Y... YEAH.
Yoo hoo!
!
JOLT
OKUBO!
OKUBO! CELL PHONE!
HUH? C-CELL PHONE ?!
DO YOU HAVE A CELL PHONE?!
GRAB
DON'T TELL ME YOU HAVE ONE TOO!
MY CELL PHONE ...
I BROKE IT WHEN I WAS SCOOPING FOR GOLDFISH.
AAGH!
SPLASH
GRIN
THANK GOOD-NESS!
Hee hee...
WHAT?! YOU'RE HAPPY ABOUT THAT?!
I'm pretty depressed myself.

GOAL ACHIEVED?

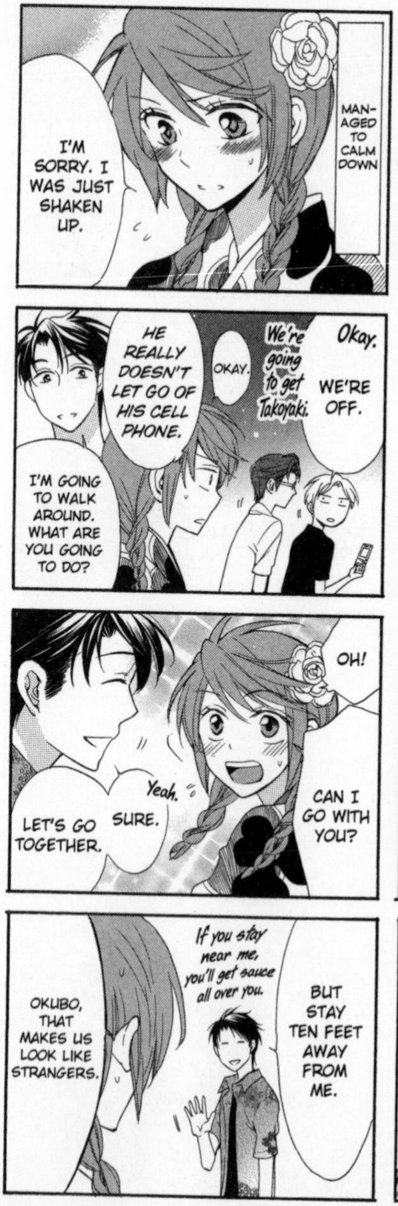
MAN-AGED TO CALM DOWN
I'M SORRY. I WAS JUST SHAKEN UP.
Okay.
WE'RE OFF.
We're going to get Takoyaki.
OKAY.
HE REALLY DOESN'T LET GO OF HIS CELL PHONE.
I'M GOING TO WALK AROUND. WHAT ARE YOU GOING TO DO?
OH!
CAN I GO WITH YOU?
Yeah.
SURE.
LET'S GO TOGETHER.
BUT STAY TEN FEET AWAY FROM ME.
If you stay near me, you'll get sauce all over you.
OKUBO, THAT MAKES US LOOK LIKE STRANGERS.

SELF-CONSCIOUS MATTER

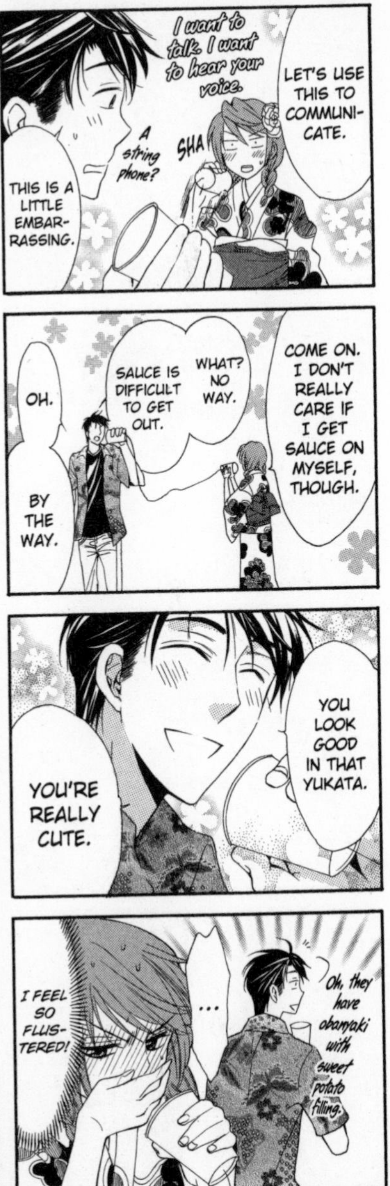
LET'S USE THIS TO COMMUNICATE.
I want to talk. I want to hear your voice.
SHA
A string phone?
THIS IS A LITTLE EMBARRASSING.
COME ON. I DON'T REALLY CARE IF I GET SAUCE ON MYSELF, THOUGH.
WHAT? NO WAY.
SAUCE IS DIFFICULT TO GET OUT.
OH.
BY THE WAY.
YOU LOOK GOOD IN THAT YUKATA.
YOU'RE REALLY CUTE.
Oh, they have obanyaki with sweet potato filling.
...
I FEEL SO FLUSTERED!

SPECIAL PRIVILEGE FOR LOVERS?

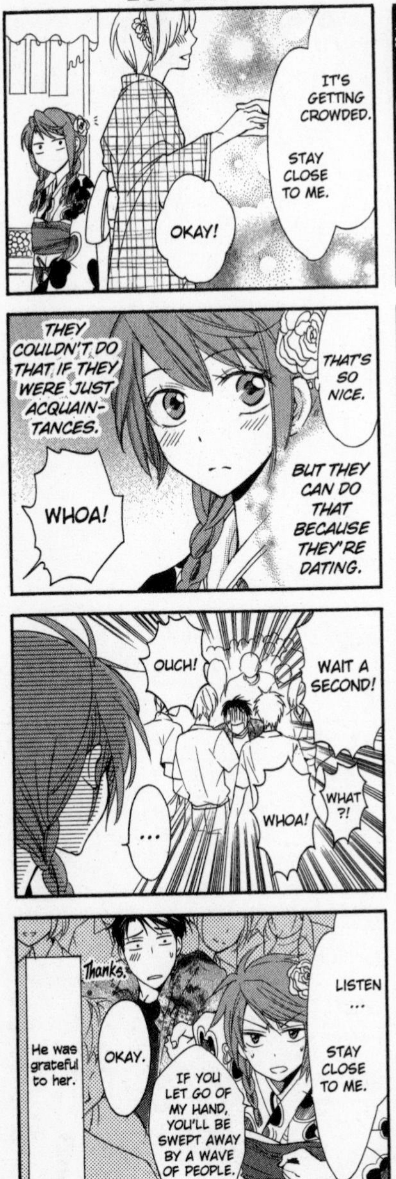
IT'S GETTING CROWDED.
STAY CLOSE TO ME.
OKAY!
THAT'S SO NICE.
BUT THEY CAN DO THAT BECAUSE THEY'RE DATING.
THEY COULDN'T DO THAT IF THEY WERE JUST ACQUAINTANCES.
WHOA!
WAIT A SECOND!
OUCH!
WHAT ?!
WHOA!
...
LISTEN ...
STAY CLOSE TO ME.
IF YOU LET GO OF MY HAND, YOU'LL BE SWEPT AWAY BY A WAVE OF PEOPLE.
OKAY.
Thanks.
He was grateful to her.

MEANWHILE, THE NORTH HIGH JUDO TEAM...

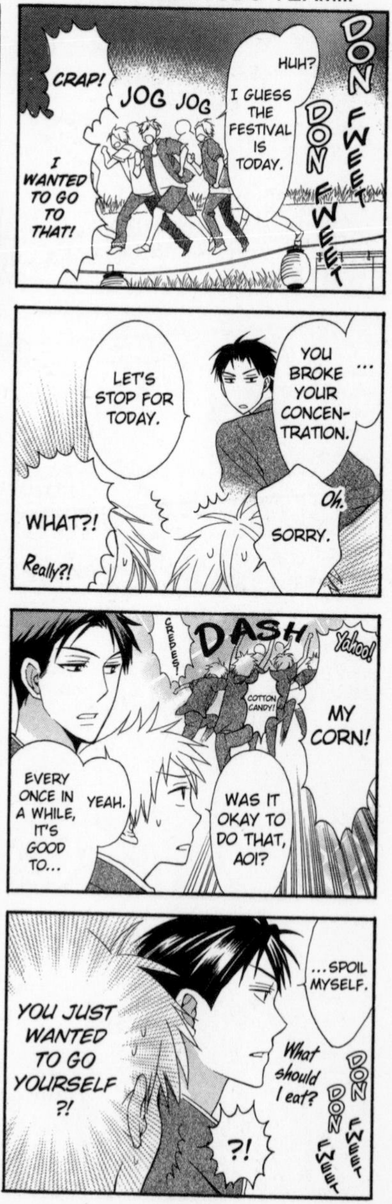
DON DON
HUH? I GUESS THE FESTIVAL IS TODAY.
JOG JOG
CRAP!
I WANTED TO GO TO THAT!
FWEET FWEET
...
YOU BROKE YOUR CONCENTRATION.
Oh.
SORRY.
LET'S STOP FOR TODAY.
WHAT?!
Really?!
Yahoo!
MY CORN!
DASH
COTTON CANDY!
WAS IT OKAY TO DO THAT, AOI?
YEAH.
EVERY ONCE IN A WHILE, IT'S GOOD TO...
...SPOIL MYSELF.
DON DON
FWEET FWEET
What should I eat?
?!
YOU JUST WANTED TO GO YOURSELF?!

RIGHT NOW, SHE'S...

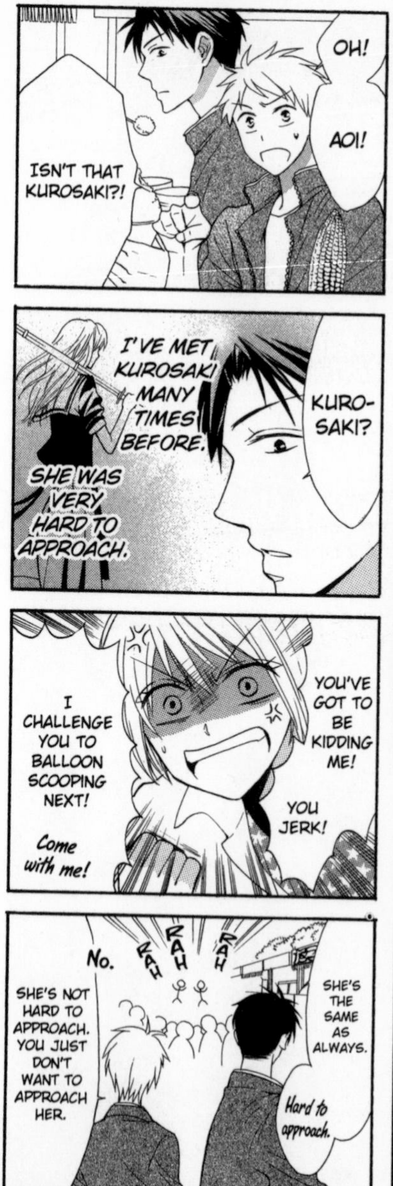
OH!
AOI!
ISN'T THAT KUROSAKI?!
KURO-SAKI?
I'VE MET KUROSAKI MANY TIMES BEFORE.
SHE WAS VERY HARD TO APPROACH.
YOU'VE GOT TO BE KIDDING ME!
YOU JERK!
I CHALLENGE YOU TO BALLOON SCOOPING NEXT!
Come with me!
SHE'S THE SAME AS ALWAYS.
Hard to approach.
RAH RAH RAH
No.
SHE'S NOT HARD TO APPROACH. YOU JUST DON'T WANT TO APPROACH HER.

GREETING

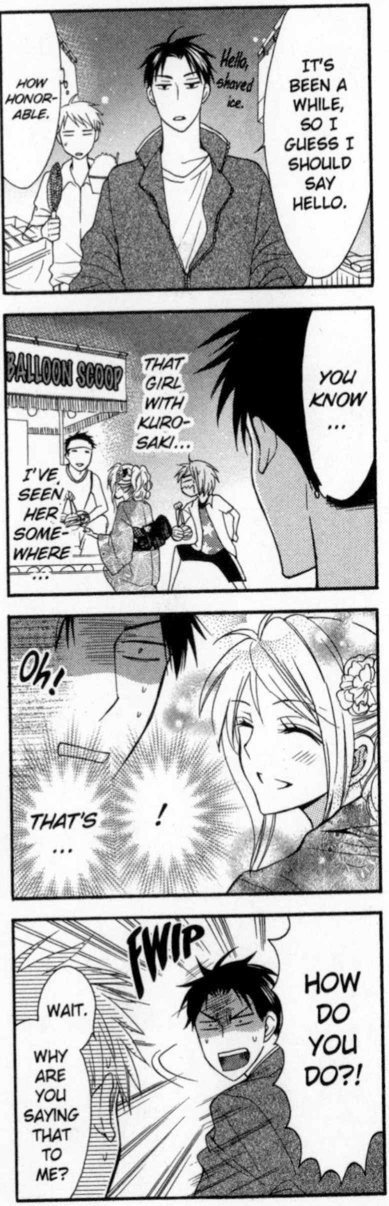
IT'S BEEN A WHILE, SO I GUESS I SHOULD SAY HELLO.
Hello, shaved ice.
HOW HONORABLE.
YOU KNOW ...
THAT GIRL WITH KURO-SAKI...
BALLOON SCOOP
I'VE SEEN HER SOMEWHERE ...
Oh!
!
THAT'S ...
FWIP
HOW DO YOU DO?!
WAIT.
WHY ARE YOU SAYING THAT TO ME?

I'M FORGETFUL

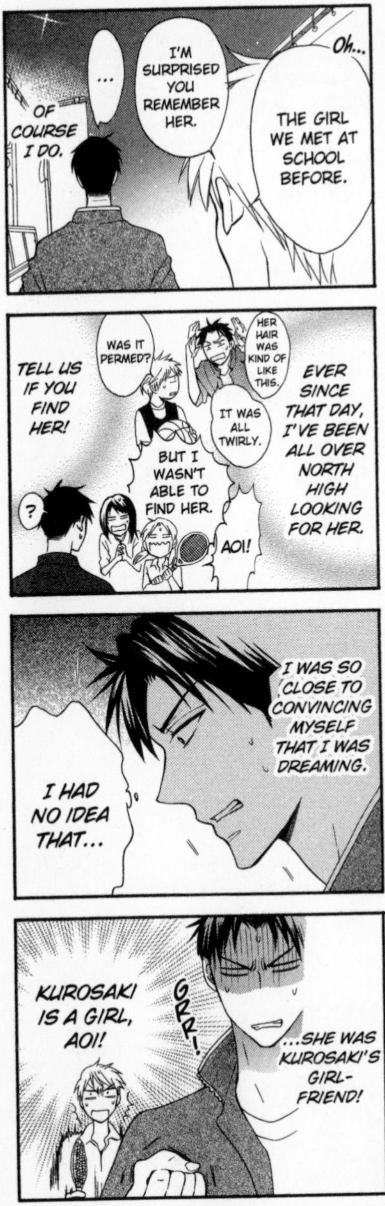
Oh...
THE GIRL WE MET AT SCHOOL BEFORE.
I'M SURPRISED YOU REMEMBER HER.
...
OF COURSE I DO.
EVER SINCE THAT DAY, I'VE BEEN ALL OVER NORTH HIGH LOOKING FOR HER.
HER HAIR WAS KIND OF LIKE THIS.
IT WAS ALL TWIRLY.
WAS IT PERMED?
TELL US IF YOU FIND HER!
BUT I WASN'T ABLE TO FIND HER.
AOI!
?
I WAS SO CLOSE TO CONVINCING MYSELF THAT I WAS DREAMING.
I HAD NO IDEA THAT...
GRR!
...SHE WAS KUROSAKI'S GIRL-FRIEND!
KUROSAKI IS A GIRL, AOI!

HIS CRIMES

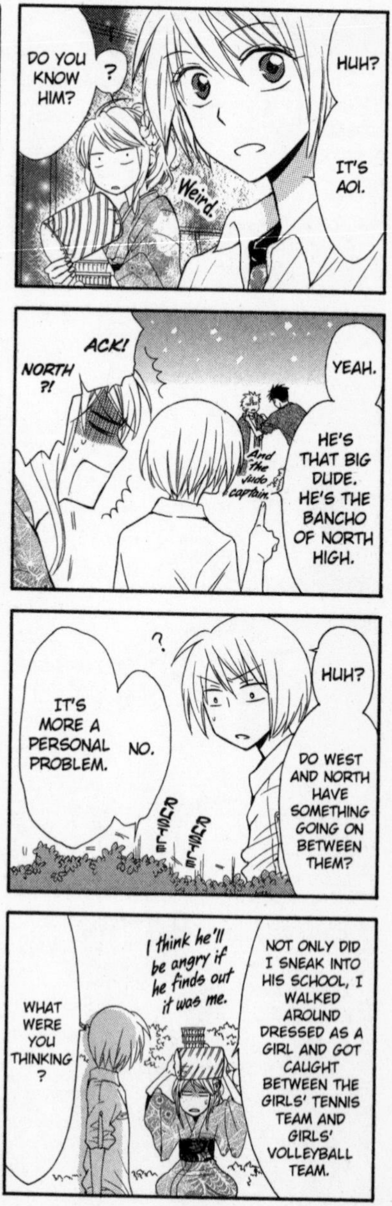
HUH?
IT'S AOI.
?
DO YOU KNOW HIM?
Weird.
YEAH.
HE'S THAT BIG DUDE. HE'S THE BANCHO OF NORTH HIGH.
And the judo captain.
ACK!
NORTH ?!
HUH?
DO WEST AND NORTH HAVE SOMETHING GOING ON BETWEEN THEM?
?
NO.
IT'S MORE A PERSONAL PROBLEM.
RUSTLE
RUSTLE
NOT ONLY DID I SNEAK INTO HIS SCHOOL, I WALKED AROUND DRESSED AS A GIRL AND GOT CAUGHT BETWEEN THE GIRLS' TENNIS TEAM AND GIRLS' VOLLEYBALL TEAM.
I think he'll be angry if he finds out it was me.
WHAT WERE YOU THINKING?

ALL HIS MIGHT

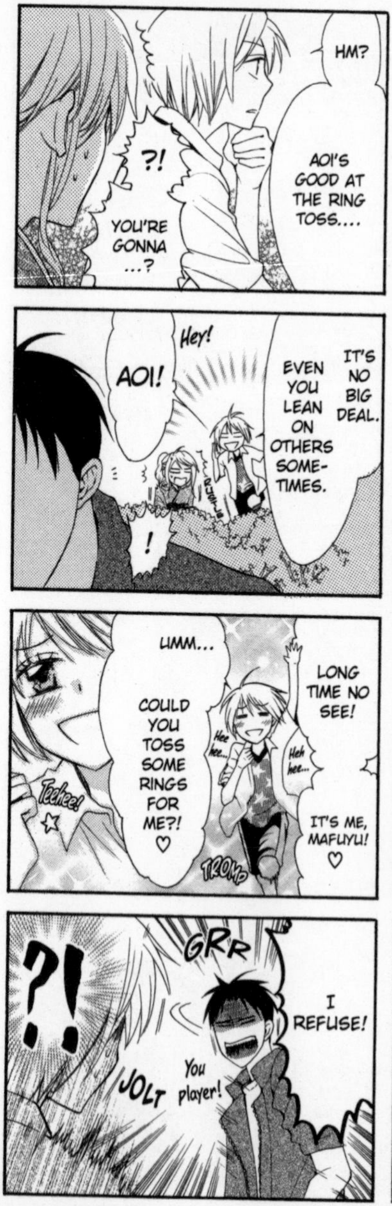
HM?
AOI'S GOOD AT THE RING TOSS....
?!
YOU'RE GONNA ...?
IT'S NO BIG DEAL.
EVEN YOU LEAN ON OTHERS SOME-TIMES.
Hey!
AOI!
RUSTLE
!
LONG TIME NO SEE!
IT'S ME, MAFUYU! ♡
Heh hee...
Hee hee...
UMM...
COULD YOU TOSS SOME RINGS FOR ME?! ♡
Teehee! ☆
GRR
I REFUSE!
You player!
JOLT
?!

AOI'S BELIEFS

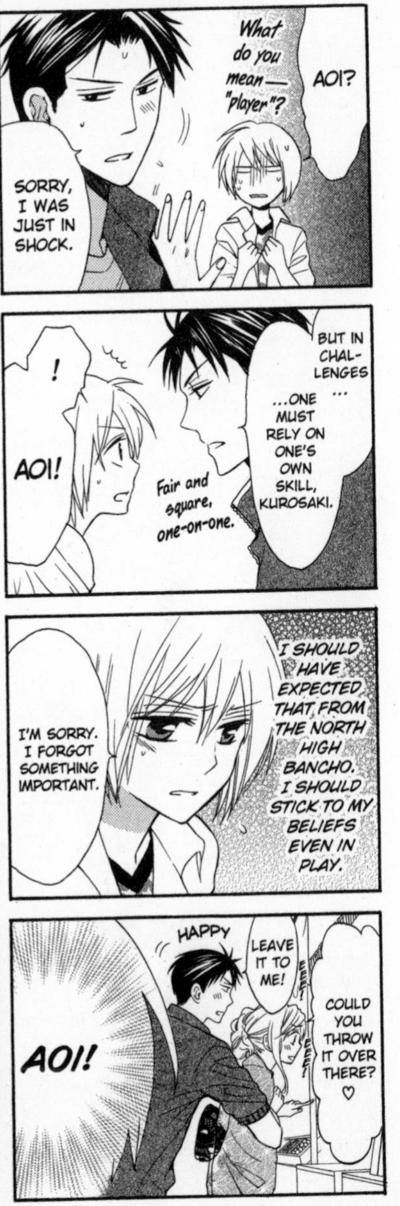
What do you mean— "player"?
AOI?
SORRY, I WAS JUST IN SHOCK.
BUT IN CHALLENGES ...
...ONE MUST RELY ON ONE'S OWN SKILL, KUROSAKI.
Fair and square, one-on-one.
!
AOI!
I SHOULD HAVE EXPECTED THAT FROM THE NORTH HIGH BANCHO. I SHOULD STICK TO MY BELIEFS EVEN IN PLAY.
I'M SORRY. I FORGOT SOMETHING IMPORTANT.
COULD YOU THROW IT OVER THERE? ♡
EEE!
EEE!
LEAVE IT TO ME!
HAPPY
AOI!

PEOPLE GETTING EXCITED

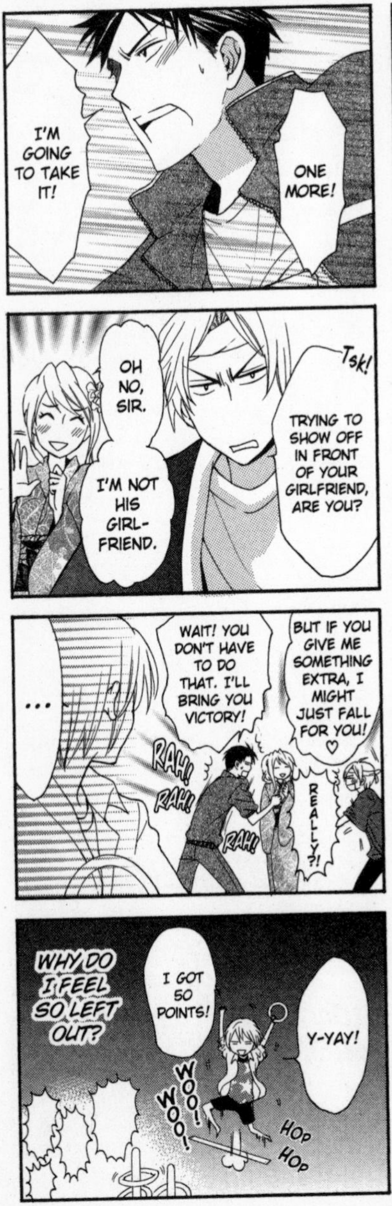
ONE MORE!
I'M GOING TO TAKE IT!
Tsk!
TRYING TO SHOW OFF IN FRONT OF YOUR GIRLFRIEND, ARE YOU?
OH NO, SIR.
I'M NOT HIS GIRLFRIEND.
BUT IF YOU GIVE ME SOMETHING EXTRA, I MIGHT JUST FALL FOR YOU! ♡
WAIT! YOU DON'T HAVE TO DO THAT. I'LL BRING YOU VICTORY!
REALLY?!
RAH!
RAH!
RAH!
...
Y-YAY!
I GOT 50 POINTS!
WHY DO I FEEL SO LEFT OUT?
WOO!
WOO!
HOP
HOP

VENTING

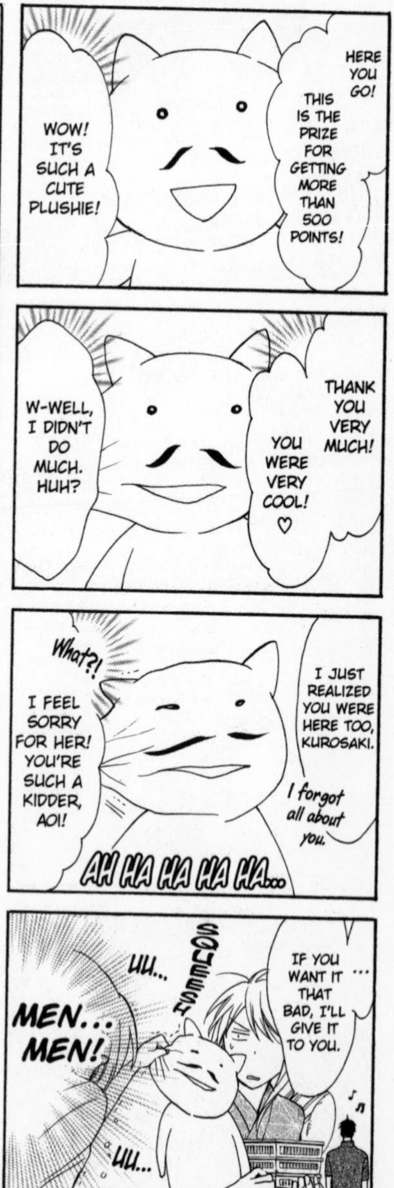

HERE YOU GO!
THIS IS THE PRIZE FOR GETTING MORE THAN 500 POINTS!
WOW! IT'S SUCH A CUTE PLUSHIE!
THANK YOU VERY MUCH!
YOU WERE VERY COOL! ♡
W-WELL, I DIDN'T DO MUCH. HUH?
I JUST REALIZED YOU WERE HERE TOO, KUROSAKI.
I forgot all about you.
What?!
I FEEL SORRY FOR HER! YOU'RE SUCH A KIDDER, AOI!
AH HA HA HA HA...
...
IF YOU WANT IT THAT BAD, I'LL GIVE IT TO YOU.
SQUEEZE
UU...
MEN... MEN!
UU...

A SKILLED MAN

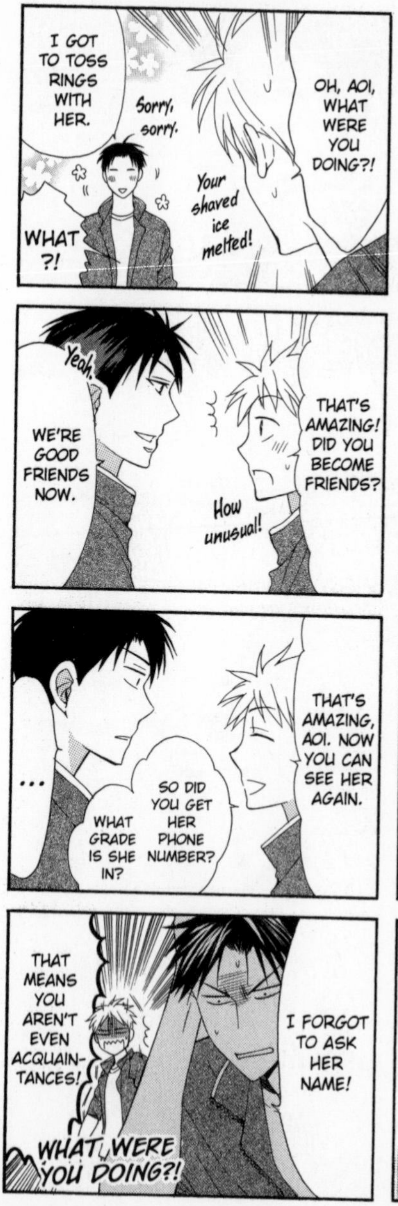

OH, AOI, WHAT WERE YOU DOING?!
Your shaved ice melted!
Sorry, sorry.
I GOT TO TOSS RINGS WITH HER.
WHAT?!
THAT'S AMAZING! DID YOU BECOME FRIENDS?
How unusual!
Yeah.
WE'RE GOOD FRIENDS NOW.
THAT'S AMAZING, AOI. NOW YOU CAN SEE HER AGAIN.
SO DID YOU GET HER PHONE NUMBER?
WHAT GRADE IS SHE IN?
...
I FORGOT TO ASK HER NAME!
THAT MEANS YOU AREN'T EVEN ACQUAINTANCES!
WHAT WERE YOU DOING?!

SLIGHT NUMBING SENSATION 1

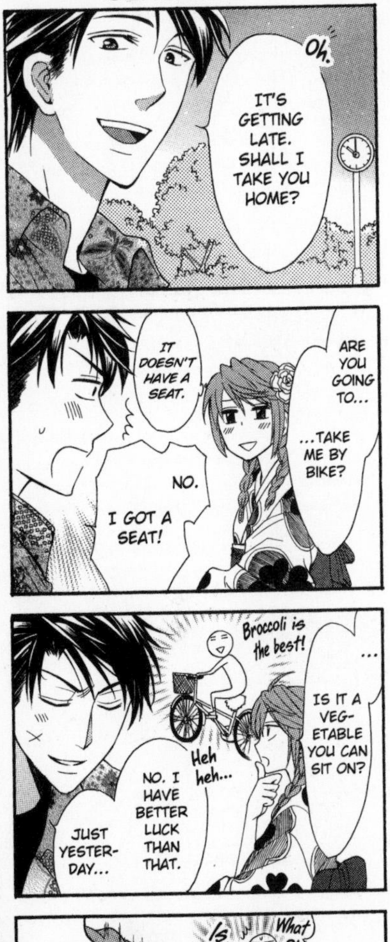
Oh.
IT'S GETTING LATE. SHALL I TAKE YOU HOME?
ARE YOU GOING TO...
...TAKE ME BY BIKE?
IT DOESN'T HAVE A SEAT.
NO.
I GOT A SEAT!
...
IS IT A VEGETABLE YOU CAN SIT ON?
Broccoli is the best!
Heh heh...
NO. I HAVE BETTER LUCK THAN THAT.
JUST YESTERDAY...
What?!
SOMEONE DUMPED GARBAGE IN THE BASKET!
Is that all?!
WHAT?! YOU CONSIDER THAT LUCKY?!

It's unlucky.

SLIGHT NUMBING SENSATION 2

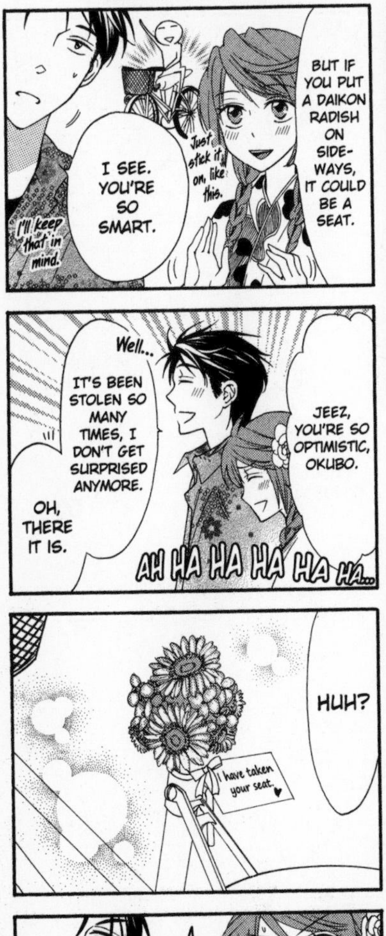
BUT IF YOU PUT A DAIKON RADISH ON SIDEWAYS, IT COULD BE A SEAT.
Just stick it on, like this.
I SEE. YOU'RE SO SMART.
I'll keep that in mind.
JEEZ, YOU'RE SO OPTIMISTIC, OKUBO.
Well...
IT'S BEEN STOLEN SO MANY TIMES, I DON'T GET SURPRISED ANYMORE.
AH HA HA HA HA HA...
OH, THERE IT IS.
HUH?
I have taken your seat. ♥
!
OH DEAR! WHAT KIND OF SETUP IS THIS?!
A noble thief?!
TH-THUMP
?!
TH-THUMP
TH-THUMP
A PROPER GREETING?! THIS IS A FIRST!

He still doesn't have a seat.

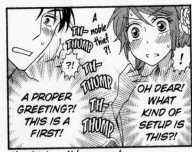

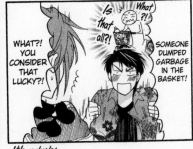

AFTERWORD

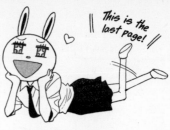

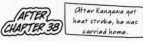

This is the last page!

Thank you very much for buying volume 7. Many people from Mafuyu's hometown appear in this volume. Summer break is the only time she can meet them!

This time I have more four-panel comic strips. There are 14 pages of them. It's a spin-off of what happened at the festival. I hope you enjoy it.

Also, there's a story of how Takaomi and Mafuyu met. It's a story about a child defeating an arrogant bastard. (On a side note, the ending connects to the fourth chapter in volume 1.)

There are two more chapters about summer break. After that, I'm going back to the main story. I hope you continue reading!

And this time, there are two Sakuradas on the cover. It's a regular Sakurada and a cross-dressing Sakurada. The next volume will have someone whom I've been saving for later.

Well, I hope to see you again in volume 8!

Special Thanks

Younger Sister / Family

Toya-san / Akino-san / Okuyama-san

Hotaka-san / Tamura-san

My editor

Thank you for all your help!

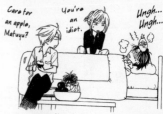

AFTER CHAPTER 38
After Kangawa got heat stroke, he was carried home.
Ungh... Ungh...
You're an idiot.
Care for an apple, Mafuyu?

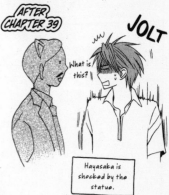

AFTER CHAPTER 39
JOLT
What is this?
Hayasaka is shocked by the statue.

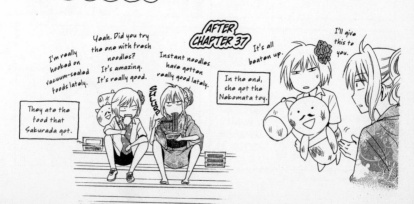

AFTER CHAPTER 37
I'll give this to you.
It's all beaten up.
In the end, she got the Nekomata toy.
Instant noodles have gotten really good lately.
SHLURP
Yeah. Did you try the one with fresh noodles? It's amazing. It's really good.
I'm really hooked on vacuum-sealed foods lately.
They ate the food that Sakurada got.

Izumi Tsubaki began drawing manga in her first year of high school. She was soon selected to be in the top ten of *Hana to Yume's* HMC (*Hana to Yume* Mangaka Course), and subsequently won *Hana to Yume's* Big Challenge contest. Her debut title, *Chijimete Distance* (Shrink the Distance), ran in 2002 in *Hana to Yume* magazine, issue 17. Her other works include *The Magic Touch* (*Oyayubi kara Romance*) and *Oresama Teacher*, which she is currently working on.

ORESAMA TEACHER
Vol. 7
Shojo Beat Edition

STORY AND ART BY
Izumi Tsubaki

English Translation & Adaptation/JN Productions
Touch-up Art & Lettering/Eric Erbes
Design/Yukiko Whitley
Editor/Pancha Diaz

Printed in the U.S.A.

Published by VIZ Media, LLC
P.O. Box 77010
San Francisco, CA 94107

10 9 8 7 6 5 4 3 2 1
First printing, March 2012

www.viz.com   www.shojobeat.com

Escape to the World of the

Young, Rich & Sexy

Ouran High School

Host Club

By Bisco Hatori

FREE online manga preview at
shojobeat.com/downloads